EUROPE AND THE THIRD WORLD

EUROPE AND THE THIRD WORLD

From Colonisation to Decolonisation
c. 1500–1998

Bernard Waites

Lecturer in European Humanities
The Open University

St. Martin's Press
New York

EUROPE AND THE THIRD WORLD

St. Martin's Press, Scholarly and Reference Division, 175 Fifth Avenue, New York, N.Y. 10010

First published in the United States of America in 1999

This book is printed on paper suitable for recycling and made from fully managed and sustained forest sources.

Printed in Hong Kong

ISBN 0–312–22207–6 clothbound
ISBN 0–312–22208–4 paperback

Library of Congress Cataloging-in-Publication Data
Waites, Bernard.
Europe and the Third World : from colonisation to decolonisation, c. 1500–1998 / Bernard Waites.
p.   cm.
Includes bibliographical references and index.
ISBN 0–312–22207–6 (cloth). — ISBN 0–312–22208–4 (pbk.)
1. Europe—Foreign economic relations—Developing countries.
2. Developing countries—Foreign economic relations—Europe.
3. Europe—Colonies.   4. Decolonization.   5. Developing countries–
–Dependency on Europe.   I. Title.
HF1531.Z4D4485   1999
337.40172'4—dc21   98–43698
                                                            CIP

For Daisy and Sam

CONTENTS

LIST OF TABLES

Preface and Acknowledgements

'Europe' and the 'Third World' are vague geographical terms with strong political and cultural resonances. Despite the ancient origin of the word, 'Europe' is a relatively modern idea. It became the common term for the civilisation occupying the western promontory of the Eurasian land mass only around 1700 when it was adopted as a secular substitute for 'Christendom' (Davies, 1996, p. 7). The Enlightenment savants who popularised the expression identified Europe with liberty and moral and material progress in a commonwealth of sovereign states, partly by contrast with the stagnant despotism of Asian empires. Even the widely admired Chinese empire was regarded as a 'stationary' polity that had scarcely changed since Marco Polo's time. When Diderot's *Encyclopédie* appeared around 1760, the pre-eminence of 'Europe' amongst the world's civilisations was a philosophical commonplace. Though the smallest of the four quarters of the globe, it was – we learn – the most fertile, had the greatest commerce and navigation, was where the arts, sciences and professions were most advanced, and where the spirit of Christianity had fostered a certain conception of human rights not found elsewhere. Europe 'had arrived at such a degree of power, that history had almost nothing with which to compare it' (*Encyclopédie* article 'Europe').

The new science of political economy offered a cogent explanation as to why Europe was the most materially progressive part of the globe, and helped articulate European self-consciousness: Adam Smith taught that national product grew through the generalisation of the social division of labour and the specialisation of economic function. The optimum preconditions for growth occurred where self-interested property owners acting under the rule of law enjoyed the greatest market freedom. These preconditions were absent in Asiatic states, where sovereigns claimed universal ownership of the land, and best realised in Holland and England. One could deduce from Smith that the more the European states abandoned their exclusive trade policies and corporate restrictions on manufacturing, then the more Europe as an emergent economic entity constituted by international trade and an international division of labour would acquire a 'real' existence. But it is debatable whether Smith would have welcomed any lessening of Europe's national and cultural diversity: in the empiricist philosophical tradition to which he belonged, the perception of human character differences, and the emulation of remarkable individuals by the mediocre, was a crucial mechanism of social progress. Smith's disciple, John Stuart Mill, was later to argue that it was 'the remarkable diversity of character and culture' in the European family of nations that had made them 'an improving, instead of a stationary portion of mankind'. Europe was wholly indebted for 'its progressive and many-sided development' to the plurality of paths taken by its individuals, classes and nations (Mill, 1859, 1975 edn, p. 89).

If Europe connoted liberty and material progress, market integration and national and cultural diversity, it was also associated with the geographic expansion of the military–political power of the Atlantic states, along with their social institutions and ideologies. Enlightened Europeans knew that the indigenous peoples had fared disastrously in the post-Columbian Americas and that commercial agriculture there was widely dependent on slavery, a mode of labour exploitation increasingly condemned on moral and economic grounds. Nevertheless, their reflections on European maritime expansion helped clarify their perception of Europe as the centre of human development, and this understanding of the world could only become engrained in subsequent generations. In the century and a half after Diderot and Smith published, the modern world's political geography was largely determined by the expansion of European states and states of European origin. By 1800, they had staked out claims to about 55 per cent of the earth's surface, and effectively controlled about 35 per cent. Apart from Europe's 4.4 million square miles, a further 13.5 million square miles of territory in the Americas, the Tsarist empire in Asia, the Indian subcontinent, the Indonesian archipelago and coastal Africa were under European or Euro-American political sway. By the late 1870s, before the onset of the 'new' imperialism, the existing political claims had been consolidated and new ones asserted, to a point where two-thirds of the world's land mass was under Western dominion. In 1914, it was about four-fifths (Clark, 1936, pp. 5–6).

Sometime between Mussolini's conquest of Ethiopia in 1935 and the British surrender of Singapore in 1942, European military–political power ceased to be the monstrous shaper of world history. The continent's partition between antagonistic blocs after 1945 so suppressed the idea of 'Europe' as a region of shared history and culture from the Atlantic to the Urals that a handful of states in the West could surreptitiously appropriate the name for their customs union. Until Mikhail Gorbachev rediscovered the 'common European home', they were abetted in their linguistic larceny by the repression of European consciousness and sentiment in the Soviet bloc. This ideological narrowing of 'Europe' was, undoubtedly, facilitated by the dramatic reduction of European power and influence in the wider world. France and Britain failed abysmally in attempting to coerce Egypt in 1956, and their colonial empires in Asia and Africa were soon to be wound up. The European international system, under whose aegis the modern state had become a universal form of political organisation, was overshadowed by opposing alliances, each dominated by an extra-European superpower. With the retreat of Europeans from the wider world, the idea of 'Europe' could more easily be attached to an inward-looking union of Western European states. I fear this book – which ignores, for reasons of space, Tsarist and Soviet Russian expansion into Asia – has imitated that casual misappropriation. The 'Europe' of my title is, first, the Atlantic Europe which turned the oceanic boundary of the continent into the highways of intercontinental exchange; second, the European metropoles that acquired formal and informal dependencies overseas; third, the 'core' national economies of an expansive capitalism; lastly, the dominant Western powers in the system of absolutely sovereign and juridically equal modern states.

My second term, the 'Third World', was coined by the French demographer, Alfred Sauvy, in August 1952 when the cold war was at its most frigid, and actual conflict dragged on in Korea. The USA and the Soviet Union could plausibly represent themselves as leading two 'worlds', with different social and political systems and ideologies, whose antagonism was so pervasive as to exclude all possibility of neutrality. In these critical international circumstances, where humanity's future seemed to lie either in general war between capitalism and communism or in indefinite hostile coexistence, it was – Sauvy argued – too easy to ignore the 'tiers monde' of 'underdeveloped' countries. Like the Third Estate in 1789, 'This third world, ignored, exploited, scorned, wishes to stand up for itself' ('Trois Mondes, une planète', an article written for *L'Observateur*, 15 August 1952). It was some years before Sauvy's coinage was given wider academic circulation in the collection of essays edited by Georges Balandier, *Le 'tiers monde', sous-développement et développement* (1956), and adopted by the review *Tiers monde* published from 1960 by the Institut Economique et Social de l'Université de Paris. More significantly, in terms of the political potency of the expression, the 'Third World' gained currency amongst émigrés from North Africa, and other French colonial territories, in Paris, many of whom were readers of *L'Observateur* (Lacoste, 1980, vol. 1, pp. 10–29).

With the outbreak of the Algerian war of independence in 1954, 'Third World' political consciousness developed in step with this increasingly bitter anti-colonial struggle. Its most eloquent voice was that of Franz Fanon, the Martinique-born doctor who had practised in Algeria, and later helped edit the National Liberation Front's newspaper from Tunis. In *The Wretched of the Earth* (first published in French in 1961), Fanon projected an eschatological vision of the redemption of humanity by the dispossessed peasantry of the 'Third World' – a vision which captured the imagination of the non-communist left during the upheavals of 1968–9, the apogee of 'tiers-mondisme' as a loosely articulated revolutionary ideology and concept of global divisions (Lacoste, 1980, p. 18). Fanon contrasted the inhuman poverty of the underdeveloped world with Europe's scandalous 'opulence' that had been founded on slavery and racist exploitation, and demanded restitution for the European plundering of the 'Third World':

> The wealth of the imperial countries is our wealth too . . . For in a very concrete way Europe has stuffed herself inordinately with the gold and raw materials of the colonial countries: Latin America, China and Africa. From all these continents, under whose eyes Europe today raises up her tower of opulence, there has flowed out for centuries towards that same Europe diamonds and oil, silk and cotton, wood and exotic products. Europe is literally the creation of the Third World (Fanon, 1969, p. 81).

During the 1960s and in 1970s, this notion of the 'Third World' as those areas of the globe exploited by Europe in the course of, and as a necessary condition for, its own development dovetailed with 'dependency' and 'world systems' theory (discussed in Chapter 1) and retains today a powerful hold on the non-Western intelligentsia. Thus, in the *Third World Guide* – a gazetteer purporting to show the world as seen by the 'Third World' – we find arguments with an obvious family resemblance to Fanon's claims. The editors regard a historical viewpoint as essential to understanding what the 'Third World' is, and identify it with the periphery of the system produced by the expansion of world capitalism whose development they regard as a global zero-sum game:

> The so-called 'underdevelopment' of the Third World is the underside of today's 'development' of the industrialised capitalist powers, whose wealth was and still is to a great extent drawn from the Third World through direct (Latin American gold) or indirect (cheap Middle-eastern oil) plunder (*Third World Guide*, *89/90*, p. 12).

The editors define the common characteristics of the 'Third World' countries as:

> First, the fact of having previously been colonies of foreign powers; second, the fact of having suffered economic exploitation which shaped their production systems to make them exporters of raw materials and deprived them of the power to make decisions on the basis of people's interest . . . Finally, cultural domination, that has created an inferiority complex with regard to the national cultures, imposing as universally valid the values of 'Western Christian Civilization' . . . (ibid., p.13).

Of course, these are the certainties of a committed publication written in a deliberately populist style. I quote them, not as a target for facile refutation, but to show how the self-understanding of the 'Third World' is bound up with the notion of a global rift between 'have' and 'have not' societies opened by the geographic expansion of capitalism from its European base.

For some time now, scholars of all persuasions have urged that the concept of the 'Third World' has outlived its usefulness in the analysis of global society. Peter Worsley, who introduced it into Anglophone social science (Worsley, 1964), made the last sustained attempt to justify its use in *The Three Worlds* (1984). He argued that

> The various meanings with which the [Third World] has been invested show family resemblances, even though they do not fully coincide. They have, that is, a common referent in the real world out there: the unequal, institutionalised distribution of wealth and poverty on a world scale (Worsley, 1984, p. 339).

Logically, a 'third' world requires the prior existence of a first and second, and it was still possible in the mid 1980s to identify these with the industrialised, capitalist 'West' under the leadership of the United States and the state socialist economies of the Soviet bloc. The 'Second Cold War' of the Reagan–Brezhnev years had re-clarified the political identities of two antagonistic social systems after a period of détente. The 'Third World' itself had some political identity in the Non-Aligned Movement – dating from 1961 – and the (overlapping) Group of 77 developing countries formed in 1964 after the first United Nations Conference on Trade and Development. Admittedly, a 'three worlds' schema blanked out the great fissure in world communism since 1963, when communist China had openly 'split' from the Soviet Union. But if the logical political conditions were just about satisfied in the mid 1980s, they had crumbled away by 1990 with the collapse of the Soviet bloc, economic liberalisation in the former 'command' economies and their closer integration with world markets.

Even before the dissolution of the 'second world', the concept of a 'third' was being challenged by the mounting evidence of economic differentiation among the developing countries, especially with the rapid industrialisation of the Pacific Rim economies. Their high growth rates were due principally to great increases in labour force participation combined with massive public and private investment, but they also exported a large proportion of their gross domestic products. An increasing prosperity due to competitiveness on world markets was quite contrary to the thesis advanced by 'dependency' theorists in the 1960s that foreign trade impoverished the developing countries and 'locked them' into a condition of 'underdevelopment'. After reviewing the experience of the newly industrialising countries, Nigel Harris pronounced the end of the 'Third World' in 1986, along with the decline of the radical ideology associated with the notion 'dependency'. For Harris, the developing countries were experiencing accelerated capitalist growth from a position of comparative backwardness, and he restated the 'classical' Marxist argument that as capitalism advanced throughout the world, so the distribution of its income and wealth would be determined by the class divisions and struggles within national economies. There were, of course, 'rich' and 'poor' countries in the sense of huge discrepancies in average per capita income but, contrary to Worsley, Harris saw no 'institutionalised' processes maintaining these differences. The 'Third World' could not be defined as those countries permanently disadvantaged by a common location in global capitalism. It was, in fact, a myth (Harris, 1986). Paul Kennedy, surveying the global divisions from the perspective of a liberal historian in the early 1990s, concurred: the term had been made redundant by the discrepancy in economic performance between East Asia and sub-Saharan Africa. The differences in non-Western economies demanded a more complex categorisation of developing countries (Kennedy, 1993, p. 194).

As with so many mythological terms, the 'Third World' has maintained a vigorous public life long after academics declared its redundancy. Whatever the empirical and conceptual objections raised against it, the expression clearly fulfils a key function in categorising human society, as a casual reading of the press will attest. To cite one instance, Harold James, a distinguished historian of Germany, referred in a review in *The Times Literary Supplement* (13 June 1997) to 'the search for a third way' between capitalism and communism in the final phase of the German Democratic Republic as 'a way into the 'Third World'. Little, one suspects, was intended apart from literary effect, but a stylistic device will not 'work' on its readers unless they and the author have some common understanding of its terms. Though I share the scepticism of Harris and Kennedy about the idea of the 'Third World', I have retained the expression partly because, bound in with the common understandings of what the 'Third World' is, are powerful though imprecise notions of how it came to be so. One such notion associates 'Third World' countries with 'post-coloniality', and so refers us both to their derivative political origins as the former colonies of the expansive European or Western states and to the hybrid subaltern cultures formed where the colonialists' languages became the media for indigenous literary expression. Of course, 'post-colonial' invokes a past not only for the 'Third World' but also for the former colonisers who exploited its plantations and mineral wealth, and induced its peasants to cultivate cash crops for export. Nearly all Western European states are 'post-colonial powers', and only a generation ago even the most parochial was seen by its national élite as having an extra-European dimension. The phrase 'Belgian-Congolese community' was on everyone's lips in the corridors of Brussels in the later 1950s (Stengers, 1989, p. 225). But, like the 'Third World', 'post-colonial' is an open invitation to sceptical empiricism: what can it mean to say that Kinshasa and Singapore are both 'post-colonial' cities? Does it help explain their extraordinarily divergent fortunes since decolonisation? I share this scepticism. Indeed, I think 'post-colonial' bundles a host of non-European states and societies into a common history almost as mythological as the present-day 'Third World'.

This book grew out of an essay on 'Europe and the Third World' that I wrote for a collaborative course *What is Europe?*, produced by a consortium of European distance-teaching universities. I am grateful to Routledge and the the Open University for permission to re-use some of the material that appeared in that essay (Waites, 1993). What interested me originally was how (or whether) European expansion related to the uneven pattern of global development and the gross inequalities in income and welfare across the world. But this could be called a 'metahistorical' interest which prompted the reading and writing: it is not a historical problem that can be addressed square-on, and it certainly has no simple answers. The best I could manage was to follow that interest but break down the messy and often imperfectly known history into discrete topics. Though some chapters refer to centuries, and depict secular processes with a broad brush, my method has been to focus on specific historical questions. Even the most problem-oriented historical writing cannot dispense altogether with a narrative framework, but

I have tried throughout to make narration serve the purposes of explanation. Each chapter can be read independently, but I hope that cumulatively they amount to a historical argument. To reduce publishing costs, I have consolidated the bibliography and used the detestable author–date referencing system.

I am grateful to the following for permission to use copyright material in statistical tables: Macmillan Press Ltd for data from B.R. Mitchell's invaluable compilations, *International Historical Statistics: Africa and Asia* and *International Historical Statistics: Europe, 1750–1988*; Editions Albin Michel for the use of data from Jacques Marseille's *Empire Colonial et Capitalisme Français*; Presses Universitaires de France for data from René Girault's contribution to the *Histoire économique et social de la France*; Columbia University Press for data from Grover Clark's *The Balance Sheets of Imperialism*; the editor of the *Revue d'Histoire Moderne et Contemporaine* and Jacques Marseille for data which first appeared in that journal; and the editor of the *Oxford Bulletin of Economics and Statistics* and Ian Livingstone for data from the bulletin.

This book has been purgatory to write; I can only hope it will be more pleasurable to read. Dr Gary Thorn read an earlier draft of Chapter 8 and the present version, however imperfect, was much improved by his comments. Otherwise, this has been a solitary task. The usual disclaimer that the mistakes are solely the author's comes from the heart. Daisy and Sam, for whom *Europe and the Third World* has long been a matter for patronising derision, would be *really* embarrassed if they knew it was dedicated to them. It's the only revenge left to me.

Bernard Waites

1

EUROPE AND THE 'THIRD WORLD': AN INTRODUCTION AND OVERVIEW

I

The themes of this book are, in a nutshell, development and underdevelopment in the course of European overseas expansion into what we call – imprecisely – the 'Third World'. It provides an inevitably selective overview of European economic relations with the other continents (and the military and political means used to secure them) in what I hope is a factually informative way. Though not a work of theory, it reviews some of the conceptual frameworks that have been used to account historically for global inequalities.

Now, 'nutshell' is a laughably inappropriate figure of speech: how could the vast tracts of history denoted by 'expansion' be compressed in such a small compass? European maritime expansion began no later than the conquest of the Canary Islands in the 1320s when, in a pattern that was to be repeated wherever Europeans came into contact with isolated populations, the natives rapidly died from diseases against which they had no natural immunities (Curtin, 1990, p. 22). Moreover, though the narrative of European empire-building is well known, the causal relationships between expansion, economic development within Europe and underdevelopment on the European periphery cannot be summarised as known quantities. There is no consensus as to the significance for the economies of Western Europe of the extension of their common economic frontier during the run-up to industrialisation – partly because there are so few data with which to gauge 'significance'. For the mid nineteenth century and beyond, we can construct statistical series to quantify the gains (in terms of commerce, raw materials and investment opportunities) accruing to industrialising Europe

1

from imperialism in the tropics. Whether the quantities are considered 'marginal' or not, there is at least broad agreement as to their magnitude. There is scarcely any such agreement about the impact of European domination on the indigenous economies and societies of Africa and Asia, and the subject remains highly controversial. In short, no single book can satisfactorily cover the themes to which I refer for reason both of their scope and of the intractably problematic nature of the questions they raise.

II

To help formulate the problems I want to address, it is better to begin with the recent rather than the distant past. If the phrase the 'Third World' serves no other purpose, it at least reminds us that we live in a world of glaring inequalities and persistent mass destitution. In the early 1980s, the two 'Brandt' reports from the Independent Commission on International Development Studies publicised the discrepancies in living standards and material resources between what were coming to be referred as the 'North' (or advanced capitalist and socialist economies) and the 'South' or 'Third World' (terms used interchangeably by Brandt). At the end of the 1970s the industrialised North, including eastern Europe, had a quarter of the world's population and four-fifths of its income; the South, including China, had three-quarters of the world's population, but lived on a fifth of the world's income. Around 1980, the 28 per cent of the world's population with incomes of $2500 or more consumed 80 per cent of the goods and services produced by global economic activity, while the 56 per cent of the population with incomes of less than $500 consumed only 15 per cent. Over 90 per cent of the world's manufacturing industry lay in the North, which dominated the world's economic system and monopolised its technology through multinational corporations (Brandt, 1980, p. 32). According to World Bank estimates, a third of the population of the developing countries, and half of those classified as 'low income' (that is with a per capita GDP of less than $600 in 1980), suffered chronic undernourishment. In the Indian subcontinent alone, somewhere between 250 to 300 million people were reckoned in the early 1980s to have had incomes barely sufficient to secure the minimum of food to sustain the human body (Drèze and Sen, 1989, pp. 33–4; Raychaudhuri, 1985, p. 801).

    It would be comforting to think that the dramatic changes in the global economy since 1980 have brought a redistribution of income and welfare to the world's poor. Certainly, the 'Third World' has always referred to an economically heterogeneous array of states that were becoming more differentiated during the 1960s and 1970s. In the post-war decades, there was a gap in the average growth rate of the richer states belonging to the Organisation for Economic Cooperation and Development and the average in the 'Third World' countries, but more significant was the sharp pulling apart of growth rates *within* the 'Third World' itself (Reynolds, 1985, p. 392). A handful of desert sheikhdoms were transformed into the world's richest societies in terms of per capita GNP as a result of world demand for oil and the quadrupling of oil prices by the OPEC cartel following the Yom Kippur War in 1973. But industrialisation and the export of competitively priced manufactures offered the best prospects for raising mass living standards in most poor countries. In the 'Third World' as a whole, manufacturing production multiplied more than 12 times between 1953 and 1990, and manufactures rose from about 7 per cent of exports to approaching 40 per cent. Unfortunately, industrialisation and export growth have been concentrated in a few economies: with only 6 per cent of the 'Third World's' population, the Asian tigers and Brazil have 25 to 27 per cent of its manufacturing capacity and provide close to 80 per cent of its manufactured exports (Bairoch, 1993, p. 92). To this we must add that the newly industrialising countries are far from homogeneous: in South Korea, for example, income and welfare have become more equally distributed, whereas Mexico and Brazil have colossal inequalities in income distribution; the latter, in particular, illustrates how little can happen in removing poverty and deprivation even with remarkably rapid growth of GNP per head (Drèze and Sen, 1990, vol. 1, p. 25; Sachs, 1990).

Against the positive trends, we have to set the truly adverse economic experiences of sub-Saharan Africa. In 12 of the world's 51 poorest states per capita national income declined between 1970 and 1980, and 11 were in Africa (Dasgupta, 1993, Table 5.4, p. 118). Though it is often suggested this is a misleading index, it correlates closely with other measures of well-being, such as per capita food availability. The negative trend was exacerbated in the early 1980s when the poorer, oil-importing countries, with export schedules dominated by a few primary products, were exposed to sharp falls in commodity prices and deteriorating trade balances. Though most of their borrowing from abroad was at concessional rates, they found debt-servicing an increasing drain on economies battered by a severe reversal in the terms of trade. The prices of their exports relative to their imports declined by about 40 per cent on average between the last quarter of 1980 and the first of 1982 (Brandt, 1983, p. 103). Total overseas development assistance to the Less developed countries fell sharply in the mid 1980s, chiefly because of the decline in lending by Arab donors. In 1984–5, the gross interest and dividends paid by the LDCs far exceeded the total net resource flows – official development financing, export credits and private investments – that they received from the developed countries (OECD, *1991 Development Review*, Table 3-1, p. 123). While the developed countries were gaining from the decline in the price of the commodities they imported from the poorest countries, the latter were becoming more impoverished. The most recent estimates of global inequality indicate that the adverse trends are affecting more people than the positive (Hirst and Thompson, 1996, pp.68–71). In the early 1990s, about 2.9 billion people lived in countries where average money incomes were below $500 a year, compared with an average of $14 000 enjoyed by the 900 million people living in the world's seventeen richest countries (P. Harrison, 'Calling it the Third World without end', *Guardian*, 19 February 1993).

III

Today's stark inequalities between the world's richest and poorest regions are not the continuation in the present of disparities stretching back into the distant past. They only became a matter of systematic enquiry for economists around 1950, when the terms 'development' and 'underdevelopment' entered their professional vocabulary. 'Development' can be non-controversially defined as the growth of labour productivity and real income per head, and causally attributed to technological innovation, the accumulation of capital and the increasing division of labour in society. In modern societies, it usually presupposes the movement of labour out of agriculture and the expansion of manufacturing and services – in other words, the structural change of industrialisation. The causal weight attached to each of the dynamic forces in development differs among rival theorists (Maddison, 1991, provides a useful introduction), but for our purposes a more germane controversy is a historical one: when did sharp differences in *rates of development* in human society begin?

One response argues for a broad similarity in productive technique and per capita income in Asia and Europe up to about 1750, and therefore focuses on the Industrial Revolution as the moment when a fault line in human society opened between the 'progressive' states with rising average living standards and the 'stationary', where the vast majority remained mired in poverty. Paul Bairoch is the leading exponent of this view: by extrapolating back from twentieth-century data, he has concluded that, apart from very small countries where trade and manufactures were heavily concentrated (such as the Netherlands) there were no strikingly rich and strikingly poor states in the pre-industrial world. Average income in even the richest country was probably only half as great again as that in the poorest. If we compare broader economic entities, such as western Europe, India, Africa or China, the per capita income gap around 1750 'was probably even more limited, in the order of 1.0 to 1.3 or even less' (Bairoch, 1986, p. 194; idem, 1993, p. 104).

Clearly, reconstructions of per capita income in Europe before the pre-statistical era ought to be treated with studied reserve, and for 'Third World' countries invite incredulity. They are arithmetical manipulations of twentieth-century data which assume a certain rate of income growth and a minimum in, say, 1750 below which starvation loomed. It is some reassurance to know that other scholars have reached similar conclusions. Bairoch has also estimated that over two-thirds of the world's manufactures were produced in the future 'Third World' in 1800 – which seems plausible simply because the great majority of humankind lived in Asia where handicraft techniques were not much less productive than Europe's. In 1830, he reckons, the proportion was still as much as three-fifths, but by 1860 had fallen to 36.6 per cent. During these decades, the division between the future developed and 'Third' worlds began to take clear shape, as industrialising countries and primary exporters were meshed more closely in the international division of labour. From the late 1840s to 1860, the volume of world trade grew 5 to 6 per cent a year (a compound rate of growth not matched until the 1950s). The export of factory-produced yarn, cloth and metal utensils undercut the market for handicraft products in the 'Third World', leading to what many have called its 'de-industrialisation' (though if the English language permitted 'de-artisanalisation' would be a more appropriate word; we will consider this issue more closely in the context of nineteenth-century India). The volume of 'Third World' manufactures declined until the beginning of the twentieth century, when output per capita was about a third of what it had been around 1750 (Bairoch, 1982, pp. 274, 278).

It may be, as Eric Jones has argued, that fixation with the classic Industrial Revolution blinds us to Europe's developmental dynamics over 'the long run' and to the many ways its economy outperformed other civilisations' by 1700. Geographic and ecological advantages, combined with political institutions more favourable to private economic activity, were such, Jones argues, as to raise average material well-being in pre-industrial Europe above that of Asian societies: 'Ordinary Europeans had better clothing, more varied food, more furniture and household utensils . . . The gulf between East and

West may have been widened by industrialisation but was not caused by it'
(Jones, 1981, p. 5). If we are to credit travellers' observations, Europe's states
and dominant élites extracted a little less from the productive economy than
their counterparts elsewhere and did a little more to provide social goods,
such as legal security for merchants. François Bernier, a doctor long resident
in Mughal India, described vast tracts of Hindustan as badly cultivated and
thinly peopled. Much good land was untilled because peasants had deserted
the tyranny of their political masters. Hindu merchants' wealth could not be
displayed for fear of the cupidity of a Muslim governing élite. 'No adequate
idea can be conveyed of the sufferings of [the] people. The cudgel and the
whip compel them to incessant labour for the benefit of others . . .' (Bernier,
1669, 1972 edn, pp. 205, 227–30). But not all Bernier's account confirms
Jones's view, for he paid glowing tribute to the fertility, wealth and
manufactures of Bengal. Such was the demand for Bengal's cotton and silk
textiles in South Asia, Japan and *Europe* that Bernier described as it as 'the
common storehouse' of these commodities (ibid., p. 439).

Indian scholars, in particular, have seen in Asia's favourable balance of
trade in manufactures with Europe evidence for an unchallenged
'supremacy in industrial technology, cost efficiency and the range of
manufactures' until the late eighteenth century (Chaudhuri, 1990, p. 301).
For reasons given in Chapter 3, I am not persuaded that the facts will bear
this construction. A much more likely explanation for the imbalance of Euro-
Asian trade is the low cost of labour in India and the greater purchasing
power of silver there. The watch, the pre-industrial world's most ingenious
machine, better indicates the respective technical accomplishments of
Europe and Asia than hand-woven textiles. The mechanical timekeeper
derives from the exceptional technological creativity Europeans had evinced
since the early Middle Ages. All the examples of labour-saving inventions
mentioned by Adam Smith dated back several centuries, and the watch
provided his most telling instance of the falling real price of manufactures.
Between the mid seventeenth century and 1776, the price of a watch fell
from 20 pounds to 20 shillings, while its quality improved (Smith, 1776, 1996
edn, p. 260). By the late eighteenth century, London and Geneva were each
producing about eighty thousand timekeepers a year *for export*, many to East
Asia where there was no indigenous tradition of mechanical clock- and
watchmaking, and no mass market for complex consumer durables (Cipolla,
1970, p. 148, p. 163).

European technological creativity and machine-building skills were
of limited economic account unless there were particular institutional
arrangements, such as patent laws and joint-stock companies, which gave
individuals an incentive to invest in innovation, and yet spread the risks of

financial loss. But here, too, European states had a head start over Asia in instituting property rights that raised the private rate of return for innovative entrepreneurs close to the social rate of return (North and Thomas, 1973). Before contact with Europe, neither India nor China had evolved the joint-stock company, despite the sophistication of their financial sectors in other respects. The final, and perhaps most compelling, reason for doubting whether the Industrial Revolution opened the developmental gap between Europe and Asia is the emergence of urban, capitalist social structures – which provided especially congenial environments for private economic activity – in north-west Europe a century before industrial 'takeoff'. The Netherlands was the most precocious in this respect: only two-fifths of employment was in agriculture around 1700, for it had developed a transport and financial services sector serving a European market as well as a wide range of processing industries. England was a close follower, partly because it had instituted exceptionally secure landed property rights that enabled the agrarian élite to dispossess the agricultural workforce of common rights in the land. As early as 1688, only a little over half the labour force was in agriculture (Maddison, 1991, p. 31).

IV

Whatever view we take of the origins of the so-called 'European miracle', we should remind ourselves that in western Europe millions died of famine and hunger-related disease in the 1840s. More intercontinental economic migrants have departed from this part of the world than any other. The Iberian peninsula, the Balkans, much of the Italian south and islands were economically backward regions up to and beyond the Second World War, with living standards generally below that of Argentina and the São Paulo region of Brazil where relatively high wages had attracted millions of European immigrants. Furthermore, it is worth emphasising that in the century or so before the 'Third World' became synonymous for the 'underdeveloped countries', many of them began to increase their per capita output. According to L.G. Reynolds's wide-ranging survey of economic growth in the 'Third World', output per capita began to grow in Chile from 1840, in Argentina from 1860, in Mexico from 1876, and in Brazil and Peru from 1880, while in Malaysia, Thailand and Burma growth began between 1850 and 1870. In Algeria growth is reckoned to have begun in 1880, and in certain West African countries from the 1890s (Reynolds, 1985, p. 32). The basic reason advanced for the shift from 'extensive' growth – where output simply keeps pace with the rise in population – to 'intensive' growth in per capita GNP was the rapid expansion of exports consequent on the great increase in world trade after 1850. 'Intensive' growth began, that is, with these countries taking advantage of the demand in newly industrialising western Europe (and later North America) both for agricultural products and industrial raw materials. Exports were not at the expense of food supply, which generally kept pace with population growth in 'Third World' countries. The shift from 'extensive' to 'intensive' growth in the aforementioned countries occurred between eighty and a hundred years earlier than the comparable turning-points in India, Pakistan and China (all reckoned as being in the late 1940s) or Iran, Iraq, Turkey and Egypt (the early 1950s) or Indonesia (1965). Nevertheless, there was considerable 'overlap' in the chronologies of growth in Europe and the 'Third World'.

The dates Reynolds gives for the 'turning-points' from 'extensive' to 'intensive' growth rely heavily on export earnings data and are, admittedly, controversial. He does not address the question of income distribution, and his data and analytic framework blot out the forms of social stratification and segregation in the colonial economies. Reynolds disregards such issues as whether mining enclaves impoverished the rural communities from which they drew their labour. Nevertheless, his survey provides a useful corrective to blanket notions of the 'Third World' as economically stagnant, without a past of any consequence, before it became the focus of 'development' strategies in the 1950s.

The stimulus exports gave to the growth of income was, only exceptionally, translated into industrial development, and may even have delayed it by channelling investment into trade and finance rather than the secondary sector. Bairoch's data show the per capita output of manufactures (whether or not produced by new industrialised processes) falling by half in the future 'Third World' as a whole between 1860 and 1913 (Bairoch, 1991, p. 3). Significantly, the exceptions were independent states in Latin America where, after 1880, export booms gave rise to sizeable domestic markets, and provided the basis for the local industrialisation of the consumer goods sector, despite competition from technologically more advanced industries in Europe and North America. Argentina provides the clearest example: once railway-building had integrated the domestic economy and steamer links were established with international markets, exports soared, encouraging mass immigration, rapid urbanisation, and a relatively egalitarian distribution of income. This combination of factors gave an impetus to industrialisation even before the First World War (Furtado, 1976, p. 102). Chile and the São Paulo region of South-East Brazil exhibited a similar pattern: by 1915, Brazil's 240 cotton textile mills employed more than 82 000 workers and were supplying about 85 per cent of domestic consumption (Reynolds, 1985, p. 98).

V

Despite the success of certain 'middle-income' Latin American countries in developing light industries before 1929, it was not fortuitous that this continent gave rise to a critique of the notion of 'underdevelopment' and to a concept of 'dependency' that has been hugely influential as an explanatory framework in 'Third World' history. 'Underdevelopment', according to this critique, is not simply the absence of development, but a discrete historical process through which economies that have already achieved a high level of development have not necessarily passed. The defining characteristic of 'dependency' is that the dynamics of capital accumulation lie outside the 'underdeveloped' economy. As far as the historical emphases of this study are concerned, its basic situations entailed either foreign investment in enclaves producing for world markets or the local ownership and control of the export sector by a hybrid élite of landowners and merchants. To better understand the arguments, it is useful to look briefly at Latin America's recent past. Apart from Cuba and the remaining 'sugar colonies', Latin America has been a region of independent states since the 1820s, but from the later nineteenth century most followed a path of development oriented 'towards the outside' (because influenced above all by foreign trade), which placed key areas of the economy in the hands of foreign investors. Foreign groups typically controlled about a third of reproducible capital in Latin American countries in 1929, and in some instances foreign ownership was virtually complete: less than a fifth of Cuba's sugar was produced in Cuban-owned mills (Furtado, 1976, p. 55; Thomas, 1971, p. 708). Latin America became more closely integrated into the international division of labour than any other underdeveloped region, not necessarily to the disadvantage of the populace. During the Argentine 'belle époque' many would have endorsed the classical economic theory that nations benefit mutually from free trade between themselves when they specialise in forms of production in which each enjoys a 'comparative advantage' (Diaz-Alejandro, 1988). This does not mean a nation should specialise in products it can produce most cheaply, but where the ratio of the costs of producing different goods gives a trading advantage. In the example used by David Ricardo, eighteenth-century Portugal could produce both wine and cloth more cheaply than England, but it was to Portugal's advantage to specialise in wine and exchange it for cloth in England because there the cost ratio was greater – one unit of wine exchanged for more cloth than it did in Portugal.

But precisely because of its integration into the international division of labour, the economic crisis that began in 1929 assumed catastrophic proportions for Latin America. By 1933, the volume of world trade had fallen by a quarter, but its value by more than half because export prices collapsed. Primary-produce exporters suffered a severe and prolonged reversal in their terms of trade and, as a consequence, between 1929 and 1939 Latin America's capacity to import fell by 43 per cent (or, if population growth is taken into account, by over 60 per cent). The flow of international capital from British and other foreign investors to Latin America was reversed as capital was repatriated to cover balance of payments deficits; throughout the 1930s, repayments of capital to Britain slightly exceeded foreign lending for the first time since the Industrial Revolution (Furtado, 1976, pp. 54–57; Pollard, 1983, p. 118).

The world economic crisis set in train an 'internally oriented' form of development in the Latin American economies to which the Second World War gave an additional impetus. Under nationalist and populist regimes, based mainly on the underemployed masses in the growing cities, the state intervened in the economy by nationalising foreign enterprises and allying with a nascent industrial bourgeoisie. 'Anti-imperialism' – directed at the USA – and a critique of economic colonialism became part of the ruling ideology. In the post-war years, the region's underdevelopment was analysed by a group of economists led by the former Argentine finance minister, Raúl Prebisch, who was the first General Secretary of the United Nations Economic Commission for Latin America, set up in 1948. The central concept of price theory in conventional economics was general equilibrium, and ECLA's originality and influence came from questioning its applicability to prices in international trade. The commission challenged the still orthodox doctrine of 'comparative advantage' and diagnosed economically retarding effects in the structure of trade between what it dubbed the 'centre' and the 'periphery'. Crucially, Prebisch advanced new arguments as to why the terms of trade for peripheral producers were deteriorating. Other economists ascribed this to the fact that demand in the developed countries for primary product exports from underdeveloped regions had not kept pace with the growth of income (or in technical terms, income elasticity of demand had declined), while demand for manufactured imports in the underdeveloped regions had proved income elastic (Myrdal, 1956, p. 52). Prebisch approached the problem on different grounds by analysing the long-term evolution of technical progress and wages in the developed and underdeveloped countries. In brief, he argued that the greater productivity gains of manufacturing had led to higher wages, rather than falling prices, for better-organised European (and American) workers, and that nominal wages had been maintained during the depression phases of the trade cycle. In the export sector of the underdeveloped regions, by contrast, a constant supply of surplus labour had kept wages down, while prices had been responsive to the cyclical pattern of demand. Over the course of a century, Prebisch argued, the disparity in wages was reflected in a structural disparity in prices. This was the origin of the concept of 'unequal exchange' which has figured so large in radical analysis of international trade since the 1960s (Prebisch, 1950; Amin, 1974, pp. 81–3; Love, 1980).

The validity of this argument is much disputed, and Bairoch has produced data to show that the terms of trade for primary products relative to manufactured goods improved by 10 to 25 per cent between the 1870s and the late 1920s (Bairoch, 1993, p. 113). The major exception was cane sugar, which was excluded from many European markets by protected beet sugar (thus France was virtually self-sufficient in sugar by the 1920s). The confusion over the real course of the terms of trade in this period arose from assuming that the terms of trade for a primary producer trading with Britain would be a reciprocal of Britain's. This overlooked the differential impact of falling transport costs, which were a larger element in the import prices of primary products than of manufactures (Bairoch, 1975, pp. 111–23). However, as an explanation for the reversals in the terms of trade for 'Third World' producers *after* 1929, and more especially in the 1980s, Prebisch's thesis appears convincing: workers in industrialised economies did maintain their nominal wages, while primary producers' incomes in underdeveloped regions were slashed.

The policy recommendation that flowed from the ECLA analysis was 'import substitution' industrialisation behind high protective barriers – a strategy later imitated in many other parts of the developing world. Prebisch did not argue that Latin American underdevelopment was due solely to the way the region had been inserted in the international division of labour; he recognised the retarding effects of great disparities in the size of land holdings, a highly unequal distribution of income (which restricted domestic demand) and its concentration in the hands of those whose preferred form of investment was real estate rather than industrial capital (Prebisch, 1967, pp. 29–52). But it was the analysis of 'centre–periphery' trade that caught the attention of the 'Third World' at large. Prebisch was chiefly responsible for persuading the United Nations to convene its first Conference on Trade and Development held at Geneva in 1964 when the 'Third World' (with which

Latin Americans were now beginning to identify themselves) first presented its collective demands to the industrialised economies for the improvement and stabilisation of primary product prices, access for its own manufactures to their markets, and greater financial flows from the rich to the poor.

VI

The indifferent success of ECLA policies encouraged a more radical critique of 'dependency' by a younger generation of social scientists, of whom André Gunder Frank was widely acclaimed on the Left in the late 1960s, though F.H. Cardoso and E. Faletto proved more enduringly influential (Frank, 1967; idem, 1973; Cardoso and Faletto, 1979. The dependency paradigm and its impact on Latin American historiography are usefully reviewed in O'Brien, 1975, and Halperîn Donghi, 1982). The vast but ephemeral enthusiasm for Frank's *Capitalism and Underdevelopment in Latin America* led him to be mistaken for the 'dependency' writer *par excellence*, though other scholars have been more influential in the analysis of Latin American economic experience. Here, it seems right to give Frank's notion of 'dependency' some prominence since it has underpinned a historical account of global inequality and remains influential within the 'Third World' to this day. It is misleading to speak – as many do – of 'dependency' *theory*, since this somewhat amorphous concept has provided a perspective on economic relations between the metropolitan and peripheral economies rather than a precise theory.

A leading target for the *dependistas* has been the model of economic development put forward by W.W. Rostow, which envisages a transition from 'traditional society' to self-sustained growth taking place through clearly defined stages (Rostow, 1960). The assumption of the model was that the 'underdeveloped' societies were in something akin to a 'traditional' state, and would replicate the transition provided certain conditions were met during the critical 'takeoff' stage (chiefly an increase in the rate of investment and improvements in labour productivity which promote rapid technical changes in production, and hence further productivity increases and further investment).

Frank forcibly rejected the idea that 'underdeveloped' societies resembled pre-industrial Europe. He viewed 'underdevelopment' not as original or traditional, but as a state of affairs resulting from the world-wide expansion of the capitalist system from the sixteenth century when the European powers first created satellite economies in Latin America and the Caribbean, using slave or otherwise coerced labour to extract mineral wealth and grow plantation crops. Since manufacturing was, largely, forbidden in European colonies under the mercantilist system, the surplus value created in them was not invested in productive enterprises, but either repatriated or used to support the parasitic lifestyle of a colonial élite. According to Frank, this pattern of metropolitan powers pumping surplus value out of their satellites persisted after former colonies won their independence and was essential to the development of capitalism on a world scale (Frank, 1973, pp. 94–5; idem, 1978). Frank contended that satellite economies industrialised most rapidly when ties with the metropoles were weakest, and that balanced autonomous growth becomes possible on the periphery only when world market relationships are severed. Not all 'dependency' writers accepted this deeply pessimistic conclusion, or the utopian revolutionary politics it supported. Numerous critics have pointed to the simplistic way Frank equates capitalism with market exchange and his cavalier disregard for the discontinuities in centre–periphery relations. Frank's central contention that capitalism formed and characterised Latin American society as early as the sixteenth-century conquest earned a stinging rebuff from the Marxist political theorist Ernesto Laclau: this demonstrated, according to Laclau, conceptual confusion between merchant capital and capitalism as a system of commodity production employing wage labour, and flew in the face of the historical evidence for the implanting or strengthening of servile labour relations in colonial Latin America (Laclau, 1971). The few peripheral countries that have chosen to sever their connections with the capitalist world market countries have not thereby promoted a more 'balanced' economic growth. Independent Burma's seclusion from international trade proved to be self-imposed impoverishment; it had been a comparatively prosperous rice-exporter before 1939.

VII

Though the dependency paradigm is generally eclipsed in academic circles, the historical concerns of the *dependistas* with the origins and persistence of economic inequalities between major regions of the world remain firmly on the scholarly agenda. The most widely discussed explanation for these structural inequalities lies in Immanuel Wallerstein's *The Modern World System*, an ambitious and as yet unfinished history of capitalism as a 'world system' whose historical origins are traced to the late-fifteenth-century crisis of European feudalism. (see Wallerstein, 1974, 1980, 1989. For an outline of his historical account see idem, 1979 and 1983; its theoretical framework is usefully expounded in Hopkins and Wallerstein, 1977.)

Wallerstein is a social scientist who has abandoned 'society' as the theoretical unit for studying social change. The arena of development, he contends, has always been geographically larger than individual 'societies' (usually identified with nation states in the modern era). The alternative unit he proposes is the 'world-system' in which there is production of bulk commodities for a unified market and at least a rudimentary division of labour among constituent regions. Such a 'world' is basically self-contained: all material necessities are produced internally, and trade with external areas is in luxury goods. Notwithstanding the cultural plurality of this 'world', its 'social system' is coextensive with the market and division of labour, and its developmental dynamics are largely internal. The Roman Empire would be a classical example, and Wallerstein proposes that all such large-scale social systems have been either *world empires* or *world economies*. A world empire's defining characteristic is subjection to a single political authority which pumps revenue out of the whole and is able to impose tributary relations on outlying or peripheral regions. A world economy – of which modern, Western capitalism is the most signal example – contains a number of states none of which imposes its authority over the whole arena in which economic factors operate, and there are reasons for thinking that expansive capitalism was feasible *only* within such a framework. The most persuasive arise from the counter-example of imperial China, where a technically and institutionally sophisticated economy became 'trapped' in an equilibrium allowing for quantitative growth but not qualitative change (Elvin, 1973).

As with Prebisch and the dependency theorists, Wallerstein regards the modern world-system as spatially structured, with economic and political power concentrated in a 'core' of strong states to which a 'periphery' and 'semi-periphery' are subordinate. Central to the core–periphery division of labour is 'the fact [*sic*] of unequal exchange', which continually reproduces a geographic division of labour despite massive changes in production processes and continual shifts in the areas constituting the core, periphery and semi-periphery (Hopkins and Wallerstein, 1977, p. 117). In the emergent world economy of the 'long sixteenth century' (1450–1640), each zone exhibited a typical form of labour control and economic class relations. In the 'core' countries of western Europe, where the most technologically advanced forms of manufacturing were concentrated, free wage labour became the norm, but in the 'peripheral' countries of central and eastern Europe serfdom was imposed on hitherto free peasantries by landlords responding to the western demand for grain. While their economic patterns diverged, the two regions became more intensively linked through Baltic trade: the eastern 'played the role of raw-materials producer for the industrialising west' and imported increasing quantities of its manufactures, with the result that native industries and towns declined. Similarly, the world market mechanism articulated 'free' and 'coerced' labour systems when the Atlantic Islands, coastal Brazil and other New World regions were incorporated into the world economy's periphery, for there plantation slavery was normal mode of labour exploitation. Sharecropping was the characteristic form of labour control in the 'semi-periphery', though frankly this seems an arbitrary construct willed into being to explain why conflict between core and periphery has not yet reached systemically destructive proportions.

The key mechanisms in Wallerstein's model of the emergence and expansion of capitalism are, therefore, the inter-regional exchange of necessities and the use of politico-military power by 'core' states to appropriate part of the economic surplus from the periphery and semi-periphery. Economic and political power were aligned, and mutually reinforcing in the European state, certainly by comparison with monolithic military empires (Ottoman Turkey, Mughal India), where the economy was shaped and constrained by the steady, increasing flow of resources to the imperial centre. But, paradoxically, European political power had more intensive potential than 'despotic' imperial power because it was limited internally and internationally. It is a commonplace that empire-building by Europe's maritime powers was an integral part of merchant capitalism's territorial expansion; trade went with dominion, and price was often determined by force. But no state has ever succeeded in imposing its imperium over all the states linked by the world market and extended division of labour. At most, individual states (the seventeenth-century Netherlands, Victorian Britain, the USA after 1945) have enjoyed periods of hegemony thanks to a combination of technological, commercial, financial and military advantage over rival powers.

One conclusion to be drawn from Wallerstein is that the 'Third World' is a misnomer: since virtually all the globe was incorporated into the capitalist 'world-system' by the early twentieth century, a term implying fundamental fissures between developed and underdeveloped regions is deeply misleading. In the world-system perspective, their interconnections explain the gross economic inequalities between regions. But though the perspective leads us to reject the term, it proffers an explanation for the concentration of material deprivation in what we (mistakenly) label the 'Third World'. According to Wallerstein, as the social division of labour was extended geographically in the course of capitalism's development, it became increasingly hierarchical:

> This hierarchisation of space in the structure of productive processes has led to an ever greater polarisation between the core and peripheral zones of the world economy, not only in terms of distributive criteria (real income levels) but in the loci of the accumulation of capital (Wallerstein, 1983, p. 101).

After new zones were incorporated into the world economy, the regular transfer of surplus value to 'core' countries through unequal exchange steadily impoverished their semi-proletarianised workforces. Boldly, Wallerstein defends the early Marxist proposition that, with capitalism's development, the proletariat suffers absolute immiseration, though in a global not a societal context:

> The vast majority of the population of the world are objectively and subjectively less well-off materially than in previous historical systems . . . the overwhelming proportion of the world's work-forces, who live in rural zones or move between them and urban slums, are worse off than their ancestors 500 years ago: they eat less well, and have a less balanced diet.

Though they are more likely to survive the first year of life, it is to be doubted whether 'life prospects of the majority of the world's population as of age one are greater than previously'. They 'unquestionably work harder for less total reward, so the rate of exploitation has escalated very sharply' (ibid.). Whether we will ever know enough about mass living standards outside Europe five centuries ago to verify or refute these contentions I rather doubt. From the chronicles of Mughal India, Irfan Habib identified about one year in three between 1554 and 1707 as a period of famine or severe scarcity. Famines rarely affected all the empire, but their threat was a permanent element in the peasantry's everyday life, and during the worst recorded children were commonly sold into slavery and the starving resorted to cannibalism (Habib, 1963, pp. 101–9). So perhaps we should treat secular immiseration circumspectly. I have attempted to summarise changes in material well-being in South Asia and sub-Saharan Africa, not over half a millennium, but during the period of modern European colonialism (Chapters 5 and 6). The issue is complex, but the evidence points in my view to altered forms of poverty rather than absolute impoverishment, and there is little question that colonial administrations were more competent to alleviate famines than the indigenous regimes they displaced. Of course, it is far easier to criticise Wallerstein's model of modern capitalist development than to put forward an alternative of comparable scope, historical detail and conceptual cogency. We can discard the absolute immiseration thesis without denying that human society has become more polarised between plenty and want. Taking 1869 as 100, the index of real national income in India was 175 in 1970, and in Britain 444. On an exchange rate basis, per capita income in India was only 4.6 per cent of average income in Britain in 1970, though this exaggerates the disparity because exchange rates reflect the prices of internationally traded commodities and underestimate real purchasing power in poor societies. In terms of purchasing power parities, average Indian income was 11.8 per cent of British. By using relative growth rates to extrapolate back, we can *hazard* that the purchasing power of per capita income in 1869 was about a third of that in Britain, which suggests that Indian relative deprivation increased threefold in the following century (Heston, 1983, pp. 415–17).

VIII

Of the broad objections levelled at Wallerstein's study, three strike me as so fundamental that they should be raised immediately. The first is his habit of explaining specific historical events in terms of their outcomes meeting the 'needs' or requirements of the 'world system'. This type of teleological reasoning is no explanation at all: economic or social systems have no 'needs' and to identify the unanticipated consequences of historical events does not explain their occurrence. If we use 'needs' in the unobjectionable sense of the conscious requirements of Europeans for economic resources then, certainly, we will find one motive for expansion into the 'Third World', but we might also be struck by how little the 'Third World' has contributed to meeting those requirements. The crude functionalism of Wallerstein's model leads him habitually to reduce organised military–political power to an epiphenomenon of economic power and economic structures: the actions of states are routinely explained as determined by the 'needs' of the world economy. One critic of Wallerstein's first volume charged him with ignoring the European states system as an autonomous factor in creating the links between Europe and the overseas dependencies in the long sixteenth century (Zolberg, 1981). This criticism could be made with equal force of Wallerstein's handling of European empire-building in India in the eighteenth.

The second is that Wallerstein's focus on inter-regional exchange relations and a regional division of labour obscures a regular and dominant feature of capitalism, namely the growth of the productivity of free labour within the individual enterprise as a result of technological innovation. Most see this as the prime source of business profits from production – or the relative surplus value appropriated by the capitalist, to use the Marxist terminology. Since productive enterprises have typically expanded by the reinvestment of profits, it must be judged the taproot of capital accumulation. The point has been well made by Robert Brenner in a critique of Wallerstein's account of the origins of structural economic inequality between 'core' western European countries and central-eastern Europe during the early modern era. *All* productive activities at the 'core' were more capital- and skill-intensive than agriculture in the 'periphery'. This was because in the Low Countries, northern France and England there existed a social system that tended to equip direct producers with capital and skill at the highest level of existing technique and that possessed the capacity to continue to do so on an increasing scale. East of the Elbe, agrarian production using coerced labour discouraged investment in fixed capital and undermined the development of skill. Since enserfment was under way about a century *before* grain exports became significant, it cannot have been (contrary to Wallerstein) a strategy of labour control adopted by seigniorial magnates seeking to maximise their profits from the 'world' grain market. It was, rather, the low level of labour productivity in serf-based economy (together with abundant land) which determined the region's role as a primary exporter in the world market. The 'underdevelopment' of the region – Brenner concludes – resulted not from the transfer of the surplus value to the 'core' but from a class structure that retarded the growth of labour productivity (Brenner, 1977).

The third objection, and the most pertinent to the themes of this book, concerns the contributions made by commerce with the extra-European 'periphery' and European colonialism in the tropics to economic development *within* western Europe itself. Here it is useful to set Wallerstein's work in the broader Marxist tradition. Marx – in one of his moods – regarded the early modern colonial system as a great accelerator of capital accumulation: sheer plunder in the Americas and elsewhere were the 'chief moments of primitive accumulation', but colonies served a more substantial purpose by providing 'a market for the budding manufactures, and [for] a vast increase in accumulation which was guaranteed by the mother country's monopoly of the market'. The chartered companies with monopolies on colonial trade were 'powerful levers for the concentration of capital', and their financial operations 'served as a forcing-house for the credit system'. Britain eventually wrested commercial supremacy from its European rivals towards the close of the pre-industrial period of manufacture and this supremacy, Marx concluded, 'produce[d] industrial predominance' (Marx, 1867, 1976 edition, pp. 915–18).

Mere quotation proves nothing, of course, but trade statistics confirm that the plantation colonies absorbed a large proportion of eighteenth-century Britain's manufacturing output. As with the other 'advanced' European states (the Netherlands and France), Britain's foreign trade expanded more quickly than total output, and in peacetime colonial commerce had a higher growth rate than other international trade. Manufactures formed a remarkably large proportion (around four-fifths) of British exports. About a third of manufactured output was exported around 1760, and exports may have represented what Adam Smith called 'a vent-for-surplus', or a market demand that meant the utilisation of production factors that would otherwise have been underemployed. Between 1700 and 1760, exports accounted for 56 per cent of the increase in the output of manufactures, and for 46 per cent during the decades 1780 to 1800, so they were almost certainly an exogenous factor in the structural change that resulted in the disproportionate growth of employment in the secondary and tertiary sectors (O'Brien and Engerman, 1991, p. 188).

Nearly all the *increment* in the volume of commodity exports was due to colonial trade during the first three-quarters of the century. One may then ask whether this vindicates Eric Hobsbawm's claim that

> Behind the Industrial Revolution there lies this concentration on the colonial and 'underdeveloped' markets overseas, the successful battle to deny them to anyone else . . . Our industrial economy grew out of our commerce, and especially our commerce with the underdeveloped world (Hobsbawm, 1969, p. 54).

The answer is 'Not entirely'. Overseas sales in colonial and neo-colonial markets were a necessary condition for industrialisation in Britain, but that process cannot 'grow' directly from trade, only from technological innovation, capital accumulation and investment. Opportunities in colonial commerce must have been a potent influence on investment decisions, but whether the profits of this trade were a major source of investment capital is debatable, and I have reviewed the main lines of argument with respect to the financing of British industrialisation in Chapter 2.

For Europe as a whole, commerce with the 'periphery' was simply too small a part of total economic activity for its profits to have played a significant role in capital accumulation during industrialisation. Around

1800, exports represented between 3.5 and 4.5 per cent of European GNP and about three-quarters went to other European states. Of the remaining quarter, about half went to the United States and half to South America, the Caribbean, Asia and Africa (the 'Third World' in modern parlance) combined. Allowing for the exports to slave states of the USA, we can hazard that the overseas 'periphery' received a fifth of European exports, representing less than 1 per cent of GNP. Bairoch does not give comparable estimates on European imports c.1800, but it is probable that about two-thirds were furnished by European countries themselves, and perhaps a quarter by the periphery (Bairoch, 1976, p. 86).

If we turn briefly to the century between 1830 and 1930, when the development gap between Europe and the 'Third World' widened critically, and vast territories in Asia, Africa and the Pacific came under European rule, then we would expect to see demonstrable evidence of colonialism's contribution to modern economic growth at the 'core'. Why else were colonies seized but to stake out economic claims on the future, to secure markets and supplies of raw materials? For continental Europe, the evidence suggests that expectations of 'social' gain were mistaken, even if individuals and groups profited handsomely. Up to the Second World War, the developed countries of Europe (excluding the USSR) and North America were basically self-sufficient in industrial raw materials, which represented a modest fraction of 'Third World' exports throughout the nineteenth century and well into the twentieth. Textile fibres accounted for about 14 per cent of 'Third World' exports in 1830 and, together with raw rubber, 19 per cent in 1936–8. Minerals (excluding precious metals) and energy sources constituted only 4 per cent of 'Third World' exports in 1911–13, and though their importance grew thereafter with oil exploitation, had still reached only 16 per cent in 1936–8 (Bairoch, 1980). As far as Europe as a whole was concerned, the 'Third World' was relatively unimportant in international trade: between 1800 and 1938, only 18 per cent of total European exports were destined for 'Third World' countries (although for exported manufactures the proportion was significantly higher). More than four-fifths of the developed world's international trade took place between developed countries. Since, on average, exports accounted for some 8 to 9 per cent of GNP in the developed countries, exports to the 'Third World' represented about 1.5 per cent of the developed world's total production (ibid.). The geographical structure of British trade was exceptionally oriented to the non-European world and, from the early nineteenth century to the Second World War, the 'Third World' of Asia, South America and Africa absorbed about 40 per cent of British exports (which were overwhelmingly comprised of manufactures). For one industry – cotton – the proportion of exports going to 'Third World' markets was as high as 67 per cent before 1914. Britain's pre-eminent role as a colonial power has, doubtless, contributed to the mistaken notion of the colonial 'estates' as positive complements to metropolitan growth, but – as Bairoch points out – the growth of output and productivity in Britain after 1870 was retarded by comparison with industrial rivals (especially Germany) much less implicated in the colonial adventure. The geographical structure of continental Europe's international trade was quite different from Britain's: in 1910 only 15 per cent of Europe's exports were destined for South America, Asia and Africa combined, and these continents provided only 22.2 per cent of European imports (Bairoch, 1976, p.88). It is true that for France protected colonial trade was becoming increasingly important before the First World War and that, while the absolute quantity did not increase greatly during the inter-war period, the proportional significance of colonial commerce rose considerably during the world economic crisis. But the French case must be a qualification (that we will pursue in more detail elsewhere) of the overall thesis that *intra*-European trade has been the dominant and dynamic element in continental Europe's development as an economic bloc. This was as much the case when the European empires spanned the world as it was during the 1950s and 1960s.

The Structure of this Book

In subsequent chapters, this book presents an overview of European expansion into the Americas, Asia and Africa, not with the intention of producing a comprehensive narrative, but to address discrete questions arising from debates over the origins of global inequality and the emergence of the 'Third World'. What economic advantages did Europeans gain from their conquests in the 'New World'? How did plantation slavery and the slave trade contribute to capitalist development in the Atlantic economy? These questions – far easier to raise than to answer satisfactorily – are examined in Chapter 2. In Chapter 3, I discuss European enterprise in Asia and ask why and how Europe's chartered trading companies were transformed into territorial powers. Did the triumph of European corporate militarism in Asia 'head off' or deform an indigenous process of capitalist development? Chapter 4 analyses relations between Europe and Africa in the centuries between the onset of the Atlantic slave trade and the subjection of the continent to European colonial rule. It can be read as a sympathetic but sceptical response to Walter Rodney's *How Europe Underdeveloped Africa*, a book that has done more than any other to popularise the thesis that African technological backwardness and impoverishment were historically rooted in the export trade in slaves and European colonialism (Rodney, 1972). Chapters 5 and 6 summarise the impact of European colonialism on the indigenous economies of South Asia and Africa: was their growth 'retarded' by specialisation on primary product exporting for international markets? Were Indians and Africans impoverished by European rule? Chapter 7 assesses the costs and benefits of modern colonialism for the European colonial powers up to the 1930s. Chapter 8 discusses the political economy of decolonisation and the association of some of the world's poorest countries with the European Economic Community through trade and aid agreements. Was the political retreat from colonial empire determined, or at least influenced, by the calculation that the economic costs of continued sovereignty were too great to bear, while the prospects of doing business with nationalist regimes were quite enticing?

This is a daunting agenda of questions and problems, and attempting to answer them has meant ransacking a large number of specialist studies. Their authors will, doubtless, cringe at the temerity with which I have pronounced on complex issues about which I know too little. But if this book has a virtue, it lies in a brash refusal to be overawed by academic specialisms. Trying to explain causal sequences and consequences over the longterm is as much part of the historian's job as the empathetic reconstruction of particular actions from documentary evidence. It cannot be done without abstract concepts, theories and hypotheses, though, in my view, there is no general theoretical perspective of global development through which we can view the tortuous interaction of an expanding Europe with a host of non-European states and societies and make everything appear coherent. Wallerstein's is the nearest approximation to one, but it is fair to say that historians of the 'Third World' increasingly view his model of the capitalist 'world economy' as something to write *against*. His basic premise that capitalism is a global economic system with a single, European point of origin has been challenged by historians of pre-colonial Asia, and is plainly controverted by the dynamic 'local' capitalisms that developed out of Chinese and indigenous merchant communities in colonial South-East and South Asia. (Pearson, 1988, provides a critique of Wallerstein's model from the perspective of pre-colonial Asia.) European economic historians are sceptical of a model that pushes the concept of a large-scale economic system, constituted by long-distance trade, back into centuries when exports and imports were small parts of total product and consumption.

As Michael Mann has so rightly remarked, societies are much *messier* than our theories of them, and this is necessarily true of attempts to 'model' their interaction over time (Mann, 1986, p. 4). Indeed, to talk of societies interacting is misleading shorthand, since they are not corporate entities that can collide together like opposing armies. My own reference to an 'expanding Europe' is even more misleading, since Europe has never had a corporate existence, has not been a single ideological or cultural community since the Reformation, was not 'represented' in international politics until recently – and even now its representation is partial and effective mainly in collective negotiations with trading partners. Since the early modern period, military–political power has been 'contained' within states and state coalitions, and remains so. There have been few if any occasions when representatives of the European states have conferred to decide 'Europe's' relations with the non-European world. (One example that is sometimes cited, the Berlin Africa Conference of 1884-5, actually demonstrates the unreality of thinking of 'Europe' as a supra-national political entity: the conference did not deal with issues of territorial sovereignty, and all the frontier demarcations in Africa were made by bilateral treaties between individual European states.) All this is commonplace, and should scarcely need saying were it not that even the finest historians refer to 'Europe' as if it was somehow a historical actor in world history. Mann's methodological approach to societies as constituted by multiple overlapping and intersecting socio-spatial networks of power should provoke historians to reconceptualise European expansion, colonialism and imperialism.

2

EUROPE AND THE AMERICAS

Introduction

Though the 'Great Discoveries' of the late fifteenth century were part of a continuum of European exploration and colonisation stretching back several centuries, the colonial conquests of Spain and Portugal in the Americas constituted a great break in human history. The indigenous peoples – possibly numbering 100 million in 1492 (Lockhart and Schwartz, 1983, p. 36) – had been isolated for so long from the rest of the human gene pool that they had no inherited immunities to 'Old World' pathogens and were tragically vulnerable to 'virgin soil' epidemics. Stricken populations were unable to resist alien conquest and, within a single generation of Cortés's expedition to Mexico (1519–22), the most densely settled regions had been brought under Spanish rule. The Catholic monarchs' new subjects practised advanced agriculture, and lived in hierarchical societies with complex political structures, but money and the payment of labour were unknown and precious metals were used for artefacts, not regular exchange. Tribute in labour and kind was rendered to the dominant strata (Gibson, 1984, p. 401). The conquerors sought to replicate the social order they had left behind in Europe by grafting the urban institutions of Castile onto the New World. To the rule over the 'Indians', they brought habits of mind formed in the centuries-long reconquest of the Iberian peninsula from Islam. The conquered would be forcibly converted and transformed, so far as possible, into the vassals of *encomenderos* – the Spaniards granted temporary lordship and tributary rights over specified Indian communities – and Spanish-style peasants. They would be made to conform to European notions of work and incorporated into a monetised and wage-labour economy (Elliott, 1984a, p. 204).

Some two centuries after this most spectacular of all colonial conquests, Adam Smith asked 'What are the advantages which Europe has derived from the discovery and colonization of America?' His question – and the answers he gave – make an apt point of departure for this chapter. Smith denied that Europe had been enriched by the fabled imports of American gold and silver: these had merely cheapened precious metals to about a third of their value in 1500, and though Europe doubtless gained 'a real conveniency' from more abundant coin, it was 'very trifling'. He divided the economic gains into those accruing to Europe, 'considered as one great country', and the particular advantages for each colonizing country. For Europe generally, the essential change was the opening of 'a new and inexhaustible market' for its surplus manufactures, though he also stressed the increased trade and consumption within Europe consequent on American imports. But his positive assessment of these commercial gains was much qualified: exclusive trade policies had artificially increased the price of colonial commodities and reduced their consumption, while implementing these policies had raised the costs of military protection. Smith further argued that the high profitability of transatlantic colonial trade had diverted commercial capital from less profitable branches of foreign trade, particularly in the Mediterranean, and so hastened their decay (Smith, 1776, 1976 edn, pp. 49, 447–8, 591–8).

What is missing from Smith's account is any quantification – however imprecise – of the gains he imputed to the rise of a transatlantic economy, but it is easy to show that for Europe *as a whole* they were trifling. Long-distance trade was significant only for favourably situated regions or small national economies. Britain exported a substantial, though fluctuating, proportion of its gross national product throughout the eighteenth century (ranging from 8.4 to 14.6 per cent) (Crafts, 1985, p. 131). But throughout Europe (including Russia but excluding Ottoman Turkey) exports were only 3 per cent of GNP on average around 1790. Three-quarters of European exports were to European states. About 10 per cent went to North America, 8 per cent to South America (including the Caribbean) and only 1 per cent to Africa, so the fraction of Europe's total product traded in the Atlantic 'triangle' was miniscule (Bairoch, 1974, pp. 561–2, 577). Imports from the Americas were mostly luxuries, such as sugar and tobacco, with markets limited by the small margin for spending on non-essentials in pre-industrial societies. Even allowing for value added through processing and distribution in Europe, it is difficult to believe they represented as much as a tenth of total European consumption. Vast though the Americas were, exiguous population meant they were a modestly sized economic bloc in relation to

Europe. Had they been a bloc of equivalent size, their exports around 1750 would have been no more than 0.5 to 1.5 per cent of total product (to allow for value added in Europe). We know, of course, that exports were a much larger proportion of American production than this, but if we fix it arbitrarily at 10 per cent we can deduce that the colonial bloc's population could not have represented more than 5 to 15 per cent of Europe's population. On assumptions highly favourable to transatlantic trade, we can surmise that, more than two centuries after its inception, it had extended the European market by, perhaps, a tenth (Bairoch, 1980, pp. 30–1). For individual countries, notably Britain and France, transatlantic trade became progressively more important throughout the eighteenth century, and we will assess its role in their economic growth below, but for early modern Europe 'considered as one great country', the Americas were economically marginal – at least from the perspective of 'Smithian' growth.

A more robust case might be made for the 'New World' discoveries as a huge increment to Europe's physical resource base in terms of fisheries, subtropical plantation lands, timber forests, prairies and granaries. The land–labour ratio in the economic space controlled and exploited by Europeans increased about six-fold in the sixteenth and early seventeenth centuries. To quote Eric Jones: 'An unparalleled share of the earth's biological resources was acquired for [Europe] on a scale that was unprecedented and is unrepeatable' (Jones, 1987, p. 82). But economic logic would suggest that the full exploitation of this natural largesse awaited the nineteenth-century transport revolution, and the empirical evidence seems to confirm this. In Spanish America, the export of bulky agricultural products of low intrinsic value to Europe was always marginal to shipments of precious metal. When silver was shipped in great quantities, merchants could economise on transport costs and export agricultural goods profitably: in 1589, for example, 144 000 hides were exported to Spain, but the number fell to a mere fraction of that total during the seventeenth century, and did not approach it again until the eighteenth century (Macleod, 1984a, p. 369). Buenos Aires has an exceptionally fertile hinterland, but for much of the colonial period it was an economic backwater, oriented not to the Atlantic but to the Andean mining industry. When a salted meat industry did evolve on the La Plata estuary in the late eighteenth century, its main market was the Brazilian and Cuban slave plantations (Scobie, 1971, pp. 70–3). American timber products failed to become a major export to Europe because high transport costs meant they were unable to compete with better-located Baltic supplies. Only the exigencies of wartime compelled the British navy to look to America for its masts and spars (Solow, 1991, p. 26). Fisheries were probably the major exception to the rule that physical resources yielding low-value 'bulk' products remained under exploited by pre-industrial Europe.

Demography and Labour in the 'New World'

Such resources are commercially valueless without inputs of labour willing or compelled to produce for market exchange, and labour shortages due to disease and demographic decline constrained the long-term development of the post-Columbian Americas. In ecological terms, they can be broadly categorised into the lowland tropics and Caribbean, the populous highland areas of Middle America, Colombia and the Andes, and the thinly populated temperate areas of North America and the Southern Cone. The admixture of 'Old World' and African diseases had a varied impact on these different regions. The tropical areas were particularly vulnerable to the ravages of imported disease, and the densely settled populations of the Greater Antilles were eliminated within a few decades of Columbus's arrival. The native Arawaks of Hispaniola may have numbered 3 to 4 million in 1492; within a generation they had been wiped out by smallpox, enslavement and the uprooting of their agricultural plots by newly introduced pigs (Watts, 1987, pp. 71–5). The Spanish originally exploited their Caribbean islands as a slave supply area, but once the natives were extinct and the placer gold reserves exhausted, they had slight economic interest in tropical dependencies chronically handicapped by labour shortage. The impact of 'virgin soil' epidemics was marginally less severe in coastal Brazil, but tantamount to the depopulation of some of the best agricultural land in the tropical world – far better land for intensive agriculture than any available in tropical Africa. Though the Portuguese attempted to establish a sugar plantation economy using Indian labour – both coerced and waged – demographic decline compelled them to import African slaves. By 1650, blacks and mulattos comprised about 70 per cent of the population of colonial Brazil; in the early nineteenth century this combined ethnic group was nearly three-quarters of the population of the lowland tropics and Caribbean.

The populous highland regions of continental Spanish America had a different demographic history. The Indians experienced absolute disease mortality on a horrendous scale, but their pre-Columban numbers were such that they did not face extinction, and it has been estimated that they still comprised 84 per cent of a total population of just less than 10 million in 1650 (Slicher van Bath, 1986, pp.19–32). Indian numbers declined throughout the colonial period but there was a compensatory increase of *mestizos* – people of mixed Spanish and Indian descent – who could satisfy the labour requirements of mining and ranching. In Spain itself, there was some demographic pressure before about 1630, followed by a population decline so severe during the epidemics of the seventeenth-century crisis that there was no net increase between 1550 and 1700. Basically for this reason, Spain provided few agricultural colonists: the peak number of annual migrants appears to have been reached before 1650, and total net immigration down to 1820 was probably as low as 750 000 – far behind the influx into temperate North America (Eltis, 1983, p. 254). Even if peasants did migrate to the Indies, it was not to perpetuate their peasantdom. The conquerors' prime concern was not to develop the land, but to extract its mineral wealth and exact labour and tribute from indigenous peoples. The rapid increase in cheap *mestizo* labour may have further discouraged agricultural immigration (Elliott, 1990; Hennessy, 1992, pp. 8–36). At Spanish American independence in the 1820s, Indians and *mestizos* comprised nearly four-fifths of the population; *criollos* – or those of entirely Spanish descent – were only 18.4 per cent.

This was an entirely different demographic history from that of the temperate English and French colonies to the north. There, the native population – reckoned at only 860 000 in 1650 (Slicher van Bath, 1986, Table 2) – was too small and scattered for tributary exploitation. The territory could be developed only by importing slave labour, or by white immigration (usually of indentured servants in the colonial period). European immigrants were much more important for population growth than imported slaves: the colonies that became the United States (and, of lesser importance quantitatively, Canada) were among the very few major areas to which, into the middle of the nineteenth century, more migrants came from Europe than from Africa. By 1825, whites were nearly 80 per cent of the total population.

As my demographic sketch has indicated, the Americas had little in common except geographic contiguity, and each found its own solutions to the problem of labour supply. Labour institutions were rarely selected on purely economic criteria: a deep-seated repugnance at the enslavement of Europeans closed off the option of transporting white slave labour, though it would have been more rational than purchasing Africans and shipping them across the Atlantic (Eltis, 1993, p. 1404). Equally, the humanitarian revulsion against the barbarous treatment of the Indians by the first colonists palpably affected the labour regime in the Spanish empire. The New Laws of 1542 – which reflected the impassioned advocacy of Bartolomé de Las

Casas – emancipated all Indian slaves and ended the Indians' obligation to provide unpaid labour to the *encomenderos*. (One must add that Las Casas did not have our sense of the universality of humanity, and recommended that African slaves be imported to serve the colonists.) (Brading, 1991, p. 61). Royal policy had long regarded obligatory labour services as an unsatisfactory expedient pending the establishment of free wage labour and, henceforth, the law required all Indians working for Spaniards to be paid a daily wage. Indian communities were supposed to provide estate and mine owners with workers through the *repartimiento* – an official form of labour service – but the system decayed where declining villages were unable to meet their quotas. In central New Spain, the core area of the Spanish empire, most Indian labour was freely engaged under individual contracts by the later seventeenth and eighteenth centuries (Gibson, 1984, pp. 404–5).

Compulsory labour levies were needed when silver-mining – the mainstay of the colonial economy – got under way in the thinly populated Mexican north and the Peruvian Andes, but their importance declined over time. After the mercury refining process was introduced from the late 1550s, mining became a more labour-intensive and technically demanding industry, staffed largely by skilled wage-earners. By the late 1590s, they were about two-thirds of the labour force in the Mexican mines, paid well enough to make the work attractive, although they were also rewarded by appropriating a 'share' of the ore for smelting in crude native ovens. Draft workers and black slaves made up the other third in roughly equal proportions. The Spanish had no compunction about exploiting Africans in the lowland gold workings of present-day Colombia, where black slaves predominated, but believed them ill-adapted to work in highlands and, therefore, a poor investment. This explains their absence from Peruvian silver mining, centred on the legendary Potosí mountain and the mercury deposits at Huancavelica, where the Inca system of draft labour, *mita*, was adapted to Spanish purposes. Introduced in the 1570s and not abolished until 1812, this compelled one man in seven from an enormous area of the Andes to spend a year at Potosí where he worked one week on, two weeks off for prescribed wages (Bakewell, 1984, p. 231; Williamson, 1992, pp.49–50). The annual draft was intended to raise 13 500 labourers, of whom 4500 were to be available for the mines and refineries at any one time. It permitted more capital-intensive methods and contributed to a quadrupling of output in the 1570s and 1580s. For the entrepreneur, *mita* had certain advantages over slavery: it did not involve him in recurrent capital outlays on slaves, and furnished labour below market rates, whose subsistence and 'reproduction' costs were covered by Indian communities (Tandeter, 1981, pp. 104–5; Stern, 1988, p. 851). Notwithstanding these advantages, the mine owners were compelled to recruit permanent, voluntary workers for skilled tasks, and these accounted for more than half Potosí's labour force by the 1600s (when the settlement's total population of all races was a staggering 160 000). Their market position was such that they, too, could insist on appropriating some of the ore for processing and sale through the native refining sector. *Mita* labour had a renewed economic importance in the context of the mid-eighteenth-century Bourbon revival of the mining industry: the quota system was manipulated to exploit the *mitayos* more intensely, which contributed signally to the Potosí mines doubling their production between the 1740s and 1790s.

Black Slavery in the Americas

No labour institution had a greater impact on American development than black slavery, and transatlantic trade links were greatly strengthened by the founding of slave-worked plantations because their whole purpose was production for export. Large-scale units of agrarian capital oriented to distant markets would not have formed without slavery or serfdom, since free white labour was insufficiently forthcoming and entailed a chronic tendency towards economic self-sufficiency. Few Europeans were willing to cross the Atlantic to work for others – particularly in the plantation agriculture suited to the climate and soils of the tropics – and the wide availability of cheap land was a constant inducement to set up on one's own account. There was so little demographic pressure in Europe before *c.*1760 that agricultural settlers had to be sought amongst Portuguese *degredados*, defeated Celtic rebels, transported sectarians, and economically marginal groups. The majority of early migrants to the French and British Caribbean and mainland colonies were indentured white servants, but they proved a notoriously transient (and truculent) class who moved on once their term of service was over (Johnson, 1984, pp. 251, 264; Dunn, 1972, p. 72). Before 1820, the total number of permanent European immigrants was not much above two million, while incoming slaves during the whole course of the slave trade totalled about 9.8 million (Lovejoy, 1982). The *net* immigration of free white labourers did not exceed slave imports until the 1840s. As David Eltis reminds us, 'In terms of immigration alone . . . America was an extension of Africa rather than Europe. . .' (Eltis, 1987, p. 24).

New World slavery is the focus of complex historical debates to which I can only allude here. The institution itself has been viewed both as 'a phenomenon of simple continuity' originating in Mediterranean and Iberian practices (an argument advanced in Verlinden, 1970, chs 1 and 2) *and* as a radically new departure in systems of bonded labour. The political economists regarded labour extorted by fear of punishment as inefficient and unproductive, and in the long run more costly than any other. Slave-based economies, they argued, could not accumulate human capital and depended on foreigners for all products requiring much skill. Since slaves were denied their reason and individuality, slavery was inimical to economic progress. New World slavery was, therefore, an atavism in the modern world – an expense of human effort that could be borne only by exceptionally profitable enterprises, such as sugar plantations. Against this notion of New World slavery as an atavism, recent scholars have emphasised its economic modernity: plantation agriculture involved a lengthy cycle of investment and profit realisation that demanded calculative rationality no less than the super-exploitation of slave labour. Many slaves were skilled, and masters responded to rising slave prices and competition in product markets by increasing labour productivity. More fundamental to debates over global modernisation is the argument (reinvigorated by Robin Blackburn and others) that the commercial development in the slave-based Atlantic economy decisively advanced the pace of capitalist industrialisation: by extending the export market for manufactures; by augmenting the funds available for investment; and by supplying a key industrial raw material – cotton fibre – at low cost.

This last theme will be taken up subsequently, but the origins and broad variants of New World slavery are worth noting immediately. To the Iberians who introduced African slavery to the Americas, the institution was as familiar and unquestioned as marriage (Lockhart and Schwartz, 1983, p. 17). Portuguese expeditions to West Africa had been returning with slaves since the 1440s, and they were about one in ten of Lisbon's population in 1551. Most were household servants or skilled artisans, and lived under codes that accorded rights to personal security and property and erected barriers to breeding slaves in captivity (Klein, 1967, pp.59–61). Metropolitan slavery continued its parallel existence and, though slave imports to Portugal were abolished in 1761, this was only to ensure adequate supplies to Brazil, where they had become scarce and expensive (Alden, 1984, p. 625). In the major colonial cities, slavery resembled the urban, codified status of the metropoles. Slaves were always a minority among a population of white criollos, Indians, *mestizos*, *mulattos* and free blacks. Because manumission was commonly ordered in slave-owners' wills, slavery ceased to be the predominant status of Africans in continental Spanish America by about 1750, when the majority were free people (Bowser, 1984, pp. 367–75).

The second variant – plantation slavery – proved the decisive factor in the burgeoning transatlantic economy, as the labour input in cane sugar production, a form of 'agro-industry' that had originated in the eastern Mediterranean and evolved into the premier institution of European economic expansion. Cane must be ground soon after cutting, for the sap quickly dries or ferments, so harvesting and basic refining had to be a virtually continuous process in the same enterprise. Plantations centred round a mill and refinery where the juice was boiled and 'raw' sugar extracted. (Subsequent refining could be – and typically was – undertaken elsewhere.) Plantation labour, whether in the fields or around the boilers, needed to be integrated and disciplined; all accounts emphasise its rebarbative and, to our eyes, anachronistically 'industrial' character. Genoese and Venetian merchants had established prototypes of this agro-industrial complex in Cyprus and Crete, mainly using serf labour (though some slaves are recorded). Genoese capital and commercial institutions largely financed its 'migration' to the Iberian dependencies in the Atlantic. Here, the sugar–slave complex was fashioned into 'the bridge over which European civilisation crossed from the Old World to the New' (Solow, 1987, p. 55). In the Canaries, sharecroppers performed much of the work, but the colonisation of the Madeiras and the Azores occurred while African slaves were becoming available in greater numbers. They were imported into Madeira from 1443 and soon became the bulk of the labour force. By 1500, the island was the world's largest sugar producer, and the Atlantic sugar plantations were attracting investment capital from financial houses in Antwerp and Augsburg, as well as Genoa. Partly because crops depleted as continuous cultivation exhausted the soil, the centre of greatest productivity (and profitability on international markets) tended to shift geographically to newly acquired islands. Older centres were left producing only for local markets (where they had an advantage in transport costs) and diversified their agriculture. In Portugal's empire, the main centre of production moved in the early sixteenth century from Madeira to the Cape Verde Islands and to São Tomé in the Gulf of Guinea which was close to the sources of slave supply and later served as an entrepôt for the transatlantic slave trade. An estimated 25 000 Africans were shipped to the Atlantic islands over the whole period of the slave trade, while São Tomé probably retained about 100 000 slave imports (Curtin, 1969, Table 4, p. 20).

By 1503, cane sugar and black slaves had both been introduced into Santo Domingo, in the Spanish Caribbean, and the first sugar was shipped to Europe by 1516. But once launched on their mainland conquests, the Spanish were content to let the Antilles serve as defensive points and way stations for their more valuable continental possessions, and the sugar–slave complex played a subordinate role in the Spanish American empire until the later eighteenth century. The decisive transatlantic shift in the sugar frontier was to the coastal strip of Bahia and Pernambuco, where it gained a foothold in the 1530s and proved the economic salvation of Brazil. By 1570, about 60 sugar mills had been established, each requiring 60 to 100 slaves. The number of mills roughly doubled in the next fifteen years as the continually rising price of sugar in Europe encouraged planters to bring new lands under cultivation, invest in refining equipment, and accelerate the transition to an African labour force. Brazil overtook the Atlantic islands as the world's largest producer and exporter around 1580 and held this position for about a century. The apogee of its sugar cycle came about 1630, when production was dislocated by the Dutch invasion of Pernambuco, and the first competitors appeared in the Caribbean (Solow, 1987; Mintz, 1985).

There are self-evident continuities in this narrative, but they should not distract from the historic shift marked by deploying huge numbers of Africans to labour for European masters in the Americas, nor the novelty of the slave plantation as a miniature 'society'. It was one in which black slaves predominated numerically over free workers, and where 'the bundle of property rights in the masters' hands was far more elaborate, all-inclusive, and permanent than its model in Europe' (Curtin, 1977, pp. 9–10). In the British and French colonies this plantation society was regulated by draconian slave laws that 'legitimized a state of war between blacks and whites, sanctified rigid segregation, and institutionalized a warning system against slave revolts' (Dunn, 1972, p. 245). Furthermore, this societal form required regular imports to sustain itself: the slave populations in sugar producing regions had a constant 'natural' tendency to decrease because of a common demographic structure, the intensity of labour exploitation and similar disease environments. Male slaves outnumbered female on the plantations, not simply because planters preferred healthy young males who were more likely to repay their capital costs before dying of disease, but also because powerful Africans preferred to sell men rather than women. With few slave unions, the numbers born in captivity were rather low, while the morbidity of African-born slaves was higher than those born on the plantations, so fresh slave imports were constantly needed to compensate for the excess of deaths over births (Curtin, 1969, p. 28). This was the fundamental factor in explaining the persistence of the slave trade well into the nineteenth century. The majority of slaves were transported between 1701 to 1810, when imports totalled 5 737 600 (with British vessels accounting for about 40 per cent of shipments, and Portuguese and French for 30 per cent and 20 per cent respectively). But 2 253 000 slaves were imported between 1811 and 1867, though Britain had forbidden the trade to its nationals and made strenuous efforts to outlaw it internationally (Lovejoy, 1982, Table 9, p. 497).

Brazil was the largest single market – absorbing more than a third of all shipments over the whole course of the trade – principally because its environment was so hostile for slave population growth that numbers required constant replenishment from Africa. In the Bahian sugar-producing districts, about 70 per cent of slaves were African-born from 1600 to the end of the colonial era (Schwartz, 1985, p. 350). Early-nineteenth-century Brazil still depended on slave imports to produce export staples when it entered the coffee 'cycle': an annual average of 37 000 slaves were imported between 1811 and 1850 for the South-Central plantations (Curtin, 1990, p. 191). This explains the tenacity with which the Brazilian slave-owners clung to the slave trade, despite growing international opprobrium. By contrast with the tropical regions, Anglophone North America proved a much healthier environment for slaves who were able to achieve a rate of natural increase approaching that of their free, white contemporaries. Only 4 to 5 per of total imports went to the British continental colonies and the independent United States after 1786, but the slave population had reached just over 1.5 million by 1825. This was significantly greater than Brazil's (reckoned at 1.15 million slaves in 1823), though the demographic discrepancy was not quite so startling because there were far more free blacks and *mulattos* in Brazil than in the USA.

Bullion, Price Inflation and the Rise of a Transatlantic Trading System

Barbara Solow has argued that 'firm and enduring trade links between Europe and America were not forged without and until the introduction of slavery' (Solow, 1991, p. 21), but she overstates her case. As early as the 1520s, nearly a hundred ships each year were trading between Spain and its American colonies; by the late sixteenth century, the yearly average was between 150 and 200 ships, and the carrying capacity of individual vessels had doubled. The total tonnage involved was about 15 000 to 20 000 modern international tons of 2.83 cubic metres. This was a substantial volume whose value was disproportionately large compared with most European commerce, though it was only about a tenth of the entire Spanish marine and a tiny fraction of the overall carrying capacity of Atlantic Europe (Braudel, 1972, p. 446; Phillips, 1990, pp. 77–8). We can put Spanish American trade in a certain perspective by noting that the number of ships passing annually between the North Sea and the Baltic was twenty or more times that of those assembled for the annual transatlantic crossing – though vessels engaged in northern European trade were smaller than the carracks of the Indies fleet (Phillips, 1990, pp. 49, 79; Parry, 1967, p. 199). Unlike the self-sufficient Asian societies, Iberian America was the economic complement of Europe, and its trade was controlled by privileged merchants who treated the transatlantic world as one unified space. There was, to be sure, a marked difference between the external commerce of the Spanish and Portuguese territories, despite the union of their crowns between 1580 and 1640. Because Portugal never possessed a merchant fleet large enough to handle its colony's bulky sugar trade, the corporation of Lisbon merchants could not maintain a strict commercial monopoly. Licensed Dutch and English ships were prominent from an early date and, even after the creation of a monopoly trading company with regular 'fleet' sailings in 1649, foreign participation in the colony's trade meant that it was oriented to Europe rather than the metropole. The Brazilians imported, via Lisbon, French and English manufactures for their own use and for re-export to Spanish America. Furthermore, sugar had to be marketed in a way that precious metals did not, so the Portuguese became dependent on the merchants and financiers – often of Jewish extraction – who internationalised Brazilian trade in a manner quite distinct from the inner-directed exclusiveness of Spanish commerce (Hennessy, 1992, p. 30). Spanish American settlers also relied on indirect imports, mostly through Seville, of the manufactures needed for a European mode of life in an American environment. They exported hides and tallow when the economies of transport permitted, but commerce was dominated by the extraction of bullion and the realisation of its value on world markets.

According to recent estimates, the Americas produced about 102 000 tonnes of silver between 1493 and c.1810, equivalent to 85 per cent of world production (Garner, 1988, p. 902; Barrett, 1990, p. 224). Over 70 per cent of the world's gold also came from the New World, but because the influx of silver was so much greater, the ratio of their values rose from about 10.5 to 1 in 1500 to 14.5 to 1 in the mid seventeenth century (Braudel and Spooner, 1967, p. 445). Some silver was retained in America and went into local circulation, and presumably this proportion rose with the growth of local markets. After 1567, about 15 tons a year was shipped from Acapulco to Manila to finance transpacific trade with China and pay for the defence costs of the Philippines. Exactly what proportion was exported to Spain is uncertain, because royal taxation and the obligation on silver exporters to share the costs of assembling the annual convoys were incentives to smuggle an unregistered part of the output, but it was probably 70 per cent or more

(Barrett, 1990, Table 7.3, p. 242). From Spain, the silver circulated very rapidly through the wider European economy, with considerable quantities flowing to the Baltic to pay for western imports of grain and naval stores. Furthermore, it permitted a deepening network of European trade with Asia, where there was little demand for Western goods and two-thirds of purchases were paid for in silver. As much as 30 to 40 per cent of American bullion may have been re-exported through the Levant or by the East India companies (Pieper, 1990, p. 113). The Spanish *real* of eight became the world's principal trading currency, and the medium for the closer integration of different centres of world production and exchange.

As we have seen, Smith dismissed this huge boost to liquidity as a trifling convenience of little consequence to European economic growth. Was he right? It would be idle to pretend that there is a simple answer, and readers must be warned that American treasure has prompted one of the most frustratingly inconclusive debates in early modern economic history. Behind the impressive facts of bullion production lie huge areas of conjecture, and placing the facts in a causal sequence linking money supply to capital accumulation is a problem for economic theory as well as historical research. Since the size of Europe's silver stock around 1530 is unknown, the initial consequences of the silver flows can only be conjectured. Many then complained of a dearth of specie, so the sudden increase in money supply *may* have relieved a bottleneck to the spread of trade and specialisation. Whether monetary shortages were seriously impeding the growth of commerce is questionable, because European merchants had long devised paper instruments as substitutes for gold and silver coins (O'Brien, 1990, p. 160). Earl J. Hamilton calculated the first reliable statistics from the returns of Seville's regulatory House of Trade, and showed that annual bullion receipts peaked around 1595, when they were valued at 42 million ducats (Hamilton's 1934 data are conveniently reproduced in Elliott, 1963, p. 175). With such an influx, the purchasing power of silver inevitably fell, and commodity prices relative to silver money inexorably rose. As early as 1556, Spanish scholars were attributing inflation to the flood of precious metal and abundant money after the discovery of the Indies (Elliott, 1963, pp. 182–3). Spain's severe inflation meant that its overpriced manufactures could not compete in international markets. Despite Seville's monopoly on exports to Spanish America, the price differential was such that it became profitable to re-export goods of French, Netherlandish and Italian origin. Spain's trade imbalance worsened because rising population and greater strategic needs increased dependence on imports of wheat, copper, tin, and naval stores, as well as on foreign shippers. As early as 1600, 'too many' of Seville's merchants were already little more than straw-men for Genoese or Dutch bankers and merchant houses (Macleod, 1984a, p. 367). Spain's mortifying sense of its imperial wealth draining away was expressed in the common remark that its kingdoms were 'the Indies of other foreign kingdoms' (Braudel, 1972, p. 476).

The Spanish scholars had an intuitive grasp of what we now call the quantity theory of money, which proposes that if the money supply increases (while its velocity of circulation remains constant) and if there is no increase in total goods and services, then the price level will rise in proportion to the increased money supply. Applying this theory, Hamilton established a close (and for him causal) correlation between bullion imports and the rise of Andalusian prices, and later propounded the more general thesis that American treasure was the principal cause of the European-wide price revolution during the sixteenth century (Hamilton, 1934, p. 301). His arguments rested on a compelling combination of theoretical cogency and empirical plausibility (for the similarity between the curves of prices – in terms of silver – and of decennial bullion shipments is, as one sceptic admits, 'astonishing') (Davis, 1973, p. 100).

The implications of inflation for economic growth depend on its differential impact on the various factors of production, and in Hamilton's view sixteenth-century price rises benefited owners of capital in whatever form. This was because price increases leapt ahead of wages – their purchasing power in England fell by half between 1500 and 1600 – so capitalists found labour costs falling in real terms while profits rose. Entrepreneurs' bigger profit margins encouraged the further concentration of capital, and for this reason Hamilton regarded New World silver as a critical ingredient in the development of modern capitalism. Wallerstein has revived this view in arguing that the circuits of silver drew economic surplus from the 'periphery' to the 'core' in the emergent 'world economy' (Hamilton, 1929; Wallerstein, 1974, p. 78). Hamilton perceived a similar sequence of monetary inflation beneficial to capital accumulation with the eighteenth-century upsurge of American bullion imports, due to Brazilian gold discoveries and the revival of Peruvian silver mining. Conversely, he attributed the severe deflation of the mid seventeenth century to a precipitous fall in bullion imports from 30 million ducats a year in 1630 to about 4 million in 1660, according to his data. However, these figures – and the monetarist explanation for the 'general crisis' of the 1640s and 50s – have become the most controversial part of the Hamilton thesis. The reliability of the House of Trade returns is suspect after 1620, and, using the reports in contemporary commercial gazettes, Michel Morineau has constructed a radically different series of bullion import data, which still show a substantial fall for 1646–55, but a spectacular recovery thereafter (Morineau, 1978, p. 83). Falling silver shipments for about a decade were due, according to Morineau, only to the disruptions of the Carrera by naval warfare. At its American source, the supply remained pretty constant, because fresh discoveries compensated for Potosí's falling output and actual, as opposed to officially recorded, bullion imports oscillated around a steadily rising curve from the late sixteenth century to the early eighteenth. This scenario at least avoids one anomaly in the Hamilton thesis: the inconsistency between the East India companies's growing bullion shipments to Asia while silver imports supposedly dwindled to a trickle. The scale of these shipments would have drained western Europe of monetary metal had Hamilton's figures for the later seventeenth century reflected accurately the inward flow of silver.

Morineau argues that we should detach price movements from the movement of precious metals, and proffers an essentially 'natural' explanation for inflation in early modern Europe. The largest international trade, by volume and value, was in cereals, and bread was by far the most important item of consumption. Fluctuations in their prices made a great impact on the general price level, and these correlated with successions of good and bad harvests. The three- to four-fold increase in European cereal prices during the sixteenth century resulted, according to Morineau, from generally poor harvests and the pressure of rising population on an insufficiently responsive agriculture. Similarly, the prolonged price fall from 1650 to the late 1680s was due to a succession of good harvests. The favourable conjuncture was broken by the miserable weather of the 1690s, which led to widespread shortages and famine prices in France and elsewhere (ibid., p. 86). This explanation needs underpinning by evidence that different parts of Europe were affected by common climatic fluctuations, but in minimising the monetary factor it vindicates Smith's opinion that all that treasure was a trifling convenience.

Dennis Fynn has gone further by asserting that the silver discoveries actually *retarded* capitalist development because the Spanish state dissipated its vast mining profits in financing warfare that devastated major commercial and manufacturing centres in the Low Countries and elsewhere. The crown's American revenues represented only about 20 per cent of its total income around 1590, but this vital proportion could be directly converted into liquid cash and pledged by the monarchy in negotiation with the German and Genoese bankers who were the paymasters of the army of Flanders. Spanish military expenditure was unparalleled in early modern history, and inconceivable without the silver receipts. It represented a waste of resources on a prodigious scale, and forced other states towards unproductive war. Early capitalism, Fynn avers, survived despite – not because of – New World bullion (Fynn, 1996). As I warned, it is a frustratingly inconclusive debate. My own sense of the literature is that the integration of a world trading economy depended on the huge increase in financial liquidity to establish a monetary 'interface' between distant regions with different price levels. Significantly, seven contributors to a collection of papers on the emergence of a world economy after 1500 deal with the integrative effects of bullion flows (see Fischer *et al.*, 1986, vol. 1, especially Chaudhuri's contribution). New World silver was not, I suspect, necessary for capitalist development in Europe, but it was for European commercial capital to establish its dominant position in Asia – a matter discussed in the next chapter.

From the second quarter of the seventeenth century, the pattern of trade in the Spanish American empire began to change with the decline of the metropolis and the colonies' growing economic autonomy. Sailings to the Indies became less frequent, fewer ships were involved and the value of the goods they carried declined precipitously (in the 1640s it may have been as little as one-thirtieth of what it had been in 1600) (Phillips, 1990, p. 88). The import–export houses based in Seville were broken in two by the 'localisation' of their branches in the New World: metropolitan firms sent merchandise only as far as Veracruz and Portobello, sites of annual trading fairs, where it was bought for resale by firms based in Mexico City and Lima (now with their own *consulados* or merchant guilds). American-based merchants began investing in mines and ranches, and furnished much of the capital needed for the diffusion of the amalgamation process in silver refining. By mid century, the merchant dynasties of Mexico and Peru contained men with fortunes comparable to those of the richest capitalists of Seville or Medina del Campo, and they were organising the American economic space more and more independently of metropolitan interests. Meanwhile, the commercial benefits and industrial 'spin-offs' from the American empire were passing inexorably out of peninsular Spanish hands. Around 1650, for example, less than a third of the Indies fleet was actually built in Spanish shipyards; Holland and the colonial shipbuilding centres in the Caribbean supplied more than a third each (Macleod, 1984b, p. 348). As the Spanish American economies became more self-sufficient in grains, ironware, woodcrafts and furniture, so they imported fewer bulk goods (in itself a significant factor in the diminishing tonnage of the Carrera). Spain tried to make the provision of wine and olive oil a metropolitan monopoly by forbidding their production in New Spain and the Caribbean, though it was permitted in Peru where markets were too distant for Spanish products to arrive intact. When the colonial economy became more regionally specialised, contraband Peruvian and Chilean wine and olive oil undercut the price of metropolitan imports in Mexico City (ibid., p. 352). An early example of 'import substitution' occurred in low-quality textiles where *obrajes* – craft workshops – began to supply local markets among the *castas* and poor Spanish, although these proto-industrial enterprises were chronically handicapped by shortages of cheap labour, and easily succumbed to European competition when trade revived (Lockhart and Schwartz, 1983, pp. 144–5; Brading, 1984, p. 431).

The economic decline of metropolitan Spain opened her American empire to import penetration by foreigners. An unknowable quantity of European manufactures and African slaves entered the Spanish colonies through a contraband trade, but legal avoidance of mercantilist regulations was far more important in undermining the colonial trade monopoly. By about 1680, Cadiz – now the principal port of the Indies trade – was a mere entrepôt for the exchange of American bullion for European goods. Only about 6 per cent of merchandise exports to Spanish America in 1689 originated in Spain (Brading, 1984, pp. 389, 410). Most of the Cadiz merchants were little more than commission agents for foreign traders resident in the city, who accounted for over seven-tenths of the declared income of the trading community in the early eighteenth century. By then, three-quarters of the Indies merchant fleet had been purchased outside Spain and her empire, mostly from the Dutch who had the cheapest and most efficient shipyards (ibid., p. 414). Despite Bourbon Spain's energetic – and in many ways successful – reassertion of metropolitan control over its American empire, foreign commercial penetration was never reversed. The colonial export economy revived under the Bourbons partly because of the steps taken to raise silver production through tax exemptions and reductions in the cost of monopoly materials such as mercury and gunpowder, but the major beneficiaries of greater trading opportunities were French master-craftsmen and traders, who were the chief suppliers of manufactured goods to Spain and the Spanish empire (Butel, 1990, p. 162). By value, Spanish products (mainly wine) probably made up less than 20 per cent of exports to the Indies in the eighteenth century; Spanish industry made a derisory contribution to colonial exports.

Although the metropolitan economy derived very little benefit from the Spanish colonial empire, the state reaped an extraordinary fiscal harvest from the administrative and commercial reforms of the late Bourbon period. Revenues raised in Spanish America from the 'royal fifth', the sale of monopoly products (including tobacco after 1768), and other sources increased sharply with the revival of economic activity, while customs receipts at Cadiz rose with the growth of imports. Bullion was still the main item in the Spanish American export schedule and accounted for most exports by value in the 1790s, but the expansion of slave-based plantation agriculture in Cuba meant that sugar, tobacco, cacao, indigo and coffee were challenging the predominance of precious metals. The British occupation of the island during the Seven Years War was a turning-point, for it opened Cuba to foreign merchants and stimulated the importation of African slaves (many re-exports from Jamaica) for the sugar plantations. Though the British soon withdrew, commercial activity was henceforth liberated from most of the restrictions of the old Spanish colonial system. In 1778, the decree of *commercio libre* formalised a liberal trade regime for the Spanish empire: Cadiz relinquished its monopoly position, the annual fleets were finally abolished, individual merchant vessels were now able to trade freely within the empire and with Spain, and the *consulados* lost many of their privileges. Colonial exports tripled within a decade, while unheard of quantities of European merchandise inundated colonial ports and saturated Spanish American markets (Brading, 1984, p. 413).

Colonial economies are often assumed to be 'export-oriented', but in the case of Spanish America this is a misconception. Even during the final, 'liberal' phase of Spanish colonial trade, exports were only a small sector of the Ibero-American economy in which the vast majority of humdrum transactions took place in the domestic market. As David Brading points out, by 1789, the produce shipped from French Saint Domingue came close to equalling the value of the exports of the entire Spanish empire in the New World. Saint Domingue's economic success resulted from deploying about 450 000 slaves. If the export earnings of the fourteen and a half million inhabitants of Spanish America barely exceeded the output of a single island, it was because the bulk of its population found occupation and sustenance in the domestic economy in which long-distance, inter-regional exchanges of foodstuffs, bullion and manufactures had been developing since the prostration of Spain in the mid seventeenth century. The existence of a complex and variegated internal economy allowed for the emergence of an equally complex and distinctive colonial society (Brading, 1984, pp. 426–7).

The 'Europeanisation' of the Caribbean and the 'Americanisation' of Europe's Long-Distance Trade

The incursions of foreign commerce into the Spanish and Portuguese empires dovetailed with the 'Europeanisation' of the intercontinental complex of production and exchange centred on the slave plantations of the American tropics. This economic ensemble functioned primarily through the exchange of European and Asian manufactures for slaves on the African coast, their sale on the marts of Brazil and the Caribbean, and the shipment to Europe of slave-grown crops. But there was a secondary level because clothing slaves, and supplying the planter class with consumer and capital goods, raised the aggregate demand for European manufactures (and for processed products, such as wine and brandy). A subsidiary extension of the complex, but by the later eighteenth century an increasingly important one, was the exchange of foodstuffs and other goods from British North America for Caribbean sugar and molasses that were processed in the refineries of New England (Curtin, 1990, is the best short introduction; Blackburn, 1997, is a superb synthesis of the voluminous scholarship).

We can trace this 'Europeanisation' to the 1630s, when the Dutch contested Iberian supremacy in the Caribbean and South Atlantic during their renewed struggle against the Habsburgs. The Dutch West India Company overran the sugar-growing region of Pernambuco in North-Eastern Brazil, and seized Portuguese slave-trading stations in West Africa. Between 1636 and 1645, the Dutch controlled the international sugar and the Atlantic slave trades, and were able to offer 'middlemen' services as carriers, refiners and re-exporters of colonial products and slaves to the English, Scottish and French planters newly established in the Antilles (largely thanks to a protective naval screen after Dutch victories over the Spanish in the Caribbean). Though driven from Brazil in 1654 by settler forces, the Dutch only renounced their claims after being accorded freedom of navigation and trade throughout the Portuguese empire.

Meanwhile, a revolutionary change in the demography and economy of the West Indies was beginning with the transformation of Barbados into the world's major sugar producer. The island was first occupied by English colonists in 1627, who, after an indifferent start growing tobacco and cotton using white indentured labour, turned to sugar production and black slaves from 1640. They were taught how to make the raw sugar by Dutch from Pernambuco who – we may surmise – calculated that much of it would be shipped to the refineries of Amsterdam in Dutch vessels (Dunn, 1972, p. 66). From the mid 1640s, market conditions for the Barbadian planters were particularly favourable, since many Brazilian plantations were devastated by resurgent conflict between the colonists and the Dutch, which interrupted the sugar supply and drove up prices. In 1651, about 3750 tons of Barbadian sugar were exported to England. By 1669, when the slave population was about 82 000, sugar imports from the island had risen to 9525 tons, and they were supplemented by modest quantities from the Leeward Islands and Jamaica where production was just beginning. By the end of the century, the British West Indies were supplying about 24 000 tons annually (ibid., Table 21, p. 203).

The hopes that the Dutch had once entertained of carrying and refining the products of the English islands were somewhat disappointed: their own success had provoked economic nationalism in the Cromwellian Protectorate, whose Navigation Act of 1651 was designed to cut out Dutch intermediaries and reserve colonial commerce for English shipping. Whatever stimulus this gave to national carriers, it scarcely affected Dutch primacy in world trade, which reached its zenith in the last decades of the seventeenth century. Admittedly, American commodity shipments formed a much smaller proportion of Dutch foreign trade than of French and British, but this was mainly a function of the huge preponderance of Dutch merchant shipping, whose volume, around 1670, considerably exceeded that of Spain, Portugal, France, England, Scotland and the German trading states combined. Thus, whereas some 28 000 tons of English merchant shipping were employed in American trade in 1690 (or one-sixth of a total merchant fleet of about 178 000 tons), the proportion of the Dutch merchant fleet employed in these trades was much smaller (only one-fourteenth) but in absolute terms this was greater: 40 000 tons out of a total of 568 000 (Parry, 1967, p. 208).

During the early eighteenth century, the political eclipse of the Republic forced Dutch shippers to cede Atlantic trade to British and French competitors, and the pattern of Dutch foreign trade steadily diverged from Britain's and France's. Dutch commercial preponderance had been based in the first instance on the low-cost shipping of bulky commodities in European waters, and despite its commercial empire in Asia and its sugar colony in Surinam, this remained the case. In 1750, about 85 per cent of Dutch trade was with Europe, while imports from Asia accounted for less than 14 per cent of total foreign trade and those from America for less than 2 per cent. Colonial merchandising in general was more important than the figures indicate, because about half of the Asian imports were re-exported, and the Dutch distributed large quantities of French colonial produce throughout northern Europe. But the Dutch had been marginalised in the most expansive branch of international commerce.

By 1750, intercontinental trade accounted directly or indirectly for more than half of Britain's foreign trade, and was clearly oriented to its transatlantic colonies (and those of Portugal, with whom Britain enjoyed an exceptionally favourable trading relationship). A third of commodity imports came from the Americas (compared with 13 per cent from Asia) and 20 per cent of exports were to America (compared with only 6 per cent to Asia). A further 19 per cent of exports were re-exports of colonial commodities to other destinations. Sales of tropical goods in the Baltic were particularly important in allowing Britain to purchase naval stores and iron (Steensgaard, 1990b, p. 145). The chief item of transatlantic trade was sugar, which represented almost a fifth of the whole import bill in 1774, far surpassing that of any other commodity. By this date, about four-fifths of Britain's exports were manufactures, and nearly half (47 per cent) were destined for Caribbean and North Atlantic markets while 8 per cent were going to Africa, the Near East, Asia and Latin America (Davis, 1973, p. 251).

For much of the eighteenth century, French foreign trade grew even more rapidly than British, and in one short period (1735–52) increased from 221 million to 500 million livres. As with its rival, commercial dynamism was due essentially to colonial trade, whose value in current prices rose nearly five times between 1716–20 and 1784–8. At the core of colonial trade was the exploitation of Caribbean plantation islands: Guadeloupe, Martinique and, above all, Saint Domingue – where production overtook Jamaica's in 1720 and made it the world's most valuable colony. Trade with Asia was not unimportant before the Seven Years War, but it was to some extent dependent on the Antilles (for Indian cloths and cowrie shells were re-exported to Africa to purchase slaves) and was always overshadowed by transatlantic trade. In 1772, commerce with America was, by value, more than seven times Asian trade. The French were notably successful in capturing much of the European re-export trade in colonial commodities – chiefly sugar, coffee and indigo – from the British. By 1750, more than half of French sales to the United Provinces and three-fifths to northern Europe were colonial re-exports (Butel, 1990, pp. 153–70).

Historians have recently turned their attention to the impact of transatlantic commerce on European consumption and the origins of 'consumer society'. In quantitative terms, what were mostly luxury imports played a small part in popular expenditure but – argue Austen and Smith – they had a considerable cultural significance, because their consumption was associated with notions of respectability that permeated broad social strata (Austen and Smith, 1992, pp. 183–99). Tobacco, sugar, and sweetened beverages became matters of choice and taste in the workers' way of life: they opened up a certain autonomy but were also 'incentive goods' that compensated for the drudgery of wage-earning. All are more or less habit-forming, and it may be that they habituated workers to a 'life sentence' of dependent labour. Sugar quite possibly disguised the real deterioration in the British popular diet after 1760 (Blackburn, 1997, pp. 558–61; Mintz, 1985, p. 180). These are interesting arguments, but when their proponents enjoin us to 'take more seriously the function of sugar in the transformation of European consumerism' (Austen and Smith, p. 185) one can only wonder where they imagine Europe to have been. Outside Britain, and less certainly the Netherlands, sugar had a socially very restricted market in Europe until after the Napoleonic wars. Competition from the French Antilles had driven British West Indian sugar out of the European markets by about 1740, but increasing domestic consumption more than compensated for the loss of the re-export trade. Partly because of the growing habit of drinking sweetened China tea, more fundamentally because of the demand from a large stratum of the 'middling sort' of consumer, the British market was the biggest in Europe: a third of all European sugar imports were consumed in Britain in the eighteenth century, where consumption per head was eight times greater than in France (despite sugar being cheaper there). The widening of the market had resulted initially from falling prices, and the major reductions were achieved in the later seventeenth century. In 1634–5, sugar retailed at 1s 2d to 1s 3d (5½p to 6p) per pound, and in 1684–9, despite the imposition of extra customs duties, at 6d to 7d (2¼p to 3p) per pound (Davis, 1973, p. 260). The retail price fell by about 40 per cent between the Treaty of Utrecht and the 1730s, but then rose again and stabilised around its pre-1713 level up to 1776. Thereafter, peacetime prices continued to rise until the 1790s. Sugar, along with tobacco and tea, had entered popular expectations of affordable luxuries, but was becoming more costly relative to other consumer goods in the later eighteenth century and any increased consumption could result only from rising incomes or a reduction of the duties which kept the price artificially high (Richardson, 1987, p. 111). By the early nineteenth century, the political economy of British taxation – which bore heavily on popular consumption – had stretched the 'income elasticity' of the market to its limit. Annual per capita sugar consumption rose from 4 lb in 1700–9 to 19 lb in 1800–9, but then dropped slightly below this amount until the reduction of the sugar duties in the 1840s encouraged a huge increase in consumption. At the end of the nineteenth century the average Briton consumed 78 lb a year; sugar refining was now an industrialised process and much was consumed 'passively' - in jams, biscuits and the like – produced by modern food and drink industries.

In a pan-European perspective, tobacco was the only consumption good originating in America to pass from luxury to commonplace item because of the elasticity of demand in relation to price. What is often forgotten, however, is that tobacco was first grown by Europeans in Europe, where it quickly proved to be an attractive cash crop for small farmers. In the early eighteenth century, between 17 million and 28 million pounds of domestically grown tobacco were being processed in the Netherlands. Tobacco was a big business: Amsterdam had thirty or forty tobacco concerns employing a workforce of around 4000, while perhaps half the workers of Gouda – some 15 000 to 16 000 people – were employed making smokers' pipes. However, much of the leaf being consumed was grown by Dutch peasants (Goodman, 1993, p. 142; Schama, 1987, pp. 194–5).

Unquestionably, transatlantic trade did foster new consumer habits in Britain of considerable cultural import, but nobody has demonstrated they were necessary conditions for industrialisation, and their significance for economic development is debatable. Neither sugar nor tobacco actually created the disposable income with which people satisfied the desire for these commodities. Their processing and sale probably called for more capital investment in shipping, wharves and refineries, and possibly created more employment, than would have been the case had the disposable income been spent on domestically produced goods (such as beer or shoes). It is arguable that in certain localised contexts the levels of investment and employment would not have been so high without the tobacco and sugar industries, but even there the notional increment can only have been a modest fraction unless we are to believe that capital and labour were substantially under-utilised in Britain or the Netherlands. Certain American crops – such as maize and the potato – when dispersed to Africa, Asia and Europe increased the calorific yield of a given acre of land, led to a better-fed labour force and indirectly spurred workers to move to other occupations. None of this can be said for processed sugar, which has little nutritional value. There are no strong reasons for thinking that mass markets for New World luxuries were a necessary condition of British industrialisation (nor even necessary for the culture of respectability, which was mostly grounded in the religious revival). It is much more plausible to look for a causal relation between transatlantic commerce and industrialisation in terms of raising the level of demand for British manufactures and the expansion of commercial credit through the lending out of trading profits.

Slavery, Capitalism and Industrialisation

Since the publication of Eric Williams's *Capitalism and Slavery*, it has been a dogma among 'Third World' intellectuals that the profits of the Caribbean slave economy contributed greatly to the Industrial Revolution in Britain by creating a stream of funds which financed industrial investment and technological change. Furthermore, and again following Williams, the suppression of the slave trade by Britain within her own empire (and as far as possible elsewhere) is commonly interpreted as an economically inspired intervention designed to meet a crisis of over-production in plantation crops and to foster the long-term interests of industrial capitalism based on free wage labour (Williams, 1944). It must be stated here that some of Williams' detailed arguments are not now accepted by scholars: the profit level of British slave trading itself has been calculated as just under 10 per cent, and if we assume that the proportion invested was the same as the national ratio, then total investment derived from the trade was only £14 000 a year (or a derisory 0.11 per cent of total investment) (Anstey, 1975, Table 1, pp. 47, 51). The abolition of the slave trade was not economically determined and did not follow inexorably from the advance of capitalism. The expansion of slavery in the British West Indies always depended on forces originating within British society which generated both the demand for plantation products and the capital for slave-based enterprises. Contrary to the Williams thesis, there was no weakening of these forces before 1807 and no undermining of the economic value of the slave plantation areas to Britain. Demand for sugar was such as to encourage the opening of new plantations on rich, virgin lands in Trinidad and British Guiana, which provided exceptional opportunities for profit. Furthermore, the fortuitous circumstances of the Saint Domingue revolution and British naval supremacy in the Caribbean ended competition from French producers and placed Britain in control of half the world's plantation exports, with more than half the slave trade in British hands (Eltis, 1987, p. 5). Britain's suppression of her own slave trade at this point in time was an instance of self-inflicted 'econocide' (Drescher, 1977). Historians are divided as to whether this was due, essentially, to an enlightened élite enforcing its own moral convictions or whether the mobilisation of public opinion around a new ideology of human and national liberty was the underlying cause (Drescher, 1987a; Drescher, 1994, pp. 116–36). In the longer-term, the necessary conditions for abolition were intellectual and ideological, rather than economic: by the 1780s, the immorality of slavery and its economic inferiority to waged labour were generally accepted in educated circles, while the antinomy between the degradation of slavery and the dignity of free waged labour was becoming an argument with which to woo the labouring classes away from an old ideal of economic independence and towards a new social order of employers and employed (Anstey, 1975, chs 15, 16; Blackburn, 1988, pp. 520–2).

But while several of Williams's particular assertions can no longer stand, the general thesis that slavery and slave-related commerce accelerated modern economic development in Britain commands renewed respect. One, paradoxical, reason is that refined macro-economic data show a lower rate of growth for manufacturing than was previously estimated, indicating rather weak internal demand factors. This has led economic historians to revise upwards the relative importance of export markets. Even in 1700, British exports were heavily concentrated in manufactures and a quarter of manufactured output was exported, with woollens being the most important item. Over four-fifths of all exports were to Europe, only 13.3 per cent to North America and the Caribbean. By the 1770s, the export ratio for manufactures in peacetime had risen to about 35 per cent, and North American and Caribbean markets were absorbing 46.9 per cent of the total. Sales in the Atlantic basin overall – including Latin America and Africa – probably took half manufactured exports. As O'Brien and Engerman say, there can be no doubt of 'the significance of sea power, imperial connections, slavery, and mercantilist regulation for the sale of British manufactures overseas' (O'Brien and Engerman, 1991, p. 186). Overseas sales were particularly important for cotton and iron – long regarded as the most dynamic and innovative industries in the Industrial Revolution. By 1801, just over three-fifths of cotton output was being sold abroad, and the industry accounted for two-fifths of all merchandise exports; its spectacular expansion is inconceivable without this export record. Not all transatlantic trade was directly related to slavery: over time, the burgeoning white population of the Thirteen Colonies – most of whom lived in states where slaves were small minorities – proved a much bigger market than the West Indian plantations (which is why the export ratio slumped during the American War of Independence). But the colonists had a trade deficit with Britain and could only maintain their capacity to import by running trade surpluses with the West Indies and West Africa. Slavery sustained two sides of a multilateral trading system. Even when independence freed white Americans from the compulsion of the Navigation Laws, they still bought nearly nine-tenths of their manufactured imports from Britain by choice. In the early 1800s, North American markets took a higher proportion of British exported manufactures than before or since. By this date, the southern states were beginning to make their signal contribution to cotton industrialisation by providing the raw material at a cost that undercut all other textile fibres: output on the cotton slave plantations rose twenty-four-fold in 1790s, and by 1800 the United States was supplying a third of Britain's cotton requirement. There were alternative sources of supply in Asia but, without the expansion of the plantation system, cotton – of generally inferior quality – would have arrived in Europe in far smaller quantities and at much higher prices.

Some thirty years ago, Phyllis Deane argued that access to overseas markets helped overcome the low level of domestic purchasing power and encouraged industrial specialisation (Deane, 1979, pp. 66–7). Bairoch and others contested this on the grounds that exports were too small a proportion of total demand during the 'genesis' of the Industrial Revolution (Bairoch, 1993, pp. 82-4). However, comparison with the industrialisation process in 'follower' European economies indicates that foreign trade was a permissive factor in 'precocious' structural change in Britain. No other economy, with a comparably low income level, has had such a large proportion of manufactures in its export schedule, and none (apart from the Netherlands) experienced such a pronounced shift of labour from agriculture to manufacturing at such an early phase of industrialisation. Joseph Inikori goes much further than Deane's position in asserting that, without the external market created by slavery, the eighteenth-century British economy would have experienced the same kind of de-industrialisation that overtook the manufacturing regions of northern Italy during the 'general crisis' of the seventeenth century. For, he argues, the insufficiency of the domestic market in every western Europe country in the seventeenth century was a major obstacle to the growth of industrial capitalism, and only the creation after 1650 of a *de facto* 'common market' in the Atlantic basin – mercantilist restrictions notwithstanding - overcame this barrier to economic development. Not only did it provide outlets abroad; it led to faster population growth at home, because workers in the buoyant export trades were encouraged to marry younger and have larger families (Inikori, 1987; idem, 1992, pp. 157–65). I am not entirely convinced: the Atlantic 'common market' absorbed between one-sixth and one-fifth of manufactured output in the last quarter of the eighteenth century; though a substantial proportion, it would seem insufficiently large to have the make-or-break developmental and demographic effects imputed to it. During the two conflicts with North America (1776–83, 1812–14), the British home market showed that it was ample enough to prevent industrial collapse. The comparison with Northern Italy, a congeries of city states, is of limited validity, for the political integration of the British Isles, the comparative efficiency of British national taxation, and the unified state power embodied in the Royal Navy had no parallels in the Italian peninsula. The most we can reasonably assert is that, without slavery, the international division of labour in which Britain specialised as a textiles manufacturer would have not emerged, or not in such a 'stark' form.

Probably the most contentious issue in the reassessment of the Williams thesis is that of capital accumulation. Generalising from some striking examples of West Indian profits being used to finance technical innovation (such as the Watt steam engine), Williams concluded that such profits were a major stream of finance capital for the new industry. This was too hasty a judgement, though it is understandable considering that he wrote before the basic quantitative data for the econometric study of industrialisation were available. The mistake was in thinking that early industrialisation depended on a large investment in fixed capital in manufacturing, whereas we now know that new investment barely sufficed to keep pace with the expanding labour force and maintain the existing capital–labour ratio (Crafts, 1985, p. 76). The growth of capital stock was much less important for the Industrial Revolution than the growth in total factor productivity. Indeed, British colonial interests – particularly in the Caribbean – may have indirectly retarded capital formation, because defending these interests involved warfare and a level of military spending so high as to 'crowd out' private investment. In two influential papers critical of the 'world system' perspective, O'Brien has argued that, even on the most favourable assumptions, *all* oceanic commerce generated a flow of profits sufficient to have funded only 16.5 per cent of gross investment in the 1780s. Nevertheless, such a modest proportion was invested in fixed industrial capital that the actual profits of oceanic trade were sufficient to cover it (O'Brien, 1982, p. 7; idem, 1990, p. 177). We have little evidence of trade profits being directly invested in manufacturing, and most detailed studies stress the roles of domestic capital and of the London and inland banks as sources of investment (Engerman, 1994, p. 203). That said, however, Robin Blackburn's thorough discussion of the role of 'triangular trade' in generating profit, and so augmenting the funds available for lending and investment, has given renewed credibility to what we may conveniently call the 'Williams' concept of primitive accumulation. As Blackburn argues, eighteenth-century manufacturers stood in great need of commercial credit and there was considerable investment in social overhead capital, such as canals, turnpike roads and docks. He demonstrates that the profits extracted from slave labour together with profits *realised* in the triangular trade (through the sale of British goods) were large enough to contribute substantially to the capital requirements of the domestic economy. Assuming that 30 per cent of profits were reinvested, just over a fifth of Britain's gross fixed capital formation in 1770 could have been financed out of slave-related trade with the West Indies and Africa. If the rate of reinvestment was as high as 50 per cent (which seems most unlikely) then it would have covered 55 per cent of capital formation. Even in the lower range, these figures are consistent with the strong version of the Williams thesis. There is good evidence (such as the opening of new territories by British planters) that triangular trade profits more than kept pace with the growth of the domestic economy in the last decades of the eighteenth century. Their role in making economic space for investment was, very probably, maintained through to the 1800s (Blackburn,1997 pp. 531–42).

It is, perhaps, foolhardy to argue for causal links between New World slavery and British industrialisation when the necessary and sufficient conditions for this lengthy and complex process are so difficult to specify. Slavery and its related trades may have been of trivial account compared with natural resource endowment and the agricultural revolution, or even the institutional advances that secured individual property rights and guaranteed a high rate of return for successful risk-takers. The arguments for (or against) causal links become clearer if we consider that industrialisation can be defined in two, analytically distinct ways: the first is in terms of a generalised process of technological innovation involving the substitution of inanimate power for human and animal effort, the mechanisation of handicrafts and the displacement of manual skills by machine operations (Landes, 1969, p. 1). The links between slavery and British industrialisation *in this sense* were tenuous to the point of irrelevance. Its dynamics – common to much of Europe – were an exceptional technical creativity in harnessing natural forces for economically productive purposes and a competence in machine-building unmatched by any other culture. There were, of course, manifest connections between cotton – the prototype machine industry – and slavery, but the causal relationship mostly worked from Britain *outwards*, with rising demand for raw cotton resulting in the extension of the slave plantation system. The mechanisation of cotton spinning is a classic instance of the shortage of an industrial input stimulating technical progress, for innovation began around 1770 in response to 'bottlenecks' in the supply of yarn when the fledgling industry still obtained much of its raw material through the Levant. The productivity gains of mechanised spinning lowered the price of yarn dramatically, and led to increased demand both for cotton textiles and the raw material. The stimulus this gave planters in the Caribbean and continental America is evident in the eight-fold increase in raw cotton imports between 1780 and

1800 (Deane, 1979, p. 87). Obviously, there was a feedback from the New World, as abundant supplies of cheap fibre became an incentive to further investment in cotton manufacturing in Britain. But mechanical innovation and the displacement of manual skills affected only the spinning and preparatory processes until the 1820s and 1830s, when power looms were introduced on a considerable scale. The cotton textiles that conquered overseas markets in the early decades of the nineteenth century were woven by domestic handicraft workers using traditional techniques. By providing handloom weavers with cheap yarn, slavery enabled them to compete with the power loom for at least twenty years after the first viable model was patented, thus *delaying* further industrialisation in the technological sense. And even when a dying trade in the 1840s, handloom weaving was not untypical of an economy that was small-scale, not generally innovative and little affected by the use of steam power and where labour productivity was no greater than in continental Europe (Crafts, 1985, p. 88).

The second, structural definition of industrialisation is in terms of a major shift in the distribution of the labour force from the primary to the secondary sector, and the argument for a positive causal link from slavery to industrialisation in this sense is stronger. Despite the slow pace of technological innovation, structural change in Britain began very early, and proceeded more quickly than in follower economies. By the mid eighteenth century, manufacturing, building, commerce and the professions already accounted for about 45 per cent of labour force allocation (ibid., p. 13). Approximately two-fifths of the manufacturing labour force depended on export markets, so there are grounds for seeing them as an exogenous factor in the disproportionate growth of secondary and tertiary employment. For a relatively small economy, such as Britain's, international trade was a necessary condition for an extended market and industrial specialisation, and as we have seen slavery had a significant role in British overseas trade.

My discussion has centred on the relationship between New World slavery and industrialisation in Britain, but it would be unfortunate if that were an exclusive focus. A brief consideration of the Portuguese case should immediately dispel any idea that slavery and the slave trade invariably contributed to economic growth: Portugal was the second greatest slaving power of the eighteenth century and, relative to the size of the metropolitan economy, must have made the largest investment in slave-related activities of all the European states. Yet Portugal experienced accelerating economic decline, despite the mercantilist reforms of the Marquis of Pombal (1750–77) that aimed to lessen dependence on British manufactures and maximise the advantages to metropolitan interests of colonial control of Brazil. The

Pombaline reforms notwithstanding, Portugal found itself more marginal than ever to the gathering pace of development around the Atlantic: economically stagnant, lacking internal transport systems, unable to feed its own population, and becoming increasingly dependent on manufactures imported from northern European trading partners. The commitment of Lisbon's merchants to slave-trading was, very probably, implicated in the increasing comparative backwardness of the national economy: the indications are that the mercantile groups in Europe, the Americas and Africa who engaged in slave-trading were those with least access to cash and credit and most reliant on archaic types of economic transaction, such as barter. Slave-traders were 'marginalised' by the financial revolution which transformed merchant capitalism in north-western Europe from the 1690s. Portugal's southern Atlantic slave trade thus repeatedly served mercantile groups in Lisbon pushed to the sidelines of the empire to compensate for their weakness relative to the merchants – increasingly British – dominant at each period of Portuguese economic history. The Portuguese became more and more specialised as slavers, while foreign suppliers and financiers and Brazilian planters led the economic growth within the empire. By the late eighteenth century, the Portuguese national economy manifested this inherent 'marginality' of slave-trading in pathological form (Miller, 1991, pp. 120–50).

The French case, by contrast, shows that the stimulus to economic growth that came from the merchandising of plantation produce and the market demand in plantation colonies for metropolitan goods was not confined to Britain. For much of the eighteenth century, France was the world's largest producer of manufactures and the most vital sector of her economy was located on the Atlantic seaboard and geared to the trade with her Caribbean islands. Commercial agriculture in the Lower Garonne was tied closely to the needs of the sugar colonies for cereals, wine and fruit. Proto-industrialisation was furthest advanced in the Atlantic provinces because they had easiest access to the American plantations (Butel, 1978, pp. 53–4). The advantageous relationship of Bordeaux and other metropolitan centres with the slave colonies was only temporarily disrupted by the Seven Years War (1756–63). In 1790, the slave population of the French empire was 50 per cent greater than that of the British. Despite this, the French cotton industry had to go to slave regions outside the empire for some of its raw materials; it was a larger market for the booming cotton plantations of late colonial Brazil than the British industry before 1785 (Eltis, 1987, pp. 37, 35). The transatlantic links were not fatally severed until the combined domestic and external crises of the 1790s, when revolutionary upheaval and naval superiority enabled the British to capture former markets for French colonial sugar, coffee and other products.

In conclusion to this section, I would suggest that there has been a paradigm shift in the way historians perceive the relationship between slavery and economic development since Williams's book appeared. He concluded that

> The commercial capitalism of the eighteenth century developed the wealth of Europe by means of slavery and monopoly. But in so doing it helped to create the industrial capitalism of the nineteenth century which turned round and destroyed the power of commercial capitalism, slavery, and all its works (Williams, 1944, p. 210).

This is in line with a broad intellectual tradition that took the maturation of capitalism and slavery to be antithetical. In Marxism, they were dominant modes of production from different epochs in human history and their co-existence in modern societies was necessarily 'contradictory'. This judgement was not exclusive to Marxism, but common to all political economists who had learnt from Adam Smith that 'work done by slaves, though it appears to cost only their maintenance, is in the end the dearest of any . . .' The received wisdom of political economy held that, with the spread of industries requiring skilled and versatile workers, slavery was doomed; the overseer's whip would inevitably yield to the greater rationality of the wage incentive. This wisdom became embedded in a historiographic tradition – well represented by Williams – which made ineluctable economic forces the prime movers in the suppression of slavery. Quantitative historical analysis of the economics of slavery has substantially revised these notions: the increase in the productivity of slaves in the British West Indies between 1750 and 1830 was about the same as the productivity increase of workers in Britain in this period. Until 1833, the British sugar colonies were still producing more sugar than Brazil and Cuba together, and were also exporting substantial quantities of coffee and cotton. Though the rate of growth in production was faster elsewhere, there was no overall indication of economic decline in the British Caribbean. Similarly, comparison of the economic performance of the northern and southern states of the USA up to 1860 has shown that growth in income per head in the slave-owning south was as rapid in the north. Indeed, throughout the Americas, the wealthiest and most dynamic regions were those that relied on coerced labour. Slavery was evidently competitive with free wage labour and not inconsistent with modernisation and productivity change. Far from decaying in the mid nineteenth century, slavery was an expanding institution that could be halted only by political and military action (Ward, 1988, pp. 7, 261; Engerman, 1986a).

If we focus only on Europe, the nineteenth century is the era when the free wage labour system became the common lot by displacing the tied labour of serfs and sharecroppers and the self-employment of peasants and artisans, and we tend to assume that the rest of the world sooner or later followed this pattern. But an intercontinental perspective reveals that, in many regions specialising in exporting tropical and subtropical commodities, slavery expanded in parallel to the growth of wage labour in the metropoles. Crippling labour problems and economic decline followed emancipation in the British (and later French) West Indies, demonstrating the intractable difficulties of producing sugar with wage labour. Many former slaves became peasants, and rather few wage labourers of any sort. The viability of the plantations depended on the influx of indentured workers, initially from Africa, slightly later from India. Between 1838 (when the 'apprenticeship' of former slaves ended) and 1918, about 470 000 bonded labourers were shipped to the British Caribbean (the great majority to Guiana and Trinidad) to work under repressive conditions resembling those of slavery (Tinker, 1974; Engerman, 1986b, Table II, p. 26). Meanwhile, plantation output had increased dramatically in the remaining major slave powers – Cuba, Brazil and the southern USA. Their economic dynamism contrasts with the stagnation in the Spanish American republics, where slavery had been marginal and was abolished during the struggle for independence. Slave prices in Cuba and Brazil rose sharply after the 1830s, more than doubled in the 1850s, and as late as the 1870s were above levels of the first half of the nineteenth century (Engerman, 1986a, p. 328). By 1850, Cuba produced over one-third of the world's output of cane sugar, and Brazil's coffee exports (which were more than double its sugar exports) accounted for over 50 per cent of the world trade in coffee. The evident vitality of slave-based production after the 1830s was deeply troubling to those who had urged the emancipation of slaves in the British West Indies in order to reap the economic 'benefits' of free labour. Capitalism and slavery, it would seem, were symbiotic rather than antithetical.

There would appear to have been a causal link between expanding consumer demand in the industrialising societies for plantation produce and the development of new areas of the Americas worked by slaves. But the relationship was complex. The new market opportunities presented to slave-owners by the collapse of colonial mercantilism were *not* in Britain, the most rapidly industrialising and most import-oriented society. Britain was the main source of demand only for cotton and, despite reducing import duties on foreign-grown sugar and coffee, took little sugar from Cuba or coffee from Brazil before 1850. The major foreign markets for these tropical groceries were the USA and continental Europe: by the 1840s, almost half of Rio's coffee was exported to the USA, with most of the remainder going to Hamburg and Antwerp. During the 1840s, about half of Cuban sugar exports went to north European ports: slave-grown sugar and, to a lesser extent coffee, were taking over markets in Europe that British West Indian producers had been forced to relinquish.

Conclusions: Europe and the New World

We will never have the data with which to measure the impetus given to Europe's early modern development by the discovery and exploitation – largely through coerced labour – of the New World. In relation to the entity of states and societies denoted by 'Europe', the impetus must have been small. Furthermore, the argument that this entity benefited from 'an unprecedented ecological windfall' (E.L. Jones) is not altogether convincing: iron-hulled vessels, steam-powered transport and the large-scale migration of free labour were required before masses of Europeans could be fed from the beef and grain of the pampas and prairies. By the time these conditions had been met, the European miracle was underway.

A more disaggregated view of 'Europe' would lead us to modulate this downbeat assessment. In the north-western part of the continent – which was at the 'cutting edge' of economic and social development – transatlantic imports nourished an important cluster of consumer habits, and transatlantic exports gave an impetus to industrial growth by raising demand for manufactures. Export-led growth, generated by colonial and African markets, transformed cotton manufacturing from a part-time handicraft to the prototype mechanised industry. The interdependence of this transformation with slave-based production needs no reiteration. In all probability, too, transatlantic commerce was an incentive to the service and financial sectors in north-western Europe to adopt economies of scale in shipping and extend networks of commercial credit.

But against the benefits individuals and groups derived from economic connections with New World must be set the state's military expenditure, financed from taxation, in winning and defending colonial territories. With respect to the Britain's richest colonies in the West Indies, these 'social costs' were such as to persuade some economic historians that national income would have increased had the sugar colonies been given away (Coelho, 1973, pp. 253–80). By the later eighteenth century, British consumers were having to pay a higher price for colonial sugar than that prevailing on the world market; relinquishing the colonies and free trade would have brought cheaper imports and lower taxes because of reduced military commitments. The counterfactual hypothesis seems somewhat 'unreal', given the endemic struggle by the European maritime states to engross colonial produce, trade and markets. A unilateral renunciation of colonialism and mercantilism is scarcely conceivable where all parties treat international commerce as a zero-sum game. A less bellicose Britain, adopting a more liberal trading policy, might have experienced a long-term economic decline similar to that of the Netherlands after 1750.

Still, the argument is useful because it prompts the comparative question: why was Britain able to absorb the social costs of exploiting transatlantic resources and commerce relatively easily, while for the Iberian powers these were a burden which more or less nullified any developmental impetus from their colonial empires in the Americas? The crux of the answer lies, I think, in the greater efficiency with which the constitutional powers coordinated civil society as compared with the absolutist regimes – a difference evident in the superiority of the fiscal machines in the Netherlands and Britain, but even more strikingly evinced in the ability of these states to maintain their credit with their wealthy subjects and borrow the money needed to finance overseas aggression. In Britain, national debt operations gave landed and mercantile groups a common interest and helped consolidate a class of 'gentlemanly' capitalists (Cain and Hopkins, 1993, pp. 66–7). Absolutist Spain, and to a lesser degree Portugal and France, were unable to tax uniformly, exempted key groups from taxation, and devolved fiscal powers onto tax farmers and local communities and magnates. The conventional contrast between lightly taxed, free-born Britons and Continentals groaning under the fiscal whip is erroneous: British taxation (which was mostly on expenditure) was more regressive and probably took a higher proportion of national income than French. The key differences were, first, that a fiscal system requiring Parliamentary consent and implemented by a voluntary magistracy was a more efficient mechanism than those devised by bureaucratic absolutism. Second, the state finances of constitutionalism reinforced the development of an organic capitalist class, whereas absolutism tended to block it or cross-cut it with other political divisions (Mann, 1986, pp. 475-83). In Britain, the operations of the military–fiscal state in undertaking colonial expansion reinforced a synergy of public and private power within and without the metropolis. The Iberians' long-term failure to exploit their conquests for their own national development clearly had many causes, from the imperial over-reach of the Habsburgs to their domestic agricultural impoverishment, but the inability of absolutist regimes to consolidate capitalist development to the mutual advantage of the state and private interests was among them.

3

EUROPE AND ASIA, C.1500 TO C.1880

Introduction

For Adam Smith, Vasco da Gama's opening of the sea route to India in 1498 ranked with the discovery of America as 'the two greatest and most important events in the recorded history of mankind' (Smith, 1776, 1976 edn, p. 626). Without belittling the achievements of Portugal's navigators and conquistadors in the East, this inflates their import for global history. The Indian Ocean had not been totally unfamiliar to medieval Europeans, and the Portuguese entered it as crusading warlords rather than venture capitalists. The Eurasian land-mass had a common stock of disease pathogens, so the Portuguese did not carry epidemics to 'virgin soil' as they did to Brazil. The states and societies they encountered were comparable to their own in every fundamental respect: monotheistic kingdoms, dominated by aristocratic warriors, served by literate clerisies and officials, and with economic structures and relations at roughly the same level of development. The intruders' sole technological advantage of any consequence was the gunned sailing ship, which could be used to terrorise harbour authorities and island principalities, though even this naval preponderance was not irreversible. Certain Asian states – Acheh in Sumatra, the Omani Arabs, the Buginese of the Moluccas – built fleets of their own to challenge European warships (Pearson, 1979). Except where they could bring their sea-power to bear, Europeans were a subordinate element in Asian politics until the eighteenth century. Their largest colony – and the only one where colonial institutions were imposed over a considerable territory – was the Philippines, acquired by Spanish expansion across the Pacific. The caravan trade had been bringing Asian spices, silks and porcelain to the eastern Mediterranean since classical times, and this ancient trading structure did not disintegrate until well into the seventeenth century. Smith himself acknowledged that Europe had derived much less advantage from its maritime commerce with Asia than from with America – a dismal result, as he saw it, of trade being monopolised by exclusive East India companies (ibid., p. 449).

This chapter has a double-sided agenda: it assesses not just the gains (or otherwise) of Western economic and military enterprise in Asia for Europeans, but their consequences for indigenous economies and societies. It asks not just whether and how European commercial and territorial advances were determined by the expansion of a European capitalist system or 'world economy', but whether and how they impacted on Asian capitalism and an Asian 'world economy'. Before embarking on the analysis we should dispel several possible misconceptions. First, 'Asia' is a European idea, and the word can hardly be used in analysing centuries earlier than our own without implying a Eurocentric perspective. There was no equivalent in any Asian language, nor was there any equivalent concept in the cartographic traditions of the Arab, Hindu or Chinese worlds before contact with Europe familiarised Asians with the idea of Asia (Chaudhuri, 1990, pp. 22–3). The notion that the vast area of the world's surface between the Levant and the Pacific constituted a single entity could only have arisen from outside: it is divided by formidable mountain and desert barriers and within it have coexisted at least four distinct, yet intersecting civilisations: Islam, Hindu India, the Buddhist lands, and Confucian China. Each has been marked by ethnic, linguistic and cultural diversity. There were family resemblances between some of the states constituted in these civilisations (between Mughal India and Safavid Persia, for example) but no common 'Asian' or 'Oriental' characteristics.

Second, the Europeans brought little new to the organisation of Asian commerce – except organised violence. They entered a trading 'world' with commercial institutions comparable to those of the Mediterranean and Atlantic and operating over a greater extent. *Before* the Portuguese arrived in India, about one-quarter of the spices traded in Asia were finally destined for European markets via the Levant. For centuries, the Asian civilisations had engaged in maritime commerce, not just in commodities of high intrinsic value, but in grains and other foodstuffs, raw materials such as timber, and manufactured goods, principally cloth and chinaware (Curtin, 1984, p. 120). When the Portuguese captured Malacca in 1511, it was an entrepôt in a zone of ecumenical trade where Indian, Javanese and Chinese merchants regularly met, and in more intermittent but direct contact with the Red Sea. Maritime South-East Asia was undergoing a vibrant commercial expansion, based upon the exchange of pepper and spices (cultivated as barter crops in the eastern Indonesian islands) for Indian and Chinese manufactures. Rapid population growth in city ports made the archipelago relatively highly urbanised. Though the Europeans helped lubricate this commercial expansion with their imports of New World silver, these were quantitatively less significant than Japanese silver flows (Reid, 1990a, pp. 1–30). The trading centres on the Indian coast were equally thriving, and for centuries after the Europeans' arrival, commerce, manufacturing and finance in maritime India continued to evolve *endogenously*, though in parallel to developments in early modern western Europe: market relations were intensified and commercial capital became more concentrated; merchants exercised a greater degree of control over artisans; and in the larger states taxation led to the wider circulation of money and more sophisticated credit structures. Indigenous shipping played a vital role in developing Asian inter-port (or 'country') trade in the sixteenth and seventeenth centuries: two-thirds of the ships leaving Surat for other Asian ports in the 1720s were owned by non-Europeans (Chaudhuri, 1985, p. 209; Perlin, 1983; Brown, 1985, p. 12).

Third, we have to disabuse ourselves of the idea – deeply engrained in Western economic thought since the Enlightenment – that Asian societies lacked the developmental dynamics of Europe, and so were inherently 'stationary'. From the eighteenth century up to the catastrophes of the twentieth century, Europe's intellectuals have believed their own quarter of the world was the most materially and morally progressive. This conviction was strengthened as their knowledge of Asian societies became systematised in a discourse – 'Orientalism' – which defined Europe as the point from which the flow of history was determined and interpreted, and opposed Europe's progress to the Orient's stasis (Said, 1978). Political philosophers, such as Montesquieu, deduced the despotic character of Asian government from climatic conditions, but the Physiocratic writers turned the concept of 'Oriental Despotism' into a rather sturdier theory of socio-economic immobilism. The basic social units of this type of political economy were thought to be unchanging villages in which the private ownership of land was unknown, and primitive self-sufficiency arose from a communal division of labour between agriculturists and village artisans. Over these communities, appropriating their surplus through taxation and claiming sole title to the soil, stood a despotic central power that invested some revenues in public irrigation works, but otherwise wasted them on military establishments and ostentatious consumption. By the early nineteenth century, the concept was part of the intellectual stock-in-trade of economics, and in the English-speaking world usually exemplified by reference to India.

In J.S. Mill, it appears as the Asiatic 'mode of appropriation', in Marx as the 'Asiatic mode of production' but the lineaments are identical. So, too, were their conclusions: the traditional Asian political economy was history's stagnant backwater, unable to progress to a higher – that is, capitalist – social form through its own energies (Mill, 1848, pp. 20–2; Marx, 1867, pp. 478–9).

Few Indologists now credit the concept of an 'Asiatic mode of production' with much explanatory power. India's village communities were less self-sufficient and more fluid than was once thought: they were integrated into regional markets by a considerable internal trade in bulk goods and by exchange between agriculturists and pastoralists (Washbrook, 1988, p. 66). Historians of the Mughal period now discern, among the complex welter of rights in land, the tendency for 'property' rights to grow and for villages to become economically stratified between larger cultivators employing hired labour, and enjoying superior rights in land, and a primitive landless proletariat, forced to undertake menial tasks for the higher classes (Raychaudhuri, 1982, pp. 176–7; Habib, 1982b, pp. 247–9). Asian 'despotism' was not so different from European absolutism. The dominant tendencies of the Mughal empire (c.1580–1707) broadly resembled those in contemporary European monarchies: an attempt at centralised government, a reformed coinage, and a concept of royal legitimacy which distinguished it from earlier sultanates (Richards, 1993). We will examine India's potential for economic development more closely, but what Marx called 'the unchangeability of Asiatic societies' is a false problem. The Indian economy lacked Europe's technological dynamism, but it was not immobile.

There is a genuine question – first posed in the Enlightenment – as to why China, the world's oldest and for so long most technically accomplished civilisation, had not kept pace economically with Europe. China had 'long been one of the richest . . . best cultivated, most industrious, and most populous countries in the world', yet seemed not to have developed since Marco Polo's visit (Smith, 1776, p. 89). However misinformed about the Chinese economy – which was growing *extensively* through demographic expansion, internal migration, the increasing density of market networks and scale of economic organisation – Smith correctly identified a great factual problem in world economic history: productive techniques reached a plateau in China by the fifteenth century, and the last centuries of pre-modern Chinese history saw less technological progress than almost any other preceding period (Elvin, 1973, p. 284). But, by whatever definition we choose, we cannot say that capitalism failed to emerge in China. Indeed, we would conclude from Elvin's study that capitalist practices and social relations were as evident in China around 1700 as they were in most of Europe: the manorial order with serfdom and serf-like tenancy was giving way to landlord–tenant relations; peasants were rational and profit-oriented, routinely producing for sale. Necessities like rice were traded over long distances. Entrepreneurs accumulated large stocks of working capital. A monetary revolution had given rise to paper currency, remittance banking and a complex credit system. Dependent labour was hired on a daily basis in at least some craft industries. If Chinese merchants only became financially involved in production in special conditions, such as to ensure supplies in highly competitive markets, this was broadly true of European merchants. The conundrum of Chinese economic history is the non-appearance of *industrialism* (not capitalism) in a society in which almost every element usually regarded by historians as a major contributory cause to industrialism was present (ibid., p. 297). Elvin explains the failure of the Chinese economy to grow *intensively* – through investment in more productive technology – in terms of the low level of return that could be expected when the economic infrastructure was already highly efficient. Late traditional techniques in agriculture, crafts and water transport had nearly reached the limits of what was possible without industrial–scientific inputs. In a vast economy which could solve bottlenecks by internal trade, there was little incentive for the type of innovations begun in eighteenth-century Lancashire (ibid., p. 312).

Whether we should extend Elvin's concept of a 'high-level equilibrium trap' to other traditional Asian economies is a matter of debate. But China was not an isolated case of capitalistic dynamics in Asia, and we should therefore think of capitalism as having many growth 'poles'. It was not a unique 'system' expanding from a single European 'core'. Europeans had an edge over Asian rivals in terms of corporate economic enterprise, but their rise to hegemony was a 'triumph' for military organisation and political power over indigenous élites, and not infrequently entrepreneurial élites. In the Chinese case, relations with Europeans were too marginal before about 1830 to be a significant factor in the late traditional economy. But India presents a different picture: the foreign trade sector accounted for a larger part of the economy than in China; its most lucrative branches were in European hands by the early eighteenth century; and Europeans dominated the most prosperous region of India by the 1760s. Whether we regard Europeans as thereby thwarting economic development will depend largely on how we assess the endogenous 'growth potential'.

Between the Asian Trade Revolution and the Beginnings of Territorial Conquest

The Portuguese monopolised Europe's maritime trade with Asia until the late 1590s, but they lacked the military and financial resources, and commercial acumen, to exploit their position to the full. Transport costs on the sea route were actually higher than on the caravan route via the Levant, and goods arrived in Europe via the Cape only because trade flows were determined by organised violence (Steensgaard, 1974, p. 40). A Portuguese blockade closed the overland route for some decades, and by depriving Mameluke Egypt of revenues may have weakened its resistance to Ottoman imperialism. But the Portuguese failure to take Aden led to a revival of the caravan trade, and after 1550 most European imports came overland (Pearson, 1987, p. 40; Boxer, 1969, pp. 59–60). The indications are that only about half the increment to intercontinental trade over the sixteenth century was due to the opening of the sea route. Since the Portuguese disrupted a Muslim trading network well able to deliver fine spices to Alexandria, it is quite plausible that the total volume reaching Europe in 1600 would have been greater had they never rounded the Cape. As it was, the *carreira* sailing to and from India represented a tiny fraction of the European marine: between 1500 and 1634, the average number of ships leaving Lisbon each year was seven, and four began the return trip (though the size of vessels did increase some four-fold during the sixteenth century) (Phillips, 1990, p. 49). The monarchy's dominant role in overseas trade had stunted the growth of Portuguese merchant capitalism, which was too feeble to exploit the military successes in Asia. The crown itself sought political rents from a redistributive enterprise and had little conception of business profit-making. It depended upon foreign capital, foreign expertise and foreign sales points to realise its monopoly profits. Lisbon was little more than a conduit between India and the rest of Europe, and most sales of imported spices were made in the Low Countries (Pearson, 1987, pp. 19–20, 43). No survey of profit and loss was ever tabulated for Portugal's maritime empire in Asia, where defence costs exceeded customs receipts long before the Dutch onslaughts in the early seventeenth century (Furber, 1976, p. 26).

The Portuguese presence had few substantial consequences for local economies. The most far-reaching were 'deepening' monetisation in India due to silver imports that reached 40 tons a year in the 1580s and 1590s, and major agronomic changes following the introduction of New World crops. Maize, tobacco, sweet potato and cocoa became staples of Javanese agriculture through contact with the Portuguese. Tobacco arrived in western coastal India around 1600, and within fifty years was being cultivated as a cash crop throughout the Mughal empire (Furnivall, 1944, p. 18; Habib, 1982b, p. 217). Otherwise, Portuguese attacks on indigenous commerce vitally disadvantaged only an atypical handful of sea-oriented principalities in western India, Ceylon and South-East Asia. Territorial potentates, such as the Mughal emperors, regarded 'wars by sea as merchants' affairs', and of no concern to their prestige. So little cognisance was taken of the Portuguese that they are scarcely mentioned in the standard Mughal chronicles (Pearson, 1987, pp. 52, 56). By holding the balance of power on the Malabar coast for about a century, they forced a rerouting of local exports and their exactions probably drove some hitherto peaceful traders to piracy (Pearson, 1979, p. 30). But, by and large, native merchants and rulers acquiesced in the tribute levied on local shipping since paying was cheaper than resistance. Asian inter-port trade was given a fillip by Portuguese officials trading 'privately', usually in partnership with high-caste *vanias* or merchants. This attracted much a greater annual investment than the *carreira*, and two thirds came from Hindu merchants (Boxer, 1980). In the later 1550s, following Ming prohibitions on Chinese maritime commerce, the Portuguese took over much of the carrying trade between Japan and China, and thereby increased the flow of Japanese silver and copper into the Asian maritime economy. In all likelihood, the Portuguese presence led to more African slaves being sold across the Indian Ocean: Goa reportedly had a 'huge' slave population, and black slaves were later to be impressed in Portuguese ships to meet a chronic manpower shortage (Boxer, 1980) .

What revolutionised Asian trade with Europe was the arrival of the north-west European monopoly trading companies from the 1600s. Unlike the Portuguese, they used their monopoly position to lower transaction costs and make the market for spices less volatile, and by internalising protection costs they secured an unbeatable advantage over the pedlars in the caravan trade. The overland route declined permanently and commerce in the eastern Mediterranean was further eclipsed by the Atlantic. Under the companies' aegis, commodity imports from Asia doubled in value during the seventeenth century, and again between 1700 and 1730. By the mid seventeenth century, 17 000 tons of shipping made voyages to Asia annually, by 1700, 25 000 tons (Pearson, 1988, p. 44).

Nearly all states chartered monopoly companies for trading in the east, but the Vereenigde Oost-Indische Compagnie (VOC) was the most heavily capitalised, had the greatest turnover, and, until the 1720s, was a more important business organisation than its only serious rival, the English East India Company (EIC). The ratio of Dutch to English trading voyages throughout the companies' existence was about seven to three (Furber, 1976, p. 78). Because of Amsterdam's position as Europe's premier commercial and financial centre, the VOC was able to serve a continental market. The EIC initially concentrated on its domestic market and, later, the re-export trade to the Caribbean and American colonies. The VOC promoted a sizeable flow of voluntary migrants: very nearly 1 million people travelled on its ships to the East Indies, of whom only 379 000 returned (Booghaart and Emmer, 1986, p. 3). The net 'drain' was significant considering the size of the Dutch population and contributed to demographic stagnation in eighteenth-century Holland. The VOC's charter created a state within the Dutch state, empowered to make war, conclude treaties, establish colonies, construct forts and coin money. The States-General exacted customs dues and retained nominal rights of supervision, but control lay with an oligarchy from Amsterdam's regent class on the governing body of seventeen directors.

The privileged trading corporation was a long-established institution, but the VOC's enormous capital – 6.5 million florins (about twelve times the amount subscribed to the EIC) – represented a new scale of corporate enterprise. Originally, the company was a union of individual capitals subscribed for ten years, but the directors refused to liquidate when the time was due, arguing that those wishing to realise their assets could do so on the Amsterdam exchange where VOC shares were trading at twice their nominal value. With the support of the political authorities, they appropriated the original investment into permanent, anonymous capital – which enhanced corporate stability and efficiency and brought the company closer to a modern business enterprise. The EIC did not take the final steps to permanent capitalisation until its restructuring in 1657 (Furber, 1976, p. 75). More than seventy trading companies were chartered in seventeenth-century Europe and most failed hopelessly as business enterprises; those operating in the Atlantic were normally unable to keep out interlopers and usually short-lived. The East India companies, by contrast, showed handsome profits over long periods of time, and defended their monopolies more successfully. The EIC's average profits were three times the rates of interest during the first half of the eighteenth century, and its dividends approximately twice the yield on government bonds (Steensgaard, 1981, p. 247). An institution combining governmental and business functions, political powers with property rights, was peculiarly 'fitted' to an environment that Europeans did not control politically and where they competed with resourceful indigenous merchants. Only the chartered company allowed for an indissoluble union of capitals, economies of scale in purchasing and protection, and corporate strategies for markets in which buyers and sellers were separated by vast distances and considerable stretches of time. It was a type of social actor that 'married' the state and private capital in a way unique to Europe, and especially north-west Europe. The companies evolved into major military powers whose ownership could be bought and sold by private citizens. Trading in their equity gave an important impetus to the development of capital markets and, when prohibitions on foreign shareholding were lifted, helped constitute a 'modern', transnational financial community (Neal, 1990, pp. 195–223).

The military and economic functions integrated within the VOC meant its operations in Asia had a dual character. The company made war on Portuguese commerce and strongholds, and violence was ruthlessly deployed in the Moluccas to secure a monopoly on fine spices. Control of the world's supply of nutmeg was achieved by conquering and depopulating Banda in 1621, and of cloves by the subjugation of the Ambon area in 1641–56. The Dutch could fix their price in Europe by the later seventeenth century, though not that of pepper, which had many more sources of supply. Meanwhile, the Javanese city of Jakarta had been seized, renamed Batavia, and turned into the hub of a sprawling trading-post empire. Had the vision of the VOC's first governor-general been realised, this would have nurtured a slave plantation economy. A slave supply existed in eastern India on which Batavia relied in its early decades for general labour and domestic service. The VOC recruited substantial numbers of slave soldiers, and land in conquered Banda had been distributed to company officials to be worked by Indian slave labour (Furber, 1976, p. 44; Boxer, 1965, p. 111; Moreland, 1923, pp. 77–8). However, the directorate refused to countenance plantation colonies, since it saw the company as a commercial organisation whose twin principles were the exclusion of competitors and 'buy cheap, sell dear'. Rather than territorial control, they preferred coercing Indonesian princes into treaties giving the Dutch exclusive rights over maritime trade. Most important trading cities in South-East Asia had been forced into monopolistic arrangements with the VOC by 1680.

The second aspect of the Dutch presence in Asia was more commercial in means as well as ends, for they, and the EIC, entered India as bulk purchasers of textiles which they exported to Europe in far greater quantities than had the Portuguese. In 1619–21, three-quarters of the VOC's outlay of nearly 3 million florins in Asia went on spices and pepper, and only a sixth on Indian textiles, which were mainly used as barter goods in archipelago. As the VOC enlarged its working capital, textiles absorbed an increasing proportion: by 1700, they accounted for 55 per cent of a total outlay of 15 million florins (though a smaller proportion of home sales), while pepper and spices together were only 23 per cent (Mauro, 1967, p. 132). The EIC had been virtually excluded from the archipelago by the Dutch, with the consequence that Indian textile purchases took a greater proportion of its investment, and by 1680 accounted for four-fifths of its merchandising. In terms of their volume, the EIC's imports peaked firstly in 1680s (when 707 000 cotton pieces were imported annually) and then in the years 1720–50 when trade was boosted by peace, a large re-export market in Europe, and booming demand for 'Guinee' cloths to barter for slaves on the African coast and clothe them on the Caribbean plantations. European manufactures only began to command a share of the African market towards the end of the eighteenth century (Lovejoy, 1983, pp. 103–4).

At their peak in the early eighteenth century, Indian textile exports – largely through the companies – totalled some 30 million yards annually (Chaudhuri, 1983, p. 842). Balances were settled in silver – which could command more goods and services in Asia than in Europe – and by importing fine spices not grown locally. All the evidence indicates that exports were a net addition to output, with significant consequences for employment in those regions where the companies concentrated their purchases. In Bengal, the richest manufacturing province, an estimated 16 000 looms would have been needed to manufacture the companies' annual procurement of textiles between 1710 and 1718, and five or six people were engaged in all the processes involved in the final output from each loom. The companies' trade probably accounted for about 10 per cent of employment in textiles, and their purchasing encouraged the localisation of weaving in *arangs* or occupational communities (Prakash, 1976). Evidently, manufacturing zones around major ports were being attached to world markets as low-cost manufacturers from the later seventeenth century; indeed, their export ratios probably equalled those in most parts of Europe. To lump, as does Wallerstein, the textile districts around Surat or Hughli into an 'external area' with which 'core' European states had a luxury or non-essential trade seems to me to derogate the impact of international trade in the decades preceding the British military advance.

To conserve the bullion needed for their Asian purchases, the companies sold shipping and other commercial services and, by the 1710s, shipments to regional markets were about twice the value of the goods shipped to Europe. The VOC had 30 000 tons of shipping in its 'country' trade and, as the principal carrier between Bengal and South-East Asia and Japan, opened new markets for Indian commodities. Its opium exports from Bengal increased from 1.7 tonnes in 1660–1 to 73 tonnes in 1717–18, while exports of coarse cotton textile pieces rose about twelve times in same period

(Prakash, 1979, p. 49). Handling the huge volume of 'country' and intercontinental trade required advances in rational business organisation which anticipated some characteristics of the modern multinational, multiproduct business corporation. Company officials had to coordinate markets by familiarising themselves with shipping schedules, the capacity of vessels, the levels of buying and selling prices, the likely volume of demand. Through the 'muster' system in India, they tried to ensure quality control in their purchases. But with this business rationality went a militant mind-set for, even in normal times, trade involved conflict with Indian political authorities and the companies were always psychologically prepared to secure their interests by force. They garrisoned their major factories, used their ships to threaten harbour authorities when their interests were jeopardised, and constantly thought of their dealings with indigenous states in terms of an 'image of dominance' (Watson, 1981).

Trade with Asia was not quantitatively very significant for either the Netherlands or England, and highly susceptible to interruption by warfare. In the early 1750s, 13 to 14 per cent of English and Dutch imports by value were from Asia, while only 6 per cent of English exports, and a trifling proportion of Dutch, were destined for Asia (Steensgaard, 1990b, pp. 147–51). But imported Asian cottons revealed a European demand for lightweight, easily washed fabrics across a wide social spectrum – which was a market innovation of great consequence. The price and quality of Indian textiles varied between different regions, and over time the bulk of purchases shifted from those supplying the cheaper to the more expensive cloths. At first, European demand was mainly for coarser fabrics, which must have been purchased by lower-income groups. Later, the more expensive chintzes from Madras and costly muslins from Bengal became fashionable in aristocratic circles and took a larger share of the market. Imports so threatened Europe's own manufactures that legislatures introduced protective tariffs and even sumptuary laws against lightweight cottons. Between 1700 and 1740, protection reduced the value of the VOC's textiles sales in Amsterdam by 30 per cent. The English parliament prohibited the wearing of Indian prints in 1701, and extended the prohibition to Indian cottons printed in Britain in 1721, though muslins, neck cloths, blue calicos and fustians were exempted. To judge by the import figures, sumptuary laws must have been widely flouted, but they formed part of a legislative framework favouring a national cotton industry. The law first allowed Indian textiles to pioneer the home market, then it moved to protect and stimulate the rapid expansion of dyeing and printing within the kingdom, and finally created a protected environment for cotton manufacture itself (O'Brien,

1990, p. 167). In terms of economic development within Europe, this was the most important consequence of international trade with India before 1760.

Neither the Dutch nor the English company sought territorial dominion in Asia, but by the 1760s both were ruling extensive lands beyond their factory enclaves and exploiting indigenous populations in new ways. Both were instances of 'expansion without design', and explanations of why they occurred must, I think, emphasise the snare of local politics. Otherwise, the situations drawing Europeans into territorial rule differed fundamentally: the VOC was the only European power in Java, where it did not tolerate 'private' European merchants. Java's princely states did not possess the fiscal machinery found in India, and could not so readily generate the revenues to defray the costs of conquest. What triggered Dutch territorial intervention in the 1670s was rebellion in Mataram, the major agrarian state in the interior, which began eighty years of almost constant warfare between rival claimants to the throne. The Dutch in Batavia bought rice and timber from Mataram and, in so far as they had a consistent purpose, it was maintaining legitimate kingship as a the sole source of honour and preferment. They wanted a single, compliant monarch who would not restrict their commercial operations for they gained nothing economically from the prolonged crisis in the native polity. Indeed, escalating military expenses were the main reason for the financial decline of the VOC in the eighteenth century (Remmelink, 1988, pp. 111–28; Ricklefs, 1993, pp. 70–1). But the VOC had made innumerable enemies in the region's trading states, some of whom were refugees in Mataram when the rebellion broke out, and its mere presence as a military power helped destabilise the political hinterland. Rebel and legitimate forces alike appealed to the Dutch for modern weaponry and military support. The ruling dynasty was restored, mainly because of the superiority of the company's forces over native levies. As the price for its intervention, a belt of territory to the south of Batavia was ceded to the Dutch in 1677, as well as a further port, and they were exempted from internal tolls and granted commercial monopolies. The incongruity of the Dutch presence is evident only to posterity: the VOC was entrenched in a Sundanese-speaking region ethnically and historically distinct from the Javanese mainstream. It was a foreign kingdom where the Dutch had grasped the sovereignty of previous Sundanese kings by virtue of military conquest (Carey, 1976, p. 53).

Successive civil wars further fragmented indigenous political structures and their settlement resulted in more territory being ceded to the VOC. But it had not achieved what a later era would call 'effective occupation' of the whole of Java when the company was formally dissolved at the end of 1795 and its assets taken over by the Batavian Republic. A hostile disease environment for Europeans, a difficult terrain and fickle native allies constantly checked territorial expansion. The VOC's strategy was essentially defensive: it protected rulers in return for payment and concessions, destroyed rebel factions and held strategic points, but it could not police all of Java (Ricklefs, 1993, p. 77). It directly exploited some of the most productive and populous regions, but elsewhere its authority was suzerain rather than sovereign: native princes were expected to regulate commerce in the company's interests and accept its appointees as subordinate ministers. In neighbouring Sumatra, the coastal sultans – save independent Acheh – were vassals of the Company, but Dutch suzerainty had virtually no impact on local society, and in any case the sultans' authority did not extend far inland.

The company sought to defray rising military expenses and compensate for declining trading profits by compelling peasants in the Priangan Highlands to deliver cash crops at fixed prices. Indigo was the first compulsory crop, but it was overtaken by coffee to cater for the burgeoning market in Europe. By the 1730s, coffee made up almost a quarter of home sales, and Java supplied 90 per cent of the company's imports. European 'coffee serjeants' supervised cultivation, and the cash return to the producer became a mere fraction of the market value of the coffee crop. Much of the income was siphoned off in perks for company officials and native regents (Furnivall, 1944, p. 40). Compulsory cropping so impoverished the peasantry as to defeat the object of the VOC's commercial monopoly: Dutch imports of European goods and Indian textiles became unaffordable, and farmers sold their produce clandestinely to Portuguese and English smugglers offering better prices. The Javanese took to growing and processing their own cotton for barter in what was becoming the 'informal' or 'native' sector (Hall, 1955, p. 270).

This syndrome of 'involution' was exacerbated by the Chinese take-over of intermediary positions in the colonial economy. The main agency in the diffusion of commercial capitalism in East and South-East Asia was a Chinese diaspora wholly ignored by the Chinese state. In Manila, they handled the transit trade generated by bullion shipments from Acapulco (Larkin, 1988). The Dutch had, initially, encouraged Chinese immigrants, whom they admired for their craftsmanship and industriousness, and Batavia became 'a Chinese colonial town'. When the British temporarily occupied Java in 1811, the community numbered 100 000. They were the most numerous, and collectively the most wealthy representatives of private enterprise in Batavia (Wills, 1993, p. 99). Despite the frequently turbulent relationship between the Chinese and the Dutch – including a veritable bloodbath in 1740 when thousands were massacred on suspicion of preparing an insurrection – the Chinese had opened craft workshops, tea-importing businesses, and sugar refineries. Tolls and taxes had been farmed out to Chinese businessmen, and Javanese village communities were leased out, both by the company and by native regents, to provide labour for Chinese sugar estates (Furnivall, 1944, p. 46).

When the VOC was dissolved, the first Dutch empire in the Indies was 'gently going to sleep' in the midst of corruption, inefficiency and financial crisis (Ricklefs, p. 105). As an intercontinental trader, the company had remained a 'going concern' until the 1770s, when about thirty ships a year sailed from the Netherlands to Batavia (Boxer, 1965, p. 314). The outbreak of war with Britain in 1780, and the Patriot Revolution, were disasters for the VOC: colonial trade was disrupted, the company's debts soared, and the political oligarchy that secured its privileges was shattered. The consequence for Java's politics was not a weakening of European power but an accelerated transition to Dutch state sovereignty, chiefly because the VOC's dissolution came at a decisive stage in the assertion of European ideological, political and military supremacy over 'Oriental despotism'. From the early 1790s, European states mobilised not only against each other, but around secular ideologies demanding limits to arbitrary rule but extending the boundaries of legitimate government. The pressures of global warfare helped to metamorphose company territories into the dependencies of nation states.

In India, the 'company state' came into existence as a regional power when the Mughal emperor vested fiscal and administrative authority (known as the *diwani*) over Bengal, Bihar and Orissa in the EIC in 1765. Only in retrospect can we see this as the beginnings of Europe's mightiest overseas empire, for the form and substance of rule remained Indo-Persian for another generation. As a political entity, the company state was not effectively integrated into the British national power structure until the French Wars, and nothing exhibits more clearly British conformity to the indigenous political culture than their exclusion of Christian missionaries from the company's territories until 1813. The company's servants had a straightforward motive in acceding to the *diwan*: to restore the company's shaky finances by seizing control of Bengal's land revenues, which were 'the key objective of policy' (Stokes, 1976, p. 27). The company's bullion imports ceased for three decades because land revenues financed its 'investments'. But its servants had no long-term imperialist strategy. They were reacting opportunistically to a crisis within Bengal's native political élite, and their intentions were conservative: to preserve the system of government of the Nawabs (Marshall, 1987, p. 75).

The company had been drawn into dominating a populous and prosperous Asian principality by the interplay of Indian state-building in the aftermath of Mughal collapse with European international competition. The Timurid dynasty was fatally weakened by the murderous disputes between Aurangzeb's heirs after 1707, and the Indo-Gangetic plain exposed to Sikh, Afghan, Persian, and Maratha invasions. Mughal provincial governors transformed themselves into *de facto* hereditary rulers with only a shadowy allegiance to Delhi, and renewed Franco-British conflict intruded into their political rivalries from the 1740s. On the European side, the initiative was taken not by the EIC but by the French Compagnie des Indes Orientales, based on Pondicherry. The French altered the diplomatic balance by allying with Indian princes in their internecine wars, and acting as their military auxiliaries. By equipping and training corps of sepoys to European standards, they brought the revolution in land warfare to the subcontinent. In recompense for his services in securing the Deccan for one of its claimants, the governor-general of the French establishments, Joseph Dupleix, was nominated Mughal governor on the Coromandel coast in 1751. By calling on British naval superiority during the Seven Years War, the EIC decisively checked French ambitions, though they revived during the maritime war of 1778–83 and the Napoleonic wars. Meanwhile, the EIC had learned to sell its services in the all-India military bazaar, and entered a string of 'subsidiary' alliance as a means of securing a stable frontier for British commercial interests and paying its own troops. In return for a 'subsidy' or the lease of productive territories, the company engaged to support client rulers. Though designed to set bounds to British territorial intervention, these alliances pointed in fact to its unlimited extension by putting intolerable strains on the finances of fragile Indian states. 'Allied' Indian rulers all fell rapidly and irremediably into arrears on their payments for the 'protective' company troops stationed on their territory. Their borrowing at usurious interest led to extortionate revenue farming, rebellion and ultimately British intervention in the internal administration to save the resources of the state (Bayly, 1988, pp. 58, 90).

Neither the London directorate nor the British government promoted belligerent expansion; the former constantly reiterated the company's commercial purpose, and the latter intervened to prevent company servants in India involving the company in unwanted wars (Marshall, 1975, p. 31). What persuaded the directors to countenance the coup which gave them territorial control in Bengal was the prospect of political profits restoring the company's finances, and even its bitterest enemies in Britain saw nothing wrong with reaping a tribute from surplus revenue. A coherent imperial policy with respect to British India emerged only with the governor-generalship of Richard Wellesley (1798–1805), when doctrines asserting the morality of conquest, British racial superiority and the power and dignity of the state were nurtured during the global struggle with revolutionary France. Only then did the political map of India acquire a recognisably modern shape and the company's administration begin the Anglicisation of the forms and personnel of British power (Bayly, 1988, p. 81). Wellesley's near contemporary, H.W. Daendels, the revolutionary 'Patriot' who served as governor-general of Batavia between 1808 and 1811, exhibited a similar confidence in Europe's capacity to master and remould native polities. He initiated a phase of more direct intervention in Javanese politics, which eventually provoked a great nativist reaction in the Java War of 1825–30 (Bayly and Kolff, 1986, p. 3).

The emphasis given so far to the political and military preconditions for territorial expansion in India is not intended to minimise economic factors, but they arose within India, not Europe. The frontier of European economic interest had moved inland long before Plassey, and had become more 'unruly' with the growth of private trade. Although the EIC retained the monopoly of trade with London, its officials made their fortunes by trading 'privately' and it tolerated 'free' merchants who settled in Calcutta and other ports, and took over much of the country trade. Before Clive intervened in Bengal's politics in 1757, company servants were systematically abusing the EIC's privilege of duty free imports to trade inland on their own account, and were selling the company's pass to Indian merchants so that they too could evade internal tolls. By law, foreigners were excluded from inland trade, and the Nawab's government, conscious of its own lost revenues, strove to protect local traders from illegal and unequal competition; the issue led to confrontation between the Nawab and the British as early as 1731. The fiscal decentralisation that followed Mughal decline, and the growing role of Hindu and Jain bankers in financing successor regimes, opened further avenues for European economic penetration. In an era of escalating military costs, the bankers rendered indispensable services by advancing cash on the security of the harvest, but relied on silver imports for liquid funds. They had, therefore, a powerful interest in smoothing the passage of European trade, and even in drawing the EIC into territorial rule when their own position was threatened. In Bengal, the house of Jagat Seth rose to prominence as the Nawab's bankers, but also became agents for British purchasers of textiles, raw cotton, opium and saltpetre in the inland markets. When the Nawab expelled the Europeans from Calcutta in 1756, Jagat Seth put himself at the head of the domestic conspiracy which, with Clive's assistance, deposed the Nawab and installed a puppet. Though making no formal claim to rule, the EIC became the dominant influence in Bengal. Its servants – with their indispensable *banians* – gained control of the most lucrative sectors of the economy.

The granting of the *diwani* set a seal on a period of raw mercantilism when, in a confusion of public and private interest, brute power served economic ends. At a village level, in both Bengal and the Carnatic, company servants claimed a prescriptive right to weavers' labour. Villages were shut off from open competition, native middlemen excluded, and weavers forced into becoming full-time wage-earners at rates so low that their employment became unremunerative. In some regions, the high-quality piece goods industry was dying long before it faced the competition of British factories. Private British merchants became involved in producing silk, sugar and above all indigo, which peasants were coerced into growing at fixed prices (Marshall, 1987, pp. 108–9; Arasaratnam, 1991). The company's administration was merely a European veneer on the *nawabi*, but its concentrated military power was used to crush Dutch rivals – who henceforth traded in Bengal only by courtesy of the EIC – and exact an immediate increase in land revenue receipts. By 1790–1, these had been forced up to more than three times the amount collected in the last year of the Nawab's regime, and on this basis the revenue demands were permanently 'settled' (Beauchamp, 1935, p. 24). What makes this revenue 'gouging' even more astonishing is that Bengal's population fell by 'at least one-third' – according to Warren Hastings's own estimate – during the great famine of 1770–1. As he advised the Court of Directors:

> It was naturally to be expected that the diminution of the revenue should have kept an equal pace with the other consequences of so great a calamity. That it did not was owing to its being *violently* kept up to its former standard (quoted in Beauchamp, p. 23, my emphasis).

New taxes were imposed on top of rising land revenues to meet escalating military and establishment costs. Opium growing, and extracting salt and saltpetre, were declared company monopolies in the early 1770s, and the salt monopoly became the largest of the company's commercial operations conducted for purely fiscal purposes. Even so, the company was in a chronic state of deficit throughout its rule.

India's Potential for Autonomous Development

British rule haunts the study of modern Indian economic history, but the ghost has appeared in dramatically different guises according to the medium's predilections. In one light, the British were the incubus stifling a transition to indigenous capitalism. In another, they represent *homo economicus*, creating a 'space' for modern economic activity in a religious and social order that had stifled the commodification of land and labour. As this implies, those upholding the second interpretation have usually held the Hindu caste system to be a socio-cultural environment in which an 'economy' – as a sphere of activity distinct from religion and politics – could not emerge. One anthropologist has asserted that, if contemporary India possesses an economy, 'it was the British government which made this possible' (Dumont, 1970, p. 165). Max Weber advanced probably the most influential argument on these lines in his comparative sociology of world religions. Work and wealth were no less esteemed in India than in the West but, Weber argued, socio-economic organisation had been stultified by the pervasive 'spirit' of ritual purity that made contact between the *jatis* (or endogamous subcastes) degrading. This mutual exclusiveness had blocked the emergence of autonomous civic communities, leaving merchants and artisans the passive subordinates of noble élites. The *jatis* are usually restricted to particular occupations and, Weber asserted:

> A ritual law in which every change of occupation, every change in work technique, could result in ritual degradation is certainly not capable of giving birth to economic and technical revolutions within itself, or even of facilitating the first germination of capitalism in its midst (Weber, 1948, p. 413).

Against this view of the British 'implanting' the culture of capitalism, Indian nationalist historiography has charged them with industrial infanticide. Drawing largely upon the evidence of British administrators, economic historians such as Romesh Dutt showed how the conquest destroyed the overseas textile trade, precipitated the decline of urban centres of craft production, and promoted general economic stagnation (Dutt, 1902; Majumbar, *et al.*, 1960). The key claim was that British rule had reversed the direction of economic change. None expressed it more clearly than the senior ex-official who told a parliamentary select committee in 1840: 'This Company has in various ways, encouraged and assisted by our great manufacturing ingenuity and skill, succeeded in converting India from a manufacturing country into a country exporting raw produce . . .' Sir Charles Trevelyan informed the same enquiry: 'We have swept away their manufactures; they have nothing to depend on but the produce of their land.' These judgements are echoed in the terms used in more recent debates on the historical trajectory of the Indian economy: 'deindustrialisation', 'retardation', 'disarticulation', 'arrested development', which all imply that growth would have been faster and more diversified under different political circumstances (Simmons, 1988). Nationalist writers influenced by Marxism gave a particular inflexion to this thesis in arguing that colonial rule halted the 'capitalistic' reorganisation of handicraft manufacturing by Indian merchants – a 'rising bourgeoisie' was, as it were, stopped in its tracks. (Jha, 1963, puts the Marxist-nationalist argument.)

The range of arguments is considerably more complex than the hoary legend of a thwarted 'Industrial Revolution' – which no historians now seriously entertain. To test them exhaustively would require a counterfactual model of the Indian economy around 1870 had British rule not been imposed, but this is an econometrician's pipe-dream. We lack reliable data on the *actual* Indian economy, and cannot extrapolate a hypothetical alternative from measurable precolonial trends. We can only speculate cautiously as to the growth potential of India from some salient features of its political economy, bearing in mind that the subcontinent is as large as Europe without Russia, with a huge variety of ecologies and subcultures. The best starting-point remains the heated controversy M.D. Morris provoked when, in 1963, he questioned the widespread assumption that British rule diverted India from some inevitable path of economic development. His basic intention was to exorcise the British ghost from India's economic past. The British imposed themselves, Morris argued, on a society for which every index of performance suggested the level of technical, economic and administrative performance of Europe five hundred years earlier. They established a 'night-watchman state' and left the economy largely to its own devices. Per capita output probably grew over the nineteenth century as political security encouraged the extension of cultivation. If modern industry still represented a tiny sector of the economy in 1914, this was only to be expected given the long 'gestation' period for industrialisation in a traditional social setting (Morris, 1963, p. 611, reprinted in Morris *et al.*, 1969). But Morris was as sceptical of the Weberian thesis of Hindu 'exceptionalism' as he was of the 'classical' nationalist interpretation of the nineteenth-century Indian economy. Hinduism is a protean and localised religion that cannot be identified with a single value system shaping social behaviour. The *jatis* function similarly to extended kin groups in other cultures, and inter-*jati* economic cooperation is well documented. Though individual social mobility was restricted, the social division of labour has been relatively fluid, because whole *jati* have changed their occupational status in a few generations (Morris, 1967). Research into eighteenth-century mercantile groups in north India has shown them developing cross-caste, urban solidarities, shedding much of their 'passivity' towards the ruling powers, and moving towards virtual civic self-government. Though it was not a 'bourgeoisie' in the European sense, there was a merchant class in formation during the decades of British conquest (Bayly, 1983, pp. 174–7).

One of Morris's points is now uncontentious: at the level of basic productive techniques, India lagged behind China and Europe in the early modern period. Farming technology was remarkably backward and stagnant. Iron – a relatively expensive material in India – was scarcely used in making agricultural implements; water power was never utilised; in many regions, sugar cane was pressed in inefficient mortar-and-pestle mills (Habib, 1979, pp. 156–60). The soil was probably manured less efficiently. What may explain this technical stasis is the abundance of fertile land and the fact that slow population growth exerted little pressure on agriculture to raise productivity. Large-scale farming of even a primitive kind was unknown. Precolonial India was a land of peasants and, though some cultivated with the help of labourers paid in money and kind, there were no concentrations of agrarian capital. Heavy taxation – assessed at half of output in fertile regions (compared with 5 to 6 per cent in China) – nullified the incentive to improve technique by investing in equipment (Raychaudhuri, 1983, p. 17; Habib, 1969, p. 38). However, since taxes were exacted in coin, they entailed monetisation and encouraged the planting of crops with a high market value. Peasants responded to market demands like farmers elsewhere, though in the knowledge that monsoons 'failed' about one year in four. Quite rationally, they allocated much land and labour to a 'famine store', which reduced the resources available for industrial crops. Even so, cotton and opium were planted to meet the requirements of the European companies and sericulture became a major enterprise in Mughal Bengal. What was precluded by the technical stasis of Indian agriculture and its peasant character were the economies of scale, rising labour productivity, and increase in the marketable surplus associated with agrarian change in early modern western Europe.

Handicraft production, metallurgy and mining (principally for diamonds) exhibited similar technical backwardness in comparative terms. High-quality iron and steel had long been smelted in India but by uneconomic methods that meant their cost relative to the price of grain was higher than in Europe.

Such mechanical devices as gearing, the belt-drive and the screw had scarcely entered the craftsman's technological repertoire, and the treadle was used only in the weaver's loom. Paradoxically, Indian textiles had achieved a dominant position in international markets in terms of price, quality and diversity, although weavers had ignored technological advances made centuries earlier in China (Raychaudhuri, 1983, p. 27). Only in certain cloth-printing techniques was handicraft technology in advance of that of other regions. Dexterity, and a minute segregation of skills amongst hereditary occupational groups, had been both substitutes for, and barriers to technical change. Indian craftsmen were certainly capable of adapting techniques from abroad; for example, working to the orders of the European companies and private traders, the subcontinent's shipwrights built considerable fleets of European-style vessels. But there was little consistent pressure for technological adaptation because of the wide availability of skilled, and by comparison with Europe, cheap labour.

The sector of the economy that was broadly comparable to Europe's was commerce and finance. Credit could be provided, money changed, and goods insured for long-distance trade by highly developed financial institutions. Their functioning was made smoother by the monetary union the Mughals imposed, with an imperial coinage whose fine silver content remained constant for nearly two centuries. Double-entry book-keeping, the use of credit notes, witnessed agreements and brokerage were all practised within the indigenous business culture before European companies and private traders penetrated into the interior; indeed, this business culture facilitated European infiltration by offering familiar services, and yet at the same time frustrated a thoroughgoing 'Westernisation' of the economy because it was embedded in kinship, caste and hierarchies of honour (Bayly, 1983, p. 262). The only form of organisation 'missing' from Indian commercial capitalism was the joint-stock association.

Whether Indian merchants were reorganising handicraft producers into the dependent workers of 'proto-industries' remains an open question. Frank Perlin has argued that, as market networks and the regional division of labour became more complex, so entrepreneurs began controlling production through advance payments. Their capitalist functions were, he suggests, essential for the extensive manufacturing in Gujarat and Bengal (Perlin, 1983, p. 70). Not everyone is so persuaded. In his generally negative assessment of Mughal India's potential for capitalist development, Irfan Habib doubted whether the urban craft workshops were evolving into true 'capitalistic' establishments. He found no evidence, for example, of employers feeling obliged to furnish tools, nor any trend towards the investment in fixed capital. The dynamic conjunction of merchant capital and dependent labour appears to have been confined to a few centres (Habib, 1969, p. 67). Elsewhere, it may have been more 'rational' for the merchants to perpetuate the tried system of self-employed craftsmen and their families producing textiles with their own relatively primitive equipment. The self-exploitation of independent piece workers probably gave the merchant as good a return as his own transformation into a proto-industrial capitalist (Bayly, 1988, p. 37).

Where counterfactual analysis becomes truly speculative is in imagining Indian political conditions had the British not imposed an imperial order. Could the post-Mughal kingdoms have become vehicles for civil development in a competitive system of states on European lines? The question would have seemed absurd to an earlier generation of imperial historians, who regarded the British as having restored India to tranquillity after 'the Great Anarchy' of the eighteenth century. Political disorder, escalating violence and the decay of cities are historical realities we cannot ignore – though without endorsing the imperial apologia for the British Raj (a state that established itself only by incessant campaigning). Agra, Delhi and Lahore all had 400 000 inhabitants or more in 1700, but each declined drastically under the impact of Persian and Afghan invasions and civil strife. But to stop at the Mughals' terminal crisis overlooks the capacity of the independent sultanates for internal strengthening and administrative reform after 1760. Their efforts to 'catch up' militarily meant that, by the 1800s, British generals were confronting native armies trained in Western military technique and with cannon cast by Indian gunmakers to European standards. The British used the allegation of a 'despotic' leeching on civil society to justify their own annexations, but the realities were more complex. The able rulers of Mysore, Haidar Ali and Tipu Sultan, encouraged the immigration of peasants from nearby territories and sought to attract foreign merchant communities. Even their British enemies had to concede that Mysore was 'well-cultivated, populous with industrious inhabitants, cities newly founded and commerce extending' (an opinion quoted in Bayly, 1988, p. 96). Tipu's regime can be compared to that of Mohammed Ali in Egypt in the use of economic monopolies to invigorate the state and expand its territorial power.

It would be equally mistaken to judge fiscal parasitism by the Mughals' exacting standards. Their land taxation had far surpassed that of contemporary European states in its scale of operation, and its repressive character was aggravated by raising the salaries of imperial officials from lands (jagirs) with which they had no permanent connection. Resources were 'drained' from agriculture and handicrafts to the imperial centre, and three-quarters spent on a vast military establishment (Richards, 1981, p. 292). But the localisation of power after 1720 mitigated this parasitism: more revenue 'leaked back' into the immediate locality because of a shift in power from jagirdars to the local Hindu élites or zamindars. These latter had been given tax-gathering responsibilities by the Mughals, which they used to obtain greater economic control over agrarian society. The most powerful contested the state's exclusive title to the land and asserted personal property rights over agrarian resources at the expense of communal rights. The so-called 'great households' felt sufficiently secure to invest in wells, market centres and new crops. Were they an incipient capitalist gentry? Washbrook implies such, just as he hints that frequent conflicts between zamindars and peasants, merchants and artisans were incipient class struggles. He concludes that the British conquered states in which the social history of capitalism was already under way, though the cultural identities of dominant and subordinate groups are difficult to perceive through Western spectacles. What the British offered the former were more secure property rights and privileges less circumscribed by custom (Washbrook, 1988, pp. 70–5).

Let there be no ambiguity: late-eighteenth-century India was a politically fissiparous civilisation, with a comparatively unproductive infrastructure by *Asian* standards. The type of state imposed on it by Muslim invaders was a less secure environment for property and commerce than that found in China and Japan, and political rents weighed more heavily on agriculture. Climate and ecology meant that most primary production was for subsistence, but the fiscal 'draining' of the surplus completed the vicious circle of agrarian stagnation. The company state, with its superior administrative and military organisation, exacerbated this situation, at least until the 1840s: legally guaranteed proprietary rights were conferred on a rentier élite, and revenue was actually extracted at a level the *ancien régime* claimed only in theory (Raychaudhuri, 1985). But the British were not required to import the 'spirit' of capitalism, and both the benign and malign consequences of their rule for the Indian economy have been inflated. Their ghost needs cutting down to size, if not laying altogether.

The Incorporation of the Indian Subcontinent into the European World Economy

The emergence of Britain's Indian empire was the most striking example of political domination securing dependent economic relations between a

European state and non-European societies. By about 1820, this empire was fundamentally affecting the 'shape' of world history: not only did it subject about a fifth of humanity to European rule, but it also provided the commodities and military manpower with which to lever open China to Western penetration. Its European-trained armies and the capacity to transport them overseas made Britain one of the nineteenth-century world's great military powers. In the 'official mind', the existence of a large empire in India was an unimpeachable reason for acquiring an even larger one beyond its frontiers.

It is tempting to discern in the British conquest the energies of an industrialising society, seeking to command the raw resources for its infant industries and the markets for its manufactures. This is entirely mistaken. Territorial rule enabled the East India Company to expand a triangular trade with China dating back to the early eighteenth century. By the 1780s, its most lucrative business was importing tea to Britain, and to balance this trade Indian raw cotton and opium were exported to China. Between 1785 and 1833, Kwantung province's annual imports of Indian cotton were six times greater than the total annual consumption of the English industry during the 1780s (Elvin, 1973, p. 313). What drove this commerce was not industrialisation, but the emergence in Britain of a mass consumer market. British political ascendancy was achieved before technological innovation, with its concomitant rise in labour productivity, radically changed the comparative costs of textile manufacturing in Europe's favour. Cotton yarn and cloth exports to India were negligible before 1814 (a mere 90 000 rupees out of total commodity imports worth about 11 million rupees). In an irenic world, India would have maintained its position as a low-cost manufacturer for much longer, since craft labour was comparatively so cheap as to compensate for relative backwardness in technique and economic organisation.

What overwhelmed this position was the aggressive 'protectionism' of the national state. In the late 1780s, a non-reciprocal tariff regime was imposed on the EIC's territories: British textiles were given additional protection against Indian imports, while Indian cloths were handicapped in international markets by export taxes on merchandise carried in foreign ships to continental Europe and the USA. When the Company's trade monopoly was ended in 1813, British import duties on calicoes and muslins were raised to prohibitive levels. Despite dissatisfaction with monopoly trading institutions, the 'common sense' of the British political class remained mercantilist in regarding international exchange as a zero-sum game. After 1815, free trade doctrines did little to modify a policy of grabbing back from neutral nations the trade their merchants had won during the war years.

The ending of monopoly trade with India and the revival of international trade after 1815 exposed Indian producers to competitive imports and inaugurated an external economic 'dependency' of a modern kind. By this date, cotton spinning in Britain was wholly mechanised and concentrated in factories. The price of factory yarn had fallen four-fold in twenty years. The quality of 'fine counts' was better than handspun equivalents (though this was not true of coarse yarns). Most cloth was still handwoven, but the cheapening and high quality of the main input brought a considerable advantage to British weaving. Because of the new-found capacity of the cotton industry, domestic and European markets were periodically saturated and merchants and manufacturers turned to the 'underdeveloped' world to compensate for insufficient demand: between 1814 and 1839–40, the value of cotton yarn and piece goods imported into India increased about twenty-nine-fold. By mid century, over 18 per cent of British cotton exports by value (and nearly a quarter of the volume) were destined for India (Farnie, 1979, p. 91). In terms of Britain's total direct exports, however, the Indian market was a disappointment: it absorbed 10 per cent in 1827, but only 6.5 per cent in 1833. The proportion rarely rose above a tenth, until large railway orders were placed in the wake of the Mutiny; India absorbed 15 per cent of British exports in 1859 (calculated from Mitchell, 1988).

The new conditions of external dependency were exhibited in the growth and changing composition of India's exports between 1814 and 1858. Exports tripled in volume and over the long term the trade balance was positive, though commodity imports – mostly from industrialising Britain – grew at a faster rate. In 1814, cloth goods were still a major item in the export schedule, but their value fell steeply, particularly after 1830 when the subcontinent became a net importer of cloth. Meanwhile, exports of agricultural commodities (indigo, opium, raw cotton, silk and jute) rose considerably (Chaudhuri, 1971). The most salient, and persistent, feature of the trading pattern was the exchange of primary produce for manufactures; textiles alone accounted for 45 per cent of Indian imports by 1870 (Latham, 1978a, Table 14, p. 78).

From his world-system perspective, Immanuel Wallerstein has interpreted the British conquest as incorporating the subcontinent into the capitalist world economy as a 'peripheral' area. There was, he argues, a two-fold process of reorganising Indian productive structures so that they participated responsively in the international division of labour, and reorganising political structures to facilitate this economic participation (Wallerstein, 1986, pp. 28–39; idem 1989, ch. 3). He rightly emphasises that, up to the 1840s, many peasants were indirectly coerced into producing cash crops by the East India Company's revenue exactions. With respect to indigo, which provided between a fifth and a quarter of total exports between 1814 and 1840, peasants were routinely forced to cultivate the crop by thugs in the hire of European planters (who were immune from the criminal law in the *mofussil*.) Planters were themselves financed through the Calcutta Agency Houses, which may have been giving subsistence to half a million native families at the height of the indigo boom in the 1820s (Greenberg, 1951, p. 34). It is possible that, at the regional level, a sizeable stratum of impoverished peasants were no longer self-sufficient in rice or other food crops. Whether, as Wallerstein claims, coercion into the market was *widely* associated with the proportion of the acreage devoted to cash crops increasing at the expense of food grains is doubtful. Before the early twentieth century, there was sufficient uncultivated land in most regions for the area under food and cash crops to expand simultaneously. Where we have quantitative data for the later nineteenth century, they show the increase in the tilled area given over to food grains keeping pace with the acres under cash crops (Harnetty, 1971; McAlpin, 1974).

Though what has been said broadly validates Wallerstein's perspective, several critical reservations must be entered. First, Indian 'dependency' on the northern industrial world was mediated through the triangular trade with China, India's most important trading partner in many of the years before 1860. Opium shipments to China displaced indigo as the most valuable item of external trade around 1850, and for a while constituted a third of all exports. It is worth reminding readers that a basic characteristic of Wallerstein's model of the capitalist world-system is the exchange of *necessities* through the international division of labour. When we learn that the mid-nineteenth-century world's 'single most valuable commodity trade' (Wakeman, 1978, p. 172) was in a narcotic drug, and that this commerce was itself founded on the British passion for tea, then we have a inkling of a historical reality unexplained by the model. Consumer demands for non-necessities (ranging from tea, sugar, coffee and cocoa to ostrich feathers and ivory) still shaped the relations between industrialising Europe and the 'dependent' underdeveloped world deep into the nineteenth century. These demands reflected economic growth in Europe, but only by the most elliptical reasoning can we imagine them as 'determined by' or meeting the 'systemic needs' of capitalist production.

Second, India's role in the international division of labour as a source of industrial materials for the European 'core' can easily be overstated. The short-staple cotton grown in India was unsuited to Lancashire's high-quality spinning industry. In 1855, only 16 per cent of British raw cotton imports were from India, and about half were re-exported. After the American Civil War disrupted the world market, the proportion of retained Indian imports rose briefly to about 18 per cent of total consumption in the early 1870s, but sank again as new sources of long-staple cotton were found in Egypt and Brazil. By then, Indian entrepreneurs had founded a mechanised spinning industry, which became a significant exporter of factory-spun yarn to East Asia. Surplus raw cotton was still exported, but to China and Japan rather than Europe. Indeed, as a source of industrial inputs, India was to be more important to Japan than she ever was to Britain. By the 1890s, most raw cotton imports for the nascent Japanese industry were coming from India. Consumers in East Asia preferred tough fabrics woven from coarse yarn for which short-staple fibre was ideally suited. British manufactures did not compete in this market, which became the platform for Japanese industrialisation. Contrary to Wallerstein's thesis of the 'polarisation' of fixed capital, the expansion of world cotton manufacturing over the nineteenth century was not a simple process of high-technology output concentrating at the Atlantic 'core'. Rather, the centres of handicraft production in Asia managed to retain certain domestic markets and, on the basis of technology imports, themselves experienced the dynamic development of cotton industrialisation (Kawakatsu, 1986, pp. 619–43).

Third, Wallerstein and other scholars broadly sharing his perspective paint a picture of exports leading, not to growth, but to immiseration and a general paralysis in the domestic economy (Wallerstein, 1986; Rothermund, 1988, p. 24). That ryots (peasant cultivators) were impoverished is undeniable, but to attribute this to external trade surely exaggerates its potential to affect mass living standards. Without a reliable estimate of India's gross national product, the proportion exported and the proportion of national income spent on foreign goods will always be unknown quantities. However, in relation to total population external trade was unquestionably small. The aggregate value of exports and imports in 1854–5 was 346 million rupees; if we divide half that sum by the estimated all-India population of 227 million, then we find that the annual per capita value of external trade was 0.76 rupees,– in sterling terms, about 8p (Chaudhuri, 1971, Table 1, p. 25). Obviously, the calculation is grossly simplifying; the per capita cash value of peasant exports must have been much higher in regions with good transport connections to the sea. But by the same token, in vast areas as yet poorly integrated into a subcontinental economy (let alone a global one) external trade must have been irrelevant to living standards. Even after 1870, when the steam revolution in internal and international transport was integrating India more closely with world markets, external trade probably accounted for only a modest proportion of total income (Chaudhuri, 1968; Chaudhuri, 1971, p. 43).

Lastly, textile imports had a more delayed and less drastic impact on Indian handicraft production than was once thought – not least by British administrators. This controversy is worth dwelling on, since the 'deindustrialisation' of Indian textiles was a formative issue in the historiography of 'underdevelopment', with something of the emotive resonance of the Atlantic slave trade. Certainly, India's trade in high quality exports was destroyed and internal demand for luxury goods choked off by the impact of British rule on aristocratic élites. Once-thriving manufacturing centres on the coast – Surat, Dacca, Murshedabad – decayed, and their hinterlands became over-dependent on agricultural employment. The Famine Commission of 1880 argued that: 'At the root of much of the poverty of the people . . . and of the risks to which they exposed in seasons of scarcity lies the unfortunate circumstances that agriculture forms almost the sole occupation of the masses . . .' (Dutt, 1906, pp. 105–6, p. 193).

Abundant qualitative evidence would suggest that textile imports induced a decline in the proportion of the labour force in manufacturing – or a structural 'reversal' of the normal pattern of development – but aggregate figures indicate that it had not gone far before 1850. Annual cloth imports then supplied about 2.25 yards per head of population, or around one-quarter of total consumption. By 1880, however, annual per capita imports were 7.5 yards, or – assuming expenditure on cloth had risen slightly – around two-thirds of total consumption (derived from data in Twomey, 1983, but using population estimates in Visaria and Visaria, 1983). Domestic spinning was better protected than weaving, because imported yarns were inferior to the handspun Indian yarn used for coarse cloth with respect to durability, washing and dyeing. They never supplied more than half of total domestic consumption. Spinning remained an important part-time occupation, especially for women, though much of their output was bartered in the extensive non-monetised sector (Specker, 1988, p. 342). Michael Twomey has *inferred* that 31/2 million full-time job equivalents were lost as a result of cotton imports between 1850 and 1880, though the estimate was 'subject to many errors' and a range of 2 to 6 million jobs 'might be more realistic' (Twomey, 1983, p. 52). This would have represented a major reversal in the structure of the labour force. Oddly, Twomey's inferences are not confirmed by the only direct quantitative data bearing on this controversy: counts of the number of looms in Madras Presidency show an *increase* of 20 to 25 per cent between the late 1850s and early 1870s. Whether the number of weavers increased by the same proportion is not known, but it could scarcely have declined. Unable to compete with imports, weavers concentrated on coarse cloth for local markets. Population growth and a fall in prices may have sustained demand, but the occupation became more precarious. The loss of popular purchasing power during famines and depressions exposed weavers to prolonged underemployment. The evidence does not indicate a long-term and constant shift of labour from the textiles to other employment, but rather sudden movements associated with mass distress when, for example, weavers migrated as contract labourers. They were certainly worse off at the end than at the beginning of the nineteenth century (Specker, 1988).

Failed 'Revolution from Above' in India?

A recurrent question in the historiography of India is whether the British had effected a social revolution by 1857 or conserved the socio-economic forms of native society while imposing themselves on the hierarchy of political power (Stokes, 1978, pp. 19–45). The ownership and control of the land is the critical 'test' in this controversy: influential nineteenth-century commentators were convinced that British rule was undermining the foundations of traditional society by imposing Western concepts of property that were a prerequisite of capitalist development. Twentieth-century historians have been much more sceptical. With the inestimable advantage of hindsight, they know that in rural India the durability of social forms was more evident than radical change up to and beyond 1947. The proposition has gained ground that the environment of law and property relations under the Raj was positively hostile to the working of a free market economy (Washbrook, 1981).

The starting-point in unravelling these issues must be the Bengal Permanent Settlement of 1793, which fixed in perpetuity the land revenue to be paid by the zamindars while securing their property rights in the land and upholding them through a Western legal system. This was part of a concerted application of Whig principles to the governance of an Asian society. Powers were to be a separated, with an independent judiciary and a political executive itself subject to the rule of law. The function of government was to be the bare task of ensuring the security of persons and property while making land the most desirable of all property. The people's industry would thus be directed to those agricultural improvements essential to their own welfare and to the prosperity of the state (Stokes, 1959, pp. 4–7). Zamindars were stripped of their right to keep armed retainers and to police their districts, and it was hoped that in the security of their new-found legal titles they would transform themselves into 'improving' estate-owners. They were vested with rights over extensive waste lands in their domain, empowered to seize the effects of peasant tenants who fell into rent arrears, and threatened with dispossession only when they defaulted on the land revenue.

Ironically, a measure intended to create a class of secure landowners led to a wholesale transfer of real property through forced sales to meet tax arrears. Nearly half the land on which the Bengal government depended for revenue was sold by 1830 (Marshall, 1987, pp.146–7). So many warrior gentry were deprived of their estates that the policy seemed 'a fearful experiment' in social levelling to one well-placed observer (Cohn, 1969, p. 53). But, rather than improving landlords, the new proprietors were usually rentiers for whom zamindari tax-gathering rights were a form of speculative investment. A minority were bankers, native officials and grain dealers already accustomed to purchasing revenue rights. In Upper India, where land transfers were on a similar scale, many new proprietors were transplanted Bengalis who had collaborated with the British and carried Western liberal ideas inland (ibid., pp.69, 76; Metcalf, 1969, p. 153). By mid century there was growing official restiveness that land control was passing steadily into the hands of the non-agricultural classes (Stokes, 1983, p. 52). Nonetheless, beneath the wholesale transfer of legal titles, the old structures of local power proved very durable. A study of Banaras province has shown that the majority 'losing' land between 1795 and 1885 retained their positions, economically, politically, and socially *within* the local areas in which they had held rights as zamindars (Cohn, 1969, p. 89). They lost rights to a ground rent from proprietary tenants but retained control over so-called *sir* land (roughly equivalent to the 'home farm') which they cultivated through tenants-at-will or hired labour, and they continued to exact tribute from caste or clan subordinates. The expansion of output and revenue were such that the rural hierarchy was able to support two different élites at its apex: the urban rentiers who had purchased zamindari rights as a form of safe investment, and the traditional local squirearchy.

Neither became a class of 'improving' landlords, and we can attribute this signal failure of imperial policy to a profound difference in the attitudes of British and Indian political élites to the land. In order to live off their rent rolls, British aristocrats had learned to look upon their estates as economic enterprises and to take an active part in their management. Traditional Indian élites were, by contrast, tribute takers for whom security, fame and respect resulted from the effective management of people grouped in families and castes. The zamindars did not think in terms of an estate-to-be-managed but rather of a village community to be managed by manipulating the rules of its hierarchy. Unlike the estate manager who maximised the net produce of his lands, the village manager maximised the number of mouths he fed (Neale, 1969, pp. 9–11). Though there were major regional variations, the large zamindars were the great men of their area because they could command status: they supported and managed the temples, organised festivals, wielded political power. Their main agricultural function throughout the nineteenth century was the maintenance of irrigation works. Only in particular places in northern and central India where they congregated with exceptional density did the landlords dissolve into a body of proprietary cultivators (Stokes, 1983, p. 39).

Over the larger part of southern India, where zamindari settlement was not introduced, the ryot was directly assessed by the state for his land-tax liability, and confirmed in his proprietorship. The government asserted the ruler's historic claim to be the universal landlord and retained its rights over waste lands. European administrators were more involved directly in agrarian governance, though heavily reliant on their native officials. Revenue assessments varied according to the type of land and crop, but were often equivalent to half the agricultural yield and represented an astonishingly oppressive burden. They held back cultivation, reduced land values and were a major cause of prolonged agricultural depression. Revisions and remissions of revenue demand were frequent, and undermined peasant confidence in investing in the future by sinking wells or purchasing fresh draught animals (Kumar, 1983, p. 219). Cash crops were cultivated not in the expectation of profit but to meet revenue and rent instalments and to pay marriage expenses.

Clearly, Indian rural society under British rule had been subjected to intense pressures before 1857, but they had resulted in an accelerated circulation of élites rather than a revolutionary change in agrarian property relations. The endeavour to 'rationalise' these relations according to liberal precepts was frustrated by the intermeshing of clan, caste and tributary hierarchies. The networks of local power were too dense for the company state to lever open a place for agrarian capitalists. Apart from forced sales due to revenue defaults, there was no land market to speak of in nineteenth-century British India, and scarcely any agrarian development brought about by large-scale, private capital investment. Rents were largely regulated by custom and, not infrequently, caste (Neale, 1962, p. 72). The economic opportunities the Raj created were snapped up by urban rentiers and moneylenders: men who assimilated easily to the status hierarchy by

claiming a share of the agricultural produce, but investing nothing to raise
the productivity of land and labour. Agrarian social relations could not be
detached from a ritualistic, honour-bound culture, nor shoe-horned into the
competitive society based on individual rights of the utilitarian vision.

That the aim fell short of achievement is partly attributable to the
ambiguities of British jurisprudence in India. Benthamite influence gave rise
to a body of codified law – finally enacted between 1859 and 1861 – intended
to make the legal process cheap, simple and accessible and individual
contracts more easily enforceable. But the evolving colonial legal system was
'distinctly Janus-faced', for besides promulgating 'Western' legal codes for
India it buttressed the customary and religious norms prevailing in local
communities (Washbrook, 1981, p. 653). On them were based the 'private'
or 'personal' law of most British Indian subjects. Although the utilitarian
strand of reforming zeal hoped to substitute reasoned, secular law for
custom, a paternalist strand saw custom as essential to conserving the social
pattern. As a consequence, the Raj attempted to define and codify Hindu
law. The British courts turned to the scriptures for guidance on moral codes,
and relied on the pandits (religious scholars) on matters of interpretation.
This inevitably resulted in personal law validating the Brahminical view of
the caste hierarchy and the varna theory of social order. With the support of
British power, the Hindu law expanded its authority across large areas of
society that had not known it before, or had followed local, non-scriptural
custom. In many ways, the conventions of Hindu law interfered with the
individual's property rights, especially in land. Kinship brought ascriptive
rights to shares in, and maintenance from land that Hindu law regarded as
the collective property of the joint family. Enforceable kinship rights greatly
restricted the buying and selling of land.

Nineteenth-Century Java: From the Cultivation System to the Liberal Era

In 1860, J.B. Money, a barrister at the Calcutta bar, contrasted the *laissez-faire*
economy of British India with another, and to him superior, mode of
colonial exploitation: the 'Cultivation System' in the Dutch East Indies. This
was the compulsory growing of export crops for delivery to government
agents at fixed prices, and in Money's eyes its advantages were threefold.
First, the Dutch state profited directly from the vast public enterprise in its
colony. Second, the colonial government's finances were healthy because a
buoyant economy yielded high revenues, mainly from indirect taxes on

consumption. Lastly, the Dutch operated the system through the native nobility, and so avoided the political disaffection that had swept through northern British India in 1857. In every respect, this was an object lesson in 'How to Manage A Colony' (Money, 1861, especially vol. 2, ch. 6.).

Money may have overdrawn the contrast between colonial mercantilism and *laissez-faire* – for there were state monopolies in British India – but essentially he was right. India did not contribute directly to the British exchequer; the corporate and national monopolies on the Indian market and carrying trade had been revoked, and foreign trade assimilated to a liberal international political economy. So completely had Britain renounced claims to tribute and exclusive trade that many argued the country would have been better off without its Indian dependency. The two empires represented different conceptions of how to tie tropical colonies to European metropoles. Indian *laissez-faire* reflected Britain's global hegemony in trade and finance, which smaller European powers could not hope to emulate. For them, the Dutch 'model' was more appropriate. Significantly, one of Money's most attentive readers was Leopold, Duc de Brabant: on becoming King of Belgians in 1866, he dedicated himself to finding his own 'Java' – an ambition realised in the Congo (Stengers, 1989, ch. 1).

The Cultivation System was imposed in the aftermath of the Java War, when an estimated 200 000 Javanese were killed, large tracts laid waste, and the inability of the native kingdoms to restore a 'pre-European' political order was brutally exposed (Carey, 1976; Bayly, 1986, pp. 111–33). With dynastic resistance broken and native society pulverised, the Dutch could concentrate Javanese and Sundanese labour on producing tropical exports to a degree rivalled only by the remaining slave plantation economies. The 'forced deliveries' imposed by the VOC in Priangan were a precedent, but the system's extent shows how 'effective' the occupation of the whole of Java had become since the later eighteenth century. During its first two decades, probably 70 per cent of agricultural families were dragooned into producing government crops, the majority in coffee, though this varied from less than half in some regions to virtually all in others. The negligent were flogged (Ricklefs, 1993, p. 121). Villagers would normally reserve a fifth to a third of their arable land for export crops, for which they received a cash payment, as well as exemption from the land tax. They also tended coffee bushes on 'waste' land declared government domain, and from January 1833, all coffee, excluding that delivered directly in lieu of cash taxes, had to be sold to the government at a fixed price. This crop always yielded the biggest profits for the Dutch administration, and forced cultivation was extended to Sumatra's west coast in 1847. Whereas the Cultivation System was largely dismantled from 1870, compulsory coffee cropping remained in force in certain regions of Java until 1915.

Tropical groceries were extracted from Javanese peasants in quantities and at prices competitive with Cuba and Brazil. Export volumes rose more than four-fold between 1830 and 1840, and their value six-fold. A state trading company handled most of the produce, and the proportion destined for the Netherlands increased from about two-thirds in the 1830s to more than 90 per cent in the 1860s. Shipment was reserved for Dutch-flagged vessels, preferably built in the home country, and national shippers, shipbuilders and wholesalers gained enormously from the exclusion of British rivals. Though regulated and largely conducted by the state, the system was a 'mixed economy' because private European entrepreneurs contracted to process sugar, the main crop grown on peasant land. By agreement between the contractors and village headmen, cane was rotated with rice on irrigated land and delivered to the water- and steam-powered factories newly constructed in the countryside. 'Private' exports – principally of sugar – were roughly equal to those of the government by 1860.

The metropolitan government, and Dutch entrepreneurs engaged in shipping, processing and marketing colonial produce, profited handsomely from this form of colonial exploitation. State trading profits were credited to the Exchequer, and averaged 19 per cent of total public revenue between 1830 and 1850. In the 1850s, rising market prices for sugar and coffee brought this proportion to 31 per cent; between 1861 and 1870, it was 24 per cent. Even when the system was being dismantled between 1871 and 1877, it averaged 13 per cent (Fasseur, 1986, p. 138). These revenues buoyed up an economy that had been depressed by the decline of its European carrying trade and the costs of attempting to retain Belgium within the Dutch kingdom by force. Dutch public debts were redeemed, taxes reduced, fortifications, waterways and the state railway built, all on the profits forced out of Javanese villages. Thanks to the Indies contributions, up to 1876 the Netherlands did not need to negotiate a single government loan. The tax burden, certainly in the higher strata of Dutch society, was significantly lower than in other western European countries. An income tax was only introduced after 1890, and even then in a very mitigated form (Fasseur, 1991, p. 43). The funds were even used to compensate the slave-owners of Surinam (Dutch Guiana) for the emancipation enacted in 1863 (Ricklefs, 1993, p. 123).

Whether the long-term development of the Dutch economy was accelerated by colonial exploitation is more debatable. Java supplied only 16.7 per cent of Dutch imports between 1865 and 1870 (as compared with

30 per cent from Britain and 25.5 per cent from Prussia) and received only 9.6 per cent of Dutch exports, despite tariff rebates favouring metropolitan goods in colonial trade. Furthermore, by comparison with her European neighbours, modern manufacturing was slow to develop in the Netherlands, which lost its most industrially advanced regions with Belgian independence. The economy remained heavily biased towards small farming and the provision of services until the last years of the nineteenth century. Although little capital was invested in Java, the existence of a profitable nucleus of colonial commerce and services in the metropolis may have retarded industrialisation by 'siphoning off' investment funds. The industrial sector most advantaged by the colonial connection was commercial food processing, in which the Dutch had long excelled. Amsterdam established itself as Europe's chief sugar centre after 1830, partly because of its privileged access to Javanese sugar. The Twente cotton industry was the only manufacturing branch to find an important outlet in Java, where it enjoyed covert tariff advantages. Even this 'easy' market had hidden costs, because Dutch cotton producers concentrated on coarser cloths and did not attempt to compete with foreign manufacturers.

The impact of the Cultivation System on indigenous society and the colonial economy has long been debated, particularly since an influential study by Clifford Geertz accorded it a decisive role in promoting agrarian underdevelopment (Geertz, 1963, ch. 4). Central to Geertz's thesis was the fact that Javanese sugar cultivation was unique in being grafted on to a traditional village agriculture in which communal rights to the land were the norm. As communities strove to accommodate greater numbers to local economies dominated by the demands of export cropping, they slipped – Geertz argued – into a static egalitarianism: agrarian society became immobilised by an 'agricultural involution' designed to provide everyone with a niche, however small, in the rural economy. Ossification of the traditional community precluded the development of indigenous rural capitalism. More recent research indicates that this influential theory needs revising, if not discarding altogether: peasant society appears to have become more differentiated and more inegalitarian. Village headmen were the pivots around which the cultivation system turned, and many used the authority vested in them by the colonial state to extend their land (which was often worked with the hired labour of landless peasants) and to acquire greater wealth and social prestige (Fasseur, 1986, pp. 141–2). Whether the mass of cultivators were impoverished by devoting so much labour to export crops is now also questioned. Compulsory crops were intended to replace direct money taxes, and a village earning more than its land tax obligation could keep the excess payment. It would seem that at least some producers benefited from this income, and from greater monetisation and increasing internal trade. Rising imports of cotton goods indicate greater purchasing power (though native handicrafts probably suffered). There was sufficient land for the per capita area given over to subsistence crops to increase slightly, and the greater use of animal power and fertiliser made it more productive (Elson, 1990, pp. 24–48).

Yet in one, incontrovertible sense, the system was deeply reactionary: tributary exactions could be imposed only because the colonial government placed itself at the pinnacle of native feudalism. Native society was structured around dependency relationships, often close to bondage, which the Dutch had always used to exact corvée labour for road-building and public works. Cultivation service was imposed on top of corvée, and enforced through the same feudal nexus. Dutch officialdom was too sparse to deal directly with the villagers, and the Javanese gentry were moulded into a parallel administration. They were paid a percentage on crop deliveries, and sometimes drafted corvée labour into the sugar factories to process the harvest, though seasonal waged employment became increasingly common. In drawing the feudal classes into the colonial power structure, the system was a model of 'indirect rule'.

From a metropolitan perspective, the dismantling of the Cultivation System after 1870 was a liberal triumph over a mercantilism now seen as reactionary and repressive, but it nevertheless fell short of unleashing economic liberalism in the colonial economy. By the 1860s, liberal factions were in a majority in Parliament and a former colonial businessman with pronounced liberal views became Minister of Colonies. He was convinced that Javanese development depended on the allocation of full property rights in land to the individual peasant. The communal arrangements whereby villages collectively agreed to supply crops to government contractors could not, liberals argued, promote a free flow of the factors of production. A bill allowing individual appropriation was placed before the Dutch Parliament, but fundamentally altered after 'a storm of protest'. The fear was that Western property law would supplant the customary *adat* law of native society. The Agrarian Law of 1870 guaranteed customary rights and ruled out the alienation of land cultivated by the Javanese to non-Javanese (though it could be rented). This reinforced the legal barriers against 'settler' colonialism – whether European or Chinese – though the long-term leasing of government domain land became easier. The law was supposed to remove official compulsion from the economy, but this persisted to some degree beyond 1900.

There was no inrush of metropolitan private investment after 1870. The commonest form of large-scale enterprise was the sugar factory, usually owned by former contractors under the Cultivation System, who raised most of their capital locally. They now rented land from village communities for periods of eighteen months, and since sugar was never grown twice running on the same land, after each crop the land reverted to native use. Exports to the world market grew very rapidly until the mid 1880s, but chiefly because of the opening of the Suez Canal and the internationalisation of Java's overseas trade. The Dutch were slow to move to steam navigation and British shippers were major beneficiaries of economic liberalisation. By 1885, private exports from all the Dutch Indies were ten times those of the government, but the immediate destination of nine-tenths of sugar exports was now London, not Amsterdam. The share of Dutch imports coming from the Indies fell from 15.9 per cent in 1870 to 6.7 per cent in 1880.

Conclusions

The third quarter of the nineteenth century is an appropriate moment to pause in this narrative both to assess what had gone before and to indicate what lay ahead. What should be emphasised immediately is the historical 'shallowness' of European rule in much of colonial Asia. Most of the territory of modern Indonesia was entered by the Dutch only in the late nineteenth century. Until then they had adopted a policy of 'abstention' towards the so-called Outer Regions, which the Minister of the Colonies deemed 'liabilities' in 1845 (Kuitenbrouwer, 1991, p. 32; Wesseling, 1988, p. 63). Colonial rule in Malaya, Upper Burma and most of French Indo-China began with a scramble for territory broadly coinciding with the partition of Africa and lasted less than eighty years. Some states, such as Johore, remained sovereign entities with which Britain simply had treaties of protection up to the 1910s, and the form of indirect rule imposed on others consisted of a Resident whose duty was to 'advise' the Sultan in all fields save those of religion and custom. The intention was to abstain, as far as possible, from the internal affairs of native states. Even where there was direct administration in 1870, it had given only hesitant and partial support to social modernisation. In British India, a handful of visionary policy-makers had hoped to unleash the forces of possessive individualism on a vast Asian society, but their achievement had fallen far short of that aim. Below the level of the warrior élite who took the full shock of conquest, such 'modernising' impact as colonialism was to have on agrarian relations had barely registered (Stokes,

1976, p. 144). The British had neither cleared the way for a native capitalist revolution on the land, nor done much to encourage 'colonisation' by European planters. Their economic exploitation of India was chiefly through expatriate control of international trade and the siphoning of revenues to satisfy London creditors of the British Indian government.

Where the Europeans had wrought a major and irreversible change was on the external economic relations of South and South-East Asia. Unlike Wallerstein, I associate this with the Asian trade revolution of the seventeenth century and the shattering impact of the chartered companies on the maritime economy of the Indian Ocean. This exogenous shock was all the greater because it came when that economy was experiencing a concatenation of problems comparable to the 'general crisis' in contemporary Europe. With remarkable economy of effort, the Europeans in Asia either took over the circuits of international commerce or destroyed them in pursuit of trade monopolies. A thriving international division of labour that had pivoted on the South-East Asian trading states was extinguished. We can only conjecture as to the consequences for indigenous development. The great increase in European demand for Indian manufactures and South-East Asian groceries, and the opening of new markets in Japan, may have compensated for the destruction of regional exchange. But in Indonesia, trading cities as populous as Europe's major commercial centres had their livelihood ruthlessly destroyed by superior military power. Seventeenth-century South-East Asia experienced what Reid calls 'a change of direction', which ended the positive interaction between inter-regional and international trade, the expansion of Islam and indigenous state-building. Henceforth, societies were more impoverished, more culturally isolated, and politically deracinated (Reid, 1993, pp. 311–25).

In India, the commercial élites that had done so much to open maritime trade were reduced to junior partners of Europeans, and the gains of trade were diverted from Asia to Europe, without any reciprocal advantage save an increase in liquidity. Those who profited most were shareholders in the giant trading companies and private traders operating on their own account. In a more diffuse way, European consumers gained from trade with Asia's 'low-wage' economy: even after the companies' huge mark-up, imported quality textiles were cheaper than comparable European products. In a purely rational world, Asian manufacturers would have been left to enjoy their comparative advantage in abundant manual dexterity, while European labour was reallocated to sectors favoured in international exchange by copious supplies of coal and iron and machine-building skills. Of course, economic behaviour was systemically irrational: much of Europe's price advantage in Asian trade was dissipated by high military and establishment costs. The bullionist dogma that bemoaned the flow of silver to Asia went with a mental set condoning the forceful extortion of working commercial capital within India. Economic relations between maritime Europe and maritime Asia were grievously disadvantageous to the latter, but not comparably beneficent to the former. Commercial intrusion into the Indian Ocean accelerated development in western Europe only by encouraging the import-substituting manufacture of cottons behind tariff barriers.

An essential element in the Europeans' success in dominating the international economy of maritime Asia was their constant renovation of the technology of naval warfare, but this is not a sufficient explanation. Success was also due to a recombination in the Asian commercial and political environment of 'public' and 'private' powers that were being consciously separated within western Europe from the later sixteenth century. The emergence of the nation state can be traced in the monopolisation of military, judicial and diplomatic functions by the sovereign power, while the rights and liberties of private individuals and corporations became legally defined. That these included property rights and economic freedoms was fundamental to that 'insulation' of the state from the economy which is a basic institutional characteristic of capitalism. Vesting sovereign powers in monopoly corporations appears quite 'aberrant', yet it has been a recurrent feature of European expansion. As we will see, the chartered trading company was the institution that first brought much of Africa under European rule. It was not just in the mercantilist era that commercial intermediaries between European and peripheral economies linked 'professionally' organised violence with business structures adapted to the pursuit of long-term corporate goals.

Further territorial expansion in Asia would have been difficult to predict in the 1860s, certainly in Britain where many were convinced India had been an expensive mistake. Economic pressures behind expansionism were more palpable in France, where Lyonnais industrialists needed to secure supplies of raw silk after pébrine infestation hit the region's silk worms, reducing the harvests in the later 1850s to about a third their normal weight. China became an essential source of supply, and the Lyon Chamber of Commerce and Ministry of Agriculture and Commerce set up a committee to consider ways of expanding Franco-Chinese trade while undermining the British monopoly on raw silk imports from Asia. Coincidentally, Lyon was a centre of Catholic missionary effort, as well as Europe's most important industrial consumer of raw silk, and the silk industrialists were able to infiltrate their material concerns into a prestigious national policy of protecting French missionaries in the Annamite empire. From the late 1860s until the early twentieth century, access to South China through Tonkin and the Red River was the principal aim of France's Annam policy, to which the organised businessmen of the Lyonnais gave consistent and, through their contacts with the Ministry of Commerce, influential backing. It is true that sub-imperialists in Saigon took the crucial decisions to advance into Tonkin, but a without powerful lobby in France favouring a forward policy there was a grave danger of metropolitan disavowal (Laffey, 1976, pp. 15–37; Albertini, 1982, p. 195; Thobie, 1983, pp. 159–67).

But the economic expansion making greatest inroads into the still independent states of South-East Asia around 1860 was Asian, not European, working through the uncoordinated migration of labour, entrepreneurship and small-scale capital. This process was centuries old, but Europeans established the preconditions for *mass* movement by introducing steam transport, suppressing piracy, and making the remittance of money much easier. Though not the only migrant group, the Chinese were by far the most numerous. An estimated 5 million entered Malaya alone in the nineteenth century, the vast majority as temporary migrants, and a further 12 million between 1900 and 1940 (Drake, 1979, p. 278). Immigrant Chinese began exploiting natural resources in typically modern ways about a generation in advance of colonial rule and some time before Western trading companies moved into mining and plantations. The best-documented case of Chinese 'pioneer capitalism' is their exploitation of rich tin deposits discovered in the Larut district of Malaya in 1848. The peninsula was then thinly populated and politically fragmented among Islamic sultanates, whose rulers controlled river communications. There was little commercial agriculture, apart from some immigrant enterprise, and few exports save for small quantities of tin. The Straits Settlements (of Penang, Malacca and Singapore) had been acquired by the East India Company in the course of its China trade as defensive points and entrepôts, but the company authorities showed no interest in exerting political control outside them. There were no tax systems to defray military expenses in the hinterland, and little to attract the merchant in a subsistence economy based on swidden agriculture. Money did not circulate widely outside the Straits Settlements, and wage labour was unknown. Apart from rice cultivation on land the peasants held on usufruct from their lords, most labour was performed either as a feudal obligation akin to corvée or took the form of debt and chattel slavery. The tin ore discoveries dramatically accelerated economic development: in return for heavy taxes on tin production, the Malay chiefs invited merchants based in the Straits Settlements to import mine labour and to move the ore to

Singapore. Though Europeans, Arabs and Eurasians invested in mining by advancing capital to leaseholders, Chinese were the key entrepreneurs, for only they could mobilise labour through the clan associations and secret societies. The main service provided by the British agency houses was marketing tin mined by the Chinese (Allen and Donnithorne, 1957, p. 55). The basic elements of Malaya's position as a primary producer – immigrant capital and labour, abundant natural resources, fairly easy access to international transport links – were present before the colonial period, and prior to Western capitalism's involvement in extraction and production. This hectic development brought political instability, as rival factions in the Triad secret societies fought over mining claims and the monopoly of supplies to the miners, and became involved in dynastic disputes. By the early 1870s, conditions inland were so chaotic as to threaten the trade and peace of the Straits Settlements, and Chinese and European merchants with investments in tin-mining states pressed for intervention (Drake, 1979, p. 272). Their representations were probably not the key factor in the British decision to establish a protectorate over Perak, the most important tin-mining state, in 1874 – a decision which reversed a settled policy of non-intervention. The extension of Dutch power in Sumatra and French in Indo-China had alarmed the Colonial Office, and it was apprehensive lest other European powers might intervene in an area flanking Singapore and the route to China (Tarling, 1966, p. 139). The government of the Straits Settlements did nothing to disturb the Chinese entrepreneurs' control of the tin trade, and it remained in their hands until the 1900s, when new mining techniques required capital on a scale that only the large European firms could mobilise. Large-scale capital imports began only in 1905.

To spell out the larger historical import of this may seem heavy-handed: as a form of economic activity, capitalism has not evolved in a unitary system. The international economy certainly acquired systemic characteristics in the later nineteenth century when the adoption of the gold standard facilitated the flow of money between the world's financial centres, but in terms of global development, this was late in the day.

4

EUROPE AND AFRICA FROM THE SLAVE TRADE TO THE COLONIAL CONQUEST

Introduction

Africa's history is as rich and diverse as that of any other continent, but little of that richness emerges in the context of its relations with Europe. Although this chapter concludes with Europeans ruling Africa and exploiting its human and material resources, it would be a spurious teleology that viewed African history as culminating in this 'end'. During the four centuries or so that separated Europeans' initial contacts with sub-Saharan Africa and the 'scramble', Africans were colonising the continent, adapting their agricultural techniques to its hostile environment, adopting new crops, founding towns, and developing complex political institutions. In the Sudan and along the east coast, the most important external influence on African societies remained – as it had been since the eighth century – the expansion of Islam, compared with which the impact of Christian Europe was slight. Admittedly, the Portuguese had opened regular commercial and diplomatic relations with the 'Guinea' states by the 1490s, and won important Catholic converts in the kings of the Kongo, who were valued allies and trading partners. Yet, except in Algeria and the south, there were to be neither dramatic conquests nor substantial settlements before 1870, when much of the continent was still unexplored by Europeans. Portugal's one attempt to found a settlement colony, in Luanda during the 1570s, failed disastrously in the terms in which it was conceived. The soils were too poor and rainfall too precarious for peasant colonists, and African bowmen defeated attempts to carve landed estates out of tribal territory. Coastal Brazil had a more hospitable ecology for plantations, and Asia offered richer commercial pickings. Portugal's

African possessions were never a major attraction for metropolitan interests before 1880 (Birmingham, 1981, p. 36; Miller, 1983, p. 129).

Tropical Africa had resisted invasion since time immemorial, for the simple reason that incomers faced the world's most formidable disease barrier. Before quinine prophylaxis, between 40 and 60 per cent of newcomers from Europe died during their first year of residence in West Africa where falciparum malaria and yellow fever were endemic (Curtin, 1984, p. 15; idem, 1976, p. 252; Headrick, 1981, pp. 62–3). The prevalence of tsetse flies – the vector of sleeping sickness trypanosomes – rendered horses and draught cattle useless through great swathes of the bush. Long-distance travel was impeded, and trade confined to goods of high intrinsic value. But the disease barrier was not the only obstacle to territorial incursions. The African chiefs from whom Europeans leased coastal strips of land for their forts and depots could usually control and isolate the foreigners whose presence was generally welcome because of the revenues from increased trade and the inflow of luxury goods. African sovereignty was normally acknowledged by an exchange of 'Notes' permitting Europeans to build and use a fort in return for a specific annual payment. Though the Portuguese occasionally mounted punitive expeditions from their forts at Elmina and elsewhere, they were directed more against European competitors encroaching on their trade monopoly than against local Africans on whom they depended for military support, fresh water, and provisions as well as trade (Fage, 1977, pp. 512–14). On the so-called 'Slave Coast' in the Bight of Benin, which was the major source for the Atlantic slave trade in the late seventeenth and early eighteenth centuries, Europeans had no military presence at all. Traders were confined to coastal ports, where they were compelled to trade on terms established by port officials (Lovejoy, 1983, pp. 54–5).

Conditions for European settlement were most favourable on the Cape of Good Hope, with its Mediterranean climate and absence of tropical disease, but the Dutch East India Company's colony experienced 'two meagre and stunted centuries' between its founding in 1652 and the development of a wool-exporting economy in the mid nineteenth century (Frankel, 1938, p. 44). Partly because of the Company's restrictions on immigration, the settlement was constantly short of labour and resorted to slave imports from the East Indies, Mozambique and Madagascar. Though there was some slave-based agricultural development (principally of wheat and wine) for the purposes of victualling East Indiamen, the Dutch settlers on the inland plateau practised a form of stock-raising closely approaching the subsistence economy of the native pastoralists whose lands they contested. Very little economic activity was directed to the permanent development of the land.

The total European population, when Britain took over the colony in 1806 was only about 20 000. There were probably an equal number of slaves – nearly all males – widely dispersed among the master class and held under a legal regime of unspeakable cruelty (Iliffe, 1995, pp. 124–5).

The Slave Trade, Slavery and African Underdevelopment

When Europeans began trading with Western Africa there were clear technological disparities between the societies they encountered and their own: Africans did not possess firearms, wheeled transport and ocean-going vessels, were not literate outside Islamicised regions, and often lacked the techniques to build in stone. But we should not conclude that the economic structures and technical competences of Europe and Africa were radically different at this time. Want of quantitative data makes it is impossible to 'rank' pre-industrial societies by objective economic criteria, but the descriptive evidence suggests that West Africa was neither static nor particularly 'backward'. There was a striking degree of urbanisation both in the savanna and the forest, with the cities of Gao, Timbuktu and Djenne having populations ranging from 15 000 to 80 000. Though towns were primarily places where agriculturists gathered for defence and trade, they also maintained specialised craft workers and served as administrative and religious centres. Indigenous techniques (in, for example, iron smelting-and-working) were of a high order and the range of handicrafts closely resembled those of other pre-industrial societies. Exchange was widespread, and facilitated by the growing use of cowrie shells as a general-purpose currency. The organisation of trade and markets was complex and efficient, and an embryonic capital market evolved at an early date (Hopkins, 1973, pp. 19, 48–51). However, one difference in economic structure had become a gross disparity in western European eyes by the later eighteenth century. To paraphrase Mungo Park, who explored the Niger during the 1790s, hired servants, voluntarily working for pay, were unknown in Africa, and the social division of labour was comparatively undifferentiated. Park ascribed this to the prevalence of slavery, and guessed that slaves outnumbered the free by nearly three to one. But he distinguished between household slaves, who could not be sold by the masters except under rather strict conditions, and slaves taken in war or purchased with money. These latter were bought and sold at regular markets, and their value increased with the distance from their place of origin. War, whether openly avowed by states or low-intensity plundering of hereditary enemies, was 'the most general and productive source of slavery, and the desolations of war often (but not always) produce the second cause of slavery, famine, in which case a free man becomes a slave to avoid a greater calamity' (Park, 1799, 1954 edn, pp. 216, 226).

Human bondage has been recorded in most societies and its occurrence in Africa is not in itself remarkable. What does require explanation is the fact that, for many centuries, the continent's sparse population was the main source of slaves for other regions. Long before Europeans began purchasing them on the Guinea Coast for the Atlantic islands, African slaves had been in demand in the Middle East and the Mahgreb as domestic servants, concubines, soldiers, and occasionally as administrators and productive workers. A tentative estimate is that 7.2 million slaves were exported via the Sahara and the Red Sea between 650 AD and 1600. In the sixteenth century, exports to the Muslim world probably outnumbered those to the Atlantic by around 3 or 4 to 1, and only after 1600 was the ratio reversed (Austen, 1979, pp. 23–76; Lovejoy, 1983, pp. 19, 25). Before about 1690, African commodity exports to the Atlantic (principally gold, with some ivory and wax) exceeded the value of slave exports – measured, that is, by the European prices of the goods for which they were exchanged (Eltis and Jennings, 1988). Exports then shifted decisively towards slaves in response to the booming demand for plantation produce, and as a result of the Brazilian gold discoveries which supplied gold more cheaply than West Africa. Powerful Africans found raiding for captives more profitable than gold-mining, and within a few years between 1700 and 1710 the export trade at Whydah switched from gold to slaves (Rodney, 1972, p. 107). During the peak years of the transatlantic slave trade in the 1780s, slaves probably accounted for 90 per cent of total African trade with the Atlantic world.

By any reckoning, the transportation of 11 863 000 Africans (as estimated in Lovejoy, 1989) to New World slavery was a major force in 'shaping' contemporary human society. Before 1840, this represented the largest overseas migration in history and was by far the most important connection between Africa and the European-dominated international economy. Ironically, a trade with such momentous consequences for humanity was a trifling part of global commerce. Around 1800, the total maritime trade (imports and exports) of West, West Central and Southern Africa was valued at around £9 million – less than 2 per cent of estimated world trade at that time, and equivalent to about only 11 per cent of Britain's foreign trade (Munro, 1976, p. 36).

Walter Rodney began an unresolved debate on the interdependence of slave-exporting and slavery in African history when he argued that, before the Portuguese opened the maritime trade on the Upper Guinea coast, there was no sizeable servile class, and no indigenous slave trade, which could serve as a launching pad for the Atlantic trade. A class society involving slaves and slave trade was, he concluded, a consequence of European demand for plantation labour. He broadened this argument in *How Europe Underdeveloped Africa* by contending that the demographic losses from exporting slaves, the social violence needed to enslave them, and the technological stasis in demographically stagnant societies, all made the 'European slave trade . . . a basic factor in African underdevelopment' (Rodney, 1966; idem, 1972, pp. 103–12). His principal critic, John Fage, pointed out that the small-scale societies of the Upper Guinea Coast may have been atypically egalitarian: the Portuguese were *importing* Kongolese slaves to larger, more hierarchical polities of West Africa before 1500, which indicates that slavery and slave-purchasing were already habitual. Fage argued that land was so abundant in West Africa as to make slavery (or conscripted dependency) the only effective means of accumulating power and mobilising labour for the economic and political needs of the state (Fage, 1969b, p. 400; idem 1989, p. 111). John Thornton's thesis is not dissimilar: even before the Atlantic trade brought external inducements to enslavement, slavery had a widespread and central economic position in tropical Africa because it was the only form of private, revenue-producing property recognised by African law, and functionally equivalent to the landlord–tenant relationship in Europe (Thornton, 1992, p. 74). Exporting slaves was, in Fage's words, an 'essentially incidental' by-product of labour coercion, the decision to supply or withhold slaves from European or mulatto traders being an economic choice made by rulers seeking to enhance the wealth and power of their states. Evidence from Kongo, the best-documented Bantu state, seems to bear this out: the Christianised King Afonso used his monopoly on prestigious European trade goods to strengthen his political position, draw neighbouring groups into a tributary status, and accelerate the slave exports that paid for European imports (Hilton, 1985, p. 60).

   The slave trade is the paradigm case of exploitative commerce, but to read into it the commercial relations of present-day 'North' and 'South' would be anachronistic. Africans controlled the supply and marketing of slaves in Africa, bringing to the enterprise formidable business and logistical skills. Few slaves were purchased by Europeans from their initial captor; the vast majority had passed through several native traders' hands before being 'bulked' for sale to Europeans on the coast by specialist brokers, many of Luso-African descent. In Senegambia and the Gold Coast, specialised long-distance traders proved particularly adept at maintaining prices by switching trade from one European competitor to another, and imposing a seasonal tariff during rainy weather to compensate for the greater costs of transporting and maintaining captives (Botte, 1991, p. 1424). Constant Atlantic demand led to a seller's market, with slave prices rising throughout most of the eighteenth century. In consequence, Africa's gross barter terms of trade improved about two and a half times over the eighteenth century in relation to Britain, which handled two-fifths of slave exports (Eltis and Jennings, 1988, Table 1, p. 943). Slaves were not exchanged for worthless baubles: the range of barter goods supplied was much the same as in other branches of early modern commerce, with textiles being the single most important item and accounting for well over half of African imports in the 1780s. The quantity of guns and gunpowder shipped to Africa is a matter of controversy, but their value was probably about 9 per cent of total imports at this time (ibid., Table 2, p. 948).

In assessing the long-term consequences of the slave trade for African populations and economies, the only reliable quantitative data are the slave exports and their distribution over time and space. Scholarly controversy has otherwise been unconstrained by 'real' numbers, and has polarised around 'minimalist' and 'maximalist' positions. The 'minimalists' argue that slave exports were less than the natural rate of population increase, could be compensated for by the tendency of polygynous societies to retain female captives, and that the trade was a small part of African economic activity. According to David Eltis:

> No reasonable estimate or manipulation of slave exports and population figures can point to this trade being of central importance to either [Africa or Europe]. This is true whether we focus on population loss or income generated. The numbers make it unlikely that long-distance trade brought any fundamental change of any kind in African societies except perhaps in select local areas (Eltis, 1987, p. 224).

For the 'maximalists', the potential population growth had slave exports remained in Africa is as important as the actual losses and, even allowing for low rates of reproduction, hypothetical projections can produce startlingly high numbers. Patrick Manning has quantified the counterfactual African population had slaves not been exported using a static demographic model, and then computer simulation to reveal changes over time. The exercise is as valid as its in-built assumptions, but these are quite conservative. Manning postulated that as an accompaniment to the estimated 9 million slaves landed in the New World between 1700 and 1850, some 21 million persons were captured in Africa, 7 million of whom were brought into domestic slavery, and 5 million of whom suffered death within a year of capture. He concluded that, as a result of absolute loss through emigration and slavery-related mortality (and relative loss because African death-rates remained high while they dropped in other regions), the tropical African population in 1850 was little more than half what it would have been in the absence of slavery and the slave trade (Manning 1991, p. 171). The African proportion of the combined population of the New World, Europe, the Middle East and Africa is reckoned to have fallen from about 30 per cent in 1600 to 10 per cent by 1900. His calculations are scarcely the last word on the subject, but they lend powerful support to the thesis that African demographic stagnation was a legacy of the slave-trade era.

This had certainly accompanied *relative* economic stagnation. Three centuries of Atlantic trade had neither encouraged structural change in handicrafts nor improved the transport system, which was the crucial bottleneck. One of its most destructive effects had been to retard commodity production (Iliffe, 1995, p. 145). The Atlantic trade's only compensatory spin-off was the introduction of American food crops – principally cassava and maize – which supported larger populations than the native plant species and profoundly affected settlement patterns over the *longue durée* (Austen, 1987, pp. 96–7). There were around 1850 no land market in Black Africa and no developed wage-labour market, while agriculture and peasant crafts were mostly uncommercialised, and subsistence production and extensive cultivation were everywhere predominant. Such simple, labour-saving technologies as the spinning wheel had not been adopted, partly – one may speculate – because the prevalence of slave labour removed the incentive to do so. Inland transport was primitive, and slaves were widely used as porters and canoemen. In Joseph Inikori's judgement, Black Africa was 'the most economically backward major region of the world' and demographic stagnation, together with the political conditions required for regular enslavement, can be seen as basic causes of its underdevelopment (Inikori, 1982, pp. 14–15). Generally, population pressure on resources in the early modern world stimulated more intensive agriculture, technological improvement, and a greater commercialisation of economic activities as a result of an extended division of labour. Conversely, low population densities allowed the continuation of extensive agriculture and herding, while negating the most essential element of any market: concentrations of buyers and sellers.

Where the 'hard' data are so exiguous, counterfactual arguments are themselves vulnerable to hypothetical speculation: could Africa's population have possibly grown more quickly given the 'Malthusian' crises which wracked the continent? We cannot know. But even were we to be persuaded that the slave trade's demographic impact was slight and its role in the totality of African economic transactions marginal, we would perforce acknowledge that it undercut the legal and moral foundations for autonomous commodity exchange within African societies and hampered production for the market by spreading a sense of insecurity. Probably two-thirds of slave exports were either taken in war or kidnapped by tribal enemies; relatively small proportions had been enslaved for debt or criminal offences (Iliffe, 1995, p. 133). The control of slave supplies was often a factor in the emergence of militaristic states, in which royal and aristocratic trade monopolies stunted private enterprise, and political leadership adapted to raiding neighbours for human wealth and defending the polity against outside attack. Pre-colonial kingdoms were deformed by their dependence on slave labour and the slave trade, and the fractures in post-colonial states still reflect the fault-lines between slavers and the enslaved.

'Legitimate Commerce' and the Traders' Frontier

Between 1802 and 1815, the most 'advanced' states in Europe and North America outlawed the slave trade for their nationals. Britain then attempted to suppress the trade completely by diplomatic persuasion, by naval patrols and by subsidising African rulers who agreed not to export slaves, but with scant success before 1850. Approximately 3.3 million slaves were shipped across the Atlantic between 1801 and 1867, and the decadal rates of shipment during the 1820s, 30s and 40s were amongst the highest in the history of the trade. Nor was this the sole transatlantic 'drain' of labour, since Africa was the largest source of contract migrants for the Caribbean sugar plantations up to 1845 (Engerman, 1984, p. 143). British cruisers had some success: in a 26-year period, 103 000 slaves were emancipated and resettled in Sierra Leone, where many were educated and Christianised. By adopting Western dress and mores and taking over petty commerce on the coast, they became important cultural brokers between Europe and Africa. But naval action mainly resulted in slave supply sources relocating to West-Central Africa (Angola and the Congo basin) and South-East Africa (Mozambique Island). In the latter region, slave exporters could profitably switch between the Atlantic market, the Mascarenes, and the Swahili coast. In Angola, there was a revival of the old slave supply link with the plantations of São Tomé and Principé. Portuguese slave-trading accounted for over two-fifths of exports from Western Africa and a third of imports in the 1820s and 30s, and 'legitimate' commodity trade for only about a fifth of total exports (Eltis, 1989, p. 205).

By 1860, 'legitimate' commerce was more valuable to both African and European trading partners than the slave trade had ever been. British imports from sub-Saharan Africa rose from £325 000 in 1815 to £5.9 million in 1860, and exports from £393 000 to £4.7 million; as proportions of total British imports and exports these were still very small (2.8 and 2.9 per cent respectively) but about five times greater than in the early nineteenth century (Austen, 1987, Table 4A, p. 277). Most of the growth of Africa's trade was due to the emergence of two export staples: the vegetable oil products of West Africa and wool from Cape Colony and Natal. Demand for both arose from urbanising societies where people in the mass were slowly becoming cleaner and better dressed. In Britain, per capita consumption of soap more than doubled between 1801 and 1861, and in the same period palm oil imports from West Africa rose from 1000 to 40 000 tons (Wilson, 1954, p. 9; Hopkins, 1973, p. 128). Up to the early 1860s, palm oil farmers and dealers benefited from a steady improvement in their terms of trade: prices of manufactured imports fell because of productivity gains in the industrialising world and cheaper transport costs. Paradoxically, though, as more Africans became involved in external trade, Africa was being marginalised in the international economy because total world trade increased at an unprecedented rate in response to industrialisation in Britain and continental Europe, while Africa's external trade grew more slowly (Austen, 1987, p. 102). As far as we are able to judge, the rate of increase in Africa's external trade between 1800 and 1870 was only 0.7 per cent per annum. From being equivalent to around 11 per cent of Britain's foreign trade in 1800, Africa's external trade had fallen to around 3 per cent by 1870 (Forbes Munro, 1976, p. 62; Hanson, 1980, p. 15). The high cost of inland transport, the relative paucity of African natural resources actually required by the industrialising economies (either as raw materials or groceries), the inefficient 'foraging' often used to supply commodities for which there was a demand – all meant that the response of tropical Africa to the expansion of world trade was comparatively sluggish. For merchants located in Britain, commerce with Africa was such a small part of foreign trade before 1880 that it scarcely impinged on the collective proceedings of chambers of commerce; if they expressed any concern with Africa, they usually opposed rather than supported interference in the internal affairs of its native states (Hynes, 1979, p. 18). Africa stirred the evangelical conscience, excited the geographer's curiosity, and was the occasional object of racist satire, but it was not a place where metropolitan interests had a serious economic stake.

Abolition had been secured in the belief that 'legitimate' commerce would have its own virtuous circle: as Africans developed a taste for European trade goods they would enter the wage labour market to acquire the means to purchase them, thus deepening the monetisation of the economy and extending the market for imported manufactures. Slavery *in* Africa would wither in competition with free labour. The actual course of events was very different. In West Africa's palm oil belt, independent petty producers and traders supplied a large part of the exports to satisfy European demand for soap and industrial lubricants, but substantial quantities were also produced by slaves. Their price had fallen with slackening external demand, making them an attractive capital investment, particularly for merchants and officials with a stake in 'legitimate' trade. Slave dealers were encouraged by favourable terms of trade to transform their slave inventories from commodities to producers of commodity exports, and so ease the transition to legitimate commerce (Hopkins, 1973, pp. 132–3). The pattern was repeated along Africa's trading frontiers: in Senegal from about 1840, European demand for groundnuts (which French firms were beginning to convert into oil on an industrial scale) encouraged landowners to settle thousands of slaves on the land to grow the crop. After the slave trade to Brazil was suppressed in 1850, a slave-worked plantation sector developed in Angola, with coffee grown in the north and cotton in the south. In the Zambezi Valley, the role of local slavery in growing copra and sesame intensified when itinerant Indian merchants linked the area to international markets (Vail and White, 1980, p. 67). In vast areas of the western Sudan, French surveys around 1900 recorded two-thirds of the population as slaves. Many were household chattel, but others were plantation slaves and bonded craft workers (Lovejoy, 1983, p. 136; Manning, 1988, p. 26).

This burgeoning of slavery within nineteenth-century Africa critically affected relations with Europeans. Indigenous African polities profiting from slavery were deemed unworthy of participating in the 'international society' of states and the continent became something of a geopolitical vacuum in European eyes. The call for the suppression of the internal slave trade and the emancipation of Africa's slaves gave the partition and conquest moral legitimacy, and from an early stage was linked to the idea of colonialism in Africa as a form of trusteeship (Louis, 1971, p. 219). African societies in which slaves and slave-owners were emerging as polarised social classes were subject to internal ruptures that attracted intervention, and provided the intervening powers with natural allies. In North Central and East Central Africa, weaker societies that had suffered at the hands of slave-raiding states welcomed European colonisers for the protection they provided (Martin, 1983, p. 21). Yet the new colonial authorities were often reluctant to enforce emancipation, because slavery was the basis of the native authority structures indispensable to indirect rule, and emancipated slaves could not be integrated into economies where wage labour scarcely existed.

At mid-century, Britain, France, the Netherlands, Portugal, Spain, and even Denmark possessed coastal enclaves dating from either the slave trade era or the struggle against it. Britain had acquired its first crown colony in tropical Africa by taking over the Sierra Leone mission for liberated slaves from private philanthropists. In 1843, France established official posts at Grand-Bassam, Assinie and Gabon, places where its missionaries and traders had been particularly active. Only the Portuguese were interested in territorial rule, and sought in the 1850s to extend their power in Angola by military expeditions to São Salvador in the north-east and the Cunene river in the south. Their forces were decimated by tropical disease; local populations fled before them; the attempt to tax those who remained provoked violence and further migration. A general retreat to the coast was ordered in the 1860s (Clarence-Smith, 1979). British interests were secured by informal paramountcy on the coasts, and reluctant interventions to cajole recalcitrant slave-trading rulers into the modern world. The deposition of the king of Lagos in 1851, and the annexation of the port ten years later, was the type of limited action that could be justified – even lauded – as inducting the natives into a civilisation of property-ownership and exchange where individuals had inalienable rights to personal liberty and the untrammelled disposal of their material goods (Hopkins, 1980). British authority was quickly extended along the coast west and east of Lagos, but Britain was unwilling to flex its military muscle at the large states beyond the ports and their immediate hinterlands. In 1863, Asante – which claimed suzerainty over Fante states on its southern frontier – was allowed to invade the Gold Coast with impunity. British prestige plummeted among supposedly 'protected' coastal peoples, but the metropolitan response was scarcely bellicose. A parliamentary select committee concluded that Britain's political obligations in West Africa were unwarranted by her commercial interests there, and recommended that all settlements except Sierra Leone be abandoned at some future date. Britain might have followed the example of the Dutch, who decided to quit their coastal enclaves for good in 1869. France, too, came close to relinquishing its small West African colonies, basically because in a free trading world they had little economic rationale. During the 1860s, in concordance with the commercial treaties negotiated with Britain, France annulled the *pacte coloniale* that had required her colonies to trade only with the metropolis and granted them partial fiscal autonomy. Some of her most successful merchants traded outside areas of French influence and relied on the authority of native rulers for protection. Those pressing for metropolitan control over areas in which they did trade – such as the Régis firm in the Bight of Benin – were largely ignored by the French political class.

That Britain did not withdraw from West Africa was principally because, after taking over Elmina from the Dutch, she became embroiled in further conflict with Asante (which still claimed sovereignty over the fort). As we know from Ivor Wilks, this formidable inland power was developing its own national cohesion and state capacity, and a war faction within its political élite hoped to restore Fante provinces to the 'empire' of greater Asante (Wilks, 1989, ch. 12). Britain was drawn into a contest for hegemony over the coastal regions that culminated in the war of 1873–4 and the sacking of Kumasi by Wolseley's expeditionary force. The war demonstrated the relaxation of some of the immemorial constraints on European territorial expansion in tropical Africa. The disparities between European and indigenous power and technology widened exponentially in the 1850s and 1860s with the adoption of the breech-loaded needle-gun by colonial forces and the invasion of African waterways by armed steamers. Quinine prophylaxis rendered the disease barrier to European advance much less formidable (Headrick, 1981, pp. 58–103). With Wolseley's display of brute power, the option of political withdrawal from the Gold Coast was effectively closed. The failure to stabilise state-to-state relations on the 'trader's frontier' created a precondition for the partition of West Africa. There *had* been an alternative route to stable relations with independent African power: educated and Europeanised Africans in the Fante Confederation had hoped to develop the country's mineral and other resources by road- and school-building. Whether the alliance of chiefdoms could have been transformed into a 'modern' state we cannot tell. But, with total ineptitude, Gold Coast officials mistook their ideal political partners as conspirators against British interests, and arrested as many as they could (Fage, 1969b, p. 144).

Despite being a tiny part of European commerce, trade with West Africa was innovative and, from the 1870s, increasingly competitive in international terms. By then, steamers were carrying nearly all West African commerce, and shipping and trading were becoming specialised businesses. Steam increased the volume of commerce, and required bigger and more permanent shore establishments at the larger ports, such as Dakar and Lagos. The traders' frontier came to involve more regular and complex transactions between European merchants and African middlemen, especially with the extension of credit (and therefore indebtedness) and the resort to local native authorities to enforce contracts and the repayment of bad debts. European merchants competing for produce imported vast quantities of cowries, thus inflating the supply of 'transitional' money, and a symptom and accelerator of economic penetration was its replacement by silver coins, especially sterling, francs and Maria Theresa dollars. Low-denomination silver coins mostly circulated where exports, and demand for European consumer goods, were expanding rapidly through the enterprise of small African producers and traders. Steam navigation allowed newcomers – notably German shippers and commercial houses – to compete with longer-established European firms. By 1880, Hamburg was importing about £350 000 worth of African goods annually. Against the international trend towards the separation of shipping and trading, the leading Hamburg merchant house of Adolf Woermann ran its own steamers to the west coast; it was to prove a major beneficiary of state support for export businesses as well as a powerful lobbyist for metropolitan intervention on behalf of German commerce in West Africa, especially when, in the early 1880s, France began to impose discriminatory tariffs in the coastal regions under its control (Wehler, 1976, p. 194; Moon, 1926, p. 102).

The first political, and at the time startling, result of German interest in Africa was the declaration of protectorates over Togo, Kamerun and South West Africa in 1884, which prompted similar moves by Britain on the Oil Rivers of the Niger Delta a year later. We should not overemphasise economic considerations in these decisions, which were interlinked with the diplomatic furore caused by Leopold II's proposal for a private state in the Congo. Bismarck was converted to a colonial policy largely because he thought it would be instrumental in securing the élite power structure of imperial Germany. Nevertheless, A.G. Hopkins has cogently argued that there were local economic preconditions for European territorial expansion in West Africa after 1880 arising from a protracted deflationary crisis in legitimate commerce. From the late 1870s, the deceleration in the growth of world trade resulted in deteriorating terms of trade for African producers, which generated chronic conflicts between buyers and sellers over the distribution of reduced profits (Hopkins, 1968). The commercial depression was especially severe during the mid-1880s, when the Liverpool price of palm oil fell by a third in a short period. European traders, faced with reduced profit margins, tried to pass their losses on to African middlemen, and both sides resorted to commercial malpractices. Europeans became convinced they could achieve economies of scale by bypassing the coastal intermediaries and purchasing directly from the producing regions of the interior. They began to press for a more active policy on the part of the metropolitan governments to persuade native rulers to abolish inland tolls, grant railway concessions and suppress slavery, their calls for action often backed by colonial administrators. European sovereignty came to be seen as desirable because it offered firm political boundaries that would prevent trade from falling into the hands of European rivals. Though not sufficient in themselves to compel the European states to authorise the partition of West Africa, the conflicts on the traders' frontier brought local peaceful coexistence between Europeans and Africans to an end.

These 'local' demands for political intervention to protect commercial interests were strongly supported from the late 1880s by organised businessmen in Britain, where the trade depression appeared to drag on interminably. Hitherto, chambers of commerce had been staunchly Cobdenite in their attachment to free trade and opposition to colonial expansion, but feared exclusion from potentially valuable markets by discriminatory tariffs as protectionism revived in Europe and French and German power intruded into Britain's 'sphere of influence'. Businessmen with African interests now regarded British formal rule as necessary to defend an 'open' trading economy in the tropics. Several important chambers of commerce pressed for intervention to forestall the inclusion of the Lagos and Gold Coast hinterlands in French or German territory (though as convinced free traders they opposed unavailingly the chartering of the Royal Niger Company to administer the Oil Rivers, rightly suspecting it would exploit its privileges to exclude commercial rivals). Significantly, where metropolitan commercial interests supported 'frontier' traders in demanding territorial acquisitions, then an unwilling British government acquiesced. In the Gambia and Sierra Leone, by contrast, the demands of expatriate merchants were not echoed at home, and could be ignored in the boundary negotiations with France. These colonies survived only as enclaves (Hynes, 1979, pp. 92–3).

The Partition of Africa and the 'New Imperialism'

About 57 per cent of Africa was still under independent rule in 1878. By 1900, European governments were claiming sovereignty over all but 6 of some 40 political units into which they had by then divided the continent, and of the 6 exceptions only 2 (Ethiopia and Liberia) were still independent states in 1914. It was the most flagrant demonstration of European power over the wider world since the conquest of New Spain. France began it all, whether we date the beginnings to the military expansion in the Senegal valley from 1878 or the occupation of Tunisia in 1881 (Wesseling, 1996, p. 65). By 1900, 3.6 million square miles and 37 million people had been added to France's African empire. Britain's acquisitions were less extensive but more populous. These powers had African interests that predated 'the scramble' and their actions were to some extent determined by existing imperial commitments. France entered Tunisia partly to protect its stake in Algeria; Britain was drawn into Egypt partly by perennial strategic concerns with the routes to India. Portugal's 'imperial vocation' appeared to be revitalised in late-nineteenth-century Angola and Mozambique, although continuities with historic forms of expansion were more rhetorical than real. From the 1870s, Portuguese colonialism was transformed by economic and political change in the metropolis, which gave the industrial bourgeoisie more power and influence within the state and led to the demand for the more effective economic exploitation of African territories. However, the indubitably novel feature of the partition of Africa was the part played by European powers with no colonial tradition whatsoever: Leopold II, Germany, and Italy which established colonies in Somaliland, Eritrea and Libya.

The partition of Africa was punctuated by the Berlin Africa Conference (1884–5). Contrary to myth, this did not deal formally with questions of sovereignty. By skilful diplomacy, Leopold secured international recognition of the Congo Independent State prior to the assembly, and European powers agreed bilaterally to partition contested areas outside the conference's proceedings. By making 'effective occupation' the prerequisite for international recognition, the conference may have accelerated the process by which paper claims became real annexations, but its deliberations were mainly concerned with trade, tariffs, slavery and the slave trade, and the protection of missionaries. The keynote of the plenary sessions – in which the USA took a prominent part – was international humanitarianism. The most important article of the General Act provided for a huge free trade zone extending to latitude 5 degrees north and the mouth of the Zambezi on the east coast. This meant freedom of trade and navigation on the Niger, Africa's most important commercial waterway and the focus of European trade in vegetable oils. By excluding discriminatory tariffs, the free trade provisions undercut the neo-mercantilist rationale for formal rule and restricted its revenue base; in effect, they were *anti-colonialist*. In the Congo itself, the provisions were largely nullified when the Leopoldian regime granted commercial monopolies to concessionary companies after 1890. Nevertheless, the Berlin Act proved the legal basis of an *international* capitalist economy in much of tropical Africa, one in which European commercial penetration was not constrained by political boundaries. To illustrate, by 1914, 44 per cent of exports from Britain's Nigerian Protectorate were palm kernel sales to German firms supplying the German margarine and soap industries; German gin was a major item in the import schedule, and alcohol sales taxes on it a significant source of government revenue (Burns, 1948,

p. 206). Germany's African colonies supplied less than 2 per cent of total imports of colonial produce, and total German trade with these colonies was only one-third of 1 per cent of Germany's foreign trade.

Explanations for this extraordinary irruption of European political power into Africa cluster around three positions: 'Eurocentric' theories have in common the claim that the critical impulsion to formal rule came from within the European states and states system. 'Excentric' theories (to use Ronald Robinson's term) locate the imperialist dynamic on the periphery where an expansive western capitalism met indigenous states. Lastly, there are explanations eschewing a general theory of imperialism and arguing that the crises on the frontiers of trade, mining and settlement which prompted the partition were largely unrelated and coincidental. This third position has a certain cogency: north of the Zambezi, the scramble was intimately connected with the mainstream of Great Power diplomacy and the participants' motives varied greatly. To the south, the scramble was driven mainly by the hostility between the Boers and English-speaking Cape capitalists, and their interaction with the federally minded politicians of London. Despite Bismarck's intervention in South West Africa in 1884-5, the fluctuating patterns of European diplomacy made little impact (Sanderson, 1975, p. 38). But this third position seems to beg the question: 'What determined that African territories should be subjected to European political power at all?'

To answer that, there is little point in disinterring the 'classic' theory of imperialism as the political expression of a new 'stage' of capitalist development in the metropolitan countries characterised by monopolies, the dominance of finance over industry, and capital exports. Even those for whom Lenin's concept is a useful analytic tool agree that, before the 1900s, the 'scramble' for Africa was 'pre-imperialist'. Monopolistic tendencies were imperceptible in France and Britain around 1880 and competition was still the norm in most sectors of the German economy, though cartels were a common feature of business organisation. In France, the most proactive colonial power, capital was widely dispersed among small and medium-sized family concerns and, even in 1914, there was little interpenetration of finance and industry. The largest industrial firms rarely depended on bankers or the stock exchange for their investment capital, but preferred to finance internal growth out of profits. The French bankers who floated the Ottoman, Egyptian and Russian state loans were not concerned to make them conditional on foreign government purchases from French industry, and capital exports bore little relation to industrial exports. In the 1900s, as international tensions increased within Europe and on its Ottoman and North African fringes, the French Foreign Ministry had to put lively pressure on the great investment banks before they agreed, often unwillingly, to tie their foreign loans to exports of armaments and capital goods. The vast colonial empire attracted less than a tenth of French capital exports before 1914 (Bouvier, 1976, pp. 305–33; Thobie, 1983).

Chronology alone indicates that any general 'Eurocentric' explanation of the 'New Imperialism' should start from advancing industrialisation, which created many centres of modern economic growth in the states system where there had been only one. Iron-hulled steamers, the telegraph and mechanised production equipped Europe's private economic actors with material and symbolic competences unmatchable in pre-industrial societies. But industrialisation also intertwined with competitive capitalism within Europe and with competition among sovereign states in international 'society'. Old and new national states learnt that 'Economic growth was now also economic struggle . . .' (Landes, 1969, pp. 240–1). Social class divisions were sharpened by the periodic slumps associated with the business cycle and optimism about a future of indefinite progress gave way to uncertainty. The liberal international political economy of the 1860s and 70s, underwritten by commercial treaties between European trading partners, was superseded from 1879 by protection of agriculture and industry. Hans-Ulrich Wehler's 'Eurocentric' theory of social imperialism attempts to relate these objective pressures of competitive industrialisation to a common ideological configuration among conservative élites. Pessimism that economic frontiers were closing, that industrial economies were chronically prone to over-production and unemployment, and that unless the state acted now burgeoning industries would be excluded from overseas markets in the future, lay behind the pre-emptive imperialism of the 1880s and 1890s (Wehler, 1979, pp. 112–34; idem, 1976).

What arouses the scepticism of the 'excentric' camp is the sheer irrelevance of poor and sparsely populated African colonies to capitalist expansion, and the fact that they were relinquished in the 1950s when their economic value was greatest. The great appeal of Robinson's theory lies in recognising the political agency of Africans themselves in the imposition of formal rule (Robinson, 1986, pp. 267–89). Clearly, many countries have been incorporated in the international division of labour without becoming political dependencies. The political outcome of capitalism's global expansion was determined by variable patterns of 'private' and 'public' interaction on the frontier between industrial and pre-industrial economies – patterns shaped by institutional differences in the underdeveloped world. Latin America had recognisably European governments advancing claims to untrammelled national sovereignty that European powers respected; Egypt and Tunisia were fragments of a moribund traditional empire where suzerain rights and extra-territorial jurisdiction did not conform to the claims of modern nation state. Normally, argues Robinson, indigenous rulers and élites collaborated with European enterprise because they gained considerably from foreign trade and finance, but their authority was often undermined in the process. They had to comply with demands from their new economic partners for concessions and monopolies, yet simultaneously command effective power over political communities increasingly disaffected by the European presence. This social contradiction was nakedly exposed when public indebtedness to European financiers required screwing taxation to punitive levels. Formal rule was imposed where collaborative arrangements were threatened or broke down. One strength of this theory is that it accommodates the imperialist process working in reverse: the relinquishing of formal control when the costs of maintaining collaborative relations rose to unacceptable levels – as they did with rising expenditure on colonial welfare and development in the 1940s and 1950s.

Europe, Egypt and Morocco

The occupation of Egypt by Britain in 1882 and of Morocco by France 1912 merit special attention. The former gave the partition an enormous impetus and has long been a test-bed for competing theories of imperialism; the latter was the 'final act' that occasioned a major diplomatic confrontation and helped solidify the opposing alliances of 1914–18. In both cases, European intervention was triggered by a crisis of indigenous government whose authority had been corroded by borrowing from Europeans and the intolerable taxation required to fund this debt. But differences between the two were as significant as the similarities: Egypt was a pashalic of the Ottoman empire which had been incorporated in the international division of labour as a producer of long-staple cotton, and thoroughly penetrated by foreign economic interests, in the quarter century *prior* to the occupation. Morocco was an independent sultanate that had kept itself a closed society.

Under Mohammed Ali (1805–48) the Egyptian governing élite had attempted to modernise 'from above' by diverting the economic surplus to the state. In a dramatic coup, the Mameluke aristocracy was massacred in 1811 and the tax-farming rights of Turkish–Circassian landlords abrogated. Every adult male was made liable for corvée on public works. A sizeable surplus was extracted by direct taxation in kind and by the monopoly purchase of all important crops at fixed prices for highly profitable sale on government account. This surplus was applied to military expansion and state-directed industrialisation behind high tariff walls. By importing machines and employing European technicians to construct them *in situ*, the state established a cotton-spinning industry that made Egypt the world's fifth largest producer of machine-spun yarn in terms of the number of spindles per inhabitant. Other large-scale production units were created for weaving and bleaching, metalworking and machine-building. By the 1830s, modern manufacturing industries probably employed 50 000 to 70 000 workers, or a fifth of the total labour force (Batou, 1991). Whether this was a feasible development policy or despotic folly is hard to judge. After a brief visit in 1836, Richard Cobden left a damning account of dilapidation and mismanagement in the state enterprises and lamented the waste of the best raw cotton, 'which ought to be sold with us' (Morley, 1879, pp. 66-7). Jean Batou has argued that the prerequisites for intensive economic growth were either present or could be easily imported: 'real' per capita product around 1800 was close to that of France because of an exceptionally productive agriculture and favourable demographic situation. Internal transport was relatively cheap and efficient, and maritime imports could compensate for deficiencies in coal and other natural resources.

If this analysis is right, then the military and diplomatic defeat suffered by Mohammed Ali in 1840 also 'blocked' a state-directed path to industrialisation that could have endowed Egypt with a modern economic structure by 1900. Egypt had become a substantial land power, and threatened to take over Ottoman Turkey's imperium in the Near East in the late 1830s. Fearing an Ottoman collapse, Britain intervened during the second Egyptian–Turkish war: Mohammed Ali was compelled to evacuate Syria, disband most of his army, and acknowledge the Sultan's sovereignty. Egypt had to abide by Ottoman law, which entailed recognising the Anglo-Turkish Convention of 1838 that had opened the empire to economic liberalism. Under this treaty, the Ottoman government had agreed to abolish state monopolies, adopt a low external tariff and remove many of the barriers to European merchant enterprise in the empire. Egypt's infant industries were not viable without tariff protection and closed during the 1840s and 50s when they could not compete with a flood of cheap consumer imports. Apart from cotton gins, it was to be almost a century before modern enterprises of comparable dimensions were established in the country. The 'autarkic' route to modernity chosen by Mohammmed Ali was barred, and his successors Said (1854–63) and Ismail (1863–79) had to modernise in the context of a *laissez-faire* 'open' economy in which the primary export sector was the fly-wheel of growth. Taxes were levied in money, and the fellah was permitted to grow what, where and as he pleased.

Cotton did not displace wheat as Egypt's main export until the early 1850s. Though improving barter terms of trade were encouraging cultivation, exports were worth less than a million sterling. Before the American Civil War, the crop was grown over only a ninth of the Nile Delta. The cotton famine of the 1860s induced an extraordinary boom: spurred on by prices that nearly quadrupled between 1861 and 1865, hundreds of thousands of cultivators in the Delta planted cotton for the first time. Export volumes rose about four-fold and their value peaked at £11.5 million in the later 1860s. There was a reorientation in export destinations: in 1840, Britain took only 17 per cent of Egyptian exports; by 1860, this proportion had risen to 59 per cent and by 1880 to two-thirds (Hanson, 1980, Table 4.6). Between the early 1870s and the British occupation in 1882, cotton exports as a proportion of total exports fluctuated around three-quarters; by the 1900s, they accounted for 93 per cent of export earnings. Export prices rose two and half times between the late 1870s and the late 1920s. There is no authoritative estimate of exports as a proportion of national income which may have been a quarter or less, because most cultivators were primarily engaged in subsistence. But exports had considerable 'multiplier effects', especially through promoting canal irrigation that extended the cultivated area and led to more double cropping. Gross income from agriculture rose approximately ten-fold in the seventy years after 1844, while population increased about three-fold to around 12 million. This rise in real income per head was most unequally distributed. Land was frequently seized for debt, and landless peasants probably formed a third of the rural workforce by the early 1870s. Rural society was becoming highly polarised: as population grew, Muslim inheritance law led to fragmentation of private real property. Bigger landowners could circumvent the law, but hundreds of thousands of fellah families came to own plots too tiny to support a household (Baer, 1966, p. 88). Nevertheless, mass living standards did improve, as evidenced by increasing per capita imports of coffee, tobacco and cotton textiles (none of which displaced domestic production). Although cotton was particularly labour-intensive, food production was not neglected and more or less kept pace with increasing population. In strictly monetary terms, the Egyptian case does not sustain the thesis that incorporation in the international division of labour as a primary producer led to mass immiseration. Per capita income in 1914 was certainly higher than in 1960 (Issawi, 1966a, p. 368). But with the spread of perennial agriculture, the health status of Egyptians deteriorated: bilharzia, a water-borne disease, was endemic in Lower Egypt by 1900 (Owen, 1969, p. 356). What the heavy commitment to exports did *not* do was accelerate structural change in the economy. In 1914, the government relied almost exclusively on revenue derived directly or indirectly from the agricultural sector, and not more than 15 per cent of the population lived in towns of any size (Owen, 1969, p. 355; idem, 1981).

Cotton exports enabled Ismail's government to embark on a hectic course of 'dependent development' financed initially by rising revenue from agriculture, and then by foreign and domestic borrowing. If railways are included, public spending on the agricultural sector totalled £30 million between 1863 and 1875, with the main item of expenditure being irrigation works. A dense railway and telegraph system was constructed, and harbour facilities improved. Alexandria was the Mediterranean's fourth most important port by 1870. Egyptian law was changed to establish private property in land and help attract European investment. In this phase of hectic growth, different foreign, predominantly European groups entrenched themselves in the export sector of the economy and began to penetrate the public administration. At a village level, Greek, Syrian and Jewish usurers advanced the working capital peasants needed to grow the crop and meet the state's onerous tax demands. Many of the skilled artisans in the major cities were Italians. In Alexandria, European merchant houses were the main bulk buyers of cotton, which they sold, via the telegraph, on the Liverpool and other cotton markets. Some established ginning factories or, exceptionally, took advantage of the 'Westernisation' of Egyptian land law to grow their own cotton. The Egyptian government's domestic and foreign borrowing attracted European brokers and commission agents. By 1877, there were eight European banks in Egypt providing telegraphic exchange on London and Paris. Some were branches of major European banks, others had been founded by foreign residents of Alexandria using, on occasions, quite considerable sums of local money. European engineers directed large-scale public works (pre-eminently the Suez Canal) and administered the system of modern communications.

On the eve of the occupation, foreign residents numbered about 91 000, the majority living in Alexandria. Most escaped local taxation and could ignore official regulations with impunity because the Ottoman capitulations exempted them from Egyptian jurisdiction. Foreigners were supposed to be policed by their own consuls, and many abused their extra-territorial privileges to smuggle contraband (Milner, 1892, pp. 39–42). In their private disputes with Egyptians, and in pursuing claims with the government for compensation for commercial losses, they could assert the diplomatic authority of their national states. In short, Egypt's ambiguous status as a less than sovereign state opened institutional 'gaps' to an informal, cosmopolitan imperialism. They allowed a diffused European political power to seep into the administration and economy. The frictions between foreigners, Egyptians and the Turkish–Circassian ruling élite created the conditions for the emergence of a modern, reactive nationalism affecting broad social strata.

Britain also imposed economic liberalisation on Morocco by the commercial treaty in 1856 (signed under threat of naval blockade), but with none of the revolutionary consequences evident in Egypt. Import duties were fixed, more ports opened to European ships, and the state's commercial monopolies abolished (except those on munitions). British subjects were exempted from taxation, apart from customs duties, and granted extra-territorial jurisdiction. This typical instrument of 'free trade imperialism' was the starting point of European economic penetration. Other European nationals obtained the same rights and legal privileges by the early 1860s, but British commerce remained 'first among equals' in Morocco's overseas trade up to the early 1900s. Unlike Egypt, however, Morocco did not have a mass of skilled cultivators ready to produce an industrial staple. The foreign trade sector was small, induced little investment and no government borrowing, and left tribal society largely undisturbed. Primary exports did not become important until the 1900s, when wool shipments to Germany expanded rapidly, and over thirty German firms established agencies to deal with the business.

The origins of great-power intervention in Egypt lay in the state's obligations to foreign bondholders. In common with Turkey, Tunisia and Greece, the Egyptian government borrowed heavily on European money markets, using a new type of finance house to tap the savings of European investors. In each case, state bankruptcy led to the international administration of government revenue and expenditure. Unlike Turkey, Egypt did not borrow for military purposes, and most of the eight foreign loans raised between 1862 and 1873 were used for public works. But the terms were usurious. Though Egypt incurred obligations totalling £68.5 million, receipts were only £46.6 million because loans were issued below par and financial agents received handsome commissions (Owen, 1981, Table 19, p. 127). Borrowing was secured against government revenues, and by the early 1870s, about 70 per cent of taxes were absorbed by debt service. Additionally, by early 1873 the Egyptian government had incurred £26 million in unfunded, floating debt (at a rate of up to 15 per cent) which had been taken up mainly by French banks. When debt repayments were suspended in early 1876, the Egyptian government's total obligations to foreign borrowers were £91 million.

The funded debt was held in roughly equal proportions in Britain and France, and the response of foreign stakeholders to state bankruptcy in

Egypt was to appeal to their national governments for political support. In Britain, there was little governmental solicitude for the bondholders: to act as sheriff's officer was, as the Foreign Secretary remarked in 1879, 'a new and embarrassing sensation' (quoted in Langer, 1950, p. 261). Private individuals had to run the risks, just as they reaped the profits, of overseas investment. True, the government had already shown that Egypt was of some strategic concern by purchasing the Khedive's shares in the Suez Canal Company, but the move had been mainly to pre-empt monopoly control of the company by a French syndicate. The canal was not a major artery of imperial communications until the 1890s. Though four-fifths of the rapidly increasing commercial traffic was British by 1880, commercial users' rights were secured by an international convention, which the company could not abrogate.

The actual outcome of Egypt's entanglement in European finance – unilateral occupation by Britain in September 1882 – was determined as much by the shifting parliamentary alliances of the French Republic as it was by British policy. France's stake in Egypt was historically and culturally deep-rooted. French was the second language of the modernising élites, who took their cultural models from Paris, not London. A French engineer had built the Suez Canal in the teeth of British opposition, and compatriots occupied key positions as officials and technicians. French financiers, in the main, had facilitated Egyptian foreign borrowing and, with their greater influence over their own government, French bondholders were a more formidable group of external creditors than their British counterparts. Until a late stage in the Egyptian crisis, the French government was more proactive than the British. But France was also a recently defeated power smarting under the loss of Alsace-Lorraine, whose most realistic objective was Franco-British condominium. This was achieved by August 1878 when a reluctant Khedive appointed British and French officials as Ministers of Finance and Public Works while about 1300 well-paid Europeans were recruited to the bureaucracy. The Franco-British entente in the Muslim Mediterranean was confirmed when Britain indicated that it would not oppose the assertion of French supremacy in Tunisia where the bankrupt Bey was also indebted to European financiers. When Khedive Ismail dismissed his 'European Cabinet', Britain and France again acted in unison to persuade the Turkish Sultan to depose his vassal in June 1879 and reassert their dual control of Egyptian state finances. By now, the two powers were concerting international European pressure on Egypt similar to that exerted over Turkey when the Ottoman government went bankrupt.

The internationally imposed solution to the debt crisis bore harshly on Egyptian taxpayers, public employees (put on half-pay or not paid at all), and the lower echelons of the officer corps, whose promotion was blocked by a Turkish–Circassian monopoly of the highest ranks. Disgruntled army officers placed themselves at the head of a national, anti-European and anti-Turkish movement enjoying broad popular support amongst the urban classes (Cole, 1993). A power struggle between the new Khedive Tewfik and the army officers hastened the emergence of populist nationalism around the slogan 'Egypt for the Egyptians'. In September 1881, when a mass demonstration led by Colonel Arabi compelled the Khedive to dismiss his ministers and convoke a Chamber of Delegates, it appeared that the collaborative arrangements for securing the interests of European creditors were breaking down. France took the initiative in issuing a joint note (January 1882) seemingly threatening Franco-British intervention should the Khedive be deposed, but its author, Léon Gambetta, soon fell from office, and it subsequently transpired that neither power seriously intended to make good the threat. Gladstone's cabinet floundered helplessly, with no consistent policy at all. The responsible ministers were loath to intervene with British forces to restore the Khedive's authority and hoped, should military action become necessary, that the Ottoman Sultan could be persuaded (at a price) to despatch an expeditionary force to relieve his vassal. This the French opposed because of their sensitivity to Muslim resistance to their rule in Algeria where the Sultan was Khalif, or religious leader, for most Muslims. Were there to be military intervention, it would have to be Franco-British (for which there were several precedents). What precluded this was the refusal of the French Chamber, by a massive majority, to vote credits for limited action to protect the Suez Canal.

It is a commonplace that more often than not historical outcomes are determined by the unintended consequences of actions. As Gladstone's biographer observed, the joint note of January 1882

> was the first link in a chain of proceedings that brought each of the two governments who were its authors, into the very position that they were most strenuously bent on averting; France eventually ousted herself from Egypt, and England was eventually landed in plenary and permanent occupation. So extraordinary a result only shows how impenetrable were the windings of the labyrinth (Morley, 1908, p. 236).

In less sonorous language, there was a cock-up. The note had the counterproductive effect of enflaming anti-Khedival (and anti-European) sentiment still further, which British representatives in Egypt systematically misrepresented as a slide into anarchy and terrorism. The nationalist ministry appointed in February acted, in fact, with ostentatious moderation. The authority of the foreign financial controllers and the obligations to the bondholders were duly acknowledged. But Edward Malet, the Consul-General, and Auckland Colvin, the Controller-General of Finance, believed the military–national movement had to be crushed to save the Khedival regime (Schölch, 1976). They urged a display of naval force to strengthen Tewfik - widely and rightly regarded as a European puppet – against his own government. It merely strengthened nationalist determination to resist external coercion and heightened popular xenophobia; on June 12 some 50 to 60 Europeans were killed in Alexandria in anti-foreign riots, possibly instigated by Tewfik to provide a pretext for European military intervention to restore his authority. Meanwhile the harbour was being fortified against naval attack. On July 3, the British naval commander was instructed to destroy the fortifications, by bombardment if necessary. Britain was left to pursue military intervention single-handedly, having late in the day seized on a spurious 'threat' to the canal as its prime justification.

British intervention was universally welcomed by European governments, for the punitive expedition was expected to do no more than restore the Khedive's authority and leave. But the declared intent to withdraw imminently was frustrated by the incapacity of Tewfik's despised regime: it could neither reorder its finances and satisfy the foreign creditors nor sustain its authority in the Sudan against the popular religious insurrection of the Mahdi. The British minister in Cairo acted as the chief executive of a 'veiled protectorate', and dual control of Egyptian finances was unilaterally abolished. The permanent occupation of Egypt had considerable consequences for European international relations: during inconclusive negotiations over Egyptian finances and the Canal's status, France's political exclusion from Egypt became manifest and deeply resented. Until the general settlement of colonial disputes in 1904, Egypt remained a running sore in Franco-British diplomacy. The rupture in their relations (and the strengthening of Germany's international position) meant the breakdown of the community of interest among the European powers in territorial forbearance in sub-Saharan Africa. With the support of Germany, France inaugurated a syndrome of 'compensatory' territorial claims in West Africa.

Egypt was an imperialist power in Africa in its own right and, in occupying the country, the British were implicated – against their will – in a vast region already destabilised by Egyptian expansion. In the 1860s, Ismail had renewed the drive towards the sources of the Nile begun by Mohammed Ali. British officers in the Khedive's service administered the Sudan in the late 1870s and suppressed much slave-trading, but in so doing had undermined support among tribal leaders for the Turkish–Circassian regime. Its authority crumbled before the Mahdi's great reform movement in 1881–3. After the Mahdist insurgents defeated an Egyptian army under General Hicks, Britain insisted on withdrawal from the Sudan against the wishes of the Khedive's government. The doctrine evolved, however, that no other European power would be allowed to dominate the valley of the Upper Nile. When this seemed a possibility, Britain effected the reconquest of the Sudan and the destruction of the Mahdist caliphate in 1896–8.

Britain's occupation of Egypt was an unpredictable event whose significance became clear only retrospectively. Much less unpredictable was the international supervision of Egyptian finances following the state bankruptcy, and this I take to be the critical sequence in the narrative I have summarised. 'Eurocentric' theories of imperialism give us the best explanatory purchase on the Egyptian crisis up to period of Dual Control, but the external forces subverting Egyptian autonomy were transnational. Analyses focusing on individual powers (whether Britain or France) are insufficiently 'European'. As we have seen, the Khedival regime was thoroughly infiltrated by, and indebted to, a cosmopolitan coterie of financiers, traders, technocrats and artisans long before the invasion. It was in hock to the Paris Bourse as much as the City of London. The initiative in imposing the first external financial control (the Caisse de la Dette Publique) came from Anglo-French representatives of the European bondholders acting in their 'private' capacity. Britain's military intervention was neither in intent nor in effect an act of pure national self-interest since all foreign creditors had their stake secured. The British government had an exceptional freedom of manoeuvre, but much of the economic power bearing on the Khedive belonged to nationals over whom it had no authority. This 'non-alignment' between European economic and military–political power in Egypt continued *after* the British occupation. Private economic interests in France were delighted when the value of Egyptian bonds soared in Paris and London immediately after the invasion. If they resented the permanent British presence, their economic decision-making certainly did not reflect this, for Egypt became a favoured field of French foreign investment. On the eve of the First World War, the Ottoman empire and Egypt attracted a larger proportion of total French foreign investment (11 per cent of capital exports) than it did British (2.3 per cent). The absolute value of French investments in Egyptian state loans was significantly greater: 53 per cent of the bonds were held by French people as compared with 39 per cent by British. French capital accounted for 52 per cent of foreign investment in Egyptian private enterprise (as against the 34 per cent share of British capital). French banks and finance houses had the dominant interest in the Egyptian banking sector and in the public utility companies of Alexandria and Cairo. Belgian capital was also active in Egypt, particularly in urban transport (Thobie, 1985, pp. 17–20). French cultural influence remained preponderant. British imperialism had proved the unwitting instrument of French finance capitalism.

There were major shifts in the European states system and the international economy of trade and investment during the decades separating the Egyptian and Moroccan crises. Unlike the Egyptian imbroglio, the Moroccan question did threaten the general peace of Europe, where diplomatic relations became significantly more tense after German foreign policy took a new course with the Naval Laws of 1898 and 1900. The ruling élite signalled its intention to make Germany a 'world power', and seized on the Moroccan issue in a clumsy attempt to divide potential enemies and to demonstrate that no international dispute could be settled in Germany's absence. Two major diplomatic crises (of 1905–6 and 1911) testified to this intensification of state rivalry.

Conflict between state actors interlaced with the dramatic growth and increasing politicisation of international investment. British investors accounted for much the biggest 'national' share of global foreign investment, but in Europe and Europe's Muslim flank the key players were French. Whereas the great majority of British issues were in the 'private sector', well over half French foreign investments in 1913 were loans to governments and so intrinsically more 'political'. Closer government supervision of the stock exchanges in France tended to politicise still further the trade in foreign securities: the Minister of Finance could forbid their sale, but government officials would also promote foreign issues when their purchase was regarded as in the national interest (Feis, 1930, ch. 5). Foreign loans became instruments of diplomacy – particularly after the floating of the first Russian loan on the Paris Bourse paved the way to the Dual Alliance in 1892 – but, equally, financiers investing abroad were seeking closer diplomatic support for their business interests. The scope of these interests was enlarged with the upsurge of European industrial growth in the mid 1890s.

Industrial concerns had hitherto benefited indirectly from foreign lending, as public works contractors or armaments suppliers, but left finance houses to mobilise capital and undertook little direct investment on their own account. If they needed mineral inputs or other primary products from the less developed world, they bought them from the specialist trading companies. By the 1900s, leading French industrial concerns were initiating foreign investments, both to win lucrative contracts tied to public loans and control their raw material sources through foreign subsidiaries. The most active in this respect was Creusot, the armaments and steel firm headed by the Schneider family.

Morocco's traditional power structure was a solid obstacle to alien intrusion, but the death in 1900 of the Grand Vizir, Ba Hamed, led to dynastic upheaval and opened the way to European economic penetration in 'depth'. A new Sultan with modernising pretensions, Abd-el-Aziz, needed funds to secure his position, and so turned to foreign lenders. Neither the London nor the Berlin money markets could accommodate him and the field was left open to two competing French consortia, one formed by Creusot and the other by the Banque de Paris et des Pays-Bas (Parisbas). The heavy industrial firms in the Creusot consortium were interested in exploiting Morocco's known or supposed mineral riches, and winning public works and railway contracts tied to international loans. In association with a mining syndicate, this consortium began negotiations for a 'personal' loan of 7.5 million francs to the Sultan as a prelude to the scramble for concessions. The French Foreign Ministry supported the consortium so enthusiastically that one of Schneider's well-placed agents declared, in 1901: 'The development of French material interests has become the dominant preoccupation of France's representatives in Morocco' (quoted in Thobie, 1983, p. 136; see also Julien, 1978, pp. 56–7). Doubtless, France had other, strategic interests arising from its position in Algeria where tribesmen were raiding its territory from Morocco. Moreover, the Algerian military and the colons constituted a 'sub-imperialist' nucleus with its own expansionist drive. But policy was determined mostly by the overlapping objectives pursued by the metropolitan state officials and leading representatives of the capitalist class. The French government at first preferred the Creusot group as the financial instrument of its North African diplomacy because it calculated that, as an industrial conglomerate reliant on state orders for armaments, Creusot would be easier to control than the Parisbas. Unfortunately, Schneider could not raise the finance needed for the loan and was obliged to turn to the Parisbas consortium, which had access to vast liquid resources and unrivalled expertise in floating foreign loans. After receiving assurances from the French Foreign Minister that the necessary steps would be taken should the Sultan forget his obligations to foreign creditors, the Parisbas consortium made the 'personal' loan, on stiff conditions but unsecured by a lien on state revenues, in December 1902. This was done in the expectation that to maintain his throne in a country drifting towards civil war the Sultan would resort to large-scale state borrowing, and egged on by French officials he duly did. In 1904, a consortium of twelve French banks (in which Creusot had a subsidiary interest) floated a Moroccan state loan with a nominal value of 62.5 million francs at an interest rate of 10 per cent. The banks may not have wanted a formal occupation, but their ancillary conditions could not have been observed without compromising Moroccan sovereignty and exacerbating xenophobic outbursts that 'demanded' armed intervention. The Paribas consortium obtained the preferential right on future loans on the same terms, as well as the privilege of buying and selling gold, and an agreement to set up a state bank. Sixty per cent of customs revenues were pledged to loan service, and the customs were to be supervised by French officials nominated by the bondholders. Meanwhile, French diplomacy had been 'squaring' rival powers with North African interests: a deal was struck with Italy in 1902 by which the latter was to have a free hand in Tripolitania in exchange for recognising French predominance in Morocco, and France agreed with Spain (whose North African coastal enclaves dated from the sixteenth century) an unequal delimitation of 'spheres'. More importantly, the Franco-British Entente Cordiale resolved the two countries' outstanding territorial disputes: Britain's position in Egypt was recognised in exchange for an acknowledgement of French paramountcy in Morocco.

The one power France neglected to 'square' was Germany, which objected vociferously to the Franco-British agreement, not on account of German merchants' sizeable commercial interest in Morocco, but because of deep suspicion of the entente's broader purpose. At German insistence, the Great Powers (including the USA) convened the Algeciras conference to settle the Moroccan question. The country's sovereignty was reaffirmed but belied by an 'international' supervision of the Moroccan state intended to secure an 'open door' for all foreign economic interests. In principle, the German banking and industrial concerns that had pressed their government to pursue a 'forward' policy in Morocco were guaranteed a stake in exploiting its economy, but this did not in practice undermine the preponderance of French finance and diplomacy. Paribas had the decisive say in the running of the new State Bank and played the major part in floating a second state loan in 1910. French companies took the majority interests in the mining and public corporations established to develop Moroccan resources. The administration created to supervise the Moroccan public debt was controlled by French officials. The telegraph service and the policing of the ports fell under French control. A French military mission was sent to modernise the Sultan's army.

It is true that German financial and industrial concerns acquired minority stakes in some of the new corporations: a consortium led by Krupps, for example, joined Creusot in an international mining syndicate in which half the capital was French and a fifth German. Such transnational cooperation by giant firms was not unusual in Europe: there was already considerable cross-border investment in the 'steel triangle' around the German–Belgian–French frontier. But can we conclude – as does David Fieldhouse – that international cooperation was 'the true imperialism of high finance'? (Fieldhouse, 1973, p. 308). This seems to overstate the case. Large companies usually invested in foreign firms in the same sector because they had common interests in lowering their costs and maintaining prices in international markets. Such minority shareholding was often more rational than attempting to achieve monopoly by destructive competition. This did not preclude the dominant partner in an international syndicate seeking special advantage from its nation state and pressing for further state action to secure its particular interest. In the Moroccan situation we have evidence for both. Despite the Algeciras agreement on equality of treatment for foreign firms, business projects requiring an accommodation of German interests were consistently blocked by the French Foreign Office (Thobie, 1983, p. 144). To profit from their Moroccan assets, European capitalists needed political security in the interior. Since French businessmen were pre-eminent among them, it was only 'natural' – in a world that had 'naturalised' the nation state – that they should have looked to France to provide it. They could no more jump out of their social identities than could officials in the Quai d'Orsay. In 1911, a new Sultan, Mulay Hafid, who had been enthroned in the turmoil created by alien penetration and high taxation, requested military aid against his domestic enemies. French forces violated the Algeciras agreement by marching on Fez. It was certain that a French protectorate would follow. Though not instigated by business interests, this was entirely welcome to the majority of them.

Germany's very hostile reaction brought on a prolonged diplomatic crisis that threatened the European peace and hardened the adversarial alignments of August 1914. From our point of view, the relevance of the crisis lies in its resolution: the German government did not expect to gain Moroccan territory, but was determined on maximum compensation for acquiescing in a French protectorate. Initially, it demanded the entire French Congo, but settled for a chunk of the 'lower' Congo adjoining its Kamerun colony. Meanwhile, Italy judged the moment propitious to fulfil its designs on Tripolitania and declared war on Turkey, the suzerain power. The absolute disposability of African territory to suit the European balance was amply confirmed. Clearly, a multitude of factors – strategic, ideological, and extra-European – had contributed to the final act of the partition of Africa. But the leading role played by French financial and industrial groups in close alliance with state officials is undeniable. The take-over of Morocco was, perhaps, the sole example of colonialist aggression which 'conformed' to the Leninist model of imperialism (ibid., p. 149).

The 'Mineral Revolution' and White Power in Southern Africa

For the historian of 'Europe' and the 'Third World', the emergence of modern South Africa as a state and regional economy presents a major analytic problem. Expressed simply, it is a problem of deciding if, when and how economic and political interests in South Africa 'escaped' from European control. In more complex terms, it means assessing degrees of autonomy and dependence amongst interacting groups in British colonies, the Boer republics, and in London. Economically, South Africa has been the site where European capital, technology and labour, and Africa's human and material resources have intermeshed most closely. This began in the mid-1840s with merino wool exports from the Cape Colony and the expansion of a market-oriented, settler society to compete with the Boers' extensive subsistence pastoralism. By 1870, three-quarters of exports through the Cape ports were wool, and they were providing 12 per cent of Britain's raw wool imports. The external trade of West Africa was then slightly larger than the Cape's, though given the disparity of populations structurally much less important (Frankel, 1938, p. 47; Munro, 1976, p. 62). Thereafter, the Cape's exports accelerated under the impact of the Kimberley diamond strikes in Griqualand West – territory claimed by the independent Boer republics, but annexed by Britain for the Cape when its mineral wealth was appreciated. Total export values for the Cape and Natal rose from £2.95 million in 1870 to £8.6 million in 1880, and with its much increased revenues the Cape government was able to raise foreign investment for railway development (Frankel, 1938, Table 5, p. 55). The gold discoveries of 1886 on the Witwatersrand, in the Transvaal, had even greater import for the region. They proved to be the world's most extensive source of auriferous ore and inaugurated the 'mineral revolution' that has determined modern South Africa's distinctive economic history and unique political economy. European capital and labour flowed in on an unprecedented scale: South Africa was the destination of nearly 10 per cent of British emigrants during the 1890s and 1900s. Immigration transformed the white social structure – the population of Johannesburg quadrupled between 1889 and 1899 – just as state revenues from the mining industry transformed the political prospects of the hitherto impoverished Transvaal. Between 1870 and 1936, the territories forming the Union of South Africa attracted 56 per cent of the foreign capital invested in British Africa (and 43 per cent of the total foreign investment in the continent) (Frankel, Table 28). On a per capita basis, foreign investment in the Union was four and half times that in the Belgian Congo, the most favoured site for foreign capital outside British Africa. Before 1914, the Union accounted for about two-thirds of Africa's exports, though it contained less than a tenth of its population, and its principal export was not 'substitutable' in a world where all major currencies were tied to the gold standard. Of the total railway mileage laid in sub-Saharan Africa by 1913, 55 per cent was located in South Africa and Rhodesia.

But while the strongest links between Africa and the European-dominated world economy of trade and investment were forged in the Union, it also developed the most robust 'national' capitalism on which was based an independent white state that resolved its ethnic, class and sectional conflicts at the expense of black and 'coloured' South Africans. The nucleus of a relatively autonomous capitalism was constituted by the diamond mining industry. Until the amalgamation of the major enterprises in the late 1880s, the industry was largely financed out of its profits and by local subscription; negligible amounts were invested by individuals and companies outside South Africa. Though the amalgamation did require foreign financial investment (mostly from the London Rothschilds), subsequently the industry was again self-financing through reinvested profits. By 1936, foreign investment in South African diamonds totalled only about £20 million, though some £340 million worth of diamonds had been produced and the companies concerned had declared dividends of more than £80 million (Katzenellenbogen, 1973, pp. 362–3).

From the amalgamation came De Beers Consolidated – the premier monopoly of its kind in the world, which controlled 90 per cent of all diamond production. Its articles of incorporation authorised the Cape-based life governors to apply the company's assets to virtually any purpose they chose. The founder, Cecil Rhodes, likened De Beers to the East India Company – aptly enough, since it proved the corporate instrument for fusing economic interest with coercive strength in a way reminiscent of the seventeenth-century chartered companies. Rhodes had already embarked on a political career in the Cape Colony, but with De Beers's assets behind him he directed the thrust of Anglophone power into central Africa. The corporation's profits subsidised first the quest for prospecting concessions in Mashonaland and Matabeleland (in modern Zimbabwe) and then the Chartered British South Africa Company (created in 1889) for which a mining monopoly had been extracted from King Lobengula by sheer duplicity. Belligerent territorial expansion would have been impossible without the financial help of the mining corporation, and foreign loans for railway-building were raised by pledging De Beers shares. During Rhodes's premiership of the Cape Colony (1890–95) the colonial Cape government constituted an embryonic South African state with its own expansionist and segregationist policies. His agents used British authority to exclude rivals from north of the Limpopo and enforce a 'native policy' subservient to the settler economy. When the Ndebele rebelled, the BSAC's forces subdued the kingdom. The official attitude in Britain was hesitancy laced with acute parsimony. The British political class was loath to spend metropolitan taxes on the occupation of the tropics. During the 1880s, the Cabinet had formulated the 'cardinal principle' that the companies enjoying the profits of private enterprise in Africa and elsewhere should bear the costs and responsibilities of government. Rhodes's scope for independent action was such that 'the men of Whitehall' were little more than his 'helpless auxiliaries' (Robinson and Gallagher, 1976, p. 121; see also Rotberg, 1988, ch. 12).

We can see further evidence for a nucleus of autonomous colonial capitalism in the role played by the Kimberley magnates in opening the Rand goldfield. They provided the initial capital and made available the skilled European labour. (British investment was not forthcoming at first, because earlier gold mining ventures in South Africa had proved unprofitable.) The magnates' initiative transformed a region hitherto comparatively marginal to the world economy into the major exporter of that economy's money commodity: by 1897 the Rand was producing about a quarter of the world's gold supply. The reefs were so extensive (though of variable quality) that gold-mining more resembled a conventional industry, with calculable economic results, than a gamble. With cyanide processing, the yield of gold from the ore was greatly increased and mining became profitable at depths of up to 4000 feet. South African gold-mining was probably the largest single capitalist development outside Europe and North America during the last two decades of the nineteenth century, absorbing a total of £44.5 million in equity capital between 1887 and 1902, and employing over 100 000 African miners by the latter date. By 1914, Witwatersrand possessed the world's biggest power station and was at the forefront of industrial electrification (Richardson and van Helten, 1984). The industry quickly became highly concentrated. A single group of companies, Wernher-Beit and Eckstein, produced about half the output on the eve of the Boer War, and about a quarter was produced by Rhodes's Consolidated Gold Fields and the Anglo-French Company.

Given the capital-intensive nature of the industry, and the insufficiency of South African financial resources, the mining finance houses had been compelled from an early stage to call upon various European sources of investment finance, often turning the connections of the immigrant entrepreneurs to advantage: Alfred Beit's background in the diamond trades of Hamburg and Amsterdam enabled Wernher-Beit to tap Jewish sources of capital in continental Europe; rival firms were supported by German banks. Reliance on inward investment does not seem to have compromised the 'South African' character of the industry, however. Most of the mining companies were locally incorporated and entrepreneurial initiative and control remained on the colonial 'periphery'. European investors were as much exploited as exploiting. All the mining finance houses raised capital by share-dealing in speculative ventures designed to fleece the gullible.

By 1899, £60 million had been invested in the Rand, and the fact that the vast capital assets of the mining corporations lay in a state outside direct British control brought a dynamic instability to southern Africa. After an interlude of colonial rule, the South African Republic had reasserted its independence by defeating British forces at Majuba in 1881. It was dominated by Calvinist farmers with a 'frontier', anti-capitalist ethos, a historic grudge against the British, and a burgeoning sense of national destiny. They excluded white immigrants from the franchise, maintained a dynamite monopoly that raised the operating costs of the mining companies, restricted the importation of African labour from other parts of the regional economy, and even encouraged labour militancy among the white miners. One of Rhodes's engineers reckoned that 'good government' would mean a saving of 6 shillings (30p) per ton on gold ore production costs, equivalent to an extra 12 million dollars a year in dividends (J.H. Hammond, quoted in Moon, 1926, p. 172). The occupation of Zambesia was partly intended to create a counterpoise that would contain Boer power south of the Limpopo. But Rhodes and associates with investments in deep mining, where labour, machinery and blasting materials imposed very high costs of production, considered the Boer government so inimical to their interests that they conspired (in collusion with the Colonial Secretary) in 1895 to overthrow it with the Jameson Raid and an Uitlander uprising. It is true that the so-called outcrop concerns found the Boer regime less irksome: these were immediately profitable; their owners were well placed to manipulate the share market, and were not compelled to think in the long term. But the fact that they stood aside from the conspiracy should not disguise the compelling economic motives behind it (Blainey, 1965; Mendelsohn, 1980).

There is an unresolved debate as to how far the major mining capitalists' desire for an accommodative state, one that would institute a political economy assuring a regular supply of cheap labour, became the objective of the British government's representatives in South Africa after 1895. Since Gallagher's and Robinson's monograph, many historians have found it impossible to sustain the view that the British annexed the Transvaal to please the gold-mining industry or international finance capital. The predominant interpretation is that the mainsprings of official British policy were imperial and strategic: an independent and wealthy Transvaal Republic would, it was thought, suborn the loyalties of Britain's Cape Dutch subjects, while Germany's support for the Republic threatened British preponderance in Southern Central Africa. The Transvaal had broken the Cape Colony's stranglehold on its commerce by opening a new railway connection to Delagoa Bay in Portuguese territory. It threatened to replace the Cape as the dominant political, economic and commercial entity in the subcontinent. The Transvaal had to be reconquered to save South Africa 'for the empire' (Gallagher and Robinson, 1981, pp. 434–55; Fieldhouse, 1973, p. 357). Shula Marks and Stanley Trapido have argued that beneath the imperial rhetoric lay an economic and strategic imperative to secure Britain's gold reserves (their precariousness having been starkly revealed by the Baring Crisis). This led to a conjunction of interest with the major mining companies who found the Kruger regime objectionable as much for its incapacity to 'organise' capitalism on the Rand as for its monopolies and taxes. These companies required a strong, regulatory state to facilitate the migration of labour to the mines and prevent competing firms 'bidding up' wages. By background and ideological conviction, Milner, High Commissioner in South Africa from early 1897, appeared to promise a political regime favourable to the collective interests of the mining magnates. Unquestionably, Milner provoked Kruger into declaring war by demanding political changes in the Transvaal incompatible with its independence. Whether the war and subsequent reconstruction were *intended* to inaugurate an interventionist, racist state capable of fulfilling the demands of the mining capitalists must remain an open question (Marks and Trapido, 1979, p. 52). But this was its most important consequence. A crucial service to the mining industry, in view of its labour difficulties in the aftermath of the war, was the official recruitment of 60 000 indentured Chinese workers for mine labour under conditions close to penal servitude.

A further result of the war was a strengthening of the 'imperial' character of capital on the Rand with the emergence of the City of London as its sole source of foreign investment. After the reincorporation of the Boer republics within the empire, those finance houses that had looked to continental European sources for investment funds turned to the City to finance post-war reconstruction (Frankel, 1938, pp. 72-7). Once the demands for new working capital had been satisfied, however, the industry showed a clear tendency to finance investment internally and reduce its dependence upon fluctuating inward investment.

To claim that South Africa had 'escaped' economically from Europe by 1914 would be simplistic: it was still a basically colonial economy exporting precious minerals and agricultural raw materials, and importing manufactures and machinery. Mining absorbed so much of the capital, skilled labour, and entrepreneurial ability that manufacturing only 'took off' when shipping shortages during the First World War gave an impulse to import substitution. Yet, constitutionally, South Africa had been unified and decolonised with remarkable speed. The Union of 1910 was, in effect, an independent white state in which English-speakers and Afrikaners were cooperating under the leadership of the former Boer generals, Botha and Smuts. South African politicians had controlled the process of unification and determined all policies relating to the Union's internal power structure (the franchise, land apportionment, labour immigration and control). Relations with neighbours were conducted from within South Africa, and the British Government's interventions were restricted to the High Commission territories. A common market – which included these territories and Rhodesia – had been established in which South African politicians maintained an 'open' economy only as long as it was in the white interest to do so. Though Britain retained the prerogative of directing an imperial foreign policy (until formally relinquished in 1931) this did not infringe South African political autonomy in any tangible way.

Colonial Regimes in Tropical Africa before 1914

The partitioning powers were steeped in *laissez-faire* traditions of government and had narrow tax bases. All were inclined to delegate the responsibilities of colonial administration to private agencies, allowing them in return economic privileges that would cover the costs of rule. Britain and Germany chartered trading companies for the Niger, East and Central Africa which took on the duties of providing roads, police and armed forces, and raising investment capital for railways and other infrastructural development. The German East Africa Company soon lost its administrative functions when, after the coastal rebellion of 1888–9, full colonial rule was implemented. None of the British companies had an officially sanctioned monopoly of trade (although the Niger Company allegedly used its administrative powers to create an effective monopsony in Northern Nigeria) and their economic privileges mostly pertained to mining rights and the levying of taxes and excise duties. Both the East Africa and Niger Companies had their charters withdrawn by 1900; the former went bankrupt and the latter was unfit for the tasks of pacification, though commercially viable.

In the Congo Independent State, French Equatorial Africa and Mozambique, the colonial powers resorted to another device – the concessionary company – which exercised some administrative functions in a specified region in return for economic privileges, though overall responsibility for the colony theoretically remained with civil servants. The CIS had the most complex administrative structure, whose 'shape' was dictated by Leopold's limited resources and the compelling need to attract large-scale finance and industrial capital. There would have been little investment without an infrastructure, so the regime implemented rigorous measures to extract the exiguous economic surplus. The central Zaïre basin was declared a state domain in 1891–2, closed to all private enterprise and its wild rubber and ivory made state monopolies. At the height of the monopoly policy, between 1897 and 1905, the CIS established close links with Belgium's largest private company, the Société Générale. From their association came the two leading mining enterprises (Union Minière and Forminière) and various railway companies that were to build the network required for the export of minerals (Peemans, 1973, p. 178). Outside the state domain, several types of concessionary zones were created by leasing land to private companies (in many of which the CIS was a major shareholder). Some, such as the Katanga Company, the Great Lakes Railway Company and the Kasai Company, played a long-term role in providing an infrastructure and developing mineral resources. But a second type of concession was granted in rubber-bearing areas to companies, such as Anglo-Belgian Indian Rubber, empowered to introduce compulsory gathering of wild rubber. Rubber exports from the CIS rose more than fifteen times in value between 1895 and 1905, and were about 5400 tons per year in the early twentieth century when (together with ivory) they accounted for 96 per cent of total exports (Frankel, 1938, p. 299; Munro, 1976, p. 104). This was achieved at a terrible cost: the concessionary companies' forces terrorised the forest populations who, through disease, flight, starvation and physical cruelty were probably reduced by half. The concessionaires were simply pillaging African resources; their main interest was stock market speculation. They invested negligible amounts in Africa, and ploughed back none of the exceptional profits gained from the doubling of European rubber prices between 1895 and 1906.

France turned to a similar concessionary regime in Equatorial Africa in 1898–9, with similar lamentable results: 40 companies were given concessions for 30 years covering some 70 per cent of the Congo, but only those that systematically despoiled the native economy and cultures were commercially successful (Coquery-Vidrovitch, 1986, pp. 341–2). At the heart of the 'pillage economy' was the demographic crisis wracking tropical Africa. For lack of capital, development was confined to labour-intensive forestry and road and railway construction which placed enormous strains on populations depleted by epidemics of venereal disease, sleeping sickness and influenza. Food supply had always been precariously balanced and it was fatally disrupted by compulsory labour. Undernourishment and famine were endemic in Ubangi-Chari (now the Central African Republic), which in 1927–32 was convulsed by the largest and longest-lasting revolt in French Black Africa. As has been remarked, it is no coincidence that 'this miserably ill-used region . . . remains one of the most deprived and politically fragile areas of the continent' (Coquery-Vidrovitch, 1988a, pp. 38–9).

In Mozambique, after the chartering of the major companies between 1888 and 1892, and the leasing of other zones to private concerns, the only district not ruled directly by agents of private capital was Mozambique Island. South-East Africa had been plagued with sand-jigger, locusts, rinderpest and smallpox during the 1890s, and famine struck the cattle-herding tribes in 1900–2, so here too underpopulation was a constraint on economic exploitation (Vail, 1983, p. 205). Each company had exclusive access to labour in its concession and used the obligatory labour clauses of the colonial code to exploit the local population ruthlessly. Illegal migration to other territories to evade company rule was severely penalised. As in other colonies, hut taxes were imposed to compel Africans to work for long periods. Capital directly invested in African colonies was usually 'national', but Mozambique was a major exception: wealthy Portuguese were too few to invest in the companies, and the bankrupt state could not borrow heavily on European money markets. British and French nationals held most of the equity in the Mozambique Company, which was effectively 'denationalised' by 1910, with administrative decisions being made by foreign committees in London and Paris. This delegation of colonial rule to international finance capitalism was contrary to Portugal's interests and disastrous for Mozambicans'. Stock speculation took pre-eminence over local investment, and the local administration was starved of funds (Vail, 1976, p. 394). Peasant production was deliberately curtailed in favour of sugar and cotton plantations (which made the colony a major supplier of the metropolitan textile industry). When the concessions were finally abolished by the Salazar regime's colonial reforms, all they left behind was a continuous tradition of violent exploitation.

The most lasting legacy of the era of company rule was the coupling of southern Mozambique to the South African mining economy. The shortest coastal railway connections from the Transvaal and Southern Rhodesia ended at Lourenço Marques and Beira. These transport linkages and the provision of migrant labour for the Witwatersrand mines created a unique degree of regional interdependence, having a greater import for economic development than the innovations made under colonial rule. By 1899, half the men required for deep mining operations were drawn from southern Mozambique through a complex network of labour migrancy. To ensure some economic return, in 1901 the Portuguese accorded the Witwatersrand Native Labour Association monopoly recruiting rights in those parts of Mozambique outside chartered company control and, as a *quid pro quo*, the Portuguese received a capitation payment for every labourer (Vail, 1983, pp. 209–212). Subsequently, Lourenço Marques was guaranteed a minimum proportion of the Transvaal's external trade. The short-term gains were considerable: customs duties on transit goods were the colony's major source of revenue, allowing it to contribute a surplus to the total colonial budget (Hammond, 1973, p. 264; Newitt, 1981, pp. 112–13). In the longer term, exporting the most productive male workers locked southern Mozambique into a dependency on the dominant regional economy.

The concessionary regimes of Central and South-East Africa were stark failures – politically, administratively and economically. The companies brought little technology, built few roads, and did not keep the peace: except that they repatriated their profits, they resembled pre-colonial predatory states in Africa. They exacted export goods from subject populations more as tribute than exchange commodities, and even when 'purchasing' produce often used barter and tax tokens rather than money. Where cash crops were introduced – as with cotton in the savanna region of French Equatorial Africa – this was through coercion rather than market incentives. Concessionary regimes brought paltry returns to the colonisers; although the value of the domestic exports of French Equatorial Africa roughly doubled between 1907 and 1928, and in Mozambique's case tripled, neither contributed more than 2 per cent to the total domestic exports of sub-Saharan Africa (Frankel, 1938, Tables 43 and 47, pp. 193 and 198).

These regimes stand in contrast to the more liberal and generally more successful economies of West Africa, where economic roles and relationships born of 'legitimate commerce' matured in the colonial period. Africans remained in control of agricultural production and European commercial firms mediated between them and international markets. Acting without external guidance, and often before roads, railways and ports were built, migrant Africans showed themselves to be innovative frontier capitalists in the virgin lands they opened up to cash cropping (Hopkins, 1973, p. 188). Their traditional values and communal loyalties did not impede individualist, market-oriented behaviour. New crops were adopted, and more use made of iron hoes, but agricultural technique was unchanged and work still organised around the social inheritance of household and kinship. Land remained abundant and cheap, and rarely became concentrated in the hands of native landlords. Despite considerable numbers of emancipated slaves up to the 1920s, the only wage labourers were seasonal migrants with families on small holdings or men accumulating the modest capital needed to become independent farmers.

Expatriate plantations were established in German Kamerun and the French Ivory Coast, but generally the 'planters' frontier' made little headway in colonial West Africa. (The major exception was the Firestone rubber plantations established during the later 1920s in Liberia, a recognised protégé of the United States.) The absence of plantations is often attributed to the protective policies of 'dual mandate' and 'trusteeship' followed by the colonial powers towards their West African subjects – policies whose cardinal tenet was the inalienability of native land. This was certainly why William Lever's proposals for palm plantations in British West Africa were received with 'frigid suspicion' on the part of the Colonial Office, and he turned to the Belgian Congo where in 1911 the authorities conceded a large territory developed as the Huileries du Congo Belge (Wilson, 1954, pp. 165–8). However, a more complex set of factors than colonial policy alone kept out concession companies and plantations: fear of political instability was one consideration, and the hostility of the powerful European commercial firms to concessionary concerns another. Furthermore, without slavery (or the disguised slavery of contract labour that persisted in the Portuguese empire) there were few economies of scale in the plantation culture of most African tropical exports. Small-scale producers, once their inhibitions against investing in new crops had been overcome, were simply more efficient.

After the colonial conquests, the native merchants who had brokered the slave trade and legitimate commerce were 'squeezed out' of international trade, either by the European joint-stock companies with their superior capital resources and easy access to colonial administrations or by Lebanese and *petits blancs* trading on an individual basis. Yet Africans continued to trade domestically on a large scale and over considerable distances, so why they retained no foothold in import–export trades is not altogether clear. Evolué families often preferred to invest in education so that their sons could enter clerical service with the European firms or the colonial administration. Perhaps, too, African cultural traditions, which measured a man's prestige by the number of his kin or dependants had some significance because native capital tended to disperse through investment in people (Iliffe, 1983, p. 20). Whatever the precise causes, the withdrawal of African entrepreneurs from the foreign trade sector meant the mercantile middle class was weaker than it might have been throughout the colonial period.

On the European side of commerce, the chief organisational change was the emergence of an oligopsony of commercial firms with a tight grip on the export sector. From the later 1880s, the private trading partnerships that had opened up West African trade mostly converted to limited liability companies, and from the turn of the century were concentrated into giant firms whose agents followed the colonial forces into the interior to establish trading depots. Numerous petty traders brought in produce, but the larger middlemen on whom the companies who had once relied were bypassed or denied credit. The biggest concerns in French West Africa – the Compagnie Française d'Afrique Occidentale (CFAO) and the Société Commerciale de l'Ouest-Africain (SCOA) – won commanding positions before the First World War, when their favourable margins on trade with African producers resulted in exceptionally high profits, and they paid dividends which began to attract French investors otherwise little interested in colonial enterprises (Coquery-Vidrovitch, 1975). The CFAO was older and more highly capitalised, and closely linked to Marseilles shipping interests. In its original centre of operations in Senegal, trading stations had been opened along the railway from Thiès to Kayes and it later branched out along the railways into other territories. The SCOA was smaller, but tied in with industrial concerns and financial interests in Lyons and Geneva, and so rather more dynamic. During the First World War, a reduced volume of trade was compensated for by a four-fold rise in value, and the companies profited by being monopoly purchasers of strategic products. Joint ownership of filial businesses led to increasing interdependence. In British West Africa, the Niger Company had a roughly comparable position before 1914, though its profit levels were lower and competition (notably from the African and Eastern Trade Corporation) was more intense.

Making Good the Claims: The Development of Colonial Africa until 1914 and its Incorporation into the World Economy

By 1900, the disappointing returns of delegated rule, humanitarian outrage at the abuses heaped on Africans, and the paucity of private investment were forcing European statesmen to reappraise their African policies. Imperial landlords sensed that their unimproved tropical estates would not turn into complementary economies without public assistance, and so called for 'constructive imperialism' or – as one French publicist put it – 'a real and lasting economic conquest!' (quoted in Marseille, 1975, p. 387). Inland freight costs prohibited development more than any other factor, but even in the southern mining economy railways did not attract private speculators; only governments concentrated sufficient power and authority to impose them on Africans. Apart from lines in Rhodesia and Nyasaland, all railways in British Africa were constructed by or on behalf of the government concerned, and were publicly owned and operated (Frankel, 1938, pp. 376–7). Despite the huge size of France's colonies, and long-standing schemes for railway development, the mileage in French sub-Saharan Africa was smaller than in either the German or British colonies (excluding Rhodesia and South Africa). The scarce resources and scanty populations of French Africa largely explain this anomaly, though the metropolitan financial restraints were also tighter than in Germany and Britain. Under the colonial budget law of 1900, France's colonies were required to be self-supporting except for military defence and such public works as were of 'imperial' interest. The colonies paid dearly for the French state's frugality. After an unsuccessful phase of construction by concession companies, all French African railways became government-owned and were financed by public loans floated on the metropolitan money market. Capital and interest were repaid from the revenues of the Federations of West and Equatorial Africa. In effect, Africans paid most of the costs of railway construction through their taxes and unpaid or underpaid labour (Thompson and Adloff, 1973, p. 129; Manning, 1988, p. 31).

Railways clearly advantaged some Africans by allowing them to cultivate export crops for the first time. In Uganda, for example, head-loading from the coast to the interior had cost £100 to £300 per ton; railway freight rates were 48 shillings (£2.40) per ton, which made cotton and coffee cultivation viable. Similarly, the arrival of the railway at Kano in Northern Nigeria gave an immediate stimulus to groundnut production (Hogendorn, 1973, p. 313; Wrigley, 1986, p. 100). Nevertheless, railways were an 'inappropriate' level of technology from the perspective of African societies. Nearly all the materials and equipment needed to construct and maintain them had to be imported (along with most of the steam coal), so they made neither forward nor backward linkages with local economies, and tended to serve only a narrow strip of territory on either side of the line. They were a 'lumpy' form of capital, whose high threshold excluded native entrepreneurs. The roads constructed under colonial authority were more 'appropriate', but often served political rather than economic ends. They were usually built and maintained with corvée labour in an act of submission to the colonial government, rather than as an investment for economic advantage (Manning, 1988, p. 30). West Africans only become agents in the transport revolution when relatively cheap Fords were introduced after 1918; Africans were soon driving and maintaining them, and acquiring them to set up transport businesses.

Internationally negotiable colonial currencies set the seal on European economic penetration. Their belated introduction must be seen in the context of the adoption of the gold standard from the 1870s and the depreciation of silver. In gold standard countries, silver ceased to be legal tender above a certain value, and it was of little consequence if the token value of a silver coin was greater than its bullion value. But metropolitan tendering regulations did not apply in West Africa, and as the 'money' economy expanded, large quantities of imported European silver coins were retained for local use. By the 1910s, almost as much sterling silver was being issued for British West Africa as for the United Kingdom. A stock of unsecured money was being accumulated with a nominal value greater than its bullion value. Were it to be repatriated during a trade depression, monetary instability could ensue. There was an evident need for a local currency conforming with the gold standard. The French solution was to charter private, profit-making institutions as issuing banks. In French West Africa, the Banque d'Afrique Occidentale was granted this privilege in 1901: it issued a currency readily convertible to the metropolitan franc within limits similar to those observed by the Bank of France. The note issue, and thus the volume of credit in the colony, were not to exceed three times the metallic reserves. For a time, there was a similar commercial monopoly in British West Africa but it was unpopular with officials and rival firms. The eventual solution was the West African Currency Board, a public institution created in 1912 that issued a visually distinct currency, convertible at par with sterling but legal only in the colonies. (Similar boards were created for East Africa in 1919 and Malaya in 1938.) The conditions governing the supply of money and credit were more restrictive than in French territories: issues had to be covered by securities held in London; 90 per cent could be in gilt-edged stock, and 10 per cent in bullion (Hopkins, 1970).

The economic conquest met its prime object of increasing sub-Saharan Africa's trade: between 1896 and 1914, the total value of exports and imports more than doubled, from £71 million to £188 million, though with great variations between regions. The fastest rate of growth was in the West African 'peasant' economies, whose integration with international markets was well under way before colonial rule: exports rose about five and half times by value between 1883 and 1913. Prices were lower at the latter date, so the volume growth was even greater, although producers' terms of trade did improve markedly from the late 1890s and rising incomes from exports probably made the new administrations more acceptable to Africans (Hopkins, 1973, p. 183). By 1909, over a quarter of world exports of vegetable oils and fats originated in Africa, making it a major supplier of raw materials to the soap and edible fats industries. West African producers now had an interest in the diet and cleanliness of European industrial workers, especially in Germany where margarine was widely consumed in working-class households before 1914. In the newly opened mining economies of Central Africa, exports grew about five-fold. Though exports declined sharply when the First World War disrupted international exchanges, they revived with the outbreak of peace. Despite the slump in world trade after 1930, the value of African exports in the years 1935–9 was five times greater than in 1905–9.

In a global perspective, Africa's commercial expansion was far less impressive: in 1913, sub-Saharan Africa accounted for only 3.7 per cent of world exports, and in 1928 for 4 per cent. Moreover, South African gold exports had such a large role that any fluctuation in their value greatly affected the pattern of the continent's trade. Even if we focus solely on the world's tropical regions lying between 30 degrees north and south of the equator, Africa was still a marginal continent in international commerce, accounting for only 6.2 per cent of all tropical trade in 1913 (Lewis, 1969, p. 15). Furthermore, the hopes vested by social imperialists in African markets for surplus manufactures proved absurdly misplaced. The proportion of French exports going to sub-Saharan Africa actually declined during the 'New Imperialism', from 1.5 per cent in 1875 to 0.5 per cent in 1905. In the case of Britain, exports to Africa (excluding the rather special case of South Africa) grew from 1 per cent to 4.7 per cent in the same period. Only for Portugal did African markets come to account for more than a tenth of a European colonial power's total exports before 1914 (Austen, 1987, Table A4, p. 278).

Conclusions

The early 1900s were the apogee of European imperial power and are an appropriate point at which to pause in this analysis of Euro-African relations. After the resolution of the Moroccan crisis, the colonial empires in Africa were insulated from international politics by a 'gentlemen's agreement' among the European states not to contest each other's position. As far as Germany was concerned, the First World War rendered the agreement null and void: the Treaty of Versailles stripped her of her colonies, which were 'mandated' by the League of Nations to France, Britain, Belgium and the Union of South Africa to be administered under 'trusteeship' conditions (in reality indistinguishable from colonial rule). But otherwise this did not disturb Europe's domination of the continent, and as long as European states held the balance of power there were no effective international restraints on, or subversions of, their positions in Africa. In the interest of the European balance, Britain and France were quite prepared to concede an Italian protectorate over most of Ethiopia in 1934, and the international community allowed Mussolini to invade the last independent African state (save Liberia) with impunity, despite his use of chemical warfare.

The preconditions for this suppression of independent African polities (and the continent's seclusion from the international states system) were the great advances in military technology, physical and symbolic communications, and preventive tropical medicine in Europe from about 1850. They combined with a normative shift in transnational values in Europe to make the conquest of tropical Africa both feasible and justifiable from a humanitarian point of view. Africa's warrior hosts could offer formidable resistance and sometimes inflicted major defeats on colonial armies (as at Isandlwana and Adwa) but in set-piece battles usually succumbed to the colonialists' superior weaponry and disciplined firepower.

In vast tracts of the continent, however, the Europeans' extensive military power was not matched by intensive political power. The central institutions of African states were easy to capture and subordinate; it was much more difficult to impose colonial authority beyond the spatial range of a marching column. The colonialists and their auxiliaries were too thin on the ground to constitute armies of occupation; meagre budgets and poor transport further limited their institutional capacity to penetrate societies and logistically implement decisions. The total area of French West Africa and French Equatorial Africa was 7 million square kilometres – 14 times the size of France – and their combined population around 16 millions. In 1914, the French presence made itself felt through 2708 white officers, assisted by 230 black interpreters and 5998 black, armed *gardes civils*. There were additionally 14 142 black troops in West Africa (Brunschwig, 1978, p. 138). Northern Nigeria, overrun by the British between 1897 and 1903, can serve as an example of an easily conquered territory where social institutions stubbornly resisted reconstruction by Europeans. The main campaign against the Sokoto Caliphate – the Muslim Fulani empire sprawling between Kamerun and French West Africa – was undertaken by about 1000 African troops under the command of 35 Europeans. The suppression of slave-raiding provided the moral justification for the conquest and, according to British accounts, was made easier by the welcome that the Hausa peasants and townspeople gave the advancing colonialists. They were exchanging one set of alien rulers for another who promised to be less oppressive. The first act of the Protectorate was to abolish the legal status of slavery, prohibit slave-trading and declare all children born after 1 April 1901 to be free. The colonial state's modest institutional capacity determined that its anti-slavery policy would be greatly compromised by the local distribution of political and economic power. Slave-raiding was suppressed and slave-dealing became a clandestine activity. However, the ownership of slaves, and the exploitation of slave labour, were far too deeply engrained in economic production and the system of social honour for the British to contemplate outright abolition. They could not tax and administer the territory without the Fulani aristocracy, whom they hoped to transform into a class of landlords employing wage labour. But Fulani power and status rested upon their slave holdings. Tribute was paid in slaves and slave stocks represented both currency and accumulated wealth in an economy where the traditional money, cowrie shells, had undergone massive inflation. To have compensated the owners monetarily would have been beyond the financial powers of the Protectorate, and a serious matter even for the imperial treasury. Fearing economic dislocation and aristocratic revolt had slaves fled *en masse*, the British administration impeded emancipation by imposing redemption payments on slaves wishing to free themselves. Bondage remained a common condition through the 1920s, making for a protracted transition to a non-slave economy. Throughout colonial Africa (but especially in Muslim-dominated areas) there were similar compromises with the traditional tributary élites (Lovejoy and Hogendorn, 1993; Cooper, 1981, p. 32).

Such compromises modulated the economic impact of colonial conquest. The Africa of the mining labour reserves moved quickly towards a free market in men's labour, and by the 1900s significant numbers had experienced waged work, at least for part of their lives. But outside the mining zones, waged workers were found only in occupations such as portering, with a status often lower than slavery. Colonial taxation impelled petty producers to enter commodity markets, but gave little immediate impetus to the spread of capitalist production relations. Whether colonialism hastened or impeded the development of African capitalism is a question I discuss in another chapter. It is worth noting here that the disappearance of African entrepreneurs from international trade in the continent's resources gave the Europeans a total control in this sector that they did not enjoy in South and South-East Asia. The arrested development of indigenous capitalism in the centuries preceding colonial conquest goes far to explain this. Before colonialism, individual Africans had amassed wealth and power from exchange, but there was little systematic accumulation of capital. There was no equivalent in Black Africa to Bombay's Parsee cotton merchants who pioneered industrial spinning in the city; nor were non-European immigrants in Africa able to play the same dynamic roles as the *chettyar* moneylenders in the Burmese rice economy and the Chinese entrepreneurs in Malayan tin-mining. By the late nineteenth century, Africa was exceptionally vulnerable to economic take-over from outside: the transport revolution made it possible for Africans to become seriously involved in producing cash crops for foreign markets before a native entrepreneurial class had emerged to profit from production. The scale of this revolution raised the capital threshold in export marketing, helping to exclude African entrepreneurs. The secular accumulation of disparities between invaders and Africans in military and productive techniques, in the capacity of state and business organisations had reached a critical mass, making the conversion of economic superiority into a 'capstone' form of political domination a fairly painless matter for Europeans by 1890. Using this political power to penetrate indigenous societies and overcome their inherited forms of 'underdevelopment' was a far more costly business, and in much of the continent not seriously attempted before 1945.

5

EUROPEAN COLONIALISM AND INDIGENOUS SOCIETY IN ASIA

Introduction: The Debate over Colonialism and Development

Modern European colonialism was not all of a piece: its essential feature was the foreign rule of Asian and African societies in which socio-cultural institutions were conserved while the administrative apex was monopolised by a white élite. But techniques of rule varied greatly, as did their impact on indigenous society and the economic change they initiated. Factors affecting the pace and trajectory of change included the relative strength of settler and expatriate minorities, the links forged between the colony and international economy, and the sheer duration of the colonial period. Colonial populations had rarely been ethnically and religiously homogeneous before the European conquests, and colonial rule in Africa and South-East Asia exaggerated their segmentary character by encouraging the influx of non-European traders, shopkeepers and moneylenders, contract labourers and plantation workers, small entrepreneurs in the rice-milling and sugar-refining trades, and so on. Modern colonies were, consequently, 'plural' societies, and though pluralism did not extend to the autocratic political sphere, it had economic, communal and juridical dimensions which insulated vertical groups (usually defined by ethnicity) from each other. Some migrants were the entrepreneurial cutting edge of capitalist expansion; the *chettyar* moneylenders whose financing of rice cultivation for export in Lower Burma encouraged absolute property ownership and the spread of wage labour are one example (Furnivall, 1948, pp. 86–7). Others supplied the wage labour not forthcoming from native peasant society. The existence of such groups complicates any assessment of the welfare gains and losses due to colonialism, and even makes it difficult to say who the 'indigenous' were. In brief, complexity was the order of the day and the historian must acknowledge this.

Three caveats have to be entered that further complicate matters: first, colonialism was not the sole cause of economic and social change during the colonial period. If, for example, there were slight improvements in living standards in India in the century before 1947, this is not evidence of the beneficial effects of British rule, while the mass poverty at Independence does not prove that colonialism was the cause of destitution. The specific institutional and economic characteristics of the traditional Indian economy may have had as much to do with what happened after 1800 as British policy (Morris, 1969, p. 123; Tomlinson, 1993, p. 8). The most profound change affecting the twentieth-century underdeveloped world, the rapid growth of population from about 1930, took place irrespective of whether a country was subject to a colonial relationship or not. Second, routines of production and exchange often persisted through the colonial period, with the result that the fundamentals of material life in South Asia in 1947 and Africa around 1960 were closer to those of a century before than to today's. Third, despite its relatively brief history, European colonialism underwent important transformations that altered its impact on the native economy and society: we have already noted the shift in the Dutch East Indies, around 1870, from the mercantilist 'Cultivation System' to a more liberal form of colonial exploitation giving freer rein to private capital. A further change came in the 1900s when the growing sense of moral responsibility towards colonial peoples led to the 'Ethical' policy that aimed to combine economic 'development' with native 'welfare'. Such was the new sensitivity to reports of Javanese impoverishment as export prices for cash crops fell that the Dutch Colonial Minister actually proposed the use of metropolitan revenue to counter the diminishing welfare of the people (Furnivall, 1944, pp. 229–32). The Dutch colonial administration faced the dilemma which sooner or later confronted all the European colonial powers: how to draw peasant societies in the underdeveloped world into the international division of labour and the process of capitalist development without subjecting traditional communal structures to excessive stresses or without these societies becoming mere objects of administrative action.

Given colonial rule's diversity and transformations, and the variety of links which it made with world markets, summarising its consequences for indigenous societies in generally valid ways is well-nigh impossible. To organise the discussion, we can begin with the verdicts delivered initially by the two parties to the colonial relationship: imperialists asserted that alien rule was the only way in which these 'backward' countries could have been modernised, and some scholars who cannot be dismissed as their apologists concur. Rudolf von Albertini, for example, concluded his comprehensive history of the colonial empires committed to the modernisation thesis: despite conserving old ruling structures, 'foreign rule in the end was destabilizing and launched social changes that characterized the Western way to modernization as the ideal way'. The colonial peace, modern administration and communications in larger territorial units, expanding education and health services, and economic development were all part of this process, but the most important change, he argues, was the introduction of Western property law, especially the law regulating the ownership of land (Albertini, 1982, p. 514, p. 499). We will give particular attention to this consequence of colonial rule.

This conception of colonialism as a powerful modernising agent within the 'Third World' has a counterpart in Marxism traceable to Marx's articles on India of the 1850s. He believed British mass manufactures were effecting 'the only *social* revolution ever heard of in Asia' by shattering the immemorial self-sufficiency of the village communities. These were the 'solid foundation' of static, ahistorical oriental despotism and, though deploring its human costs, Marx welcomed their disruption. Humanity's 'self-developing social state' had been petrified into 'never changing natural destiny' by the stasis of village life whose ideological concomitants were degrading religious practices requiring 'man, the sovereign of nature' to adore the monkey and the cow. British rule would lead, Marx believed, to the capitalist transformation of the forces and relations of production: British-built railways would integrate the market, hasten the dissolution of the hereditary division of labour, and – because they required coal, iron and steel, and machinery – become 'the forerunners of modern industry'. Ultimately, British rule would be justified by the socialisation of the modern economy developing under its aegis; they were 'laying down the material premises' for the development of the productive powers of Indian society and their appropriation by the Indian people (Marx, 1853, 1959 edn, pp. 35–41, 81–7). In sum, Marx's arguments exhibited ethnocentric incomprehension of other cultures, an amalgam of naïve historical and technological determinism, and a vulgar utilitarianism that regarded future progress as a warrant for present suffering.

Modern Marxists have not, on the whole, shared Marx's conception of nineteenth-century imperialism as destined to effect the full-blown capitalist transformation of the societies brought under its sway. Quite reasonably, they have not felt bound by views formed when industrial capitalism was still largely confined to Britain and competition for colonial empires among industrialised states lay in the future. Lenin, rather than Marx, was for much of the twentieth century the principal inspiration for Marxist accounts of the capitalist transformation wrought by imperialism in the 'Third World'. Though he said very little about the impact of modern colonialism on indigenous societies, Lenin believed that capitalism had exhausted its progressive potential and in its parasitic colonial form could only retard industrialisation. The late Bill Warren created something of a stir by attacking – to devastating effect – Lenin's theory of imperialism from within Marxism and proffering a robust defence of the progressive role of the modern colonial empires as 'pioneers' of capitalism. As with Marx in the 1850s, Warren credited the colonial era with launching, almost from its inception, a process of development through the integration of economically backward regions into world markets. But whereas Marx focused on railway-building, Warren emphasised improvements in health and education, and the provision of new types of consumer goods, which were all particularly favourable to the long-term expansion of the productive forces. He cited approvingly the estimate of W.K. Hancock that, by money measurement, the cocoa farmers of the colonial Gold Coast were better off than the majority of peasants in Romania and south-eastern Europe during the 1930s, and in welfare terms immeasurably better off. (He might have added that mass cultural development also compared quite favourably with the more backward parts of southern and eastern Europe: by 1940, half the Gold Coast's children received some primary education.) In Warren's view, the material impact of colonialism in the underdeveloped world brought a corresponding dissolution of traditional outlooks as they were exposed to the individualism and rationality of Western culture (Warren, 1980, pp. 129–31, 135).

Warren's style was uncluttered by nuance and even a die-hard imperialist might jib at his encomium of colonialism's modernising drive. The health status of colonial populations rarely improved before 1920, and throughout Africa had deteriorated catastrophically during the preceding generation. Java was probably the only colony where Western medicine (in the form of smallpox inoculation) and sanitary measures made a significant impact on death-rates before the inter-war period. Public health policies in colonial West Africa, for example, were fragmentary and largely ineffective until 1945 (Coquery-Vidrovitch, 1988a, p. 41; Hopkins, 1973, p. 224). But more of a problem for Warren's thesis is the anti-capitalistic ethic of much colonial administration and its collaboration with 'traditional' élites whose power and legitimacy could not have survived thoroughgoing economic and social liberalisation. The explicit purpose of this alliance in colonial Africa was ensuring continuity with the past: colonialists utilised indigenous institutions and authorities in order to conserve them. In India, the situation was more fluid and complex, but by 1870 the Indian Civil Service had acquired an anti-capitalist ethic and was beginning to shield agrarian society from market forces. Commercial and mercantile groups were legally excluded from land-ownership in certain provinces, and their credit operations were frustrated. Official indifference (at best) to urban, entrepreneurial interests eventually drove Indian businessmen into opposition (Washbrook, 1981, pp. 686, 690).

By contrast with the proponents of colonialism as 'progressive' and modernising, as and when Westernised educated groups began to form in colonial societies they articulated the idea that colonialism was not only unnecessary but positively harmful to their general political and social development. After the founding of the Communist International in 1919, and of Asian communist parties in subsequent years, the nationalist critique of colonialism assimilated the Leninist concept of imperialism as the final, decadent stage of finance capitalism. Lenin's thesis that capitalism in its parasitic colonial form could only retard industrialisation was adopted by the Sixth Congress of the Communist International in 1928, and subsequently became an important inspiration for notions of 'underdevelopment' (Warren, 1980, p. 85). Out of this intellectual and political opposition to colonialism, radical scholarship has formed a negative view which emphasises such features of the colonial economy as over-specialisation in cash crops or other primary products (such as copper) for export earnings; the neglect of food production; 'de-industrialisation' of handicrafts; the fact that large-scale capital units tended to be confined to mining and processing primary products, and were foreign-owned. Some have posited the concept of a 'colonial mode of production' in which local exchange between artisans and peasants was superseded by the international exchange of raw materials for imported manufactures, with the result that the different segments of the internal economy no longer traded with or complemented each other and were consequently 'disarticulated'. With respect to India, Hamza Alavi has argued that the elements of the Indian economy were integrated only by virtue of their separate ties with the metropolitan economy. Extended reproduction – or, in a different jargon, economic growth – could not be realised within the economy of the colony but only through the imperialist centre (Alavi, 1975; idem, 1982).

One particularly influential theory, put forward by Geoffrey Kay, contends that colonial 'underdevelopment' and metropolitan development were reciprocally connected by Western merchant capitalists' pivotal role in integrating the colonies with world markets. From their monopoly of oceanic trade and their use of the telegraph to connect distant markets, western merchants gained critical advantages in price information and market situation. They acquired primary products at less than their value to the European producers who processed them, and were able to import overpriced manufactures. This double 'mark-up' supposedly accelerated the accumulation process in the metropolis by providing cheap raw materials, and retarded it in the colonial periphery by 'draining' away poorly requited exports. According to the theory, Western merchant capital had an ambiguous impact upon the colonial economies: native producers were encouraged to enter the market, but merchants profited as much (if not more) from exchange with peasant smallholders as they did from investing in production. The consequences were innovative yet conservative: more people were drawn into the exchange economy, and more land given over to cash crops, but agricultural techniques were unaltered and the productivity of land and labour remained much the same. European indirect rule through compliant traditional élites – which was the norm in practice – reproduced at the level of the state all the ambiguities that merchant capital created in the economy: it established a centralised political authority upholding private property and money, but rested its power in part on local pre-capitalist groups (Kay, 1975, pp. 96–105).

India

For obvious reasons, most of my substantive discussion concerns India: in 1939, about three-fifths of all the people under European colonial rule lived in India, which long exhibited the mass poverty and low level of industrialisation so characteristic of 'Third World' underdevelopment. For some, this was the classic case of the colonial remoulding of a pre-modern economy that in 1800 still produced – if we are to credit Paul Bairoch – a fifth of world manufacturing output (Bairoch, 1982; Habib, 1985). Furthermore, the debates I have outlined were anticipated from the 1890s by early nationalist intellectuals, who charged British rule with distorting India's economy and impoverishing her people. The 'imperialist' orthodoxy was that growing prosperity and economic development were by-products of the pax Britannica, with its efficient and honest administration, railway-building, and government-sponsored irrigation. No-one could seriously maintain that the state in British India had been interventionist, but it had, purportedly, provided the political security and legal framework necessary for great increases in cultivated area and commercial cropping, and stimulated foreign commerce.

   In rebutting this orthodoxy, Indian scholars (pre-eminently Dadabhai Naoroji and R.C. Dutt) certainly identified aspects of British rule they considered positively harmful, most notably the 'drain' of wealth to Britain and the Indian tariff regime. But it is essential to grasp that an implied criticism of the Raj was that it had not been interventionist enough: British rule, they argued, was not leading to industrial growth and had produced economic changes without generating economic development. For the early nationalists, this stasis was the inevitable result of the way the British secured their rule in collaboration with the traditional élites, and they saw the removal of British rule as an *essential*, though not sufficient, condition of Indian modernisation (For a convenient summary, see Chandra, 1969, p. 36).

Since the 'tributary' subjection of India to Britain was a central and emotive issue for early nationalism, this is a convenient point to enquire into the size and character of the notorious 'Home Charges' – the payments the Secretary of State for India made in London both to meet obligations to bondholders and to defray the 'Anglocentric' expenses of Indian civil and military administration. India's colonial status was made manifest in these financial transactions, which diverted part of the stream of national income abroad. The charges were eventually met by Indian taxpayers, and because the weight of taxation shifted in the later nineteenth century away from rural producers towards urban consumers, they were by 1900 especially galling to educated city-dwellers attracted to modern nationalism. As a proportion of public expenditure, the burden was large and growing: the Home Charges absorbed 16 per cent of current revenues between 1875–6 and 1898–9, and 27 per cent by 1933. Since total tax revenue has been estimated at 5 to 7 per cent of national income, we can hazard that the Home Charges were 'draining away' less than 0.5 per cent of gross domestic income in the 1870s and approaching 2 per cent between the wars (Kumar, 1983b, pp. 937, 905; Sen, 1992, ch. 2). Even the latter may not seem very consequential, but compounded over sixty years it would have sufficed to wipe out the gains of economic growth in, say, Britain between 1850 and 1914 and left individuals, on average, worse off. For a very poor country to transfer even a small part of its wealth to a rich one for the best part of century would have severely impeded economic growth had the transfer been sheer tribute. One part certainly was: the British military expenses imposed on India (accounting for more than a quarter of the aggregate Home Charges), and her considerable contribution towards the cost of British administration in Aden, China and Persia. But, in large measure, the Home Charges met economically productive expenditure: the major item from the 1860s to 1933–4 (accounting for about 51 per cent) was guaranteed interest payments to British investors in Indian railways and public works. The Indian economy benefited from these investments by a steep fall in inland freight charges: to have transported the goods shipped by rail in India in 1900 by the cheapest alternative methods would have cost an additional 1.2 billion rupees or about 9 per cent of national income (Hurd, 1983, p. 741). It is most unlikely that Indian capitalists would have financed the railways, since the rate of return on equity and debentures – 4.97 per cent and 3.65 per cent respectively – was less than they were accustomed to expect from commercial speculations. To Western eyes, interest rates in India were 'exhorbitant' and there was a considerable social saving in having what was the world's fourth largest railway system by 1910 financed by the cheap money available in London. The only other item in the Home Charges worth mentioning was the purchase of government stores in Britain (including railway equipment). In the view of the Indian Industrial Commission – an official enquiry of 1916–18 which provided a fund of evidence on factors behind tardy industrialisation – stores purchasing was 'conducted in such a way as to handicap Indian manufacturers in competing for orders and to retard industrial development in India' (Indian Industrial Commission, 1919, Summary). But compared with the obstacles to industrialisation inherent in the Indian economy – irrespective of the colonial superstructure – the deterrent effect must have been small, and from the mid-1920s new purchase rules began to favour the Indian as opposed to the foreign entrepreneur.

Indian 'Underdevelopment' and the International Economy

In the more recent phase of the debate over the relationship between British rule and Indian 'improvement' (or 'stagnation'), great emphasis has been given to India's place in the international economy, particularly during 1870–1914 when the subcontinent ran a considerable export surplus and acquired a pivotal role in the settlement of international balances (Bagchi, 1982, pp. 88–90). With the transport revolution, a widening range of commodities could be marketed internationally and there were striking changes in the geography and organisation of Indian trade. Until the early 1860s, the most important export was opium, an easily stored commodity of high intrinsic value and low freight costs serving a captive but static market. Negligible market information was required to sell opium, and overseas sales were extraordinarily stable until 1880, after which their value slowly declined. But cotton, jute, tea and rice, which found expanding markets throughout the world, faced competition from alternative suppliers. High-quality commercial information was indispensable for international trade in these commodities, and from the 1870s this was provided by means of the telegraph, which not only linked India and Europe but unified the market in South-East Asia by connecting Calcutta with Rangoon, Singapore and Batavia (Latham, 1978a, pp. 32–7). The telegraph transmitted prices and orders intercontinentally; it promoted forward selling and speedier transactions by substituting telegraphic transfer for bills of exchange. Fortuitously, monetary factors made Indian goods increasingly price competitive from the early 1870s. The rupee was a silver-based currency, and the price of silver relative to gold fell while most of the world's major currencies adopted the gold standard (though curiously Indian imports grew at a faster annual rate than exports between 1871–3 and 1896–8, which is quite contrary to what one would expect of a country with a depreciating exchange rate).

Whatever the benefits (or drawbacks) to Indian producers of participating in the international division of labour, there cannot be much doubt as to the advantages for British exporters and consumers, particularly after 1890. British needs for staple foodstuffs were partly met by the subcontinent: with steam transport via the Suez Canal, Indian wheat could be exported without deteriorating on a long sea voyage and, by 1904–13, a sixth of Britain's wheat imports were coming from India, though only 13 per cent of the crop was actually being exported. British commodity trade with India went into surplus, and in the early twentieth century there was a very favourable balance. (see Table 5.1) The surplus in Indian trade compensated for about 30 to 40 per cent of Britain's deficit in commodity trade with Europe and North America. In terms of their impact on British incomes and employment, British exports to Asia in the early twentieth century were virtually as important as exports to industrial Europe, and a great deal more important than exports to the USA (Saul, 1960, ch. 7).

Table 5.1   British trade with India, 1870–1914 : annual average worth and as a percentage of total British trade

	British imports from India		British exports to India	
	Total worth (£m)	Share of all British imports (%)	Total worth (£m)	Share of British direct exports (%)
1870–9	£29.4	8.2	£21.6	9.9
1880–9	£33.8	9.6	£30.7	13.3
1890–9	£28.2	6.6	£29.4	12.5
1900–14	£37.7	6.1	£46.4	12.3

Source: Data from B.R. Mitchell (1992).

Scholars who assert that there was some amelioration in Indian living standards under British rule argue that the communications revolution, by allowing Indian producers to satisfy demands for wheat and oilseeds in Europe and for cotton in Japan, opened better markets, stimulated cultivation, and probably raised peasants' real incomes – though all admit that the dearth of worthwhile statistics makes the last point highly speculative (McAlpin, 1983a, p. 891). Nationalists long contested this optimistic interpretation, asserting that a chronic imbalance in foreign trade 'drained' the economy of real resources. Merchandise imports into India were less than two-thirds the value of Indian exports in the late nineteenth and early twentieth century. (See Table 5.2.) Exporters were duly paid for their goods, but about a third of the export surplus was met by bullion imports, the rest by the sale of Council Bills. A large part of this money capital was re-exported to reimburse British investors and bondholders, repatriate the profits of British business, and pay the Home Charges, so we can see why nationalists regarded 'unrequited' exports as symptomatic of colonial dependency. Nevertheless, the value of the export surplus normally exceeded the capital flows from India, with the result that the country was a net importer of gold and silver from the later nineteenth century up to 1914 (Latham, 1978b). 'Ameliorists' regard this as grist to their mill, arguing that purchasing power increased as bullion imports entered the income stream and Council Bills were redeemed. However, little of the precious metal appears to have made its way into productive investment, and there is evidence that imported gold ended up in the hands of 'parasitic' groups (landlords and usurers) or 'hoarded' against drought and famine. The Royal Commission on Indian Currency and Finance (1914) was advised that hoarding had become more extensive after the rupee became a token coinage in the 1890s and Indians lost confidence in it as a store of value. If this was so, then real assets – cotton, jute, etc. – were exchanged for monetary metal and effectively amortised. So where does this leave us with the 'drain' thesis? In the terms stated by its proponents, it does not seem defensible. Export surpluses *could* have been a source of structural change and growth in the economy. What was dysfunctional was not the fact of surpluses in themselves, but institutional blockages that stopped earnings in foreign trade being channelled into investment and capital goods imports.

Whether India's foreign trade sector was ever large enough to have a considerable impact on Indian popular welfare for good or ill is debatable. As a proportion of national income, exports from colonial India were probably never more than the 11 per cent attained just before the First World War, when their per capita annual value was around £0.56. In the

Dutch East Indies their estimated value in 1913 was twice as high (£1.15), but for a truly exported-oriented economy in South Asia we have to turn to Ceylon, a small specialist tea producer with per capita exports estimated at £3.89 (Maddison, 1971, p. 59; Hanson, 1980, Table 2.6, pp. 26–7). A measure of the per capita value of Indian external trade is presented in Table 5.2 by dividing half the sum of exports and imports by the total population of the subcontinent at each census year between 1871 and 1931. Up until 1937, Indian trade statistics included Burma, which must inflate the export figures somewhat since a large proportion of Burmese gross domestic product was exported. Furthermore, the currency fluctuations during the period disguise the increase in the *volume* of exports, particularly between 1873 and 1893, when (as we have noted) the international value of the rupee declined substantially. From 1914, agricultural prices rose very quickly and the increase in the money value of exports hides the fact that their volume remained roughly constant. During the 1920s, though prices had fallen from their 1919–20 peak, they were approximately twice as high as in the 1900s, so in real terms the per capita value of international trade was much the same (price movements are shown in McAlpin, 1983b, Table 11A, p. 903).

Qualifications aside, foreign trade was modest relative to the size of the population, even allowing for pitifully low average per capita incomes. A supposedly 'optimistic' estimate put them at 42 rupees a year in the 1900s when the per capita value of international trade was 4 to 5 rupees (Bagchi, 1972, p. 3). Can a domestic economy really be described as integrated into the early twentieth international division of labour when its annual per capita imports were worth around five shillings and sixpence (27.5p)? Poverty and the relative self-sufficiency of a subcontinental economy imposed a meagre level of import penetration, much below that achieved in other tropical colonies. In British West and East Africa, for example, foreign trade was worth about £2 per head of population by 1935–9 (Munro, 1984, p. 21). India's ties to the world economy were surely more tenuous than both the 'ameliorists' and 'pessimists' would have us believe, and would seem too weak to have the 'disarticulating' effects posited by Alavi except in regions with good transport connections to the sea. In the pre-1914 decades, when exports were the motive force of most tropical development, Indian exports actually grew *comparatively* sluggishly: while the agricultural exports of the tropics (excluding India) increased at an average of 3.0 per cent per annum between 1883 and 1913, India's agricultural exports rose by only 1.4 per cent per annum, and non-food agricultural production by 1.9 per cent per annum. As Arthur Lewis argued, the average Indian farmer failed to get himself a cash crop, in the way the Japanese got silk, the Brazilian coffee, the Ghanaian cocoa, the Burmese rice:

India was locked in the poverty of subsistence agriculture, unable to exploit the opportunities created by the expansion of world trade so abundantly because it had little additional fertile land to cultivate; it was already heavily populated, its soils exhausted, and its yields notoriously low (Lewis, 1969, pp. 11–12).

A real awakening to Indian self-sufficiency, to the persistence of barter in the countryside, and to the low-level equilibrium in which the agricultural sector was trapped, came after independence, when economic planners realised how grossly exaggerated was the impression that the domestic economy had been largely commercialised and simultaneously integrated into the world economy by railways and imperialist policies (Morris, 1983, pp. 608, 610).

Table 5.2   Annual per capita value of India's international merchandise trade (current prices)

		Annual average		
	Population (millions)	Total imports (million rupees)	Total exports (million rupees)	Per capita imports + exports / 2 (rupees)
1870-9	255.2	387.8	546.8	1.83
1880-9	257.4	631.3	924.9	3.02
1890-9	282.1	737.6	937.0	2.97
1900-9	285.3	1143.1	1590.4	4.79
1910-19	303.0	1765.3	2497.9	7.03
1920-9	305.7	2704.3	3358.8	9.92
1930-9	338.2	1522.8	1818.0	4.94

Note: In 1870, the rupee's exchange value was approximately 2 shillings (10p). In 1893, the Indian mints were closed to the free coining of silver, and after some years the exchange value stabilised at 1 shilling and 4 pence (6½p). This official rate of exchange lasted until 1920, when it briefly rose again to 2 shillings. From 1923, the official rate was driven downwards and in 1927 stabilised at 1 shilling and 6 pence (7½p).
Sources: Mitchell (1982); Maddison (1971).

Whether the 'openness' of colonial India's economy delayed structural change is a different issue from the impact of primary exporting on popular welfare. A well-lubricated international trade sector can have major consequences at critical economic margins, even if the sector's size relative to total economic activity is not particularly large. Venture capitalists are a minority in any market economy and only relatively small numbers need be persuaded that trade in primary products is more profitable than investment in processing or manufacturing to block structural change. The Indian Industrial Commission concluded from the evidence of Indian and expatriate businessmen that the stunted growth of modern manufacturing was 'predetermined by the existence of a very large trade in raw materials, and by the ease with which most classes of manufactured articles could be imported from abroad. . .' Primary exports had not been matched by a sufficient import of capital goods to exploit industrial raw materials (such as mica) or to establish agricultural processing industries. (Thus, while India was the world's leading supplier of oilseeds, she had imported very little crushing and refining machinery.) Though metalworking was an ancient craft, agricultural tools were mainly imported, and the country had 'not a machine to make nails or screws'. The Indian bankers and moneylenders who furnished all the credit in the domestic economy preferred to finance external trade rather than run the greater initial risks of industrial enterprise, with the result that capital was notoriously 'shy'. Commercial firms, the Commission concluded, had 'prospered too well along conservative and stereotyped lines to trouble about undeveloped industries with uncertain prospects'. Tariffs were too politically sensitive to be included in the Commission's terms of reference, but it documented how other commercial policies encouraged the flow of primary exports to the detriment of domestic manufacturing. Differential rail freight rates made transporting industrial raw materials to the ports much cheaper than moving them inland. In the case of hides, port rates were nearly 50 per cent less than internal rates. This discriminatory pricing 'greatly discouraged Indian tanning, and aided certain foreign industrialists to obtain a hold on a class of raw material of which India possesses a partial monopoly' (IIC, 1919, pp. 45–8, 171).

This is evidence for the 'disarticulation' of the parts of the domestic economy posited by theorists of the 'colonial mode of production' but these concepts are not, I think, especially illuminating as to the overall trajectory of change in the economy. Up to *c*.1870 the subcontinent was divided into small, relatively isolated markets because high transport costs prevented regular trade in bulky commodities of low intrinsic value. Prices in these markets were determined by local factors of supply and demand, with no predictable relationship between the different price levels. Modern communications integrated the subcontinent by allowing regions with a surplus to respond to the price signals of regions in shortage, and so reduced the spread of prices between different places (McAlpin, 1983a, pp. 885–6). Without hammering the point unduly, we could say that the different regions were spatially and symbolically linked up (or 'articulated'). By the same logic, modern communications could only enhance regional specialisation, and a regional division of labour, which were prerequisites for the development of a 'national' economy. As a result, manufacturing concentrated in particular *regions*, and declined in others; in Rajasthan, for example, secondary employment declined substantially after 1881 because the transport revolution exposed a wide range of local manufactures to national and international competition, and the labour force was 'agriculturalised'. But the Indian occupational structure as a whole altered very little between the late nineteenth century and Independence (Krishnamurty, 1983, pp. 546, 548).

Furthermore, the 'disarticulation' argument oversimplifies the impact of imports on artisanal production, for they were often semi-manufactures to which value was added in Indian cottage industries before retailing. The Industrial Commission found no real ground for believing these industries were generally decaying. Many had lessened their costs of production and extended their markets by adapting to technical progress in the industrialised world. Dyers had taken to synthetic dyes, brass and copper smiths to sheet metal, blacksmiths to iron rolled in convenient sections. Tailors invariably employed sewing-machines, and town artisans used European and American tools (IIC, 1919, p. 162). After 1900, there was a belated technical improvement in handloom-weaving when the slay flying shuttle was widely adopted, enabling the sector to defend its market share. Output per weaver rose, more than compensating for the fall in employment: an estimated 965 million yards was produced on handlooms between 1902–3 and 1912–13 and not less than 1068 million between 1930–1 and 1937–38 (Morris, 1983, p. 577; Krishnamurty, 1983, p. 540).

And what of Kay's thesis postulating the exchange of over-priced European manufactured imports for under-valued primary exports? Historians of modern colonialism have found empirical confirmation for this 'unequal exchange' in the trading profits of the major firms operating in colonial West Africa (which are the real inspiration for the theory). But these were quasi-monopsonies in colonial–metropolitan trade which dominated the external commerce of the Black African colonies. With respect to India, conditions were different and the theory is scarcely persuasive. All 'upcountry' commodity trade was handled by Indian merchants well able to obtain the maximum price for the goods they bulked and traded. Their commercial information about the industrialised economies may have been deficient, but for Indian commodities to have been consistently undervalued we must envisage them being sold in markets where buyers would not 'bid up' prices. This is an unreal assumption: external commercial relations were genuinely multilateral by 1900, and Indian exports were selling in world markets where competition among buyers ensured that the price to the seller was what the market would bear. (See Table 5.3.) As we would predict, India's barter and income terms of trade improved overall between 1870 and 1914 (Lal, 1988, p. 180). Though always the largest single customer, Britain's share of Indian exports fell from about 48 per cent during the 1870s to 34 per cent by the 1900s. In 1913, 10 per cent of India's total exports went to Germany, nearly 9 per cent to Japan, and about 8.5 per cent to the United States. In the five years before the First World War, Germany and Austria provided about 9 per cent of Indian imports, while she was importing iron and steel, textiles, chemicals and oil in sizeable quantities from the USA, Belgium and other industrial countries. The development of modern manufacturing contributed to the diversification of the export schedule and the widening of foreign markets. Typically, colonial exports were exclusively raw materials and mostly despatched to the imperial metropolis. By the pre-war decade, India had departed quite significantly from this pattern: in 1914, manufactures and semi-manufactures accounted for 22.4 per cent of total exports by value (Chaudhuri, 1983, pp. 856–63; see Table 5.4).

Table 5.3   Indian exports to main trading partners (million rupees)

	China (inc. Hong Kong)	Japan	UK	USA	Australia	Germany
1879	105	1.0	278	33	—	—
1889	108	12	396	38	—	—
1899	145	64	337	76	13	75
1909	193	126	525	145	27	180

Source: Mitchell (1982).

Table 5.4   Main Indian commodity exports (million rupees)

	Raw cotton	Cotton goods	Jute	Jute goods	Opium	Rice	Tea
1879	111	27	44	12	143	84	31
1889	187	86	86	28	101	101	54
1899	99	96	81	63	82	131	92
1909	314	131	151	170	93	183	117

Source: Mitchell (1982).

The Dutch East Indies in the International Economy

India's links with the international economy are worth comparing with those of the Dutch East Indies, both to elucidate common features before 1914 and to highlight their divergence between the wars. Indonesian foreign commerce grew and fluctuated more or less in parallel with Indian from 1874 (when reasonably comprehensive data for Dutch territories outside Java become available) up to 1914. Exports values rose more than four-fold, from about 160 million guilders to 690 million. Imports were never more than 470 million guilders, and the surplus of exports over imports was proportionately much the same as in India. As was the case throughout the tropics, commerce expanded erratically, and for much of the time Indonesian net barter terms of trade deteriorated. Coffee, sugar, tobacco and indigo shipments accelerated with the opening of the Suez Canal, but this boom petered out around 1880, and from the mid-1880s to the mid-1890s export volumes grew very slowly while prices for the traditional colonial staples slumped. The rate of growth then accelerated in the 1900s, reaching over 8 per cent per annum. The Dutch were pushing out the political frontier, and exports boomed with the effective occupation of the 'Outer Islands' (i.e. the territories outside Java, where their authority had hitherto been merely suzerain). International capital and migrant contract labour flowed into rubber, tobacco and tea plantations in underpopulated Sumatra, with the result that by 1913 only about half the agricultural investment in the island was Dutch. The capital invested in mineral exploitation in Dutch Borneo was even more international in character (Furnivall, 1944, p. 311). The share of the Outer Islands in total exports quickly rose to 25 to 30 per cent and reached two-fifths just before the First World War; by 1925 it was over half. The export schedule diversified away from the staple tropical groceries to include tin, rubber and petroleum or petroleum products. At the same time the Dutch East Indies became reliant on imports of rice and other foodstuffs through Singapore.

As with India, commercial liberalisation after the abolition of the Cultivation System allowed for an increasing number of important trading partners for Indonesian produce, and Dutch ties with their prime colonial possession became unusually loose. Their share of Indonesian exports dropped from about three-fifths in 1870 to barely two-fifths in the latter half of the 1880s (while there was a compensatory rise in the share of intra-Asian trade). During the general expansionary phase between 1900 and 1914 the Dutch share was forced down to less than one-third. The Netherlands was a small economy, strongly committed to free trade because of a large international service sector, and it was not in the national interest to maintain a mercantilist relationship between colony and metropolis, such as the Salazarist regime imposed on Portuguese Africa. At the peak of the inter-war boom in 1925, the Netherlands was receiving only 15 per cent of Indonesia exports and furnishing a fifth of imports. Asian markets were more important for Indonesian exports than European, and Asia provided almost as large a proportion of imports as Europe. By the mid-1930s, Japan was the single most important source of Indonesian imports.

Whereas there was a broadly parallel movement in the growth of Indonesian and Indian external trade up to 1914, from that date there was a striking divergence, demonstrating the relative 'closure' of the Indian economy and the continued 'openness' of the Indonesian. If we take 1913 to be 100, the Indian index of export volumes fluctuated around this figure throughout the inter-war period. Export quantities fell fairly gently between 1928 and 1932 (though the price fall was much steeper), recovered slightly thereafter and by 1937 that index was about 105. By 1928, the index of Indonesian export volumes had risen to 330 and they were accounting for over a third of national income. The index fluctuated wildly during the 1930s, touched 440 in 1937, and fell back immediately before the outbreak of the Second World War (Booth, 1990, Figure.12.2, p. 281). Only the Philippines had a comparable volume growth in the 1920s and 1930s.

Did Indonesia's people benefit from this impressive expansion of external trade? There is considerable evidence that living standards were declining in late-nineteenth-century Java, and international trade was charged with 'draining' away surplus revenue to the Dutch entrepreneurs who handled exports and to the Chinese who imported consumer goods. The island's population was approaching 30 million by 1900, creating serious pressure on land resources, and village agriculture had become over-committed to sugar, a crop which exhausted the soil and whose price was falling on international markets. An official commission documented widespread immiseration, but by the time its reports appeared popular welfare was improving. This is an inescapable inference from the rapid rise in mass consumer imports and a great increase in the amount of rice available per head. A key factor was the recovery in Indonesia's commodity terms of trade after 1908 and the trickling down of welfare gains from export expansion to the primary producers (Lindblad, 1986, pp. 665–705). After the First World War, a sharp disparity emerged between the economic fortunes of the Javanese and those of the smallholders who turned to export cropping in the Outer Islands. The irrigated land rented by the sugar companies from Javanese villagers could have been more productively employed growing food crops; the rents villagers received from the industry did not properly compensate for the rising price of imported rice. In retrospect, it is clear that Java should have been devoting its resources to labour-intensive, land-saving crops, and to manufactures. That this did not happen was due partly to important vested interests within the colonial power structure (Booth, 1990, p. 290). The living standards of the Javanese were sustained to some extent by public works expenditure on irrigation, which raised agricultural output but, ironically, real improvements came with the dramatic collapse of the sugar trade in the 1930s and a switch to food crops. In the Outer Islands, exports were produced by capital-intensive European enterprises that housed and fed hundreds of thousands of contract workers, and native smallholders (many of them migrants from Java). The European estates accounted for most of the output, but yields per acre achieved by smallholders were the same, with much lower development costs, and their sector was serviced by a network of skilled Chinese entrepreneurs. (In Malaya, Chinese were the majority of smallholders and owned many medium-sized plantations, but under the 'Ethical' policy they were forbidden to hold land in the Dutch East Indies.) Smallholder rubber production in Indonesia owed nothing to government policy, depended on navigable rivers for its transport links, and (with its parallel development in Malaya) must be counted a remarkable instance of indigenous response to export opportunities (Barlow and Drabble, 1990, pp. 187–209). Once the trees had matured, a smallholder's returns were much greater than plantation wages, and his life was free of the severe discipline imposed on contract workers. The major problem for the smallholder was coordinating his long-term investment in seeds and land with rubber prices in the advanced economies. During the industrial slumps of 1920–2 and 1930–3 rubber prices fell by as much as five-fold, and migrants who had developed their holdings on credit were sunk in indebtedness. On balance, however, the smallholders were less adversely affected by the Depression than the large estates: the prices of their consumption goods also fell and they could revert to subsistence cropping. They recovered more rapidly than the estates during the later 1930s, increasing their share of production of rubber and coffee.

Between the wars, Indonesian exports as a proportion of gross domestic product fluctuated wildly between 23 and 37 per cent, but even at the trough of the Depression they represented a considerable export orientation by international standards. There are few easy generalisations as to how external trade impacted on native welfare, save that autonomous migrants in the Outer Islands gained from producing rubber and copra, while Javanese villagers tended to lose out from sugar. More important in the long term, however, was that the indigenous peoples were largely excluded by history and their cultural traditions from the ancillary services where the real profits were made. Chinese entrepreneurs were the chief intermediaries between native cultivators and large foreign concerns, and owned the small and medium-sized factories that began food processing and consumer manufacturing during the late 1920s and 1930s.

Retarded Industrialisation in India: 1870–1914

A striking paradox of Indian development under British rule was industrialism without industrialisation. The steam-powered factory arrived early in India during the 1850s, and by 1914 she was the world's fourth cotton manufacturing nation. Her 264 cotton mills, employing about 260 000 workers, gave her a spinning capacity three times greater than Japan's. Output from her coalmines was 15.7 million tons, making her self-sufficient in steam fuel and a net exporter from the 1900s. Yet, at Independence, large-scale manufacturing accounted for only 7.2 per cent of total net output, and relied heavily on foreign technology and capital goods imports. Handicrafts still produced a larger share of total output (8.9 per cent). The few patches of rapid growth had not served as nuclei from which economic expansion proliferated, and the structure of the labour force was unchanged. This seems still more puzzling when we consider that cotton, the fastest growing sector before 1914, faced Lancashire competition and was the industry against which official policy worked most harshly. To what extent did this paradoxical situation result from the 'open' political economy imposed on colonial India? We have already argued that the preference of Indian entrepreneurs for overseas trade and the high cost of borrowing investment capital discouraged industrial enterprise. Were there more profound obstacles in the traditional Indian economy and society inhibiting industrialisation, obstacles which colonial rule neither eroded nor reinforced?

Before attempting to answer, we should note that pre-1914 industrial growth was sharply bifurcated between Indian-owned cotton enterprises concentrated around Bombay and expatriate jute factories in Calcutta, for this division reveals the openings for, and constraints on, indigenous industrial capital. That factory-based production began in cotton-spinning was typical of early industrialisation everywhere, for the machine technology is relatively simple and the productivity gains are enormous, but there was to be no replication of a pattern laid down in western Europe and North America. Millowners, like other Indian businessmen, were restricted by the capital and consumer markets, and their factories were sometimes no more than ramshackle sheds, using simple, often hand-built machinery. They operated in a business environment lacking the complex system of signals and incentives of the developed market economies and without the cultural homogeneity of Japan. It was a necessarily more 'uncertain' context for business decision-making. There was scarcely any production for stock, and output was regulated according to market fluctuations. Labour was used in the factories in much same way as in the small 'informal' workshops (Chandavarkar, 1985, p. 638).

Capital for the first Parsee-owned mills came from the profits of opium-trading. They enjoyed geographic advantages in their proximity to raw materials and sold most of the output of coarse yarn to the still considerable handloom market. After erratic beginnings, and a cycle of boom and slump associated with the US Civil War and its aftermath, the mechanised industry expanded quickly in the 1870s. Ownership was predominantly Indian and the managers and technical employees were mostly Indian from about 1880. The rate of founding of new enterprises was particularly rapid after 1885, and by the mid 1890s there were 144 Indian cotton factories, with over 3.7 million spindles and 140 000 employees. The industry had captured the entire home market in coarse yarns and practically extinguished commercial domestic spinning. Yarn exports had also risen about six times in volume between 1879–80 and 1890–1, chiefly because of the growth of sales to China and Japan. During the famine and plague years of 1895–1900, domestic trade was severely depressed and industrial growth retarded by the destitution of many handloom weavers. Sustained recovery began only about 1905. Though the weaving sector of the industry remained subordinate, it was nonetheless growing more quickly in the pre-war decades because the export market for yarn had proved very volatile, and Indian businessmen were turning to the more stable domestic market for coarse cloth (Gadgil, 1971; Morris, 1983, pp. 574–5).

The mechanised jute industry established with expatriate British capital in Bengal – using locally supplied raw materials – differed radically in its market orientation and scale of organisation. The Indian home market for jute manufactures was much smaller than that for cotton goods, and since so many products (such as gunny-bags) were used in international transport, the industry's export-led growth closely mirrored that of world trade. By the later 1870s, cheap labour costs had made Indian mills the world's major exporter, and their products had virtually excluded those of Dundee from Asiatic and Australian markets. After the upsurge in world trade from the late 1890s, Indian jute products took over the US market from the British.

In per capita terms, it was more heavily capitalised than cotton, with larger units of production: though the labour force was about four-fifths the size of cotton's around 1913, cotton mills outnumbered jute four to one. Unlike cotton, the jute industry was initiated, managed and until the First World War entirely controlled by Europeans (though the large majority of firms were rupee companies financed directly by British investors in India). Why they had an exclusive role in jute industrialisation, while cotton was overwhelmingly the preserve of Indians, is not immediately obvious, since there were no bars to entry in either case. Morris explains the situation in terms of differential access to market information: British entrepreneurs in India were ideally placed to predict demand in Britain or foreign markets and so concentrated on exported-oriented businesses such as tea plantations. In the Indian domestic market, however, they enjoyed no such advantage: Indian merchants controlled 'up country' trade and Indian industrialists were better placed to estimate demand (Morris, 1979).

The most obvious feature of an 'open' political economy is the absence of tariff protection for native industries, and this was a key charge in the nationalist indictment of colonialism as retarding industrialisation. Undeniably, British tariff policy towards later nineteenth-century India was guided by a doctrinaire commitment to free trade and 'comparative advantage', and the self-interest of Lancashire cotton manufacturers who saw a 'captive' market where artisans would be more usefully employed growing cotton. Much of the pressure for changes in land tenure and Indian government expenditure on infrastructure came from Lancashire industrialists hoping for a shift of wage labour to cotton growing and an increased flow of primary exports. Largely because of their influence, Indian import duties on piece goods and yarns (originally imposed for revenue purposes after the Mutiny) were reduced to 5 and 3.5 per cent in 1862. Twenty years later, Lancashire manufacturers were instrumental in securing the abolition of all general import duties. When, in the mid 1890s, the financially hard-pressed Indian government secured an import duty of 3.5 per cent, Lancashire's fierce and effective lobbying led to the imposition of a countervailing excise on equivalent Indian products – which penalised consumers and exporters (Harnetty, 1972; Charlesworth, 1982, p. 63). Nothing better illustrates India's special place in the British imperial system. She perforce abided by free trade while the 'white' Dominions, together with Tsarist Russia, Brazil and Argentina, introduced tariffs to nurture 'infant industries' and their savers acquired the habits and expectations of investors. The low rate of return to be expected from Indian enterprises denied protection was one factor in discouraging private investment (Bagchi, 1972,

p. 25). But, though it was clearly a disadvantage to Indian entrepreneurs, nobody has yet specified counterfactually how much more rapid industrial growth would have been with protection, and our assumptions on this score should be cautious. The Bombay mills thrived during the period of greatest trade liberalisation after 1882, when the duties were abolished. The growth rate of value added in factory manufacturing was higher between 1900 and 1913 than between 1919 and 1939, when industry enjoyed protection (Lal, 1988, p. 192). Tariffs have the drawback of raising consumer prices and protecting inefficient producers, and the policy of promoting industrial growth without any regard to these social costs followed by independent Indian governments has disabused many of the utility of protection as a way of engineering structural change.

The domestic counterpart to free trade was *laissez-faire* government, which had the negative virtue of being cheap by comparison with the past and contemporary societies (or even Indian princely states where the fiscal burden was often considerably higher). The total government revenues of British India amounted to about 9 per cent of national income in 1872–3, and the proportion declined slightly in the early twentieth century. Public expenditure only rose above a tenth of GNP during wartime. The comparison with Japan, where public expenditure rose from 10 per cent of GNP in 1879–83 to 25 per cent in 1905–12, is instructive (Kumar, 1983b, p. 927). It reflects both the modernising policies of the Meiji government and the greater power of a cohesive national élite to impose higher taxes in the face of popular resistance. British authority was too brittle to withstand the political strains of a publicly financed development policy. In Japan, public investments in social overhead capital were consciously directed to industrial growth, and the state accumulated 'human capital' by promoting technical education and near universal literacy. Specialists argue about the relative significance of state intervention and private entrepreneurial initiative, but there can be no question that Japan's government had a strategy for developing the nation's manufacturing base decades before one was contemplated by the government of India. Even so, the contrast should not be over-drawn. The economic functions assumed by the Raj in constructing railways and other public works compared favourably with responses in equivalent late developers. Official attitudes to Indian industrialisation became more positive as foreign imports displaced British: by 1900, India was importing more steel from Belgium than from Britain, which was a factor in persuading the government to assist the Tata Company in founding the Jamshedpur iron and steel plant in Bihar. The company's transport costs were reduced, access to land eased and the government guaranteed the purchase of a large proportion of rail output for ten years. What state initiatives lacked before 1919 was a consistent developmental dynamic (Morris, 1983, p. 598; Charlesworth, 1982, p. 59).

The Indian economy was as much affected by British private enterprise as it was by public power, and whether expatriate capital on balance hastened or retarded industrial transformation is a complex issue. Controversy has focused on the key Western commercial institution in colonial Asia, the managing agency house. Its distinctive feature was that, as well as trading on its own account, the agency sold managerial services to British-owned businesses operating in an environment where professional management was scarce, and later diversified into managing Indian-owned businesses. The price paid for agency management was high: typically, the agency was represented on the board of a joint firm, no matter what proportion of the capital it held, and one of its partners acted, ex officio, as chairman. The agency would receive a percentage of turnover or profits, a commission on purchases or sales, and a 'head office allowance' for its services; it would normally expect to receive interest on loans advanced and various other fees. In practice, it usually became the decisive partner. Originally, the agencies concentrated in the export and extractive industries – and organised the 'drain' in nationalist eyes – but the largest acquired diverse business portfolios: in 1911, the 32 enterprises managed by Andrew Yule's included 5 jute factories, 12 collieries and 8 tea plantations. Through interlocking directorships, the major agencies achieved a considerable concentration of control across a broad swathe of large-scale enterprise. The agency system was repeatedly pilloried for its speculative tendencies and potential for malpractice, as well as for entrepreneurial conservatism. Despite instances of stock market manipulation and inflated fees, the hostility was mostly unwarranted. The agency houses were not simply managers of other people's money: by 1914, they had become heavily involved in setting up rupee companies that attracted native investors no less than British civil servants and other expatriates. Compared with expatriate European business in the Dutch East Indies and French Indo-China, the extent to which the agency houses went beyond the usual enclave enterprises is rather striking. In 1915 almost half the employment in the organised industrial sector (excluding public enterprises and mining) was provided by European-controlled concerns, and so far as large-scale factory industry was concerned, the proportion of employment provided by the expatriate firms was much higher (Tomlinson, 1989, p. 97). The agencies drew native capitalists away from their traditional rentier preferences into industrial investment, and so contributed to the emergence of a modern Indian bourgeoisie. In this way, the managing agency system was 'indigenised' from within. By the mid-1920s, it was almost impossible to distinguish British from Indian interests in regard to invested capital, for companies floated and managed by British managing agents were often largely owned by Indians, while many companies regarded as Indian had considerable numbers of British shareholders (Tomlinson, 1978, p. 670).

To attribute the slowness of the Indian industrialisation simply to the political economy of colonialism and 'insertion' in the international division of labour would be a fantasy. The great majority of economic transactions resulted from Indian businessmen's decision-making within the domestic economy, where nine-tenths of total internal trade was financed by indigenous bankers. They were rational and risk-taking, but were caught in 'a web of relationships which dampened the absolute level of performance and inhibited the rate of change' (Morris, 1983, p. 558). Expansion in a single sector, however successful, could not permeate the broader economy, where the low productivity of agriculture left little margin for expenditure over and above the needs of subsistence. Yields of cotton and rice per acre were substantially below those obtained in Egypt and Japan, for example, and the ratio of labour employed to land use was high by international standards (Indian Industrial Commission, 1919, p. 53). This meant that, on the demand side, the market for mass manufactures was restricted by the poverty of the village community, as well as its relative self-sufficiency. Rural autarky may have been exaggerated but is not entirely mythical. Artisanal village servants produced many of the goods needed by India's cultivators and often bartered them for grain. Official report described the late-nineteenth-century Punjab village as follows:

> eminently self-sustaining, it grows its own food, it makes its own implements, moulds its own domestic vessels . . . [it] looks to the outside world for little more than its salt, its spices, the fine cloth for its holiday clothes, and the coin in which it pays its revenues (*Report of the Census of the Punjab* (1881), cited in Gadgil, 1971, p. 10).

Because of the self-sufficiency of Indian village life, barter may still have accounted for two-fifths of the trade in consumer goods in the early 1950s (Morris, 1979, p. 344). For basically the same reason, regional specialisation in agriculture was hampered: typically, for example, cotton was grown in small patches around the village and used locally. The peasant cultivator was torn between specialising in remunerative commercial crops well-suited to local conditions, and a caution inculcated by the chronic uncertainty of monsoon agriculture. Quite rationally, he would invest most of his family's labour resources in crops that could be consumed if necessary, and a surplus that could be stored against dearth (McAlpin, 1974). Government-sponsored irrigation, and cheaper transport allowing for grain shipments into famine-stricken regions, helped break down this caution, encouraging regional specialisation in industrial and export crops after 1880. But the famines of the late 1890s reversed the trend: peasants substituted inferior but hardy food crops – such as millet – for more delicate cash crops. On the supply side, Indian entrepreneurs had to rely primarily on caste and kinship for investment capital and faced a deficit of technically qualified workers. The exploitation of raw labour from the countryside often made more economic sense than investment in expensive imported machinery (as well as imported management and technical skill), particularly in view of the high cost of investment capital for industrial enterprises. The preconditions for the rapid, broad-based expansion of modern mass manufacturing were more complex, and harder to achieve than national sovereignty.

The Origins of Economic Sovereignty and Withdrawal from the International Economy: 1914–39

Industrial growth in India during the inter-war years was closely related to her partial retreat from the international economy and emerging self-determination in economic affairs. Considering the size of India's population, her share of world trade has never been large: in value terms, it was 3.75 per cent in 1913. This fell to 3.2 per cent in 1928, and then, as total world trade shrank, to 2.5 per cent in 1937. Malaya took over India's function in the settlement of Britain's international trading accounts: by 1929, the positive balance in Malayan trade with the USA was about two and half times greater than that of India, and Malayan imports from Britain were now the main means by which dollars were acquired to meet Britain's deficit in trade with the USA. Many of the realities of economic sovereignty devolved to the government of India by the 1930s, and government itself became more representative of Indian interests. Some of the cultural bias and racist hauteur which had kept the administration and Indian entrepreneurship at arm's length were softened by Indianization of the civil service, and the greater participation of Indian businessmen in the political process. To defend the interests of British creditors, Britain reserved control of exchange rate and monetary policy. Indian exports were, allegedly, damaged by the official overvaluation of the rupee in 1920, but since its sterling value on the market was driven down by a quarter between 1923 and 1927 this handicap was not so severe in practice. The result of these changes was the dismantling of the 'open' political economy of the Raj and the origins of a much more positive policy of controlling her international economic relations, which was to become characteristic of official thinking after Independence (Chaudhuri, 1983, p. 869).

The 1914–18 war gave some impetus to established industries by restricting manufactured imports, though there was little import substitution in other sectors because capital goods imports were also choked off. Cotton imports fell by two-thirds during the war, creating exceptionally favourable conditions for the Bombay mills: their total profits quadrupled between 1913 and 1920. However, these were not reinvested primarily in the industry's capital equipment but in purchasing managing agencies and converting proprietary concerns to joint-stock companies. When the boom ended in 1922, the manufacturers were no less dependent on imported machinery (the first ring frame was not built in India until 1946) and many mills were working at a loss in the mid 1920s. Of greater long-term significance was the fact that Lancashire's ability to dictate Indian tariffs ended when the finances of the Indian government deteriorated with massive increases in military expenditure, and the reintroduction of revenue tariffs became inevitable. In 1917 the government of India was permitted to raise the duty on cotton imports from 3.5 to 7.5 per cent, without any corresponding increase in the countervailing excise, and it publicly declared industrialisation to be the paramount objective of fiscal policy. Henceforth, British pressure groups had no role in setting Indian tariffs. Fiscal autonomy was conceded in a tariff convention of 1919 by which the imperial government resolved not to interfere with Indian tariffs so long as the Viceroy and his Executive Council were in agreement with the Indian legislature. Under this convention, the government of India initiated a policy of 'discriminating protection' for industries enjoying a natural advantage but unlikely to develop without tariffs or considered viable without them in the long run. During the 1920s and 1930s, a tariff wall was progressively erected with levels (25 per cent on British piece goods and 50 per cent on foreign) that effectively excluded Lancashire cottons from what had been their largest export market. Imports had provided nearly three-fifths of domestic cloth supply in 1905–6, but only 7 per cent by 1936–7. Indian mill output soared, and by 1939 was satisfying nearly 86 per cent of domestic demand. Machinery and millwork were by then the largest single class of Indian imports.

Industrial production increased about two and half times between 1913 and 1936–8, a rate of growth well above the world average (Lal, 1988,

p. 188). The manufacturing base broadened; new centres, such as Ahmedabad, came to rival Bombay and Calcutta; and heavy industry took an increasing share of output. Between 1920 and 1937, pig-iron production grew by about 400 per cent, and steel by even more, under the stimulus of protection and government patronage. After 1939, industrial growth accelerated still faster with massive defence expenditure within India, making her the world's tenth largest producer of manufactured goods by 1945 (Tomlinson, 1979, pp. 30–1). But, despite a striking absolute growth in manufacturing employment, it scarcely rose as a proportion of total labour force. Structural change was smothered by 'Malthusian' demography.

Economic policy and performance in India during the Depression had more in common with independent states in the 'periphery' than other colonial dependencies. A process of economic decolonisation was hastened by the diminishing role of the expatriate business community and the 'indigenisation' of company ownership. The British sector of the managing agency system had attracted little metropolitan capital since the early 1920s. Nearly all the new investment came from native business communities that had emerged from the financial and trading castes, such as the Marwaris, who began opening textile and other industrial plants in Calcutta and other cities, and the Naidus of southern India. Ownership of the jute industry – once the preserve of expatriate capital – passed increasingly into Indian hands. In Bombay province, the British share in the gross assets of public listed companies declined from 43 per cent in 1912 to 10 per cent in 1935 (Jha, 1963, p. 174). But a process parallel to the decline of expatriate business was the emergence of direct investment in manufacturing by multinational corporations. Tariffs, and the Swadeshi boycott of foreign products, changed the market conditions for European imports and prompted British-based exporters to consider subsidiary manufacturing in India. The best-documented case is Unilever Hindustan, set up after 1931 by the Anglo-Dutch giant in response to a 25 per cent *ad valorem* tariff on imported soaps. It was the first Unilever business in any underdeveloped country whose products replaced the staple imports from the parent companies in Britain (Fieldhouse, 1978, p. 148). In all, twenty-one Indian subsidiaries were created by British-based multinationals during the 1930s, and represented about half of British capital holdings at independence (Tomlinson, 1993, p. 143). It was one of several ways in which the transition to a new political economy predated the transfer of sovereignty.

With some truth, Bagchi has asserted that 'between 1937 and 1946 India exchanged a state of unilateral dependence on Britain for that of multilateral dependence on the advanced capitalist countries' (Bagchi, 1982, p. 94). The loosening of colonial economic ties was not a release from the thralls of underdevelopment. As a backward, predominantly illiterate country India depended on imported technology and expertise for her industrial development, and on food imports to make good the grain deficit in most years. Industrialisation had not yet 'taken off' in 1947, and industrial growth still had a predominantly 'enclave' character, even where the capital was in Indian hands. The backward linkages from urban industry to the countryside were tenuous in most regions, and even where robust do not seem to have favoured either an improvement in rural living standards or an increase in labour productivity in agriculture.

The nationalists came into their political inheritance convinced that the colonial relationship had depleted the stock of national resources and denied Indians the opportunity to develop a modern industrial economy as a basis for national prosperity, but British rule and the expatriate business community had been less of an incubus than they believed. The balance of the evidence indicates that the tariff and purchasing policies of the Government of India before the 1920s were hindrances rather than major obstacles to industrialisation. Economic expansion was obstructed more by the absence of a rapidly growing indigenous market than by government policy, which, though not vigorous, was not as hostile to local developments as has often been suggested (Morris, 1983, p. 598). Even with protection and the preferential treatment for Indian producers in the purchase of government stores, it seems unlikely that the flow of investment in the private sector from agriculture and trade to manufacturing would have been greatly augmented. From the 1920s, the charge of indifference to developmental issues cannot be levelled against the Government of India. Indeed, there was to be considerable continuity between the late colonial state's attempts to formulate policies favourable to industry and those of independent India. Whether this was for good or ill is now very contentious: the autarkic route to industrialisation, once favoured by nationalists in awe of the Soviet achievement, has been discredited by the glacial pace of structural change in the highly protected economy of independent India. Deepak Lal sees Indian economic policy after 1920 as having embarked on a disastrous road to an inward-looking, increasingly inefficient, and capital-intensive form of industrialisation that culminated in stagnation after the 1960s when the limits of import substitution were reached. By providing the Westernised élite with 'the poisoned chalice of protection . . . the British left their worst and bitterest legacy to Indian's labouring millions' (Lal, 1988, pp. 202–3).

To pursue that argument would take us into an analysis of post-Independence economic policy and beyond the confines of this study. It would also distract us from the more fundamental problem confronting government, whether British or Congress-led: that of trying to accelerate development in a society with low levels of productivity and savings, and in which markets for produce and labour, and the borrowing and lending that took place at village level, tended to lock millions in a self-perpetuating cycle of poverty. Whether the agrarian policies of the colonial state inadvertently exacerbated this syndrome of underdevelopment is a question we should now address.

India: The Land and the Law

Three-quarters of India's labour force won a livelihood from agriculture, so British rule inevitably had its greatest impact on economic structures and relationships where it affected the ownership of land, and the rights to its use. This has generated a large scholarly literature, and assessments of how policy affected land use and agrarian relations have been implicated in both 'deleterious' and 'ameliorist' accounts of the consequences of British rule (a good summary of the main issues is in Charlesworth, 1982, ch. 2). Tapan Raychaudhuri has briefly but powerfully restated the thesis that the emergence of mass agrarian poverty was the direct result of the revolution in land tenure engineered by the British. He argues that, by conferring legally guaranteed proprietary rights on about 4 per cent of the agricultural population, the British polarised agrarian society into an élite of landholders and rich peasants and a mass of landless labourers and sharecroppers. Usufruct rights that were once inviolable now had to be purchased from zamindars who could turn to the British courts to evict defaulting tenants. The pyramid of power relations became more asymmetrical for the mass of smallholders, whether tenants or proprietors, who were deprived of nearly all their surplus by high rents and usurious credit. Many – he argues – were driven into landless destitution, particularly during the famines of 1865–6, 1876–8 and 1896–7 (Raychaudhuri, 1985, pp. 805–6).

The central propositions of this thesis have long been questioned by 'revisionist' scholars. It can no longer be assumed that the abundance of land and the ease with which whole villages fled oppressive taxation made landlessness rare in pre-colonial society. There was a demand for dependent labour within the ritual hierarchy, because most Brahmins regarded manual work as polluting, and a supply in the form of the hereditary servile castes for whom landlessness was a common condition. They formed a wide stratum of bonded labourers, especially in the south where about 15 per cent of the population around 1810 was in some form of servitude, though in parts of Malabar the proportion was 1 in 4. (Kumar, 1965, p. 181; Hjejle, 1967) Some, such as the *paraiyan* of the Tamil country, were the joint property of the village, and could not be sold separately from the land they cultivated, nor could the land be sold separately from them. Others were the personal property of their owners and could be sold, mortgaged and rented out. In Gujarat, in central west India, families of tribal origin were commonly bound as farm servants to Brahmin landlords, and probably formed one-tenth of the population (Breman, 1992, p. 252). In a formal sense, the status of the servile improved with the British decree abolishing Indian slavery (1843), but for decades the legal statute was irrelevant to the real condition of the servile groups. Many slaves and their descendants remained bonded to landlords under contracts that were enforceable in British courts, and the outcaste groups continued to be miserably oppressed. Even after the legislation was more widely enforced, there was a continuity with the pre-colonial forms of labour exploitation, since the servile castes, not dispossessed peasants, constituted the landless labour force of southern India. The proportion classified as dependent agricultural wage earners in the census of 1901 is close to the estimated size of the servile castes in 1810, a firm indication that landlessness increased little, if at all. Indeed, Dharma Kumar's pioneer study actually showed greater numbers and a larger proportion of land*owners* in Madras Presidency in 1901 than in 1881 (Kumar, 1965, p. 179).

Amelioration, like immiseration, is a relative concept. Those arguing that material conditions for the majority improved slightly deny neither the daily grind of peasant life nor the horrendous famine mortality of the last quarter of the nineteenth century (when an estimated 26 million died). The argument for modest general improvement from about 1850 lies, first, in the rapid and general extension of cultivation while population growth was sluggish. In southern India, the area of tilled peasant land increased 50 per cent faster than population between 1856 and 1874 (Kumar, 1983a, p. 230). The land–labour ratio improved in most regions up to the about 1920. As a result, there were both more food grain available per capita and more land on which to grow higher value cash crops. Second, agricultural prices generally rose faster than those of consumption goods, which meant increased incomes for those able to market a surplus. Third, revenue demands became less onerous. Land revenue, the government's main income, probably took at least a quarter of gross agricultural output in the early nineteenth century; by 1901, it was only 5 per cent. McAlpin's analysis of the Bombay ryotwari settlement elucidates the interlocking processes that reduced the state's 'take' from agriculture: although the total revenue collected in twelve 'settled' districts rose fairly steadily from about 1830, this was more than compensated for by the increase in the area of cultivated and taxable land, so that the revenue collected per acre generally fell from about 1840. If revenue payments are compared with the rise in the price of food grains, then their real cost to the peasant cultivator fell steeply, particularly during the 1860s when speculation in cotton led to rising prices throughout the agricultural sector. Though there was considerable variation between districts, in all of them the share of produce paid as land revenue declined, often very dramatically (McAlpin, 1983a, p. 125). After 1920, the political difficulties in collecting land revenue mounted, and its share of total agricultural output was only 1.7 per cent by the late 1930s.

The indices of per capita income calculated by Heston and others support the 'ameliorist' position in showing a 37 per cent improvement between 1868–9 and 1920 (Heston, 1983, Table 4.5, p. 402). We ought to be sceptical of numbers derived from fragile evidence, but other indicators point in the same direction: imports of sugar, a widely consumed luxury food, rose from 2 per cent of total imports in 1870 to over 9 per cent in 1910 (Latham, 1978a, p. 73). There are no data on the distribution of income, and an overall rise on average would not be inconsistent with greater social polarisation if village headmen, moneylenders and rich farmers engrossed nearly all the surplus. Commonplace though such exploitation was, it seems not to have negated the ameliorative tendency. Increased income went primarily to those who cultivated and controlled the land and, in the districts McAlpin examined, four-fifths of taxable land was cultivated by its owners, either singly or in partnership, during the 1880s (McAlpin, 1983a, pp. 127–31). All the qualitative evidence – showing agricultural cattle and carts used more widely, increased digging of wells and the construction of 'superior' houses - reinforces the inference that improvements were widely diffused.

The expansion of the agricultural market economy may even have benefited the servile castes by creating opportunities for migrant labour on the Ceylonese coffee and tea plantations after 1850. About 4.9 million Indian labourers migrated to Ceylon between 1843 and 1903 (some 1.5 million permanently) and a large proportion going from Madras were from the servile castes. Though conditions on the tea estates were harsh, they were an improvement on the outcaste's misery: one month's pay equalled two years' income at home (Hjejle, 1967, pp. 103, 107). In certain districts some returning migrant workers were able to invest their earnings in proprietary rights.

By 1920, Indian agriculture could extend no more without sharply diminishing returns, and incomes stagnated for the rest of the colonial period. The amount of food grain available per head declined between 1920 and 1940 by perhaps a quarter (Heston, 1983, Table 4.6, p. 410). Population pressure on the land had been evident in Bengal, in particular, from the 1900s but became quite general between the wars. More and more families found their plots too small for subsistence, and the proportion of male wage-earners in the total workforce began to increase, though they were often seasonally employed and some even leased out their land when casually employed during the peak season when wages were high. Whereas India as a whole was shielded from the Depression by its comparatively small export sector, the great contraction of world trade between 1929 and 1933 had a traumatic impact on the agriculturists of East Bengal. Exports of raw jute fell by a fifth, and of gunny by over half, while raw jute prices crashed by 61 per cent. The real income of the jute- and rice-growing peasantry in the region fell by over a third between 1929 and 1933–4. As a result of indebtedness and distress sales, 1.6 million acres of land transferred hands and holdings became more polarised (Goswami, 1986). The crisis laid bare how externally oriented industrialisation in Bengal had brought dualistic development, not pervasive transformation. Because the growth of secondary employment had not kept pace with demographic expansion, there had been a perceptible shift in the workforce *towards* agriculture and away from manufacturing. By 1939, wage labourers and their families constituted 22.5 per cent of Bengal's agricultural households, and a further 12.2 per cent were sharecroppers whose condition was no better. More than a third of Bengali rural families totally lacked rights in land on the eve of the 1943 famine, while another two-fifths held less than two acres. Agrarian proletarianisation and mass immiseration were virtually synonymous. Wage labourers were responsible for only an eighth of total cultivation, so at least half were redundant workers trapped in the countryside by the slow growth of secondary employment in the towns and the loss of rural craft occupations (Greenhough, 1982, pp. 63–70). Even the better-off cultivating tenants could not escape the vicious circle of population growth, the subdivision of holdings by partible inheritance, and their inefficient parcellisation into scattered strips.

The most serious charge levelled against colonialism in India was that it exacerbated, and could not function without parasitic landlordism. In his famous study of agrarian relations in the making of the modern world, Barrington Moore asked whether the Raj was a landlords' paradise. His subtle and lucid analysis was heavily qualified: the British, he acknowledged, strove to protect tenants and there were vast numbers of impoverished petty landlords. Yet his answer was, basically, yes: 'the main effects of British rule were a shortage of land among the peasants and the emergence of a small, enormously wealthy, and indolent class of landlords' (Moore, 1966, p. 355). The policy of conciliating the traditional agrarian élite in the aftermath of 1857 gives some support to this argument. During the revolt, the talukdar landlords of northern India – who performed scarcely any economic function – had shown they could still command communal loyalties and the government was determined to recognise their rights and status as proprietors of land. The British even legislated to protect them from being sued for debt: in return their property was turned over to managers who undertook to pay arrears and revenue to the government. It was the first explicit legislative admission that the maintenance of status and social stability was more important to the Raj than economic efficiency and entrepreneurial risk-taking (Neale, 1962, pp. 74–5). But when considering the consequences of British rule in the long run, the charge of bolstering 'parasitic landlordism' cannot be sustained: the peasant producing a marketable surplus who farmed his holding with family and (more occasionally) hired labour was the chief beneficiary of British legislation.

'Landlord' is an imprecise term, but students of British agrarian history usually associate it with a large estate-owner, frequently leasing part of his land to businessmen tenants, but also farming on his own account with hired labour and exploiting other assets, such as mineral rights. This 'landlord' was an agrarian capitalist and profit-maximiser. The British signally failed to implant his like in Indian soil. Perhaps the most remarkable finding of revisionist scholarship is that there was precious little change in the concentration of land ownership between 1850 and 1950. Land was very unequally distributed in the early nineteenth century and there was no secular trend towards either the dispossession of smallholders or the emergence of latifundia (Lal, 1988, pp. 165–6). Large-scale commercial agriculture remained very exceptional and usually consisted of expatriate enterprise on the frontier of settlement, such as the Assam tea plantations. Indian farm-holdings had never been large by European standards, and even before population outstripped land supply they tended to diminish and fragment into separate plots – partly under the influence of Hindu and Muslim inheritance law but also, it has been argued, because the colonial state sustained the conditions permitting the widespread access to land that caused fragmentation (Charlesworth, 1992, p. 215). Holdings were too small to achieve significant economies of scale or generate substantial farm incomes, and inevitably undercapitalised and technologically backward: in 1951, wooden ploughs outnumbered iron by 30 to one (Charlesworth, 1982, p. 22). In two-thirds of the agricultural land of north and central India, the typical holding was around 8 acres in 1940. This could maintain a family of five adequately and, well beyond Independence, the family generally remained the principal unit of labour organisation, growing much of its own food. Even in the most thriving districts of the north, the largest category of cultivating holding around 1950 was no more than 40 acres on average (Stokes, 1983, p. 62). Where zamindari rent-collecting rights were heavily concentrated in big 'estates', these often had no physical existence as large land holdings, but were simply bundles of rentier rights over scattered parcels of land. The substantial farms by Indian standards belonged to a peasant élite: in 1947, two-thirds of farmers in the United Provinces were confined to one-fifth of the land, while just over 1 million cultivators, or a mere 9 per cent of the total, occupied as much as 43 per cent, though each cultivated on average only 16 acres. By Western standards, these were smallholders, but in India they were the socially conservative yeomanry who gained most from zamindari abolition after 1947, and proved the principal upholders of the Congress Raj in the countryside.

Rather than securing a landlords' paradise, British rule had succoured 'a mass of petty peasant privilege' (Charlesworth, 1992, p. 215). The political authorities were forced, from the 1850s, to adapt their ideological preferences for a free market in land and a strong landlord class to the requirements of political and social stability. The project of engineering a tenurial revolution by agrarian *laissez-faire* was vitiated by legislation interfering with the rental market wherever it seemed to bear oppressively upon the cultivator. Beginning with legislation applied in Bengal and Bihar in 1859, a series of acts sought to protect tenants in northern and central India by curbing landlords' power of eviction and by increasingly stringent measures of rent control. Tenants' occupancy rights became heritable but not saleable, and some of the powers and profits of ownership were transferred to them. By 1900 any surviving feudal aristocracy had received short shrift. The appearance of authority might persist, but typically at the price of lack of direct control over events on the ground. Restrictions were also placed on the alienation of land to 'non-agricultural castes' – which usually meant urban moneylenders. A prime example was the Punjab Land Alienation Act of 1900, introduced to protect Muslim peasants of the western Punjab (a major recruiting ground for the Indian Army) from economically more successful Hindus and Sikhs. The latter were effectively prohibited from acquiring agricultural land in satisfaction of unpaid debt. At the time, the responsible official commented illuminatingly that it would be extremely dangerous to persist further 'in the principles of free trade in land and the survival of the intellectually fittest' (quoted in Cell, 1992, p. 20).

The land and rental market as the British had originally visualised them did not materialise, because their legislation divorced the ownership of the land from its control, imposed severe conditions on its sale, and limited the influence of market forces on rents. The protected tenant became virtually the owner of the land he tilled with his family, apart from his liability to pay a controlled ground rent. By 1926, when even the former tenant-at-will became a statutory tenant in northern India, the law had almost completely divorced the non-occupying owner of land from control of his land; tenants had become so legally secure in their occupancy as to be transformed into sub-proprietors, though the frequency with which illegal cesses were being exacted in the early twentieth century suggests a certain gap between law and reality (Neale, 1962, pp. 102, 105). Indian rural society was divided not between landlords and tenants (as the West would understand these terms) but between a mass of peasant sub-proprietors confronting absentee owners of a rent charge or ground rent – broadly, the zamindars. In Bengal, site of the Permanent Settlement, the development of a thoroughgoing landlord capitalism had never got off the ground. The dominant tendency from about 1920 was the sharpening of the conflicts between the richer peasants – who now shaded off into the moneylending and trading groups – and the smaller peasants, impoverished smallholders, sharecroppers and labourers (Chatterjee, 1986). As elsewhere in India, the non-cultivating landed proprietors were in eclipse. Their fortunes declined partly because rent increases failed to keep pace with the rise in agricultural prices: in 1840 rents were worth 32 per cent of output in the United Provinces, but only 13 per cent by 1924 (Neale, 1962, p. 164). The commercialisation of agriculture whittled away the roots of zamindari power: the larger, more enterprising cultivators on a zamindar's lands prospered from cotton and tobacco and depended less on him for credit or patronage. The rise of Congress nationalism, which drew its most solid support from the better-off peasants, and the inter-war depression in agriculture, further enfeebled the zamindar class. The lesser rentiers – especially widows, the elderly and infirm – were particularly affected by the 'stickiness' of occupancy tenant rents and legal restrictions, but all non-cultivating proprietors were exposed to more intense political pressure. As part of its civil disobedience campaigns, Congress orchestrated rent and revenue strikes, which led to violent clashes between landlords and tenants. The price fall between 1930 and 1932 threw rent-fixing procedures into still greater disarray: to maintain social order, officialdom waived rent arrears on a massive scale. As the zamindars found their rent increasingly difficult to collect, so they defaulted on the government's revenue demands. The Raj's powers of

collection were now not so very much better than the zamindars'. When
the Congress came to power in the provinces in 1937 with the intention of
abolishing zamindari rights, many zamindars were reconciled to their
fate, but the Second World War postponed the end till 1948 (Kumar,
1983b, p. 228).

If there is a connecting thread in colonial land legislation, it was not
constructing an alliance with landlordism but restricting the social
development of market relations in the countryside. The British feared that
if market competition were let loose, the resulting social conflict would
destroy the Raj's own governing institutions and political security. They
met every crisis by efforts to defend and shore up the agrarian community's
'antique' mode of production. Peasant tenants and landowners were
protected from the consequences of their own indebtedness, and the links
between the land and the money markets were much attenuated. This
protective strategy represented a very strange way for any capitalist state, or
at least a state attached to a capitalist metropolitan base to behave
(Washbrook, 1981, p. 685). Some of its 'natural' allies were alienated by the
cosseting of the rural community and went over to Congress. Many
professional bania groups quit agricultural finance and their roles were
taken over by wealthier peasants. Mercantile capital left for East and South
Africa and South-East Asia. This policy of insulating agrarian society from
market forces went with the state continuing to uphold in its courts the
Hindu personal law that was so inimical to 'Western' possessive
individualism. Astonishingly – to European eyes at least – up to the 1930s
even professional earnings in South India could be legally construed as
joint family property where it could be shown that kin had contributed to
the education of a particular individual. As David Washbrook has argued in
an influential paper, the juridical changes in India under British rule are
extraordinarily difficult to interpret either in terms of modernisation
through the introduction of Western property law (as von Albertini argues:
1982) or as 'pioneering' capitalist transformation (Warren, 1980). Legal
conventions did not move very far or fast to accommodate the social
imperatives of market capitalism. They served at least as much to shore up
pre-capitalist social institutions and rights as they did to pave the way
towards a society based upon individualism and competition. The political
and legal context in which the Raj invited capital to work was not very
conducive to the development of the forces of production. It contained a
series of restrictions on the social competition which, at least in Marxian
theories of economic change, drive forward the revolution in the means of
production (Washbrook, 1981, pp. 674–81).

Conclusions: Colonialism, Modernity and Capitalism in Asia

The impact of British colonialism in India cannot be summarised in terms suggesting either a unidirectional movement towards 'Western' modernity or an accelerated process of capitalist transformation. Modern technologies and institutions were, of course, introduced into India, while expatriate and indigenous capitalists both developed corporate business sectors that began to fuse together between the wars. But in 1947 'modernity' was a thin layer of administration and economic organisation stretched over a pre-industrial civilisation that had somehow absorbed its conquerors and deflected their zeal for change. Ninety years before, Marx had been wrong – but provocatively wrong – about what was happening in India; it was another instance of his exaggerated respect for the capitalist bourgeoisie as an agent of social transformation. He probably assumed that British economic organisation would have primacy in the colonial power structure or somehow 'rule through' the civil bureaucracy and military. If so, he was mistaken. However much racial solidarity and easy social intercourse facilitated the operations of British business interests, the colonial state was never their tool, and proved ill-adapted to enforcing the market imperatives of capitalist development. As B.R. Tomlinson remarks, one fruitful way to write the history of Indian economic development from 1850 onwards is as the story of forces that opposed and frustrated the development of market capitalism. We should avoid an over-simple identification of these forces with the Hindu value system and the supposedly rigid caste hierarchy it supported. There was no single 'Hindu' – and therefore no single Indian – ideological position to shape social behaviour. Traditional values did not constrain Indian entrepreneurship in the Bombay textile industry where economic responses to available technology and factor–price relationships were as 'rational' as those in the West. There are numerous instances of economic cooperation among the jati or regionally based endogamous groups who were the real 'carriers' of the Brahminical ideology of ritual purity. Static, sociological descriptions of the religiously prescribed occupational division of labour do not capture its fluidity over time (Morris, 1967). It is true, nonetheless, that Indian social forces, values and institutions – including but not exclusively those rooted in religion – impacted on and 'indigenised' the colonial power structure. The result was a complex interleaving of the archaic and the traditional with modernity. British rule did not just adapt to Indian cultures and social systems; it reinforced them: by adopting the conventions of Hindu personal law in its courts, by giving legal weight to the obligations to the extended family, by acknowledging the claims of caste status in its revenue assessments, by delineating certain groups as 'martial castes' and others as 'non-agricultural', and in many other ways. Expatriate enterprise was compelled to make adaptations that were parallel to those made in the political and administrative sphere, and had to use Indian intermediaries to extract resources from the domestic economy. Foreign capitalism could never achieve much more because of the efficiency of native merchants and traders, and the sheer paucity of British investment in relation to the total population. Partly as a result, foreign control of the 'commanding heights' of modern enterprise proved surprisingly short-lived. Above all, of course, modernisation and capitalist development were least evident where most Indians lived: on the land. Here, colonialism chose security over development: its officials knew they lacked the power resources to engineer a massive dispossession of the peasantry – and most were too humane to contemplate it. Instead, it entrenched the cultivator's right to use the land, and to bequeath that right to his heirs so solidly that a vast class of petty sub-proprietors was created. This so-called 'peasantisation' of agriculture, and its partial insulation from market forces, can now be perceived as central to the painfully slow economic growth in the subcontinent – but that is the blessing of hindsight. It is hard to see realistic historical alternatives to policies of social conservation for an alien state committed to peace and cheap government. The history of the Indian economy since 1947 has revealed many of the same problems of low productivity and non-developmental social organisation that were apparent in the colonial period.

6

THE ECONOMIC AND SOCIAL CONSEQUENCES OF MODERN COLONIALISM IN AFRICA

Introduction

Did colonialism in Africa act 'as a powerful engine of progressive social change advancing capitalist development far more rapidly than was conceivable in any other way'? (Warren, 1980, p. 9). The litmus test for scholars addressing this question (whether Marxist or non-Marxist) is the emergence of free wage labour employed by profit-maximising entrepreneurs in producing commodities for the market. As with all such tests, dispute arises not so much about the empirical data they yield as the data's significance: in 1960, wage-earners were no more than one-third of the labour force in any sub-Saharan country other than South Africa, and in only one country did they constitute more than 10 per cent of the total population (Harwitz, 1964, p. 16). Some might reasonably cite this as evidence of the speed of economic advance in colonial Africa – particularly after 1945 – given that free wage labour was virtually unknown outside porterage around 1900 and that pre-capitalist relations of production (involving kinship, slavery, pawnship and clientage) were still widespread in native societies until the 1920s (Iliffe, 1983, p. 29). But for others, the data confirm the colonialists' deep-seated reluctance to foster a permanent proletariat, and their preference for types of economic exploitation which 'fossilised' the native smallholder in agriculture, while relying on migrant, contract labour in the towns and mines. Though the British, French and Belgian colonies were experiencing the accelerated growth of a wage-earning class from the 1950s onwards, with a reorientation of labour policy towards the stabilisation of urban workforces, they rested on a great mass of peasant producers only partly involved in the modern economy when they became independent states. In Nigeria, one-twentieth of the labour force was in waged employment at independence, in Ghana a fifth (Munro, 1984, p. 52). When Portuguese Africa became independent in 1975, the evolution of a wage-earning, cash-oriented society was far from complete. An autonomous African agricultural sector had not only survived but had also become more geographically widespread with the extensive internal colonisation during the late colonial period (Newitt, 1981, pp. 134–7).

If there is no immediate, unambiguous answer as to whether colonialism greatly accelerated capitalist development, a similar uncertainty surrounds its impact on African living standards. Mortality rates declined as modern transport facilitated famine relief and colonial states took the first effective measures to control the epidemics that had decimated African populations in the generation before 1920. But whether the colonial peace enabled Africans to eat a little better is debatable. In his revised *African Survey*, Malcolm Hailey recorded that native diets were 'universally poor in quality', with excessive starch food, such as maize, and insufficient protein, mineral salts and vitamins. Poor diet was 'reflected in low standards of health and efficiency'. During the Second World War, about half the so-called able-bodied men selected for conscription in rural Nigeria were unfit for heavy manual labour (Hailey, 1957, p. 1283). Though this did not prove that nutritional standards had declined during the colonial period, the possibility was seriously considered by Hailey, and has been asserted by others since. Jean Suret-Canale has blamed endemic malnutrition in French West Africa on increased production for international markets (Suret-Canale, 1971, p. 297). In the Quelimane district of Mozambique, decades of forced labour – which removed men from the villages at key times of the year – and compulsory cotton-growing created serious food shortages by the 1940s, and a sharp decline in the nutritional value of what could be produced. Cassava had become the basic diet of a region that had once fed itself with maize and millet and exported groundnuts and sesame (Vail and White, 1980, p. 378).

To begin this chapter by posing the stark alternatives of 'progressive' capitalist development versus peasant 'fossilisation', rising living standards versus immiseration, may seem factitious: no empirical assessment of the socio-economic consequences of colonial rule over a vast continent, with all its environmental and climatic variation, could arrive at an 'all-or-nothing' conclusion either way. The *persistence*, over a Biblical lifetime, of traditional techniques and social forms of production in much of tropical Africa would scarcely be surprising, given the low level of investment in agriculture and the virtual exclusion of immigrant capitalist settlers from West Africa, the most populous region. But far-reaching economic *change*, associated primarily with 'the cash crop revolution' that linked peasant producers to foreign markets via the modern transport systems built by the colonialists, would be an essential counterpoint. Similarly, any calculus of the welfare gains and losses resulting from African production for international markets would have to take account of fluctuating terms of trade for different commodities: in certain periods, export producers' prices and incomes rose in relation to consumer imports (1900–13 and 1947–60 were, generally, the most favourable); in others, prices and incomes collapsed (there was a severe and universal decline in West African real incomes during, and immediately after the Second World War, for example) (Hopkins, 1973, pp. 180–3; Berg, 1964, pp. 199–229). Though it would seem that producing for export helped raise incomes in the long run, nobody would deny that there were losers as well as winners, and that progress in raising living and health standards was slow and patchy. A sensible person could predict a 'two-handed' conclusion in advance of the discussion.

Indirect Rule and 'Native Policy'

That there is genuine controversy as to whether colonialism in Africa was, on balance, 'progressive' or 'conservative' will, I trust, become evident. But in focusing on economic processes we cannot ignore the common political context of indirect rule in which they worked. The British practice of ruling through native authorities used to be contrasted with Portuguese authoritarianism and French assimilatory centralisation, but these stereotypes were overdrawn. The dearth of European personnel compelled all colonialists to transmit their demands through carefully chosen political allies. As Governor-General Merlin of Upper Volta acknowledged in 1909, 'In the colonies, it is impossible to practise direct administration . . . Everywhere . . . one must pursue a policy of co-operation and collaboration with the indigenous chiefs' (quoted in Coquery-Vidrovitch, 1988a, p. 91; see also Kiwanuka, 1970). The shortage of administrators led the French to create salariats of tribal chiefs, liable to promotion and demotion, whose job was to transmit orders and supervise their application: tax-collection, the inspection and harvesting of famine crops, bush-clearing to control sleeping sickness, latrine and water-hole digging – these all became responsibilities of chiefs and sub-chiefs, some of whom continued to preside over native courts. In their drive to extract produce from the Congo, the Belgians placed their police force at the chiefs' disposal and made them retrospective annual payments on the basis of the productivity of their territory. Transforming chiefs, whose authority had rested on lineage and sacral or ritual functions, into salaried officials in charge of simple administrative divisions may have 'impersonalised' the chiefly class in African eyes, but it effectively 'veiled' the colonial regimes until the final phase of European rule.

More germane to our concerns is that, in both intention and effect, indirect rule strengthened the chiefs' autocratic authority within tribal structures. Frederick Lugard, who had an unrivalled influence on the ethic of British administration, defined the district officer's task as building up a tribal authority, even where non-existent, and according it legal standing as a bulwark against social chaos. The consistent aim was to maintain and augment the prestige of the native ruler, and encourage his initiative. Through the native court, he was to become the judge and executor of customary law 'provided it is not repugnant to humanity'. 'Backward' Africans at the 'patriarchal' stage of development, where authority was located in the household, had to be hurried into the tribal stage. Small tribes, or sections of a tribe, were to be grouped together so as to form a single administrative unit (Lugard, 1922, pp. 216–18). The practical consequence of these doctrines was that good district officers in romantic revolt from their own industrial society cheerfully upheld petty despots whose dubiously traditional authority was supposedly unsullied by market relations. Thus, Charles Temple saw his duty in Northern Nigeria as 'protecting the virtues of northern aristocratic life and its communal economy from the "barbarising" effects of European capitalism, democracy and individualism'. A colleague identified good government in colonial Africa with 'a reasonable hut tax, the preservation of tribal customs, young men respectful of their elders, proper care of native agriculture' (Pedler, 1973, p. 100; Ehrlich, 1973, p. 652). Except in Southern Rhodesia, European governments were uniformly hostile to African rural capitalism, seeing it not only as socially and politically dangerous but as somehow improper for Africans, like guitars or three-piece suits (Iliffe, 1983, p. 37). Yet, notoriously, chiefs made free use of the authority vested in them to enrich themselves. They exacted labour for their own fields from dependents, and the obligation to provide men for public works routinely occasioned the extortion of 'presents' from those seeking excusal. Corruption – as we would call it - was an organic part of the system of 'indirect rule', especially in Northern Nigeria (Bayart, 1993, p. 71). Wealth and power accumulated in African societies, but in a segregated institutional context which obliged indigenous entrepreneurs to work with the grain of 'tribalised' authority. Free markets in labour and land, open access to public office and positive law, would have undermined the 'decentralised despotisms' that were the solid foundation of indirect rule, and which persist in much of rural Africa (Mamdani, 1996, ch. 2).

'Settler' and 'Peasant' Regimes

African colonial economies were embedded in a variety of political forms, but we can draw a basic analytic distinction between 'étatiste–peasant' regimes and 'regimes of competitive exploitation'. (The terms are borrowed from Austen, 1987, chs 6 and 7.) In the first, a European bureaucracy were the ultimate rulers of native smallholders who continued to control most production, whether of subsistence agriculture or of export crops, although expatriate firms dominated import–export trade. In the second, white settlers, backed by the authority of the colonial state, competed with African farmers for land, labour and political influence. Racial restrictions on the occupational movement of labour became the norm in settler colonies and differential prices for European and African agricultural produce were common. The distinction roughly corresponds to that between 'external' colonialism (with political control and the dominant economic interests impinging on the colony from outside) and 'internal' colonialism (where the political and economic power of white minorities worked from within).

South Africa exhibited the purest form of competitive exploitation, where the alienation of native land went to extreme lengths and, though not a colonial economy in constitutional terms, cannot be ignored in this discussion. Institutions and practices developed there to secure white domination were hugely influential wherever Europeans settled in Central and East Africa, and it blazed a trail to decolonisation that many hoped to follow. The legislative cornerstone of territorial segregation in the Union was the Natives' Land Act of 1913, which created a racial monopoly of the best land and, by outlawing African squatters and sharecroppers from white-owned land, sought to drive black men into poorly paid dependent labour while their families subsisted on the native reserves. Independent black farmers were finally eliminated from market agriculture, which was wholly 'Europeanised'. The Act was a 'model' for Southern Rhodesia's white settlers when they achieved internal self-government in 1923. Similarly, the industrial 'colour bar' on the Rand – legally defined by Union legislation from 1911 onwards – was imitated in the Northern Rhodesian copper belt.

In more abstract terms, the Union's experience bears on our concerns because from it has been abstracted an 'ideal type' of how capitalism has combined with anterior modes of production in modern Africa. The term used – 'tributary articulation' – denotes the linking of the centres of capitalist growth with the subsistence communities of the 'native reserves' through the more or less coerced flow of male migrant labour to the mines and white commercial agriculture. As an analytic tool for disclosing the mechanisms of 'internal' colonialism in Central and Southern Africa, and for understanding the dynamics of rural impoverishment, the concept remains useful. But there is a danger of over-generalising from the Union's experience, which was unique in three respects: the state's coercive power was unequivocally derived from the representative politics of local white society (whose class and national conflicts were at best composed at the expense of blacks); South Africa's gold meant that white farmers could, in effect, be subsidised; and South Africa had the power and the political reasons to constrict African homelands to the supply of tributary labour and, critically, the financial resources with which to ignore the economic consequences (Lonsdale, 1981). Because these conditions were not reproduced further north, the imitations of South Africa's political economy were necessarily imperfect copies.

Land alienation in Southern Rhodesia mirrored South African experience in being designed both to secure a settlers' monopoly of the best land and to destroy independent black farmers who competed with them in the market economy and 'blocked' the emergence of a waged labour force. African market farming in the colony flourished from about 1900 in response to the influx of mining enterprise and railway-building. In 1903, black farmers earned around £350 000 from grain and livestock sales, and over the next twenty years, the number of African-owned cattle rose seven-fold, partly because of investments in ox-drawn ploughs and carts (Arrighi, 1970, p. 214). The high price paid for their produce and the lack of population pressure on land made black farmers reluctant to enter the labour market. They had lower labour costs and were generally as productive per acre as white settlers, so the competition they presented could only be met by political means. As more European settlers were attracted to the colony, white farmers led a clamour for 'segregation' which would exclude African landowners (though not labourers and rent-paying tenants) from designated areas. Before its dissolution in 1923, the Chartered administration had already alienated to about 3000 white farmers 32 per cent of all the land and enacted 'Masters and Servants' legislation that criminalised a migrant worker's desertion (Gann and Duignan, 1971, p. 106). Having achieved direct control over internal government, the settlers brought in the Land Apportionment Act 1930, reserving just over half the territory's land for white settlement, about a fifth for tribal reservations where land was held under communal tenure, and designating less than a tenth as open to individual African purchasers. African squatters and sharecropping tenants were prohibited in the white areas. Agricultural policies adopted during the Depression discriminated harshly against African participation in the produce market: state monopoly marketing of maize, for example, introduced a two-price system which protected the white farmer and penalised the black. Nevertheless, whites were too few to take over all commercial agriculture and the regime was unable to engineer the comprehensive Europeanisation of farming on South African lines. Equally, the Shona and Ndebele were so doggedly resistant to leaving the land that immigrants from other territories were between half and two-thirds of the colony's wage labour force up to the 1950s. Territorial segregation was economically dysfunctional as well as morally despicable. It created artificially swollen populations and land scarcity in the reserves, which experienced ecological deterioration from overstocking of pastures and deep-ploughing of thin topsoils. Meanwhile, much of the land from which Africans had been excluded lay idle (Palmer, 1977, p. 242).

Distant Kenya was in some ways the most northerly extension of the South African frontier, for the Union's pass laws and native reserves were consciously imitated, and Indian immigrants excluded from areas of designated white settlement (Bennett, 1971, pp. 60–4). Europeans formed a wafer-thin stratum of landowners, urban and rural capitalists and professionals. There was no economic space for unskilled and semi-skilled white immigrants because the presence of African labour power drove down the market price of white labour, and Asian artisans and small traders were unbeatable competitors. The economic structure was grossly distorted by the alienation of land to white settlers and an elaborate system of economic discrimination on their behalf. By 1939, about 6 million acres of the highlands were, theoretically, occupied by less than 3 thousand settlers who had paid nominal prices to the colonial administration. Since they were far too few to exploit this vast area profitably, Africans had to be compelled to work white farms for wages that were considerably lower than their returns from growing the same crops on their own land. African 'squatters' with plots on land purchased by Europeans were one source of labour: the Resident Labourers' Ordinance 1918 converted them into colonial serfs, bound to work for the owners of their plots for a minimum of 180 days a year. More importantly, in terms of the total labour supply, high rates of taxation compelled African men to enter the money economy as seasonal contract workers. By the mid-1920s, more than half the able-bodied men in the Kikuyu and Luo tribes were seasonally employed by Europeans and, according to Colin Leys, three quarters of their cash wages were absorbed by direct and indirect taxation (Leys, 1975, p. 32). The Masters and Servants Ordinance bound the worker to serve out his contract on pain of imprisonment. White farmers were able to weather the Depression partly because their workers' real wages declined sharply. From the mid 1920s to the late 1940s, settlers exerted an influence on official policy, through committees of the legislative council, quite disproportionate to their numbers. That white 'mixed' farms were of vital economic importance became an article of faith in official circles, and they were truly pampered by the state. In response to the Depression, marketing and regulatory boards under settler control used their sweeping powers over domestic and external trade to protect white farmers' prices. Public subsidies, rebates and the Land Bank were introduced to help settlers diversify their crops, and control arrangements implemented to give them a monopoly of the domestic food market. Investment in roads and railways was channelled into the settler highlands on a liberal scale, while very little support was given to African food-producers (ibid., p. 35). Although Africans paid the bulk of taxation, virtually the entire benefit of government services (railways, schools) went to the Europeans. The prices white farmers obtained for their produce within Kenya were subsidised by the customs tariff (especially after its revision in 1923) and they had privileged access to profitable markets Uganda and Tanganyika (Brett, 1973). Under common currency arrangements, the large gap between Kenyan imports and exports was financed by its neighbours' trade surpluses. The railway rates charged for Ugandan cotton exports helped to subsidise the specially low rates enjoyed by settler maize exports. African farmers were, meanwhile, virtually excluded from export production. Down to 1912–13, they had accounted for at least 70 per cent of exports. By 1928, their proportion had fallen to less than 20 per cent, and from 1925 the absolute value of African export production declined as the 'reserves' relapsed into subsistence farming to support expanding populations. Africans were denied a major market opportunity by being prevented from growing coffee on a significant scale and, until the mid 1950s the purchasing power of the great majority was kept as low as possible.

Étatiste–peasant regimes in their purest form were located between Senegal and Nigeria, and the petty producer character of West African economies was all the more marked because mining never had as much impact there during the colonial period as it did in the south. The foreign-trade multiplier was stronger and the capacity for structural change greater than in those regions where enclave production predominated. Since the European population was small and transient, racial conflict was minimised and the political struggle at the close of the colonial era was on the whole orderly and evolutionary. These regimes gave freest play to endogenous enterprise and economic forces, and presided over a trajectory of development broadly continuous with the pre-colonial economy. As Hopkins has argued, colonial rule in West Africa did not create modernity out of backwardness by suddenly disrupting a traditional state of low-level equilibrium:

> On the contrary, the nature and pace of economic development in the early colonial period can be understood only when it is realised that the main function of the new rulers was to give impetus to a process which was already under way (Hopkins, 1973, p. 235).

Discontinuity was far more pronounced in the Congo basin of Central-West Africa, where severe demographic losses during the partition and the brutalities of the concessionary companies had pulverised native polities and the colonial state stepped into a political void. In this vast, underpopulated region there was considerable uniformity and comparability of experience during the high colonial period: labour coercion, especially for road- and railway-building, compulsory crop-planting, and low investment of risk capital outside mining were the basic features of the colonial economy whether the formal rulers were French, Belgian or Portuguese. The most 'étatiste' regime in the region – and in colonial Africa as a whole – was that imposed on the Belgian Congo after 1908. The colonial government participated in the promotion of industrial undertakings on an unparalleled scale and was instrumental in shifting the economy from its 'gathering' phase to mineral exploitation and the cultivation of palm products and cotton. During the 1920s, rural Congolese producers were able to enter a free agricultural market created by the needs of the mining enclaves, but conditions changed profoundly with the economic crisis at the end of the decade. In 1928, the administration began to plan the exploitation of rural societies in a systematic way, seeking to compensate for declining mineral exports by increased agricultural exports. The area under cotton, which most Africans would cultivate only under fiscal compulsion, was greatly extended, and exports of ginned cotton rose from about 2000 tonnes in the early 1920s to over 30 000 during the later 1930s (Harwitz, 1964, Table 2.7, p. 35). The processing and marketing of agricultural products became the monopoly of European companies to whom peasants were forced to sell cash-crops for sale at fixed prices under threat of flogging and imprisonment. The administration intervened closely in the rural economy, partly to release African men for employment elsewhere: cassava planting, for example, was encouraged and often imposed because its cultivation required minimal field labour. Shifting patterns of agriculture were modified and rural societies transformed into vast work camps rationally managed to meet exterior needs. Fiscal devices drove people to sell agricultural goods and labour at any price, and effectively eliminated the nominal freedom to sell one's harvest. The bureaucratic control of village agriculture became still stricter during the 1950s, with a system of land apportionment to peasant families who were required to follow a pre-established crop rotation. The state sponsored cooperatives to cultivate African perennials such as palm products, coffee and hevea rubber for processing by local European entrepreneurs (Jewsiewicki, 1983, p. 101).

Abortive Late 'Settlement' in Portuguese Africa

The distinctions between 'peasant' and 'settler' economies were, to some extent dynamic, for metropolitan policy modified the economic character of colonial territories over time. The attempted transformation of Portuguese Africa into white settler colonies came late in the day: the territories' 72 800 white inhabitants in 1940 (who included transient officials, military personnel and convicts) testified to the comparative failure of a century's continuous effort to promote European immigration. The overwhelming majority of Portuguese emigrants had left for South America; Brazil alone received 1.5 million between 1850 and 1950. It was partly to compensate for this haemorrhaging of population that both the late-nineteenth-century monarchy and the republic sponsored migration to Africa. Colonists were to be attracted by free grants of land, remission of taxation, free tools and other subsidies. What was envisaged was 'a new Brazil', organically tied to the mother country, which would absorb Portugal's excess population and in rather unspecified ways promote metropolitan development (Newitt, 1981, pp. 152–3).

As it transpired, the white rural settlement planned by Salazarist bureaucrats was more of a nightmare than a coherent reality, partly because Angola (the favoured destination for agricultural colonists) lacked the requisite infrastructure for most of the colonial period. The long-projected Benguela Railway was completed only in 1929, and as late as 1953 a country twice the size of France boasted a mere 53 miles of asphalted roads. Furthermore, the typical settler was barely educated, unskilled and without capital. He tended to believe that 'only blacks should work in Africa' and his reliance on government handouts made him more of a state pensioner than an independent farmer. In the interior of Angola, settlers often lived in total misery, begging for food from neighbouring Africans. The tiny, generally unstable and impoverished *colono* population had impinged little on African rural society before the 1950s, and contributed an infinitesimally small percentage to gross agricultural production. Most gravitated to unskilled urban jobs, with the result that in 1950 less than 10 per cent of the active white male population were working in agriculture. Even though the post-war coffee boom generated a scramble for land in the north and the forcible expulsion of Africans from their holdings, the regions where Europeans competed for land were a mere fraction of the territory. In 1960, 97.3 per cent of the land was either vacant or in African hands (ibid., p. 103). European colonisation under the government settlement agency made a trifling impact: as late as 1968, it could claim only 840 *colonos* within its planned settlement programme in rural Angola, among a total population of more than 6 million (Bender, 1978, pp. 100–3). Large-scale physical dislocation of Africans from their home lands to accommodate white settlers did not occur until the last years of the colonial regime, with the creation of subsidised settlement colonies (colonatos) in the Central Highlands. Remarkably, in the early 1970s there were more European requests for land than at any other time in Angolan history (ibid., p. 149).

By far the most numerous colonists in twentieth-century Angola were Africans taking advantage of the colonial *pax* to move into vacant land. Improvements in communications made possible the commercial farming of remoter inland areas by African smallholders, a process best documented in the case of the Ovimbundu after about 1920. They moved south and east into thinly populated or unoccupied land, establishing small family farms where maize and coffee were grown for the market. By the 1930s, the Ovimbundu had colonised vast tracts that were unsettled at the time of the pacification, and had greatly extended the area of Angola which was 'theirs'. Similar processes took place in Guiné and Mozambique, and indeed throughout much of colonial Africa. What we can call the 'peasantisation' of Angola's economy accentuated in the late colonial period, notwithstanding international investment in the mining and plantation sectors: despite a 15 per cent increase in the African population, the number of rural wage-earners *fell* from 314 543 to 241 351 between 1950 and 1964, when 87 per cent of the labour force worked on their own account (Newitt, 1981, p. 135).

The 'Cash Crop Revolution' and 'Incomplete' Capitalist Development

The phrase 'cash crop revolution' can deceive. Around 1960, as the colonial era closed, African farmers devoted a much larger proportion of their resources to subsistence than cash crops. About 70 per cent of the total cultivated land and 60 per cent of total adult male labour in tropical Africa were still utilised in subsistence production (Myint, 1973, p. 37; Adedeji, 1986, p. 211). Nevertheless, the *dynamic* economic experience of Africa's smallholders in the colonial era was the voluntary investment in crops for final sale in distant markets, both overseas and in the new urban and mining centres. Though its origins lay in nineteenth-century 'legitimate trade', colonialism gave export production a great impetus, especially in the 'peasant' economies. With the notable exception of palm products, the quantum of peasant exports rose at least ten-fold between 1905 and 1955 – an increase far outstripping population growth (Harwitz, 1964, p. 16). It was dynamic because it induced innovation in land use and the social pattern - though the overall trajectory of change has been much contested by scholars of different theoretical persuasions. All would agree that what made the cash crop revolution possible was a reallocation of labour between the sexes, and greater regional specialisation. In pre-colonial Africa, men felled trees and cleared the ground, but normally left hoe agriculture to women. Because of chronic political insecurity, the lives of older African males revolved around military, ritual and judicial functions, functions which colonialism did without. Their labour was underutilised in pre-colonial Africa, and this 'spare capacity' was still being tapped in the 1930s, though a new sexual division often incorporated customary notions of male and female 'spheres'. In Kenya, for example, ox-ploughs were bought by men, and each roughly doubled a cultivator's tillage. But the plough did not replace or supplement a woman's hoe labour; it was worked alongside her on separate areas of land, whose produce the male household head appropriated for his own use (Kitching, 1980, pp. 14–25, 51).

In the analytic model informing liberal interpretations, trade acts as a 'vent for surplus' in economies where factors of production were not utilised for want of a market. The model has been much criticised for overlooking the fiscal and physical coercion behind much cash cropping and for not differentiating between ecological regions in terms of the ease with which cash crops could be introduced (Tosh, 1980). Coffee and cocoa adapted easily to the lengthy growing season in humid forest areas where staple foods were root vegetables requiring little labour. Cash cropping posed no threat to food production, and in the cocoa-and-coffee belt of West Africa and the cotton-and-coffee zone on the northern and western sides of Lake Victoria, men quickly turned their energies to export agriculture with little prompting from the government. A desire for cash income was widespread: it enabled Africans to pay their tax and to satisfy their 'new wants' (for permanent roofing materials, bicycles, sewing machines) with the least disruption to their way of life (Wrigley, 1986, p. 126). Agriculture was and is much more intensive in the short growing season of the savanna, where the vent-for-surplus model has more limited application. Ecological conditions frequently required a diversion of resources from subsistence if cash crops were to be cultivated, and this caused serious social strain. Diets often deteriorated in quality because cassava was substituted for labour-intensive grains. Rain-grown cotton, in particular, placed a heavy burden on an already an exacting working routine, and would usually be grown only under sustained administrative compulsion and with a miserably low return. Colonial Chad provides a glaring example, though the same misguided attempt to impose cotton on the 'coping' pattern of life in the Sahel continued after independence under the guise of Franco-Chadian cooperation.

But this qualifies the model that I think remains indispensable in explaining both the extent of change and the limits to it. African smallholders had very modest durable capital equipment, rarely resorted to employing wage-labour, and called on few if any outside resources. The expansion in export quantities was achieved with few major improvements in agricultural technique (ox-ploughing was the most important) and without significantly reducing the amount of land and time involved in producing for subsistence or for internal trade. Usually, subsistence and export cropping expanded simultaneously; in Uganda, for example, the area under cotton increased about eleven times between 1918 and 1950, and the area under subsistence food crops about seven times. Those instances where export crops came to be cultivated at the expense of foodstuffs were exceptional: in Senegal, concentration on groundnuts was such that locally grown grains were insufficient and large quantities of rice had to be imported from the 1930s onwards. Dahomey was gradually transformed during the colonial era from a net exporter of foodstuffs to a net importer (Manning, 1982, p. 240). But Africa as a whole entered the post-colonial age self-sufficient in foodstuffs, and even exported a small surplus.

A more fundamental critique of the *économie de traite* of French tropical Africa, levelled by the respected Marxist, Jean Suret-Canale, is that it impoverished the peasantry and 'blocked' technical and structural change: the oligopoly of European trading firms in control of foreign trade paid so little for peasant produce and sold European goods (cloth, hardware, processed foodstuffs) so dear that the transaction 'drained' off all surplus wealth, leaving nothing for saving and investment (Suret-Canale, 1971, pp. 159–67). The analysis of their trading accounts confirms that profitability came from the 'mark up' on buying and selling in many small quantities: the net rates of profit in relation to turnover of the Campagnie Française d'Afrique Occidentale fluctuated around 15 and 30 per cent in the 1920s, a much higher return than could be obtained in the French economy (Coquery-Vidrovitch, 1975, p. 598). Suret-Canale argues that export prices were too low for wage labour to be profitably employed in agriculture, and capitalist accumulation through the surplus value created by labour could not begin. In 1936, wage-earners in French West Africa numbered 167 000 (scarcely 1 per cent of the population) and were mostly employed in transport. The commercial companies themselves invested negligible amounts in agricultural production, and greatly increased output was achieved simply by extending the area under cultivation and by longer and more intense labour using traditional methods. Commerce, he asserts, extracted more than surplus produce; it took part of the produce required for natural growth, and reduced the producer to penury. 'Monopoly, mercantilism, parasitism, stagnation: these were the main features of French colonialism in tropical Africa' (Suret-Canale, 1971, p. 160).

This pessimism is not easy to square with the assessment of West Africa's 'open economy' in Hopkins's classic economic history, written from a liberal perspective. Admittedly, the French colonies were poorer and less populous. They accounted for only a quarter of West Africa's total trade and attracted only one-fifth of total investment up the late 1930s (Frankel, 1938, Table 28). Barter, which disadvantaged the African producer, survived longer in the French Federation. But it could be argued that what was impoverishing was the narrow and 'primitive' character of French colonial trade, rather than international trade in itself. The business decisions of French firms rather bear this out. They expanded into the Gold Coast cocoa trade, and Nigerian palm products and tin, between the wars. The competition was sharper, so profit margins must have been smaller, but there was far more trade to be done in colonies that had attained a more advanced stage of development and which produced and consumed more. Hopkins charts several reversals in the native producers' barter terms of trade – with fluctuations around a falling trend from 1913 to 1945, and then a recovery between 1945 and 1960 – but concludes they gained considerably from participating in international commerce, though the benefits were unevenly distributed, both geographically and socially. Africans' income terms of trade tended to move upwards, as is shown by the increase in per capita imports. By 1960, West Africa's total import-purchasing power was about four times what it had been in 1900; allowing for a two-fold population growth, average import-purchasing capacity approximately doubled. It was those areas *outside* the ambit of international commerce (such Mauritania or the area around Lake Chad) that probably suffered an absolute fall in living standards (Hopkins, 1973, p. 183).

A more difficult issue than whether foreign trade impoverishes is why economic growth led by peasant exports encountered definite limits to sustained development. By common consent, the Gold Coast cocoa industry provides the most impressive illustration of vent-for-surplus theory, but also demonstrates 'incomplete' capitalist transformation. No Africans elected to enter the money economy more rapidly and with such large sums available for spending as the Akwapim cocoa-farmers. In response solely to market incentives, they migrated into thinly inhabited forest lands where tens of millions of trees, each requiring about seven years to mature, were planted annually. Cocoa exports were worth only £500 in 1895, but by 1900 were valued at £27 000 and on the eve of the First World War, £2.49 million. The farmers created much of their own infrastructure by building roads, and also employed migrant and seasonal labour on a considerable scale. The labour intake of the industry, excluding transport, rose from 100 000 labour days in 1891 to 37 million in 1911 (Hill, 1963; Hogendorn, 1973, pp. 305–22). They bear comparison with rural entrepreneurs in any frontier society.

Inland freight rates fell twelve-fold between 1909 and 1930, thereby effecting a critical external economy for primary producers. Production became profitable over a wider area and the scarce labour of head-carriers was released for other employment. Food output comfortably matched demographic growth, and the economic gains from world market participation were widely diffused. In one village studied by a District Agricultural Officer, about two-thirds of the average family income (nearly £22 in all) came from the sale of cocoa – which meant prosperity by rural African or Indian standards. Paradoxically, however, collective and individual indebtedness had accompanied economic progress, and the village creditors formed a circle of *rentier* capitalists gaining an increasing lien over the cocoa produced by their debtors (Hancock, 1942, pp. 275–84, summarising the study of W.H. Beckett). The 'multiplier' effect of the industry was 'patent to the eye' in the larger towns where, according to Keith Hancock,

> Whole streets are occupied by African tailors with their sewing machines, or by shoe-makers or tinsmiths: there are general retailers and provision merchants and porters and boatmen and clerks, all pursuing their specialised tasks and making a living by satisfying the diverse demands which originate in the sale of cocoa overseas (ibid., p. 274).

In a longer perspective, the relations between trade and internal development appear much more ambiguous than they did to Hancock, for independent Ghana inherited an 'undiversified' economic structure dominated by monocrop exporting and exposed to unstable and usually declining terms of trade for cocoa. Foreign trade accounted for 58 per cent of GDP in 1960 (as opposed to 38 per cent in 1911) and cocoa provided 54 per cent of total exports in 1960 (as against 45 per cent in 1911). The wealth generated by cocoa had stimulated local manufacturing only to a small degree, as is indicated by the high proportion of imports (71 per cent) destined for final demand uses in 1960. (The comparable figure in 1911 had been 91 per cent.) The domestic economy remained fragmented and compartmentalised, with a poorly articulated price system and persistently localised markets. Production factors did not move easily into entrepreneurial activities outside cocoa farming, and the 'carry-over' effects of the industry on the so-called learning rate of the economy had been inhibited. Around 1950, over half the labour and land were still utilised in subsistence agriculture which market institutions had touched only superficially (Meier, 1973, pp. 450–52). The extension of cocoa cultivation had been essentially a widening process, with more labour being applied to more land, but without a significant increase in productivity through technical innovations. Moreover, because of easy access to land and the simple technology required, cocoa farming provided an ideal environment for the petty entrepreneur relying mostly on his own and family labour. Between about 1900 and 1930, wage labour was widely employed on a piecework and contract basis, and about 200 000 annual migrants from outside the colony were employed in the 1950s. But the dominant trend was towards sharecropping, the least profitable form of labour exploitation, though the easiest to supervise and finance. Sharecroppers themselves expected to become independent farmers. The ratio of family labour to hired labour in cocoa cultivation was reckoned, in 1950, to be about 5:1. In short, cocoa-farming was 'capitalistic' in that it promoted saving and long-term investment in a production cycle, but it did not give rise to a capitalist class.

Had the nexus of public and private institutions constituting the colonial 'establishment' restricted autonomous development, as proponents of the 'underdevelopmentalist' paradigm have argued? (Kay, 1972, pp. 3–37). No legal obstacles had been placed in the way of rural enterprise: by not exercising sovereign right to vacant land, nor making it available to European planters, the state had allowed tenure arrangements in the cocoa villages to evolve out of traditional practice. Asante, in which slave labour was extensively used in agriculture, would have been a less benign political environment for the cocoa planters. Agreed, the mental horizons of British rule were bounded by the liberal nostrums of the 'night-watchman' state until the Second World War opened a new era of state intervention. Government revenue was raised largely from customs duties for the greater part of the colonial period; nearly half went on the salaries and pensions of expatriate officials, and the funds available for government economic departments, such as agriculture and forestry, were minute (ibid., p. 192). The colonial government was generally hostile to industrialisation before the 1940s – for an urbanised working class was equated with political disaffection – and preferred to import skilled manpower rather than develop human resources. Inevitably, the Royal Commission on Higher Education in West Africa (1945) reported startling shortages of trained personnel in education, medicine, agriculture, industry, commerce and administration (Hailey, 1957, p. 1231). Not until the 1951 Development Plan, and the inauguration of responsible self-government, were substantial public resources devoted to education. Until then, the impressive increases in primary school enrolment were the work of mission schools that had long been staffed by Africans. The administration's orthodox monetary policy – implemented through the West African Currency Board – served expatriate trading interests rather than the domestic economy. The locally issued currency was held at parity with and readily convertible to sterling, but the total money supply in the colony was strictly tied to export earnings. This resulted in price fluctuations in the world market being transmitted automatically to the domestic economy. The British banks operating in British West Africa proved 'very efficient and reliable lubricators of Africa's international exchanges, but not equipped to act as agents of its internal development'. They found it hard to discern suitable opportunities for local investment, and most of the funds entrusted to them by the colonial government and expatriate businesses were transferred to London (Wrigley, 1986, p. 120).

These limitations notwithstanding, the notion of the classic colonial state as an 'incubus' is easily over-drawn. Civil peace, honest administration and sound money appear solid achievements in the light of disastrous economic mismanagement in independent Ghana. More restrictive of native enterprise was the dominant position of European companies in international trade, and the success of Levantine and Asian immigrants in occupying intermediary positions in the domestic economy, which relegated Africans to a minor role as unorganised petty traders. Doubtless, without the expatriate firms there would have been less investment in commerce and a much smaller foreign trade sector, but they were overloaded with costly European managers whose cautious business practices contributed little to local economic development before the run-up to independence. The United Africa Company, which conducted nearly half of West Africa's foreign trade, had virtually no industrial interests in West (or East) Africa in 1945. The firms restricted competition by agreeing not to bid up the price of cocoa and allocating the crop among themselves according to fixed proportions – a 'pool' system bitterly resented by farmers. In retailing, the firms could not compete with Levantine traders operating on smaller profit margins in conditions European employees would have found intolerable, and in the 1940s had to give ground in international trade too. By independence, the Levantine community numbering about 1370 was responsible for two-fifths of the country's imports (Hailey, 1957, p. 412). There was considerable Levantine investment in houses and land, and a few firms combined moneylending with commerce, thereby profiting from the habitual caution of the European banks when it came to advancing credit to African entrepreneurs.

What poses the most difficult problem of historical judgement is the legacy, not of the 'open economy', but of late colonial neo-mercantilism. The British government purchased the entire cocoa crop on the outbreak of war, partly to provide farmers cut off from their normal market with some income, and instituted other emergency measures with the aim of conserving dollars. Few of these controls were relinquished after 1945 when Britain's commitment to colonial development provided further justification for state economic management. Purchasing boards for the major crops were set up in 1947–9, and a range of measures restricted the free operation of the market in the years preceding independence: import licensing, large-scale subsidies to certain activities and enterprises, restrictions on employment, and even minimum wages (Bauer, 1973, pp. 644–5). The liberal economist, Peter Bauer, condemned these measures for restricting the movement of labour and commodities and slowing down the spread of the exchange economy. Even more damaging to long-term development, he argued, was the fact that state-controlled marketing became a mechanism for penally taxing primary producers, one eagerly seized upon by nationalist politicians to accumulate development capital, acquire private wealth and reward political supporters. Taxation and corruption helped to reduce the real prices paid to cocoa-growers by about 93 per cent between 1957 and 1983 (Iliffe, 1995, p. 254). Though not personally corrupt, Kwame Nkrumah used the accumulated funds of the Cocoa Purchasing Board as the financial basis of his political operations and allowed his associates to profit from the control of public office and institutions in a way that became commonplace in post-colonial Africa. Ghana has belonged to the long list of African states that can, without exaggeration, be described as kleptocracies (Bayart, 1993, p. 88).

But behind a degree of institutional continuity between the late colonial state and independent Ghana lay an African determination to break decisively with the past. Nkrumah believed that private enterprise was incapable of modernising Ghana at the breakneck speed he envisaged, and in mid-1960 engineered a clear change in economic direction involving massive expansion of the public sector and discrimination against private entrepreneurs, both domestic and foreign. The state borrowed to finance development on a scale the colonial authorities would not have permitted and the productive economy became burdened with ruinously inefficient public enterprises (Iliffe, 1983, pp. 77–8). Ghana's reckless experiment with state socialism was scarcely a linear development from late colonial neo-mercantilism.

Mining and Economic 'Dualism'

Cutting across our broad classification between 'peasant' and 'settler' colonies is a further distinction – already familiar from the discussion of the chartered and concessionary regimes of Central Africa – between mining enclaves that acted as 'poles' of capital-intensive enterprise, and their hinterlands (sometimes under a different sovereign power). Mining was the principal matrix for the transfer of advanced technology, technical skills and the wage labour system from the industrialised societies, and attracted more than two-thirds of foreign investment (Katzenellenbogen, 1973, pp. 360–425). Outside South Africa, the secondary impact of mining on labour catchment and food supply areas made it more disruptive of the existing economic and social pattern than European agriculture, but it did little to foster wider economic development. This was partly a matter of scale: in 1939, the Transvaal gold mines alone employed twice the workforce of the combined Belgian Congo and Northern Rhodesian mining zones. More important, however, was the nature of the colonial political economy. The colonies' primary function was to provide their metropoles with markets for manufactures and furnish raw materials, and colonial policy restricted mining's forward and backward linkages to rest of the economy. Moreover, access to mineral deposits was granted to mining companies on very easy terms and they paid peppercorn rents to colonial governments, with the result that only a tiny fraction of the product of mining enterprise was recirculated in the local economy. The contrast with South Africa is instructive: there political forces were strong enough to extract substantial mineral rents, and a national industrial policy was adopted by the dominant coalition from the mid-1920s. As a consequence, mining ceased to be an 'enclave' and began to act as the leading sector in the economy.

For Hailey, Northern Rhodesia, 'provide[d] the most striking example of the geographical limitations of economic development based on mining' (Hailey, 1957, p. 1317). American and South African firms had led a spectacular expansion of copper mining during the 1930s, and their influence in the colonial political economy had eclipsed that of the relatively few white settlers. A formal industrial colour bar, intended to restrict the African work force to migratory unskilled labour, had been added to the apparatus of colonialism. The colony's transport system functioned according to the copper industry's requirements: the only railway joined the northern Copperbelt to its southern outlet, and facilitated the influx of cheaper food from Southern Rhodesian farms. The handful of modern townships and few stretches of macadamised roads clustered along the railway line. A narrow belt of country beside the line was the only significant source of African cash crops, and native commercial farming was further inhibited by the fact that white settlers controlled the most fertile areas with the best transport connections. Hailey found that

> Away from the railway belt, in the outer provinces where the bulk of the African population lives and a low subsistence level of production prevails, the pace of development is all the slower because the best of the labour force has been attracted to the centres of industry (ibid.).

The sheer moderation of this observation brings out the parasitic character of enclave development all the more effectively.

The Belgian Congo was somewhat exceptional because the metropolitan economy was too small to benefit from a colonial dependency of the classic type. As a specialised exporter of machinery, Belgium was better served by providing the capital goods for expatriate light industry in the Congo, for which a market lay in the concentrated populations of relatively well-paid workers in the mining enclaves. Even so, in 1939 industrial output in the Congo still accounted for a tiny proportion of 'modern' economic activity. Import-substituting industrialisation was boosted after 1945 by policies favouring European settlement which extended the market for consumer manufactures and processed food and drink. By the end of the 1950s the total value of industrial output was equivalent to 43 per cent of the colony's mineral exports and local industry satisfied more than two-fifths of consumer goods demand (Peemans, 1973, pp. 186, 193; Austen, 1987, p. 183). How far the mining and industrial sector had transcended its 'enclave' character on the eve of decolonisation is debatable: some regard the linkages with the rural hinterlands and traditional agriculture – which still occupied the great majority – as very tenuous. In this view, the rural poor remained the 'leftovers' of colonial growth, with life chances and health status far inferior to those working in the European sector (Vellut, 1983, pp. 151–52). Jean Stengers agrees that striking improvements in urban living standards had not been matched in the countryside before 1947–8, but argues that a widening circle of Congolese benefited from economic growth thereafter. African expenditure on consumption goods rose by three-quarters between 1950 and 1957. There had only been 50 000 bicycles in the colony in 1946; ten years later there were 700 000. The peasantry who represented about three-quarters of the population still obtained only 28 per cent of national income, but their deprivation relative to urban wage-earners was becoming less marked (Stengers, 1989, p. 189).

Rather than generalised development, mining in colonial Africa is associated with economic 'dualism', or the cohabitation in one society or region of a modern, industrialised money economy with the traditional agrarian subsistence economy. As a descriptive term, 'dualism' is unexceptionable but controversy has raged around applying W.A. Lewis's explanatory model of 'dualist' development to African colonial history. The nub of the argument is whether dualism was a 'natural' state progressively *reduced* by market forces or whether capitalist development, aided by the political force of the colonising power, actually intensified dualist disparities. From the 1960s, Africanists – taking their cue from the 'dependency' school – began to argue that 'underdevelopment' was generated by the articulation of subsistence agriculture in the reserves with the mining industry. In Africa's traditional pattern of shifting agriculture, men's labour regularly cleared the bush and broke new ground; without them, agricultural productivity fell and nutritional levels declined. The labour 'tribute' rendered to capitalist mining resulted – so it has been argued – in chronic malnutrition and rural immiseration in the labour-supply areas where women and children subsisted on stagnant agriculture (see the editors' introduction to Palmer and Parsons, 1977).

Case studies of rural impoverishment confirm the reality of this process, but we must question whether it was an ineluctable part of 'dualist' development. No colony contributed more labour to mining in proportion to its total population than Mozambique: in 1926, 45 per cent of black miners employed by the South African Chamber of Mines came from Mozambique where, not unusually, a quarter of the able-bodied men in recruitment districts would work on the Rand. At the time, supposedly dispassionate observers commented that figures of this magnitude had no serious adverse effect on the labour supply within Mozambique, and represented a surplus to the requirements of African agriculture, which was traditionally carried on by women. The truth of their observation is borne out by a 65 per cent increase in Mozambique's population between 1930 and 1960 – this despite massive emigration. (In Angola, where labour migration to the mines was far less frequent, population increased by 39 per cent.) (Newitt, 1981, p. 142.) Though the labour supply areas of Mozambique were comparatively slow in adopting cash-crop farming, and so considered economically 'backward', this may have been because the remittance of migrant miners' earnings alleviated the fiscal pressures on their families to enter the money economy. According to one authority, a black miner on the Rand in the 1920s might earn between £5 and £8 a month out of which he paid taxes. Earnings were five times those of a worker in Mozambique, and taking into account the fact that he received free food and lodging and did not have to support his family, a miner's pay compared very favourably with that even of a skilled worker in Britain. Indeed, 'up to 1940 the South African miners can be considered an élite among the world's working class' (Newitt, 1981, p. 114). Newitt's wage data may be inaccurate – according to Katzenellenbogen, average wages on the Rand for African miners were about 58 shillings (£2.90) per month between the wars (Katzenellenbogen, 1973, p. 412)).

We should recall, too, that the mining industry's demand for a healthy, stable labour force was instrumental in promoting preventive medicine and sanitary living conditions for African populations, and so removing a serious obstacle to economic growth. Initially, mining employers had calculated that by recruiting across political boundaries they could shrug aside the costs of improving industrial welfare; horrendous mortality rates from accidents and the diseases harboured in insalubrious labour compounds testify to their indifference to the well-being of the first generation of black miners. Between 1902 and 1914, 43 484 men from Mozambique alone died in employment on the Rand (Iliffe, 1987, p. 125). But even before 1914 it was evident that malign neglect spelt economic inefficiency, and effective steps were being taken to curb disease among compound-dwellers and eliminate accidents. Such was the success in controlling malaria, pneumonia, sleeping sickness and other diseases that by the mid 1930s the African and European mortality rates in the labour force were much the same. Africans were no longer averse to mining work, and recruitment ceased to depend on fiscal coercion. The health and housing facilities provided by the mining companies served as an example for other industries, notably the railways (Katzenellenbogen, 1973, pp. 383–8). Welfare provision in the mining towns of the Belgian Congo gradually reduced urban mortality to rates as low as in industrialised countries (Vellut, 1983, p. 156).

Africans and the Land

Probably the most drastic of all long-term consequences of the colonial intervention was that Africans began to evaluate the lands they used in new ways (Wrigley, 1986, p. 139). Tradition normally accorded a household the right to use the land controlled by the political community to which it belonged, and made no distinction between rights of ownership and rights of sovereignty. Land tenure rules were often extremely vague: the real limits on the acreage any household could work effectively were set by shifting cultivation, simple agricultural technology and reliance on family labour. There was rarely a clear distinction between 'waste' and cultivated land. Under colonialism, African communities were familiarised with land as a limited economic resource, subject to exclusive property rights. The old idea that all members of a political community had a general right of access to the land began to conflict with the notion that a household might enjoy the fruits of its labour and pre-empt land for profitable use (Colson, 1971, pp. 193–212). Land claims then came to be tested in the native courts, where adjudication encouraged the development of fairly comprehensive bodies of customary law governing the allocation and use of land. Because customary courts were under the ultimate jurisdiction of colonial officials, and driven to formulate more precise rules, European concepts of land tenure were transmitted to native society.

Colonialists and colonised started to share the assumption that 'no land is without an owner' (whether communal or individual) and to define rules of tenure. In 'settler' regimes, and in much of Central Africa, the Roman Law principle that all uncultivated land belonged to the state justified its public appropriation and sale to individuals and corporations. Where this sovereign prerogative was not exercised, newly codified rules concerning communal holdings sometimes inhibited the development of individual rights in waste land. But, more generally, the provisioning of external and internal markets encouraged individuals and families to exploit land more systematically, and led to a rising demand for the recognition of individual tenure with full proprietary rights. Land markets had existed in very limited regions of pre-colonial West Africa, but elsewhere colonialism introduced 'the European idea that land is something that can be measured, plotted, and subdivided into units which become "things" in themselves and subject to rights assigned to holders' (ibid., p. 198). Thus, by 1931, under the pressures of white settlement, the Kikuyu had come to conceptualise their present and past occupation of the land in European terms as property that could be personally owned, bought, sold, or rented by a tenant. Mission-educated Kikuyu in skilled or semi-skilled urban jobs had begun to use their savings to buy land and employ others to work it. They 'straddled' the divide between the modern, waged economy and tribal society. This process by which educated employees became rural capitalists has been documented elsewhere in East and Central Africa, and appears to have been one of the most general sources of structural change in African societies (Kitching, 1980, p. 285; Iliffe, 1983, p. 31). As land became valued as a commodity, class divisions opened between those with property rights and those without them.

Such social stratification appeared even in the 'peasant' regimes, where the colonial authorities aimed, in the words of one administrator, to 'preserve for future generations the unlimited ownership of the land by the tribe as against any form of freehold' (Burns, 1948, pp. 247–8). By acting as the trustee for tribal society the colonialists restricted the alienation of land to foreigners: in French West Africa, where the consent of the governor-general in council was required before communal land could be alienated, Europeans held only 75 000 hectares on permanent title in 1938 and some 80 000 on provisional title (Fieldhouse, 1971, p. 620). But individual appropriation by Africans seizing opportunities in the export market evidently did occur. By the 1950s, just over two-fifths of the land under cocoa in Nigeria was held by about a tenth of the farmers in virtual freehold, and a parallel process was occurring in the Ivory Coast (Hopkins, 1973, p. 239).

Algeria: French Property Law and Muslim Rural Society

As we have seen (Chapter 5), the diffusion of European law governing landed property is considered central to colonialism's modernising dynamic, and there is no better context in which to observe its impact than Algeria. The 'conquest phase' of the French occupation was completed by 1845, and Algeria was then divided into civil territory, assimilated into the metropolitan system of government, and territory under military administration. European agricultural settlement was forbidden in the military zone but encouraged in the civil territory, and plots of supposedly vacant (and therefore state-owned) land were granted to concessionaires with the long-term aim of implanting a French-speaking peasantry. Rural colonisation remained the principal concern of France's Algerian policy until 1930, despite the fact that most Europeans were townspeople, either independent artisans and businessmen or white-collar employees throughout the colonial period. By the end of 1851, there were 33 000 rural colons out of a total 131 000 Europeans (of whom only 66 000 were French, since cheap passages brought a flood of poor immigrants from Mediterranean Europe). Much concessionary land was actually grazed by nomads, or had been left fallow by native farmers practising extensive, low-yield agriculture, so these early grants seriously disrupted the subsistence economy and were a causal factor in the famine of the late 1860s. Under the Second Republic, legislators intended to assimilate property rights in Algeria with those of France, but retreated from this drastic measure for fear of violent reaction and, instead, decided that land in native ownership was either '*melk*' (private) or '*arch*' (tribal). Up till 1922, tribal property held in common under customary law could not be alienated, though tribes were restricted to a fraction of their former territory by the practice of *cantonnement* or delimitation.

A major turning-point in Algeria's history came with the fall of the Second Empire, and the Arab insurrection of 1871. Rebel land was sequestrated in the revolt's aftermath and colon opinion became the determining voice in Algerian policy. The Republican goal of *francisation* or assimilation to France had the paradoxical effect of placing Algeria in the hands of its European citizens, whose elected deputies and local representatives normally wielded more power than the governors appointed by Paris. Reacting against the pro-Arab policies of Napoleon III, republican Algeria committed itself to official colonisation, hoping to bring about French settlement in rural areas by free grants of land conditional upon obligatory residence. Emigrés from Alsace-Lorraine were targeted for state munificence. Some 687 000 hectares of 'public' land were granted to concessionaires between 1871 and 1900 (Ageron, 1991a, p. 58). Meanwhile, 'private' colonisation was greatly facilitated by the Warnier law of 1873, which allowed undivided tribal property held under the Islamic law of *melk* to be broken up for sale provided just one of the joint owners so desired. This legal instrument encouraged the speculative purchase (normally by European companies) of vast estates at little cost and ruined many native communities. From 1880 to 1908, the colons acquired 451 000 hectares through the private purchase of land. The result of the combined processes of 'public' and 'private' appropriation was that by the mid 1930s nearly 2½ million hectares of farm land belonged to the colons.

Contrary to French official intentions, after 1880 the European rural population grew much less rapidly than the rate of land acquisition.

Corporate capitalism, rather than the individual settler, was the key actor in promoting rural change. From the first, many concessionaries circumvented their conditions of obligatory residence, and farmed their land with native sharecroppers. The introduction of the vine, after Europe's stock was devastated by phylloxera, and the adoption of American dry farming techniques, were accompanied by the amalgamation of small properties into great estates producing for the export market. By 1930, there were actually only 26 153 European properties, and a fifth of them accounted for three-quarters of the 'European' acreage. The rural European population had ceased to grow, and 43 per cent were wage-earners (ibid., p. 61).

Meanwhile, the Muslim rural population had begun to feel the insistent pressures of population growth, the morcellisation of holdings and agricultural unemployment. Because Arab agriculture was extensive and left the land fallow for periods of two years, it was highly sensitive to the shrinkage of cultivable area at its disposal, and its contribution to total output fell steeply. By 1938, the Muslim harvest accounted for only 44 per cent of Algeria's wheat. The numbers of sheep and cattle declined relative to the Muslim rural population, and at the end of the inter-war period many fellahin were no longer able to eke a living from their plots. Opportunities for wage labour in the highly capitalised European agriculture sector were limited by its rapid mechanisation. The small-scale fellah farmer realised that, with less than 10 hectares, he was working at a loss. As soon as he had broken free of group control, he found that it was to his material advantage to go elsewhere, either as a farm labourer or, better, as a factory worker. From 1935 onwards, these uprooted peasants flocked into the urban areas (Berque, 1967, p. 56).

On the eve of the 1954 insurrection, agrarian society was grossly inegalitarian and racked by unemployment and undernourishment. Although the total area cultivated by Muslim peasants had been enlarged since the late 1940s, the annual quantity of grain it produced per capita fell from 2.5 quintals in 1940 to 1.5 quintals in 1954. Native agriculture was beset by diminishing returns and surplus labour. In 1954, of the 2.7 million men of working age in the rural population, only 1.7 million were employed for more than 100 days a year. European enterprises numbering 22 037 occupied 2.726 million hectares, while 630 732 Muslim farms covered 7.349 million hectares, and most were too small to support the average family. In the highly productive areas around Oran, Bône and Philippeville, four-fifths of the land was in the hands of colons, who had easier access to agricultural credit and technical assistance than Muslim cultivators. Europeans produced 55 per cent of the gross agricultural income and the Muslims 45 per cent.

Two-fifths of Muslim agriculture was absorbed in subsistence, as against 3 to 4 per cent for the colons. A not unreasonable guess is that 80 per cent of the native rural population were undernourished.

What the disparities between European and Muslim agriculture masked, however, was the increasing inequality within indigenous rural society. Muslim inheritance law and the opening of a land market by French property law had generated contradictory tendencies: the equal rights of male heirs hastened the fragmentation of holdings in a rapidly growing population, but wealthier Muslims – often townsmen – were consolidating properties and employing permanent workers in considerable numbers. In the early 1950s, 70 per cent of individual proprietors had on average no more than 4 hectares, or a mere 23 per cent of the farm land owned by Muslims; 1.13 per cent of proprietors accounted for a fifth of the privately owned land in Muslim possession.

Governor-General Léonard warned a conference of higher civil servants in 1954: 'The vital problems of Algeria must be resolved if we are to avoid the birth of the Algerian problem'. It was too late. There had been insufficient 'compensatory' assimilation of native Algerians to offset the polarisation and immiseration of Muslim rural society. Only 12.75 per cent of children of primary school age were being educated. Muslims accounted for nine-tenths of the population, but only 18 per cent of lycée and college students, and 11 per cent of those enrolled at Algiers University. A tiny number had entered public service and they were virtually absent from the upper administrative echelons. Despite more than a century of French rule, the great majority of Algerians could not even speak the language of their political masters. According to the 1948 census, only 15 per cent of Algerian men and 6 per cent of women spoke even rudimentary French, while 6 per cent of men and 2 per cent of women could write it. Among European men, only 20 per cent could speak Arabic or Kabyle, and among women about 10 per cent (Rachid bencheneb, 1986, pp. 415–30).

Did Colonialism Impoverish Africans?

Pre-colonial Africa was land-rich, and this has helped sustain 'the myth of Merrie Africa' as a continent without paupers as Europe knew them. According to this rosy image of the African past, the free availability of productive resources, the fact that societies were relatively unstratified, and the support given by the 'extended family' to its less fortunate members, all meant that a distinct, stigmatised category of poor people was unknown.

Only with the coming of colonial rule, market economies, and urbanisation, so it is often claimed, did things begin to fall apart. In its cruder versions the myth is scarcely worth refuting. Colonialism did, however, alter the balance between the fundamental causes of poverty in a way best clarified by distinguishing between the conjunctural poverty suffered by nearly all during temporary crises (such as drought) and the structural poverty to which specific groups were chronically prone (my analysis is indebted to Iliffe, 1987, pp. 4–8).

In pre-colonial Africa, inability to work or lack of access to labour was the prime cause of structural poverty. The poor were, usually, the physically incapacitated, those without kin, and the newly enslaved. Possession of a family was an insurance against impoverishment, and chronic poverty among the able-bodied was rare outside the Muslim Sudan or Christian Ethiopia. On the other hand, all groups in pre-colonial Africa save the very rich and powerful were vulnerable to the conjunctural poverty resulting from periodic droughts, epidemic disease, locust and other infestations, and political insecurity.

Colonialism had its greatest ameliorative impact on the conjunctural poverty arising from natural disasters and political insecurity. The reduction in famine mortality began in South Africa in the 1890s, about a generation ahead of tropical Africa. Mass death from starvation was more or less eliminated by more efficient transport and government, wider markets, and better opportunities to earn wages. This pattern was repeated in Southern Rhodesia, where abnormal mortality was avoided during the serious droughts of the early twentieth century because, being then more intensively governed than other colonies, it had better trade and transport systems (ibid., p. 159). From the later 1920s, famines causing great mortality disappeared from colonial Africa except in localised and temporary circumstances (such as the disruptions to trade and transport consequent on the Second World War). Fortuitously, higher and less erratic rainfall during the mid-colonial period reduced the incidence of crop failure, but the stable administrations imposed by the Europeans were also increasingly competent in foreseeing and alleviating famine. The introduction of motor vehicles helped control famine mortality further by widening the grain markets. Moreover, the officially encouraged cultivation of drought- and locust-resistant root crops, such as cassava, brought African populations larger reserves of starchy foods which could at least sustain life during dearth, though their consumption as a staple was often associated with the protein deficiency disease kwashiorkor. Lastly, we should note that food shortages became less of a threat to life as the colonial administrations eradicated, through vaccination and sanitary measures, such diseases as smallpox and cholera that had always struck hardest among the under-nourished. Demographic recovery and growth in tropical Africa after the 1920s was the indisputable result of the disappearance of famine and the curbing of epidemic diseases. That the major exception to this ameliorative trend was independent (but feudal) Ethiopia, which lacked modern transport, medicine and government, confirms the key part played by colonial administrations (ibid., p. 157).

But though the colonial economies relieved the epidemic starvation of conjunctural poverty for nearly all, they tended to condemn the very poor to endemic undernutrition, and created novel forms of impoverishment for both rural and urban Africans. The flat-rate taxes indiscriminately levied by colonial administrations drove those least able to pay into deep poverty, particularly during the inter-war depression when direct taxation was screwed up in response to declining customs revenue. In Dahomey, for example, the burden of taxation during 1931–5 was astronomical by all previous standards and denuded the population of money (Manning, 1982, p. 249). As elsewhere in Francophone Black Africa, the conjunctural poverty caused by the trade cycle was magnified by the rapacity of the state. In Futa Jalon, people pawned their crops and children or sold their stock, grain, pots, and even their Korans to pay their taxes. Taxation drained away money from rural communities and made debt a pervasive feature of rural life, even in the prosperous Gold Coast. By contrast, poverty due to landlessness, which is commonplace in contemporary Africa, was relatively rare in the colonial era. South Africa was the glaring exception, and in the 'reserves' the women contending with the harsh climate, poor soils, and large numbers of dependents constituted a new category of rural poor. They experienced an extreme version of the deepening inequality between town and the country that was a general feature of the colonial period. With urbanisation, rural crafts congregated in the towns, leaving agriculture the only occupation in the countryside. In the urban economy, males were at least protected from unemployment by labour shortages, and the poverty of the unemployed emerged only slowly in twentieth-century Africa.

Whether labour migration to the mines across frontiers was a universally impoverishing process (as proponents of the 'tributary articulation' concept have argued) is a more complex issue. Partly it is a question of when we are talking about, for as 'a way of life' labour migration was transformed under colonialism. In the late nineteenth century, migrants appear to have sought cash chiefly to pay bridewealth, expand the homestead, or relieve famine, but in the early twentieth century taxation and lower real wages gradually converted migration into an essential means of family survival. As we have seen, up to 1914 or thereabouts, Mozambicans – who were the largest group of migrants – paid a heavy toll in injury and death. In all probability, they and their families led more impoverished lives. But the social history of labour migration did not stop at this point. Improving real wages and working conditions made mining positively attractive and there were growing numbers of clandestine migrants. Remitted mine earnings kept poorer peasants afloat through the hardest of times. The Portuguese authorities insisted on the deferred payment of part of the miner's earnings and this had the desired effect of stimulating consumption within Mozambique itself, so that mine wages were the mainstay of the commercial economy of the villages right up till independence. For some, they provided a way of accumulating capital with which to rent land or purchase cattle, ploughs, cashew trees and even tractors. Samora Machel's father used mine earnings to build up a large herd of cattle and to work 30 acres of land. He represented a relatively prosperous 'middle peasantry' brought into being by over a century's emigration to the mines (Newitt, 1995, p. 454).

Compared with the changes wrought in the pattern of conjunctural poverty, structural poverty remained much as it had always been throughout the colonial period. Chiefly because land was still so abundant, the very poor continued to be those who lacked labour and family support: the orphaned, the crippled, the outcast. Africans were rarely impoverished by having too many mouths to feed, though their reciprocal obligations may have impeded the accumulation of wealth and capital. In West Africa, the responsibility of the wealthy to support dependent relatives, indigent members of the same tribe, and a large number of professional beggars tended to reduce their freely disposable income. According to Hailey's informants, the wealthy were even inhibited from using banks effectively for fear of exposing their wealth to the claims of their relatives. The fragmentation of incomes among kin was an obstacle to the emergence of a substantial class of African capitalists (Hailey, 1957, p. 1303). The converse of the undoubted amelioration of conjunctural poverty, and the disappearance of mass famine mortality, was the greater incidence of chronic malnutrition among the poor. The sacrifice of subsistence to cash cropping, and the adoption of protein-deficient staples, had some part in this, but their 'net' impact has probably been exaggerated. Cash incomes allowed Africans to diversify their diets by buying food imports, such as condensed milk. With local exceptions, the internal trade in foodstuffs expanded because transport became so much cheaper. Cassava probably saved more lives than were blighted by kwashiorkor.

The economic experience of colonial Africa varied so much that only the rash would attempt a conclusive answer to the question 'Did colonialism impoverish Africans?' Some respected scholars are certain that in particular colonies Africans were worse off in 1960 than in the 1900s, and that the proximate cause for virtually all their economic woes was colonial government. In the case of Dahomey, Patrick Manning has documented a decline in per capita import purchasing power out of export revenue (and thus a decline in per capita income) and the colonial state's dominance of the economy through excessive taxation. In Dahomey, he asserts, 'the replacement of [pre-colonial economic] growth with stagnation must be attributed primarily to the policies of the colonial state, rather than to the workings of the capitalist-led world economy in general' (Manning, 1982, p. 244). As we have seen, in colonial Algeria, explosive demographic growth from 1930 and land shortages brought absolute impoverishment to most rural Muslims. It would be naïve to think that European domination and settlement were the sole cause, though they were implicated, and we should note that in metropolitan Algeria post-war poverty was alleviated through the social security system, as in other parts of France (see Chapter 8). In other colonies, Africans experienced considerable deprivation *relative* to settler communities, and their consciousness of gross differences in material conditions was sharpened by systematic social and legal discrimination. But we must remember that colonial societies were almost invariably segmented into groups speaking different languages, with different creeds, dietary codes and styles of dress, and filling different occupational 'niches', especially in the towns. These segmentary groups were stratified in hierarchies of power, in which some African groups won considerable advantages over others. In the Mozambican sugar company town of Luabo in the 1950s, the Ngoni formed a labour aristocracy, better paid than any other field workers, and very conscious of the company's special regard for them and their own ethnic separateness. Below a whole chain of groups, and despised by everyone, were Anguru migrants who formed the majority of field workers (Vail and White, 1980, p. 379). In such hierarchies, there were inevitably low-status, often immigrant groups whose lives were impoverished compared with the past, and with more powerful communities.

Still, with due qualifications, the balance of the evidence indicates that colonialism did not impoverish Africans. There were generalised gains in living standards, though they mostly accrued during the late, 'constructive' colonialism after 1945. If Dahomey was impoverished, this was not typical of French West Africa as a whole, where real GNP increased by 8.5 per cent a year between 1947 and 1956. In Dakar, the index for hourly unskilled labour rose from 100 in 1949 to 240 in 1959, and in Abidjan to 394. In 1954, French West Africa imported twice as many cotton goods, three times as much sugar, four times as much condensed milk, and five times as much wheat flour as in 1938. Consumer imports grew at a similar rate in Cameroon and French Equatorial Africa where GNP increased by 10 per cent a year between 1948 and 1955. With such evidence for increasing consumption, it would be quite misleading to speak of a regression of living standards (Ageron, 1991b, p. 118). It is true that the proximate cause of this widespread material improvement was not colonialism, but favourable export prices for peasants' crops: on average, they rose by a factor of 3.65 from 1947 to 1958. Some did much better than others: taking 1949 as 100, the producer's price index for groundnuts was 147 in 1957–8, 343 for cocoa and 409 for coffee. In Ivory Coast, which specialised in coffee and cocoa, the real value of exports increased by more than 10 per cent a year, and in French West Africa as a whole by about 7 per cent. But the role of French policy was far from negligible: price stabilisation funds were established for certain products and public investment in infrastructure and social services raised the level of economic activity.

Field studies undertaken in West Africa in the late colonial era give us a better sense of what the aggregate data meant 'on the ground'. In one Gambian village observed between the late 1940s and early 1970s, agricultural innovations such as cattle-keeping and ox-ploughing resulted in food production more than keeping pace with population growth. The traditional hungry season largely disappeared, but at the cost of greater inequality, for the village was increasingly dominated by longer-settled wealthier households who owned oxen, had access to swamp-rice fields, and controlled relations with the outside world. Below this stratum, there was increasing indebtedness and proletarianisation. By the early 1970s, a class of landless labourers had emerged, as population outstripped the available land (this research is reported in Iliffe, 1987, pp. 162–3; for a detailed case study of Hausaland, see Hill, 1977). Finally, we should note the considerable increase in peasant prosperity during the last years of Portuguese rule in Mozambique. With the ending of compulsory cropping in 1960, the peasants switched to less labour-intensive cash crops, such as coconut and cashew. Income from these crops rose so that it overhauled mining wages as the main source of peasant cash (Newitt, 1995, p. 458).

In one post-colonial generation, Africa's population rose about two and half times, reaching something over 600 million in 1990. This colossal human progress – resulting from the control of endemic diseases and dramatic reductions in infant mortality – has put intense pressure on finite agrarian resources. More people have come to depend on cultivating marginal land and rural wage labour at starvation rates – or migrated to the cities where underemployment is rife. The absolute numbers of chronically undernourished people have increased, and in rural Africa they probably constitute a greater *proportion* of the population than was the case around 1900. But we must not project the syndrome of modern impoverishment back into the colonial past: when decolonisation came to Europe's African empires, it was a revolution of rising expectations.

Conclusions

Africa's historians do not agree among themselves about the impact of European colonialism on African economies and societies. Summing up the economic achievements of the colonisers, P. Duignan and L.H. Gann wrote that

> Within the lifetime of a single worker, Africa pulled out of the Early Iron Age into the era of steam power and the internal combustion engine . . . African labour and resources were important in laying the bases for modern economies in Africa; but without the capital and skills and markets provided by Europe, development would have been greatly retarded (Duignan and Gann, 1973b, pp. 689–90).

Yet Joseph Ajayi, who was doubtless thinking of Nigeria, has dismissed colonialism as a transient phenomenon which did not significantly divert African societies from a trajectory of development underway before 1880 (Ajayi, 1968, p. 194; see also Adu Boahen, 1987, ch. 7). Similarly, one historian of East Africa in the late stages of colonial rule has concluded that 'government did not impinge very much on the lives of the people' (Wrigley, 1976, p. 509). Such minimalist assessments appear to discount that, at the very least, the European governments created a new infrastructure of administration, transport and social services which influenced all aspects of exchange and production (Austen, 1987, p. 122). Others have argued that the 'social reach' of the colonial state went far beyond the provision of infrastructure and penetrated deep into native societies. John Lonsdale and Bruce Berman, for example, discern societal engineering of a truly totalitarian kind in the containment and regulation of Kenya's native peoples (Lonsdale and Berman, 1992, especially p. 144).

Steering a path between such divergent views towards coherent conclusions is not easy. In the terms posed at the outset of this chapter, Bill Warren was wrong: colonialism could, quite conceivably, have done much more to promote capitalist development. Import and export taxes could have been manipulated to provide incentives for investment in the local processing of primary produce and manufacturing. There could have been less stringent restrictions on credit and the supply of money. Colonial governments could have invested more, and much earlier in African human capital. Administrators everywhere could have been better disposed towards African entrepreneurs; some of them could have been better disposed to European capitalists. That these are not sheer flights of fancy is suggested, firstly, by comparison with parts of the underdeveloped world where the exercise of economic sovereignty palpably made a difference to capitalist development (Brazil, or British India between the wars) and – more emphatically – by comparing colonial economies in Africa. For the fact is that there were significant differences in the degree to which metropolitan states and their colonial regimes created environments favourable for European business, the development of secondary industry and the emergence of an urban wage-earning class. The hostility of the 'night-watchman' state in British West Africa to local industrialisation was at one end of a spectrum. At the other, 'benign' and cooperative end stood Belgium, where metropolitan bureaucrats were persuaded that the *mise en valeur* of the Congo was a national duty, and its colonial administrators gave a free hand to the corporations that had invested in minerals, plantations and railways in the colony. Despite being a major shareholder in the mining and other companies, the colonial state made no attempt to direct and influence business decision-making. Its roles were not, as some have argued, to participate in a 'mixed economy', but to provide honest administration, mobilise labour for major projects, and ensure that the Congolese got some return from European enterprise in the form of corporate taxation, company welfare and high wages (by African standards) for permanent urban workers. By contrast with British Africa, there was no cultural antipathy between colonial officialdom and colonial corporate management, and considerable career movement from one bureaucracy to the other (Stengers, 1989, p. 222). The example of the Congo demonstrates that colonial capitalism was able to move beyond its 'enclave' or purely commercial character in the right political circumstances. On the eve of the Belgian Congo's hasty and chaotic independence, nearly half its consumer goods requirements were satisfied by local manufacturing industries. Only South Africa and Southern Rhodesia witnessed a greater degree of industrialisation before 1960. There were, in short, realistic alternatives to the *économie de traite* practised across the Zaïre River in the French Congo.

That said, it would be unrealistic not to recognise basic and fairly intractable constraints on the promotion of capitalist development by the colonial regimes. First, apart from independent South Africa, Africa was economically marginal as a trading partner or field of investment by comparison with North America, Europe and Australasia. The one exceptional period was after 1945, when there was a world shortage of certain primary products and the export earnings of African colonies helped overcome the dollar shortages of the European powers (see Chapter 8). Second, given the financial orthodoxy practised by European governments, both in the metropoles and their colonies, there were political and ideological obstacles to the state substituting itself for the missing private investor. Colonies had to be cheap or they were not worth having. Lastly, the balance of production factors in much of Africa often meant that it was more economically rational for European businesses to trade with peasants than employ workers on plantations or in secondary production. Abundant land enabled most rural peoples to preserve their household economies and ensured that wage-earners generally had to be drawn as temporary migrants from remote areas. Migrant labour checked the formation of capitalist and proletarian classes. To maintain acquiescence in their rule, and out of humanitarian concern for African welfare, colonial administrators were happy to conserve customary land law, and so hinder if not entirely prevent the emergence of rural capitalists from African peasantries.

While all this is true, we should not slip into a facile elision of colonialism with Western capitalism nor overrate 'purely' economic mechanisms in considering the colonial impact on Africa. At decolonisation, productive routines and local markets in many parts of Africa still resembled descriptions of them given a hundred years or more before by European explorers. Bornu, in northern Nigeria, provides an apt instance: farming techniques and the general run of subsistence crops were the same as before colonialism, and they were harvested and marketed in the same time-honoured ways. The colonial regime had contributed materially to local infrastructures by digging deep wells and in other important ways, but these had been evolutionary increments to African resources, not revolutionary changes (Cohen, 1971, p. 124). Colonialism, it is worth insisting, was primarily an authoritarian system of *rule* that combined and organised military and political power in local armies, police forces, courts of law, civil administrations and salaried chiefs. Economic production was not a central purpose of colonialism, though its authoritative power was used in economically consequential ways to tax goods and people, and compel them to work, and from the 1940s monopoly state agencies marketed tropical exports and determined prices administratively in British and French Africa. The public purse was the main source of investment in transport infrastructure, but the economic functions of investment in production and technological innovation were left largely to private individuals and companies. Expatriate interests were heavily concentrated in the primary sector and the sphere of exchange, and the best-organised merchant capitalist corporations operated across colonial frontiers. Few European multinationals contemplated investment in manufacturing in Africa before 1945. The result was that within colonial states organised forms of coercive power predominated over the diffused, collective power generated by economic organisations. This was to prove colonialism's crucial and damnable legacy: centralised repressive apparatuses were implanted in segmented societies where economic organisation was overshadowed by military–political power and the sense of national community was weak. In something like a reversal to the pre-colonial pattern of African history, authoritative power – wielded by 'the man on horseback' – has been used in many independent states to amass private wealth and distribute economic resources among client groups.

The plundering of Zaïre by Mobutu Sese Seko, installed as president by an army coup in 1965, was an extreme but not wholly unrepresentative example of this degeneracy. After the chaos of the early 1960s, Mobutu promised a new order based upon a strong, unitary, depoliticised regime. He used the colonial state heritage of centralised, bureaucratic, authoritarian rule to dissolve political parties. The provinces, where regional ethnic groups had tried to establish self-government, were reduced to administrative subdivisions as in colonial times. His regime became a synthesis of European authoritarianism and African patrimonialism. Mobutu acted as if he and his clients 'owned' the economy, and in a real sense they did. In 1973–5, in the name of the 'Zairianisation' of foreign assets, the political class received by patrimonial distribution title to a broad swathe of the economy. The patrimonial state degenerated into institutionalised corruption, and made opportunities for illicit gain an integral part of the political system. The state required enormous resources just to sustain itself, and in 1974 consumed no less than 59 per cent of the GNP (Young, 1983, pp. 322–3). When the Mobutu regime collapsed in civil war and bankruptcy in 1997, the years of Belgian colonial rule appear as an interlude of social progress and sound administration in the long history of pillage and tributary exploitation in Central Africa. Nor, of course, is Zaïre the only state whose experience since independence throws such a favourable light on the colonial era. To those who believe that democratic self-determination is the essence of the 'good' political society, this is profoundly troubling.

7

THE BALANCE SHEET OF
MODERN COLONIALISM

Introduction: From Colonisation to Colonialism

It was no secret that the modern colonial empires were acquired for the advantages they brought the European states. As one colonial propagandist wrote in 1912:

> if colonies, the foundation of which nearly always costs the metropolis so much money and sacrifices and which exposes them to such great risks, were not made to serve those metropoles, they would have no raison d'être (Jules Harmand, *Domination et colonisation*, quoted in Young, 1994, p. 100).

Even Lugard admitted that

> European brains, capital and energy have not been, and never will be, expended in developing the resources of Africa from motives of pure philanthropy . . . Europe is in Africa for the mutual benefit of her own industrial classes, and of the native races in their progress to a higher plane. [As well as bringing civilisation to Africans, the colonialists were] ministering to the material needs of [their] own civilisation (Lugard, 1922, p. 617).

In this chapter, I will try to draw up the balance sheet of modern colonialism's advantages and disadvantages for the national economies of the European powers, concentrating on two sub-periods, 1870–1914 and 1918–39, when the colonial contribution to metropolitan trade and investment opportunities was significantly different. The final phase of the European empires (1945–60) is discussed in Chapter 8. Before proceeding, a few points of historical semantics and contextualisation will be useful. Until quite late in the nineteenth century, a 'colony' was generally understood to be a derivative community of European settlement that remained politically connected in a relation of dependence with the parent community. John Seeley, for example, did not consider India part of the 'Colonial Empire', because it was not colonised in the classical sense (Seeley, 1883, pp. 44–54). The theory of 'colonisation' had been an important branch of political economy in Britain where the Colonial Reform movement advocated state-promoted emigration to Australia and elsewhere as a solution to the economic stagnation and social malaise of the 1830s. The movement's publicists claimed that colonies presented new opportunities for investment and new employment markets for an economy confronted by surplus labour and with a diminishing rate of return from agrarian and industrial capital. J.S. Mill was so persuaded of these arguments as to overcome his usual preference for *laissez-faire* and endorse the promotion of colonisation as a legitimate and necessary function of government, without compromising his hostility to the mercantilist trade policies required by the 'old' colonial system. (Winch, 1965, is a lucid guide to this literature; see also Kittrell, 1970.)

What distinguished the colonialism undertaken after the 1870s was that it made little pretence of attracting colonists, and its rationale did not presuppose a problem of surplus labour. It is perhaps not surprising that we should find the case for 'modern colonisation' first systematically propounded in France, in 1874, by a young academic economist (Leroy-Beaulieu, 1886). France's population was scarcely growing, so Malthusian-inspired arguments for 'colonisation' were obsolescent, but the industrialising economy was subject to crises of over-production. Colonies' most useful function, Leroy-Beaulieu argued, was as ready-made markets for metropolitan manufactures: by raising the level of effective demand they would increase profits and wages in the metropolis. The advantages of colonies as sources of supply and as profitable fields of investment for surplus capital were supplementary to their primary function of increasing consumption. Leroy-Beaulieu was an economic liberal and opposed any return to exclusive colonial commerce: 'the whole world would benefit' from freedom of trade with the colonial markets. But he recognised that these commercial gains could not be achieved without large-scale investment in colonial infrastructure. When first published, Leroy-Beaulieu's arguments for colonial expansion found little favour among French economists, but subsequent editions of his book in the mid-1880s, after the French occupations of Tunisia and Tonkin, enjoyed a more favourable reception, particularly among republican nationalists (Thobie, 1983, p. 83; Ganiage, 1968, p. 21). Jules Ferry, who as premier authorised the occupations, defended them before the Chamber in July 1885 in terms indebted to Leroy-Beaulieu:

> [I]nvestment colonialism [was a policy] suitable for peoples who have either too much capital or too many products . . . it is of greatest importance . . . in the midst of this crisis which is affecting all European industries, to remember that when one founds a colony, one is supplying an outlet for trade (quoted in Brunschwig, 1966, p. 76).

As it happens, colonisation in something like its *classical* sense was the most dynamic force in late-nineteenth- and early-twentieth-century global economic development: nearly nine-tenths of Europe's 20 million permanent emigrants between 1880 and 1930 went to the Americas. European overseas investment was also mostly located in relatively developed, culturally familiar economies where the yield of capital was generally higher because of the presence of social overhead facilities. Investments in countries of European settlement amounted to about 131 dollars per habitant in 1913, while in other countries the figure was about 11 dollars (Bairoch, 1976, p. 97). On a per capita basis, the countries with the highest level of European investment in 1913 were Canada, Argentina, Australia, New Zealand and South Africa. International trade was similarly concentrated in the European trading bloc and among countries of European settlement: though Europe had only 26 per cent of the world's population in 1900, it accounted for 59.5 per cent of world exports. Between 1880 and 1910, over two-thirds of European exports were destined for other European countries; less than a quarter went to Asia, Africa and South America combined. Most European imports were from other European countries and the most important source of supply outside Europe was North America (ibid., p. 18, 82).

Colonial Accounting

In strict truth, modern colonialism was not exclusively European (for Japan and the United States had colonies in fact if not in name), but for about seventy years it was by far the most important political nexus between Europe and the underdeveloped regions. Ever since economic arguments were advanced for modern colonialism, publicists and scholars have alluded to its costs and benefits in terms of the national accounts of the colonial powers: on the credit side are colonial markets for metropolitan exports, colonial sources of industrial raw materials and foodstuffs, and profitable fields of investment in the colonies for metropolitan businesses. On the debit side are the military and administrative costs of acquiring and maintaining colonies. Of course, this accounting can create an illusion of meagre profits from the colonies if it lulls us into thinking that red-letter items were deducted from the returns. Colonial costs were a public charge, and metropolitan consumers gained only when they obtained products at below world market prices (which they rarely did). Profits mostly accrued to tiny minorities of shareholders. Furthermore, the methodology of such a balance sheet is fraught with problems, the trickiest being what to measure the putative gains of colonialism *against*. To put the matter simply: to itemise the colonial proportion of European trade as an absolute gain falsely assumes that colonialism was a necessary condition for this commerce in its entirety, when as we know European merchants traded with African and Asian states before they were colonised and would surely have continued to do so had they remained independent. The real measure of the commercial benefits of colonialism is the difference between the volume of trade in the counterfactual situation, where a large part of the underdeveloped world was not subjected to European rule, and the actual volume of trade after a specified period. The same reasoning applies to the gains from colonial investment. Calculating this hypothetical increment with any precision is impossible, but it should be a conceptual parameter of the discussion.

The European colonial empires (including mandates which were effectively colonies) were at their greatest extent on the eve of the Second World War, when their combined populations totalled about 584 millions or rather more than a quarter of the world's population (Michel, 1993, p. 16). The empires were not especially important as sources of supply for the industrialised world: no colonial power received from the overseas territories it controlled as much as a fifth of its requirements in raw materials and foodstuffs (Clark, 1936, p. 4). As we have already noted in Chapter 1, the developed countries of Europe (excluding the USSR) and North America were basically self-sufficient in industrial raw materials up to the Second World War. On the eve of the inter-war Depression, they were together responsible for 88 per cent of the world's coal output and 91 per cent of the world's iron ore. Africa, Asia and Latin America are poorly endowed with these key resources for heavy industry: their combined output of coal in the late 1920s represented just over 8 per cent of the world's coal production and they produced about 7 per cent of the world's iron ore (Table 7.1). Before 1930, the only industrial mineral not found in abundance in North America and Europe was tin.

Table 7.1   World output of industrial resources in the late 1920s (data from *Balance Sheets of Imperialism*)

	Share of world production (%)				
	Coal (average 1926–9)	Iron ore (average 1925–8)	Copper (average 1925–8)	Tin (average 1925–9)	Oil (average 1925–9)
Africa	1.13	2.21	7.46	6.51	0.13
North America	44.83	40.69	54.84	—	68.89
Latin America	0.26	1.23	23.21	22.70	15.58
Asia	6.88	2.74	5.09	66.91	6.51
Europe (excluding the USSR)	43.06	50.11	7.35	2.15	2.66

Source: Clark (1936, Tables L–E, L–F, pp. 106–7).

With respect to energy sources, more were produced than consumed in the developed countries and until the Second World War their energy exports to the 'Third World' slightly exceeded their imports from the 'Third World'. Western dependence on 'Third World' oil has, of course, reversed this situation, but it is of comparatively recent origin. In 1939, 77 per cent of the world's crude oil output (totalling about 285 million tonnes) came from the Americas – 60 per cent from the USA, which was still the most important exporter. Only about 10 per cent of world output of crude petroleum came from areas under European political tutelage, though mostly outside the formal colonial empires. The Persian oil fields under British control produced 10.3 million tons, Iraq (a former mandate and still a client state) produced 3.8 million, Trinidad 2.7 million. The Dutch East Indies produced 7.9 million tons and, considering the size of the metropolitan economy, was the richest colonial domain in terms of the provision of industrial raw materials. Apart from its rubber, tin and oil, it was the world's largest producer of copra.

The converse of the industrialised world's near self-sufficiency in terms of inputs was that, in 1939, raw materials formed only a small proportion (18 per cent) of the exports of the 'Third World' as a whole – which, of course, embraced far more than the colonial empires (Bairoch, 1980). But we need to probe beneath that crude statistic: disaggregated analysis shows that colonial production accounted for more than half the world output of two strategic commodities, rubber and tin, and was important for other non-ferrous metals, vegetable oils and cotton. Asian rubber, tapped from the transplanted *Hevea brasiliensis*, was a triumph of arboreal imperialism. Total world shipments of rubber touched a pre-war peak of 1157 metric tons in 1937; 41 per cent came from British Malaya and 38 per cent from the Dutch East Indies, while other Asian colonies (French Indo-China, Burma, Ceylon, Borneo) produced most of the remainder. Malaya and the Dutch East Indies provided well over half the world's output of tin ore between them, while Nigeria and the Belgian Congo also produced significant quantities. During the 1930s, the proportion of the world's copper mined in the Central African copper belt had doubled, reaching about a fifth in 1938 (400 000 tonnes out of 2.026 million tonnes). The Belgian Congo produced 80 per cent of the world's uranium – a strategic commodity of world-shattering importance by 1945.

The case of cotton is interesting because the world's largest manufacturer had not relied on colonial supplies to any great degree before 1914, but became more dependent on them between the wars as the industry went into decline. In 1913, when Britain consumed nearly a fifth of the world's raw cotton, three-quarters of her supplies were imported from the United States, and 19 per cent from the 'veiled protectorate' of Egypt. Imports from India and other colonies provided less than 4 per cent of Lancashire's raw materials. By the late 1920s, the US share had declined to 51 per cent of total raw cotton imports, the Egyptian share was down to 16 per cent, and the Indian and colonial share had risen to 14 per cent (Clark, 1936, table XLVIII). As the industry contracted in the 1930s, raw cotton inputs from the empire and Egypt became proportionately more important, principally because the price advantages these countries gained in exporting to Britain with the inauguration of the sterling bloc (see below). But it was a bigger share of a greatly diminished whole: in 1937, Britain consumed only 9.6 per cent of the world's raw cotton output. For France, the picture is different: despite the best efforts of the colonial authorities to encourage production, the colonies furnished only 1.7 per cent of the metropolitan industry's needs in 1937 (Marseille, 1975). The one European cotton industry ever to achieve colonial self-sufficiency in raw material supply was the Portuguese – and that after the Second World War.

Though only a small part of industrial Europe's inputs, colonial commodities were certainly extracted on terms very favourable to capital. This was not necessarily because labour was any more exploited than it would have been had European enterprises been operating in independent countries. Rather, colonial governments allowed them access to land and minerals on very easy terms, which meant a tiny share of the product of European enterprise going to rent and taxes. In Malaya and Indonesia, for example, land was made available to plantation companies on long leases at charges amounting to 4 per cent or less of total development costs (Barlow and Drabble, 1990, p. 198). Mining in the Northern Rhodesian copper belt was a particularly gross instance of enclave enterprise bringing negligible returns to native labour and the colonial government. In 1937, copper exports were valued at £10.7 million or 90 per cent of the colony's total exports. Total imports were only about half this, leaving a net drain of £5 millions, from an exceptionally poor territory. The total paid in wages to the native workers in the copper mines was about £250 000. As against this, over £5 million was made in profits by the three leading mining companies; and nearly £3 millions of this was paid out in current dividends. The British Treasury got about £500 000 in taxes – apart from the taxes levied in the colony itself. Since the total public revenue of Northern Rhodesia was about £1 million, and a significant proportion came from hut and poll taxes, the fiscal charge on the companies cannot have been onerous (Cole, 1947, pp. 878–9).

The French and British Colonial Accounts: 1870–1914 and 1918–39

Let us begin with France, the second greatest colonial power in 1914 and the one which had gained most territorially from the European division of the world. Ostensibly, the commercial returns to the Third Republic of the 'colonial adventure' were modest, and did little to arrest France's declining importance in world trade: French exports were 13 per cent of global exports in 1860, only 7 per cent in 1913. (By comparison, Britain's share fell from about 25 per cent to 17 per cent.) Nor did the empire alter the European orientation of French commerce: in 1860, European markets took 65.1 per cent of French exports and in 1910, 69.8 per cent. The geographical structure of imports is less easy to determine, but approximately 55 per cent were of European origin in 1910. French export markets in North America had contracted in the late nineteenth century – as had other European trading nations, – and Africa had partly compensated. The African share in the geographic structure of French exports had fallen from 10.1 per cent in 1860 to 6.6 per cent in 1880, but rose to 12.3 per cent by 1910, when trade with Africa was more or less in equilibrium. Asia was not a significant market for French goods, but furnished 10 to 12 per cent of imports by 1910 (Bairoch, 1974; Thobie, 1983, p. 65). About 21 to 23 per cent of French exports went to what we now call the 'Third World' in the pre-war years, and it supplied 34 per cent of imports, but about half this trade was with countries *outside* the French empire. Less than a tenth of French imports were being provided by the empire in 1913, and only 13 per cent of exports were going to colonial markets. This was an unimpressive commercial return for a country whose empire had increased from 900 000 square kilometres to about 10 million, whose colonial population had risen from about 3 million to 50 million, and which had instituted a protected colonial market between 1889 and 1892. Apart from those territories affected by international agreements to maintain an 'open door' (Equatorial Africa, Dahomey, the Ivory Coast and later Morocco), the empire was 'assimilated' to the metropolitan tariff, meaning French goods entered duty-free while foreign imports paid the same tariffs as they would entering France.

Table 7.2   The part of the French empire in French external trade (millions of current francs)

	Imports			Exports		
	Total	Empire		Total	Empire	
	worth	worth	Share of total	worth	worth	Share of total
	(francs)	(francs)	(%)	(francs)	(francs)	(%)
1880	5033.2	244.6	4.8	3467.9	219.5	6.3
1890	4436.9	362.9	8.1	3753.5	296.1	7.8
1900	4698.8	363.6	7.7	4108.7	477.7	11.6
1913	8421.3	797.2	9.4	6880.2	894.8	13
1928–31	51603.5	6656.9	12.9	43696.3	8608.2	19.7
1932–8	30882.9	7720.7	25	20220.9	6207.8	30.7

Sources: Marseille (1984b); Mitchell (1992).

The commercial returns were all the more disappointing because foreign commerce was gaining more from markets acquired at the expense of the French taxpayer. The report on the colonial estimates prepared for the Chamber of Deputies in 1896 complained: 'Outlets worth 95 million francs [to France] cost us 80 million francs a year; foreign countries have outlets in our colonies worth 126 million, for which they make no preliminary expenditure' (quoted in Brunschwig, 1966, p. 138). The failure of French commerce to make the most of colonial markets was particularly evident if we exclude from the accounting the North African territories that were not strictly colonies but protectorates and *départements*. In 1909, foreign imports into the colonies juridically defined were worth 267 million francs as against 246 million from France; the colonies' exports to foreign markets were worth 316 million francs as against 258 million. Private gains from the colonial adventure had required significant amounts of public expenditure: in 1885, the Colonial Ministry's estimates were about 42.7 million francs; by 1902, its actual expenditure was almost 116 million francs. This represented nothing like the full public costs of colonial expansion, because the Colonial Ministry was not responsible for many overseas territories, and part of the expenditure fell to other ministries' budgets (ibid. pp. 95, 135–6).

Capital exports are the heart of theoretical controversies over imperialism, and the brute figures for French exports to the empire demonstrate that French investors had largely ignored Leroy-Beaulieu's call for a new 'capitalist' colonialism. The cumulative total of French external investment grew more than three and half times between 1870 and 1913, but most was located in Europe on the eve of the war and less than a quarter in Africa and Asia combined. The proportion going to the colonies actually fell between 1882 and 1902 (Table 7.3), though there were significant investments in the African colonies of other European powers during these decades. In the Belgian Congo 72 million francs were invested, with 1592 millions in British Africa and 40 millions in Portuguese Africa. Annual capital flows rose and fell broadly in line with the pace of economic growth. When the economy grew rapidly, flows abroad increased, and they decreased when economic growth was sluggish. This rather contradicts the theory that the declining rate of profit led to a capital 'surplus' that had to be exported to maintain the accumulation process, and it indicates that overseas investments were not made at the expense of the French domestic economy. Capital flows during the period between 1876 and 1894–5 – the years of colonial expansion – were significantly less than during 1855–70 and 1896–1913. During the age of 'high' imperialism, Latin America was the favoured location for new French investment outside Europe. Table 7.3 shows that there was a considerable surge in colonial investment in the early twentieth century, but probably 70 per cent was on public account. Since the metropolitan state was legally debarred from subsidising colonial civil expenditure, nearly all public investment was covered by loans floated on the French money market, and redeemed by local taxation in the colonies. A large number of such loans were promoted in 1897–1909: according to an incomplete survey of colonial territories for the Vichy Government in 1943, two-fifths of all public investments in them between the assumption of French sovereignty and 1940 were made in this period (Marseille, 1974).

Table 7.3   French external investments: 1882, 1902, 1914 (%)

	1882	1902	1914
North-West Europe	3.87	7.9	4.4
Central Europe	18.67	11.68	8.79
Mediterranean Europe	35.86	16.84	9.01
Eastern Europe and the Balkans	1.53	3.10	5.93
Russia	7.33	23.72	27.03
Turkey and Egypt	23.06	12.03	9.01
Asia and Oceania (excl. colonies)	0.67	2.40	2.64
Americas (excl. colonies)	4.0	12.72	20.44
Africa (excl. colonies)	0.67	6.18	3.96
Colonies	4.34	3.43	8.79

Source: R. Girault (1979, p. 238).

The aggregate figures help us understand the defeatism of 'parti colonial' on the eve of the war – the feeling it had lost the struggle to excite public interest in the empire – and why Henri Brunschwig concluded that economic imperialism was essentially a 'myth'. French expansion, he argued, was a costly, politically determined expression of late-nineteenth-century nationalism (Brunschwig, 1966). But this interpretation needs to be heavily qualified on a number of counts. First, the analysis of French public expenditure confirms that the empire was acquired pretty cheaply. Between 1850 and 1913 French colonial expenditure of *all* kinds – whether on conquests, administration or development (and including Algerian) – never accounted for as much as 10 per cent of the annual budget. From 1881 to 1913, 6 to 7 per cent of the budget was normally devoted to colonial expenditure, with a peak of 9.6 per cent in 1896 as a result of the conquest of Madagascar (Bobrie, 1976). Central government expenditure in France was about 9 per cent of GNP in 1850; by 1890, it had risen to 14 per cent but fell back to 11 per cent by 1910 (Mann, 1993, table 11.3, p. 366). We should bear in mind, too, when calculating the costs of empire, that the expenses were not borne, and the gains made, by exactly the same body of people. Over half of French fiscal receipts came from regressive indirect taxes between 1880 and 1913. Those French people with savings to spare who invested in (very secure) colonial loans were not the same as those French consumers whose taxes paid for the conquest of the colonies.

Second, time series and disaggregated data show that colonial trade was exceptionally dynamic and becoming important for certain sectors of French industry. Colonial trade grew at 3.8 per cent annually after 1880, as opposed to 1.5 per cent for foreign trade, and by 1913 the colonial empire ranked behind Britain and Germany as France's third most important trading partner. Colonies acquired *before* 1870 – Algeria, the French Antilles, Cochin–China and Senegal – always accounted for at least 70 per cent of colonial trade, so it was not the acquisition of new territories that explains the dynamism so much as the shift to protectionism. Before 1890, imports from the empire exceeded exports, but after that date the trade balance became favourable to France. This was partly because greater public investment in the infrastructure of the colonies led to the imports of equipment (such as rails and rolling stock). These investments in turn encouraged colonial production and exports. By 1913, the colonies furnished France with most of her imported rice, wine and raw sugar, a large part of her groundnuts and palm oil imports, and significant quantities of phosphates and rubber. The impact of protectionism at the behest of French farmers had greatly reduced the proportion of agricultural primary products in total imports (down from 33.5 per cent in 1880 to only 13.6 per cent in 1913) *but raised the empire's share of this declining whole* (from 8.4 per cent to 40.1 per cent). The movement of relative prices had made colonial trade increasingly advantageous to metropolitan interests. The barter terms of trade are not known precisely, but Jacques Marseille has estimated that average colonial export prices declined by approximately a third, relative to the price of imports from France, between 1880 and 1913 (Marseille, 1984a, p. 300). We may conclude that, as infrastructural development accelerated the transfer of colonial resources to the metropole before 1914, so the colonies' declining terms of trade helped repay the sums invested. By this means, and through the redemption of state loans, the empire was paying dear for its own development.

Sectoral analysis demonstrates that specific industries relied heavily on colonial markets for export outlets: in 1913, 67.6 per cent of the sugar industry's exports went to the colonies, 65.1 per cent the soap industry's, 41.4 per cent of the metallurgical industry's, and 33.1 per cent of cotton textile industry's (although for cheap bleached cloth the proportion was 86.2 per cent). Nevertheless, the colonies' contribution to raising total demand for metropolitan manufactures, and creating employment in France, was small – certainly by comparison with Britain and its empire. In terms of employment and value added, cotton textiles was France's largest manufacturing industry: the growth of output accelerated between 1880 and 1913, and while other French textile exports declined as a proportion of total exports, those of cotton cloth rose. But exports accounted for 18 per cent of output between 1905 and 1913, so the colonies absorbed only 6 per cent of the industry's production. On the basis of this evidence, Jacques Marseille's judgement that, even before 1914, the colonial market was playing 'a fundamental role in France's economic growth' is overstating the case in my view (Marseille, 1984b, p. 225). To put matters in perspective, the much larger Lancashire cotton industry exported over three-quarters of its output in 1914, and nearly two-fifths of cloth exports were to India. In 1914, the role of the French empire as virtually the sole export market for French cotton cloth lay in the future, whereas the contraction of the British industry's Indian market was already evident: the proportion of yarn exports destined for India fell from 19.6 per cent of the total in 1900–4 to 15.7 per in 1910–11; cloth exports declined from 41.6 per cent to 38.7 per cent.

Third, and most significantly, the analysis of private capital exports to the colonies has dispelled the view that they consisted largely of investments by merchant firms in the primitive *économie de traite*. This may have been true of Black Africa, but the favoured fields of colonial investment were Algeria and Indo-China, and banking firms and mining companies accounted for much more of the issued capital than commercial companies. Private sector investment was, of course, only a fraction of total French foreign investment, which was mostly in state loans, but by 1914 the colonies were absorbing a substantial proportion of this fraction. There was almost as much French capital invested in private enterprise in the colonies as there was in private enterprise in the Tsarist empire. Of the 469 companies primarily engaged in business in the colonies in the late 1950s, 200 had been formed before the First World War. Among the 32 most profitable colonial companies in 1958, as many as 20 originated before 1914. Much of their success was due to the very high profits made in this early period: not unrepresentative were the dividends equal to between 30 and 35 per cent of the nominal share price paid by the Tonkin Coal Mines before 1914. Returns on equity are difficult to compare, but colonial investments seem to have been more profitable than foreign (Marseille, 1987, p. 131). Our focus here is primarily that of the metropolitan economy, but it is important to add that the raising of capital on the French Bourse by companies with 'colonial' prospectuses does not mean that the subscribed sums were necessarily invested in productive or commercial enterprises in the colonies. The Compagnie Occidentale de Madagascar is but one example of heavily subscribed colonial companies that more or less fraudulently extorted millions from gullible investors without 'implanting' any capital overseas (Marseille, 1984b, pp. 125–8).

Drawing up a comparable balance for Britain is complicated by the fact that the British and French empires were very dissimilar entities. The 'white' Dominions were not economic dependencies in any real sense, but were the most important fields of imperial investment (receiving over 70 per cent of the finance directed to the empire) and major trading partners. They were increasing their share of primary produce sold to Britain before 1914 – while that of India and the Crown Colonies remained static – and after the war were collectively more important as suppliers and markets. It is reasonable to suppose that the Dominions would have continued to trade with Britain, and attract British capital, had they been fully independent countries like Argentina. Indeed, Britain would have *gained* economically from dissolving formal ties because the Dominions refused to assume their 'share' of imperial defence. While British defence expenditure was the highest in the late-nineteenth–early-twentieth-century world on a per capita basis, the Dominions spent little on their defence by comparison with other countries at a similar level of development (Davis and Huttenback, 1988, pp. 131–2).

The further dissimilarity is that, unlike France, Britain remained a free trading nation until 1931 and where possible compelled its colonies to do the same until the Second World War. This complicates assessment of the gains from trade with the empire, for all countries enjoyed 'most favoured nation status' in Britain's dependencies, which sent only about a quarter to a third of their exports to Britain before 1914, and much the same proportion in 1938. During the preceding half-century, British sovereignty was the context, if not the cause, for the remarkable growth in the colonial empire's external trade: although containing only 2.6 per cent of world population, it accounted for 7.5 per of world trade between 1936 and 1938, as compared with 2.9 per cent in 1911–13 (an increase which more than compensated for the partial retreat of India from international trade). The colonial Empire was the fourth largest trading entity in the world on the eve of the Second World War. Although invariably the largest supplier, Britain furnished only a quarter of her colonies' imports on average (Meyer, 1948, pp. 1–6). The colonies' multilateral trading relations worked to Britain's advantage by liquidating some of her deficit in commodity trade with the rest of the world, and by generating demand for financial services and transport.

British officialdom could plausibly claim it set 'a fair field and no favours' for compatriot traders and manufacturers, which has some validity in relation to other European trading nations. German manufacturers increased their exports to 'open' British empire markets by 129 per cent between 1895 and 1907 (Aldcroft, 1968, p. 20). In relation to potential domestic competitors in the dependencies, the reality was that free trade gave British manufactures considerable advantages by hampering import substitution. The Indian market for Lancashire yarn and cloth was much larger than it would have been had Britain been trading with independent countries in South Asia. Nevertheless, even with tariff protection of 20 to 40 per cent *ad valorem*, some British cotton goods would still have been competitive (as we know from the level of yarn exports to protected markets in Europe and the USA before 1914). British services, such as shipping, competed world-wide and would presumably have continued to carry much colonial trade had political connections with the metropolis been severed. So, one measure of the economic gain of empire to the metropolis is to ask what would have been 'lost' had the colonies and dominions imposed tariffs comparable to those of independent states. Michael Edelstein has calculated that British exports of goods and services to the empire (including the dominions) represented 7.9 per cent of GNP in 1870 and 11.9 per cent in 1913. By his counter-factual reckoning, the net gain from 'imperial free trade' in 1870 was only 1.0 per cent of GNP, and in 1913, 2.5 per cent. Since this refers to the empire as a whole, and not just the 'non-white' colonial dependencies that are our concern, we need to reduce the figures to 0.55 per cent in 1870 and 1.4 per cent in 1914. But this calculation assumes that the only economic difference made by British rule in the colonial dependencies was the inability to implement tariffs, whereas it is virtually certain they would not have participated in the international economy to the same extent. Using Edelstein's 'strong' counterfactual hypothesis that trade with tropical and subtropical colonies would only have been a quarter of what it actually was had they never been conquered by Britain, we can hazard that the 'commercial gain from colonialism' was about 2.2 per cent of GNP in 1870 and 3.4 per cent in 1913 (Edelstein, 1981, pp. 90–3; idem 1994, pp. 200–4).

The significance of this arithmetic is debatable. Any economic activity expressed as a proportion of national product appears trifling, but in the context of a slowly growing economy (such as late-nineteenth-century Britain) this *may* have represented a major source of expansion. My sense is that it did not. It is wholly implausible to suppose that the economic resources employed in production for colonial markets could not have been profitably relocated had these markets closed (O'Brien, 1988). There is some evidence that the increment to national income from the colonial empire had its hidden cost because British industry avoided renovation and restructuring by 'sheltering' in empire markets where there was less competition from more efficient German and American producers. Between 1900 and 1910, the exports of British iron and steel, hardware, cutlery, railway rolling stock, tools, ships and other iron and steel products, increased by about £23.5 million; but of this increase, £14 million represented new 'imperial' business. The British empire, which took 33 per cent of these exports in 1900, took 40 per cent in 1910 (Moon, 1926, p. 534). Markets of impoverished consumers, such as India, generate little demand for high-value-added products or capital goods imports and stimulate little industrial innovation. Significantly, India and the other tropical dependencies received only about 12 per cent of investment exported from Britain between 1865 and 1914 (Simon, 1968). This was not because British stockholders were averse to such secure issues as Indian railways; rather the indigent dependencies required few capital goods imports that were the underlying cause of inward foreign investment. We have not reckoned other 'gains' to the metropolitan economy that came with the repatriation of savings by British residents in the colonies, and the payment of officials' pensions out of colonial taxes. Nevertheless, if we exclude the dominions from the balance sheet of colonialism, then the returns to Britain before 1914 begin to look as exiguous as those to France.

For want of a conclusive crunching of numbers, imperial Germany affords an interesting counter-example of an economy that was strikingly successful in raising its exports to the underdeveloped countries before 1913, yet whose colonial empire in Africa and the Pacific was commercially quite insignificant. By the eve of the war, German exports to primary producing countries substantially exceeded British (Aldcroft, 1968, Table III, p. 19). As far as German manufacturers were concerned, their own colonialism was profitless, yet they gained more from the widening of the international division of labour than any other European capitalist class.

The First World War altered the relationship between the metropolitan powers and their colonial empires both directly and indirectly. The French colonies contributed to the war effort by mobilising 607 000 soldiers and about 200 000 civilian war workers, and supplied strategic products in useful quantities. The empire enjoyed considerable public esteem and for a while the Minister for the Colonies, Albert Sarraut, received broad political support for an ambitious programme of colonial development that envisaged spending about 3½ milliard francs over ten to fifteen years (Coquery-Vidrovitch, 1979). In the event, the demands of domestic reconstruction were so great that none of the credits materialised, though Sarraut's plan did serve as model for subsequent projects and stimulated efforts to improve public health in the colonies. The major indirect effect came from the loss of a large proportion of French external investments through the collapse of Tsarist Russia and Ottoman Turkey. This was a harsh lesson in the value of political security when placing capital overseas, and made colonial issues that much more attractive. The franc's weakness on the foreign exchanges after 1919, and the need to reduce purchases in foreign currency, was an additional incentive to developing the empire as an economic resource. (However, a weak franc favoured exports to foreign, not colonial markets.

The fluctuating value of the franc explains much of the variation in the geography of French exports.) There was a boom in colonial trade up to the late 1920s, when French West African coffee exports tripled and cocoa quadrupled, and this attracted further investment. 'Finance capital' made its belated appearance in the political economy of French colonialism at the beginning of the decade, when the major investment banks first became active in mobilising capital for the colonies. Paribas, for example, founded the Compagnie Générale des Colonies and participated in the capital formation of several important mining and commercial concerns. Michelin, which purchased rubber plantations in Indo-China, was one instance of a leading manufacturer investing in the empire to secure raw material inputs. Largely because of the investment banks' activities, flows of private capital to the empire in the 1920s were much greater than public investments. The state had played a role in the economic life of the colonies often attributed to it only at a later date: before the war, it had 'pioneered' the way for private investment, eliminating many of the risks inherent in new enterprise in underdeveloped regions and assuring its profitability. By 1930, the empire was France's most important trading partner and most important recipient of capital exports. Even before the great slump, France had initiated imperial preference measures designed to create a protectionist economic bloc, the 'Unité Economique de la France Totale'.

To talk of France 'falling back' on the empire in the 1930s is misleading. Certainly, the global economic crisis strengthened an existing trend towards imperial economic autarky, but the empire was *already* the principal means by which France participated in the international economy (Marseille, 1984b, p. 155). The crisis accentuated the empire's value to France by reducing most external trade to vestigial proportions while having a lesser effect on colonial commerce. Reductions in both the price and volume of world exports led to the worst slump ever in global trade: total European exports tumbled from a peak of $16.1 milliards in 1929 to $5.9 milliards in 1933 (Bairoch, 1973, p. 12). The French government's mistaken policy of defending an overvalued franc during the early 1930s meant that French exports were worse and longer affected than those of other trading nations: from a 1929 peak of 50 139 million francs in current values, exports fell to a nadir of 15 492 millions in 1936 (data from Mitchell, 1992). Though French colonial commerce was badly hit by the crisis, reductions in the value of imports and exports of major colonies were *proportionally* less severe than they were for the metropolis, and volumes frequently rose. Algerian exports, for example, fell by about two-fifths in value between 1930 and 1935, and imports by about half, but this was a matter of falling prices concealing quantitative increases. The volume of Algerian wine exports to France doubled between 1927 and 1933. French markets for wine and wheat cushioned the impact of the trade slump on colon producers: despite quota restrictions, French credits allowed imports to be sustained at a higher level than would have been the case had Algeria been independent. Algerian terms of trade improved over the medium term because prices of manufactured imports fell more than those of primary products. The European colons gained most from improving terms of trade, but even Muslim farmers benefited. To a greater or lesser degree, the same pattern of an initial deterioration in the terms of trade followed by a more than compensatory improvement was observable in the other African colonies. Indeed, in purely commercial terms, the Depression was a not unfavourable conjuncture for primary producers in French Africa (Coquery-Vidrovitch, 1977).

As part of its strategy of dealing with the international economic crisis, France integrated the empire more effectively into a coherent economic bloc: African territories hitherto covered by the Congo free trade convention (described on p. 131) were assimilated to the metropolitan tariff, and the state responded to private disinvestment in the colonies after 1930 with a programme of public works financed by metropolitan loans. Fixed prices were introduced for colonial imports and restrictions were placed on the convertibility of colonial currencies tied to the franc so as to conserve foreign exchange. Colonial governments were authorised to borrow more freely on the French money market for infrastructural development. Another 40 per cent of the total public investment in the French colonies before 1940 was made between 1931 and 1935 under the Maginot Plan (named after the Minister for the Colonies at the beginning of the decade). These measures helped sustain the volume of French exports to the colonies, although their value (expressed in 1928 francs) fell from 9.7 milliard francs in 1929 to 3.6 milliards in 1938. Even more striking was the way protectionism worked for the benefit of colonial exports to France, provided they did not compete with French products. In the mid-1920s, only about a fifth of Indo-Chinese exports went to the metropolis, but by 1938 the proportion was 56 per cent. Two-thirds of French West African exports went to France in 1933, and four-fifths by 1935. Imperial preference raised the colonial share of French cocoa imports from 56.1 per cent in 1929 to 88.4 per cent in 1938, while for coffee the corresponding figures were 3.7 per cent and 42.7 per cent, and for rubber 9.3 per cent and 25.1 per cent (Ageron, 1991b, p. 40). Imports of Algerian and Tunisian wine had become such a threat to French producers that the government was compelled to limit their entry by quotas even before the onset of the Depression – which nicely illustrates how the colonial political economy was ultimately defined by national interests. By 1938, colonial commerce represented 27 per cent of France's total foreign trade. The empire had cushioned the impact of the collapse of external trade, and the public investment made under the Maginot Plan encouraged a revival of private capital exports to the colonies in the later 1930s. According to statistics published in 1935, 51.6 per cent of French capital holdings abroad were in foreign countries and 48.4 per cent in colonial titles. Most of the foreign issues were fixed-term state loans, whereas colonial titles were more stable and flows were more regular. Bearing in mind that the empire had accounted for less than a tenth of France's external portfolio on the eve of the First World War, this was a remarkable transformation. It was thanks to the empire that France was able to maintain capital exports at the same level as in 1914.

Apart from greatly strengthening the colonies' commercial ties with France, the Depression had the further impact of increasing – usually substantially – their public indebtedness. Government revenues came mainly from trade, and were severely reduced by the fall in the value of exports and imports, which began as early as 1926–7 in most of Black Africa. There was no crisis of overproduction as in the industrialised countries: African farmers strove to maintain their incomes by increasing their output as unit prices fell, and all their extra produce was marketed. But colonial budgets were severely strained by the loss of revenue and by continuing obligations incurred in easier times. Moreover, the retreat of private capital in 1930–1 threw the whole burden of equipping the colonies with social overhead capital onto the public sector. As noted above, metropolitan France agreed to finance public investment by means of loans, repayable over a fifty-year period at an interest rate ranging from 4 to 5.5 per cent. These loans – rather than the commercial recession – were the crucial factor in exacerbating public indebtedness, and increasing the fiscal burden on the peasantry. Budgets could be balanced only by imposing new, direct taxes at the time peasant producers were least able to afford them. French scholars have discerned in this policy of development loans the origins of a vicious cycle of 'aid' and indebtedness so characteristic of the 'Third World' in 1970s and 80s (Coquery-Vidrovitch, 1977, p. 407).

In a superficial sense, the colonial balance sheet was most positive for the French national economy during the 1930s, but even then some industrialists and administrators discerned unreckoned debits in the account. The prices of colonial groceries and raw materials that now formed a large proportion of French imports were on average twice those prevailing on

240 Europe and the Third World

world markets (Ageron, 1991b, pp. 40–1). The metropolitan industries which looked to the empire for their exports generally represented the more archaic sectors of French manufacturing, organised in family firms, with a diminishing share of total output. Cotton textiles provide the pre-eminent example (Marseille, 1975). In the 1920s, while French industry as a whole increased its output by a quarter as compared with 1913, the output of cotton manufacturing lagged behind its pre-war level. Because synthetic textiles were squeezing cottons out of the home market, a larger proportion of the output was being exported. (about 30 per cent in 1930, compared with 18 per cent in 1913.) Increasingly, however, French cottons were unable to compete abroad with Japanese and American producers, and exports were heavily concentrated on the empire, which accounted for nearly nine-tenths of overseas sales by the later 1930s. The French cotton industry's growing dependence on its protected markets was contrary to the 'logic' of comparative advantage in twentieth-century global development – a logic that has determined the relocation of textile manufacturing to non-European regions where labour and raw material costs are lower. As a result, the developed countries have provided a diminishing share of world textile exports. The trend was already evident in the 1920s when, throughout the industrialised world, textiles' share in total manufactured exports declined sharply: in the case of France, it fell from 42.8 per cent in 1928 to 24.8 per cent in 1938. The French empire was sustaining a stagnating industry and a relationship between core and periphery that was becoming outmoded in economic terms. Meanwhile, the technologically progressive branches of French manufacturing – such as motor engineering – were being 'asphyxiated' by the overvaluation of the franc and protectionism. Colonialism may have been the 'lifebuoy' of French capitalism between the two world wars, but it did not keep it afloat on the wave of the future.

The First World War had a far-reaching impact on Britain's position as the world's major source of investment capital over and above the compulsory liquidation of foreign assets to help meet the immediate costs of the conflict. Between 1919 and 1931, a considerable sum was invested abroad (about £1300 million), but in money terms it was a quarter less than during the corresponding period prior to 1914 and in real terms approximately half. Far fewer calls were made on the post-war London money market by foreign companies and governments (partly because borrowers' terms were more attractive in New York), and as a consequence empire securities were a bigger proportion of the diminished whole. About 65 per cent of new overseas issues were located in the empire, and 'imperial' public securities amounted to £591.5 million or 45 per cent of the total. Most public 'imperial' public capital was raised on behalf of the dominions, but India and the tropical colonies were relatively more important recipients than they had been before 1914. They took 36 per cent of the public capital invested in the empire, and the government of India was the largest single borrower on the London money market (Atkin, 1977, Table 14, p. 130 and app. A). What proportion of the private 'empire' capital was located in the tropical colonies and India cannot be determined from published sources, but since the Malayan rubber plantations alone attracted 13 per cent, the total share of the dependent colonies and India cannot have been much less than a quarter. Clearly, the colonies and India were rather important in sustaining London's position as a major capital market in the 1920s; the investment opportunities afforded by their public loans partly compensated for the end of the global railway boom and the fact that so many Latin American governments were now looking to New York for finance. Political and legislative factors reinforced the dominant position of empire issues: to encourage development lending, colonial stocks had been accorded trustee status and various privileges meant that the effective interest on empire public authority loans in London was less than the interest on foreign government loans floated in New York.

The collapse of the international economy in 1931 forced Britain, like France, into a preferential commercial system centred on the formal empire, though one in which colonialism played a subordinate part. Unlike France, exhausted reserves compelled Britain to leave the gold standard and allow the pound's international value to float. The empire (except Canada) and various trading partners and client states in the Sterling Bloc continued to peg their exchange rates to sterling and use it as their reserve currency, but there was no common exchange control system, no pooling of reserves, and all sterling assets were fully convertible to other currencies or gold. The first substantial tariffs had originated with the so-called McKenna Duties on imported luxuries, imposed in 1915 to save shipping space. They had been extended in the 1920s to cover motor vehicles, and had afforded considerable protection to motor manufacturing. Other industries had been protected by import restrictions in the 1920s, but in relation to total annual imports these *ad hoc* measures did not constitute a major violation of free trade principles. The economic blizzard of 1931, by creating a large unfavourable balance of payments, made tariffs politically irresistible, and under emergency legislation 50 per cent *ad valorem* duties were temporarily imposed on a wide range of manufactured goods. The Import Duties Act of 1932 formally inaugurated imperial preference by exempting empire goods from the new general tariff that ranged from 20 to 33 per cent according to the type of import. Foodstuffs were for the moment excluded, which kept the British market open to such specialist primary producers as Denmark and Argentina. Later in the year, the Imperial Economic Conference was convened at Ottawa with the objective of expanding free trade within the Empire–Commonwealth by removing dominion and Indian tariffs on British imports. The colonies were not represented, but were expected to acquiesce in the Ottawa agreements. In the event, it proved impossible for Britain to reconstruct the empire as an autarkic free trade association. Britain, Canada and India, and to a lesser degree Australia and South Africa, depended heavily on non-empire outlets for their exports. Empire countries could not replace these markets, and in their own interests the dominions would not allow imperial preference to destroy reciprocal trade with foreigners. More fundamentally, the dominions and India were determined on industrialisation and the protection of their infant industries against British competition. Industrial protectionism was already rampant in Australia and Canada by 1914, and the Indian government had been protecting a widening range of industries since the 1920s. The most they would concede to British exporters was further increases in the tariffs charged on foreign goods.

The old mercantilist conception of an industrialised mother country linked with primary producer dependencies could be maintained only with respect to the directly governed tropical colonies, and they were a relatively unimportant part of the imperial political economy Britain was attempting to construct in the 1930s. Though the proportion of imports from the empire to Britain increased from 32.9 per cent in the late 1920s to 41.2 per cent in 1934–8, and the proportion of exports to the empire rose from 37.2 per cent to 41.3 per cent, most of this was due to increased trade with the dominions, and represented the continuation of a long-term trend. The share of exports going to India declined from 11.6 per cent in the late 1920s to 8 per cent in 1930s. Between 1920 and 1939, exports to Australia, Canada and New Zealand combined totalled £1751 million, comfortably exceeding exports to India (£1340 million) (calculated from Mitchell, 1992; Cain and Hopkins, Table 3.3, p. 37). It is true that the African share of British trade rose impressively: by 1938 Africa was taking 13.2 per cent of British exports, whereas the USA took only 4.3 per cent and Canada 5 per cent. But over 70 per cent of Britain's African exports went to South Africa, which boomed after 1931 because of the rising value of its gold exports. The tropical colonies of Africa, South-East Asia and the Caribbean received 5 per cent of British exports in the late 1920s and 7.4 per cent in the late 1930s. Their combined contribution to British imports rose from 9.9 per cent to 11.4 per cent (Cain and Hopkins, 1993, Table 3.3, p. 37).

The Depression's impact on the trade of Britain's tropical colonies was broadly comparable to its impact on France's colonial empire: colonial export earnings plummeted from £207 million in 1929 to a low point of £93 million in 1932, though volumes did not fall proportionally because producers responded to collapsing prices by increasing output. There was no consistent movement in the terms of trade. Contrary to the experience of French Africa, the peasant economies of British West Africa fared badly: taking the late 1920s as a baseline, the purchasing power of the Gold Coast's exports relative to imports fell by nearly half up to 1934; the terms of trade recovered strongly in 1937, but then worsened again. By contrast, over the decade 1929–39, the purchasing power of Malayan exports relative to imports rose three-fold. Public debt increased throughout the tropical colonies, chiefly because the collapse of export earnings made the servicing of loans raised on the British capital market in the 1920s that much more onerous. But, though the Depression's impact was broadly the same, the political response of the metropolis was different. The British government did not act so forcefully as the French to integrate the colonies into a commercial bloc; indeed, the Colonial Office continued to advocate strict free trade for the colonies at a time when all other countries, including Britain, had abandoned the principle. The level of tariff preference for colonial tropical products entering Britain was generally too small to ensure a reorientation of exports to the British market, and in some cases (cocoa for example) Britain could not absorb all the crop. The average proportion of the colonies' exports consigned to Britain in 1927–9 was 25 per cent, and in 1937–9 it was 29.6 per cent (Havinden and Meredith, 1993, p. 179). There thus emerged a striking difference in the degree of dependence on metropolitan markets in adjacent tropical colonies: British West Africa, for example, sent 40.5 per cent of its exports to Britain in 1937, whereas the French West African Federation sent 82 per cent of its exports to France in 1938.

There were also significant differences in the development policies pursued by the colonial powers with regard to their tropical dependencies. From the early 1920s, British governments regarded public works in the colonies as a palliative to high unemployment at home and a solution to an (alleged) shortage in the supply of raw cotton. The Colonial Development Act 1929, which authorised grants and loans to colonial governments from a Development Fund, was chiefly conceived as a stimulus to the British economy that would increase exports of machinery and capital equipment and have a 'multiplier effect' on the demand for labour (Abbott, 1971). With the collapse of international trade and the huge rise in unemployment, the

Act became virtually irrelevant to Britain's economic problems. By January 1931, it was directly providing work for 13 000 people, while 2.7 million were unemployed. For the rest of the decade, expenditure under the Act represented a modest assumption by Britain of its sovereign obligation to improve the welfare of its colonial subjects (an obligation assumed much earlier by the Dutch government in the 'Ethical policy' for the East Indies). Up to 1940, the Development Fund paid out £6.5 million to finance schemes put forward by colonial governments. Unlike the Maginot loans, the Act did not significantly contribute to the growth of public indebtedness in the colonies, for three-fifths of disbursements were free grants, and loans were on easy terms with an interest free period in most cases. But neither did the frugal expenditure foster development by promoting secondary industry and diversifying colonial export schedules. Few proposals with these objectives were actually made by colonial administrators who were usually wary of modern economic growth as a threat to indigenous political institutions. In London, the mercantilist view of colonies as the primary producing complements of industrial economies and markets for manufactured imports still dominated Whitehall's thinking. As the Assistant Secretary of State at the Colonial Office complained, in any conflict of economic interests, British commerce ranked first, dominion interests second, and those of the colonies last (Meredith, 1975, p. 498). Those colonies outside London's direct control that had abandoned the 'open door' were expected to give a tariff preference to British manufactures and to refrain from encouraging local manufacturing enterprise. Where this did arise (Hong Kong and Malaya), it was considered an especially unwelcome form of industrial competition, because 'sweated labour' was, allegedly, exploited to the detriment of home producers. Some valuable public health and sanitation measures were initiated under the Act, but it failed to promote economic diversification. The Depression cruelly exposed the dangers inherent in growth led by a narrow range of primary products, especially those tropical groceries for which demand in the industrialised showed limited 'income elasticity'. Yet by 1939, the export schedules of most colonies had become even more concentrated on a narrow range of primary exports than they had been two decades earlier.

The British government's attempts to develop colonial markets for British exports during the Depression were largely ineffectual and their overall impact on the domestic economy was minute. The British share of colonial commodity imports steadily declined; for all British Africa, it fell from 60.3 per cent in 1920 to 44 per cent in 1937. True, the balance of colonial commodity trade remained favourable to Britain, and British predominance in financing, insurance and shipping in the colonies brought further advantages from the sale of 'invisible' exports. Thus, though offering few returns to industry, the colonial empire was a handy asset in terms of maintaining the international stability of sterling in the 1930s (which was a central objective of the political élite). Whether the objective accounting of social costs, such as Davis and Huttenback essayed for the pre-war period, would show it to have been any less of a liability is doubtful. Despite retrenchment in defence spending, the military costs of empire continued to impose a comparatively high burden on the British taxpayer.

The Balance Sheet of Dutch Colonialism

Colonialism was the handiwork of small powers, as well as great ones, and there is suggestive evidence that their economic gains from dominion in the underdeveloped world were larger than those of Britain and France, bearing in mind their smaller populations. Comparing the balance sheet of Dutch colonialism in Indonesia with British rule in India is instructive in this context. Relative to the size of the Netherlands population (8.8 million in 1939), Dutch involvement in colonialism, in both the private and public sectors, was certainly greater. Those classified as Europeans in the 1930 Dutch East Indies census numbered 240 000 (or 0.4 per cent of the total population), and on average they received 10.6 per cent of Indonesian net domestic product at factor cost between 1921 and 1939 (Maddison, 1990, pp. 322–35). We should note, though, that two-thirds of 'Europeans' were of mixed descent, and that they tended to monopolise the lower-ranks in the colonial administration while the highest posts were filled by metropolitan Dutchmen. Additionally, 5 per cent of national income in Indonesia accrued to non-residents (mainly Dutch) and to government entrepreneurship. Some European income earned in the Indies was consumed or reinvested locally, but a substantial proportion was remitted to the Netherlands, where it represented 8 per cent of Dutch net domestic product between 1921 and 1938. One-quarter of all direct taxes collected in the Netherlands came from colonial remittances (Albertini, 1982, p. 177). An informed guess was that from one-fifth to one-tenth of the Netherlands population either directly depended on, or had an indirect financial interest in, the commerce or industries of Indonesia (Keller, 1940). At the same period, there were 168 000 British people living in India. Only 26 000 were engaged in the private sector (compared with the 63 600 Europeans working in the Indonesian private sector) and they were less likely to be born in Asia. Angus Maddison has estimated that the British share of income of all kinds in India was about 5 per cent in the 1930s. The proportion transferred to Britain was comparatively small: 1.5 per cent of Indian product according to Maddison. Assuming this is correct, the transfer represented 0.8 per cent of British net product between 1921 and 1938. The surplus of exports to imports in Indonesia was proportionately more than twice as high as in India between the wars (75 per cent as opposed to 33.4 per cent), and this reflects the larger 'drain' to the Netherlands on Dutch account through residents' home remittances, remittances to non-residential commercial interests, and government transfers.

The impression of a more 'extractive' form of colonialism, in which Indonesia was conceived as a major business asset – to be valued for its pecuniary returns to Dutch nationals – is strengthened by comparing patterns of foreign investment (Tomlinson, 1986). In per capita terms, this was around four times greater in the Dutch Indies in 1930, and mostly the result of private business ventures. Government borrowing was approximately 20 per cent of the total. Foreign capital was heavily skewed towards direct agricultural production for the export market, with over half invested in agricultural industries and financial services, and a further 19 per cent in mineral extraction for use abroad. In Java, 84 per cent of the foreign agricultural capital was Dutch-owned in 1929, and seven-tenths of their holdings were invested in sugar that was mainly grown on village land rented to nearby factories. (The Dutch proportion of foreign investment was much smaller in Sumatra.) (See Furnivall, 1944, p. 311.) In India, by contrast, government debt represented about half the total foreign investment, and this had been mainly used to provide infrastructure serving the domestic economy as well as external trade. Private foreign investment in India was concerned mostly with the processing of peasant production, and was more evenly spread within the major sectors of the domestic economy.

The two colonial economies responded rather differently to the Depression: as we have noted elsewhere, Indian entrepreneurs were then taking over much expatriate business, and they accounted for most new investment in the 1930s. The only exception to this was the direct investment in local subsidiaries by British multinational manufacturers. In Indonesia, real investment was drastically curtailed with the collapse in world prices for tropical exports. Three-quarters of the Javanese sugar factories were sold off for their break-up value, and there was real hardship among European employees and owners of small businesses. The Dutch had been wedded to economic 'openness' for their colonial subjects since the late nineteenth century, and abandoned its principles very reluctantly. The Netherlands' share of Indonesian imports had steadily diminished since the early twentieth century, but the decline accelerated in the early thirties (falling from 17.8 per cent in 1929 to 12.9 per cent in 1934). This was partly due to the guilder remaining on the gold standard and the over-pricing of Dutch goods in international markets, but more to intensifying Japanese competition. By 1930, Japan dominated the market in cotton imports and was the chief source of pottery, cement and glassware. With the devaluation of the yen in December 1931, it became practically impossible for European or American manufactured imports to compete, whether the category of goods was electrical equipment, bicycles or sheet iron. The Japanese even began retailing in Indonesia, recruiting the first native shop assistants to serve in stores on the Woolworth model. Under a Crisis Ordinance of 1933, the government introduced quotas to restrict imports of textiles, cement and beer, and it raised duties on manufactures and reduced them on machinery. The policy objective was to wean the economy from its external trade dependence and foster infant consumer industries. Chinese entrepreneurs led the way in food, drink and tobacco processing, though European trading firms also diversified into manufacturing and some Indonesians set up small businesses making 'native' cigarettes, soap and leather goods. The Swadeshi movement and the government's Textile Institute stimulated local crafts, with the result that handweaving – usually undertaken by thirty or more workers in small factories – enjoyed a spectacular revival. The number of handlooms rose from 500 in 1930 to 35 000 in 1940, which encouraged the development of dyeing and improved the loom-building techniques of local carpenters. But there was no institutional structure to enable Indonesian entrepreneurs to penetrate the domestic market for consumer goods on a significant scale, and no parallel to the 'indigenisation' of large-scale enterprise in inter-war India. Even businesses nominally owned by Indonesians were often capitalised or controlled by men of different ethnicity, and at independence there were few native private businesses capable of taking the places hitherto occupied by Europeans and Chinese (Allen and Donnithorne; 1957, pp. 65, 268). For some manufacturing multinationals, the controls on foreign trade were an incentive to direct investment in production for the local market: General Motors had already set up an assembly plant in the late 1920s, and British American Tobacco opened a cigarette factory. Unilever, Bata and Goodyear were among the major multinationals investing in subsidiaries in the 1930s. Much of this new inward investment was non-Dutch, and publicists commented uneasily on the scarcity of Dutch interests in Indonesia's industries, whether capital-intensive implantations or smaller-scale enterprises of local origin (in which the Chinese predominated). Only 2 per cent of Dutch investment was in manufacturing industries in 1940 (Furnivall, p. 435; Allen and Donnithorne, 1957, app. II). This caution is slightly puzzling, given the colonial government's energetic support for manufacturing and industry, and its proclaimed intention of remaining in Indonesia for another three centuries. It may be that the Dutch were so entrenched in profitable enterprise geared to agricultural exports that they could not easily envisage alternative avenues for economic activity when external trade collapsed. It must be said that not all the 'signals' pointed to the end of the 'old' political economy based on the culture, processing and distribution of tropical staples. From 1934, some lines of colonial trade were salvaged by a quota system providing for the direct exchange of goods between the Netherlands and Indonesia: rice, copra and palm oil were 'swapped' for unbleached cottons, fertilisers, lightbulbs, and sanitary earthenware.

The fact that the Indies had been a large source of profit to the Dutch in Europe, while Dutch multinationals had not engaged in direct investment to the same degree as British MNEs in India, helps explain the different patterns of economic disengagement that accompanied independence. By 1939, the British political élite mostly accepted that there was no major national economic interest in India, and wanted to retain her in the Empire–Commonwealth for strategic reasons. British corporations that had directly invested in import-substituting industrialisation behind tariff walls adjusted fairly easily to independence, despite the Indian government's assumption of strict economic controls. The Dutch, by contrast, acted in the belief that independence would be a severe blow to the national economy. Their 'stake' was in the direct exploitation of Indonesian resources, and this made it much harder than in the British case to envisage a *modus vivendi* with nationalism. Dutch intransigence had the effect of a self-fulfilling prophecy, for independent Indonesia moved quickly to nationalise expatriate economic interests.

The Balance Sheet of Portuguese Colonialism

The final balance sheet we must consider is that of Portugal. There was a once pervasive view that this poor and backward European country retained its African possessions during the 'Scramble' for reasons of national pride and in defiance of economic good sense (Hammond, 1966; idem 1973). That orthodoxy is now somewhat discredited. Gervase Clarence-Smith has argued that the metropolitan bourgeoisie – which was the dominant class in the Portuguese state from the mid nineteenth century – exercised rational, class-based economic choices with respect to the empire, and was the most economically motivated of all European ruling groups during the partition of Africa (Clarence-Smith, 1979; idem, 1985). Discriminatory tariffs of 1892 were intended to secure a market for Portuguese consumer exports (especially textiles and wine) and compel colonial raw materials to come to Lisbon, even if they were to be re-exported. Though they could not be implemented in those parts of Angola and Mozambique covered by the Congo free trade convention, elsewhere tariffs severely restricted foreign imports. They also made it financially crippling not to send goods in Portuguese ships to the metropolis for re-export to their final destination. The colonial market proved critically important for the rapid, export-led expansion of the textiles industry (which employed more than a third of Portuguese working in units of more than ten workers by 1911) and took a third of wine exports by the 1900s (Newitt, 1981, p. 72). Financial interests involved in the Banco Nacional Ultramarino obtained lucrative monopolies in colonial banking and transport. However, while the evidence clearly indicates that Portugal's colonial revival was motivated by economic interest, and rewarded some sectors, it remains debatable whether the colonies added to national income before the Salazar era. Colonial trade amounted to only 8.8 per cent of total trade in 1910 and 6.7 per cent in 1920. The principal colonies, Angola and Mozambique, were poorly endowed, thinly populated territories that took decades to pacify, and their budgets required constant subsidisation by the metropolis. Though the output of the Portuguese textile industry nearly quadrupled between 1900 and 1924, only 5 per cent of raw cotton imports came from the colonies in the mid 1920s. Portuguese capital resources were insufficient to monopolise the colonial domain, with the result that foreign concession companies took over large areas of Mozambique. Economic relations with Brazil were more important, because Portugal depended on emigrants' remittances to cover a large and chronic deficit in the overall balance of trade. Clarence-Smith hazards that the colonies made little difference either way to the Portuguese national economy, though the country 'would probably have been somewhat poorer and less developed had it remained an isolated economic unit'. However, he adds that

an Iberian federation of an effective kind would almost certainly have brought greater benefits. To the extent that the colonies were a political and ideological obstacle to Iberian unity, they indirectly exercised a negative influence on economic development (Clarence-Smith, 1985, p. 19).

The republican interlude (1910–26) witnessed the rapid deterioration in colonial public finances, and a relative decline in Portugal's share of colonial imports. During the First World War, Portugal had supplied about 60 per cent of Angola's imports, but by 1927 this figure had sunk to 23 per cent and was by no means compensated for by the increased volume of trade. Short-term fiscal decisions prompted by the ravages of inflation reduced cotton textile exports to the empire and blocked moves to obtain more raw materials from the colonies. When Antonio Salazar – a gifted academic economist – came to power in the New State he may well have looked upon colonies as an economic liability. Although he had no immediate plans for turning them into an asset, in subsequent years his regime attempted to construct a unified escudo economy in which the colonies would take a larger share of Portuguese exports than hitherto, supply the mother country with primary products at advantageous prices, and strengthen the common currency by achieving positive balances in third-party trade. These objectives were not simply a neo-mercantilist defence of the *status quo*, but part of a development strategy for a metropolis that had itself long depended on the export of labour and its agricultural products to wealthier countries. To break out of its own dependency, Portugal and her colonies were to form a protected trading area in which there would be heavy tariff and quota preferences for imperial products. Rural areas were to achieve self-sufficiency in food, produce raw materials, and maintain a steady supply of cheap labour, all of which would enable urban Portugal to industrialise. Foreign capital was to be largely excluded, and where private Portuguese capital was not available, the state would finance investment. In this scheme of things, the colonies were viewed essentially as parts of rural Portugal, supplying the urban economy with industrial raw materials and essential foodstuffs and achieving import substitution in as wide a range of products as possible. They were also to provide the labour whose cheapness would keep the Portuguese economy competitive (Newitt, 1981, p. 190).

The most novel feature of the Salazarist colonial pact – which probably did most to strengthen the metropolitan economy – was the system of exchange control that allowed Portugal to exploit the colonies' exports to foreign countries more efficiently than the cumbersome re-exporting of colonial produce through Lisbon. The basis of Salazar's economic policy for Portugal and her colonies was monetary stability, achieved through rigid limits on public expenditure. Exchange control reinforced this deflationary political economy by helping sustain the international value of the escudo (long an inherently weak currency because of Portugal's huge trade imbalance). Before 1930, emigrants' remittances, and the repatriation of business profits, had been relied on to cover the Portuguese commercial deficit. With the world Depression, economic relations with Brazil were ruptured in a way that threatened the deflationary thrust of national economic policy. A new Brazilian government halted immigration, prohibited capital exports and imposed tariffs that severely reduced Portuguese wine and foodstuff exports. The flow of emigrants' remittances was abruptly cut off – throwing many Portuguese families into penury – the balance of payments deteriorated, and Portuguese banks in Brazil were ruined. This brutal severing of economic ties with Brazil brought the empire into greater prominence as the salvation of the Portuguese economy. To conserve foreign exchange, colonial currencies ceased to be convertible and licences had to be sought for a broad range of imports. Colonial re-exporting was replaced by the pooling of the colonies' foreign exchange earnings in a special fund which converted a large part into metropolitan escudos. Foreign exchange obtained from the empire took over the role played in earlier decades by the emigrants' remittances in covering Portugal's trade deficit. Since the metropolis controlled the colonies' access to foreign currency, it could also manipulate the exchange controls to boost sales of Portuguese products on the imperial market. Coupled with the regime's insistence on meeting all public expenditure in greater Portugal from current fiscal receipts, the system made the escudo one of Europe's strongest currencies.

Greater Portugal was the first European empire to be constituted into a monetary bloc–the escudo zone – and its provisions (inconvertibility, import licensing, pooled foreign exchange) anticipated those in the sterling area from 1939 and the franc zone. The indications are that these arrangements became very advantageous to the Portuguese economy from the later 1940s – and probably a great deal more advantageous in relative terms than the franc zone was to France. The major colonies ran considerable surpluses in foreign transactions (Angola through its commodity exports and Mozambique through invisible earnings) and much was transferred to the metropolis by the large favourable trade balance that Portugal had with her empire. This was without the considerable subsidies to colonial budgets that were needed to operate the franc zone, and which I discuss later in the context of the political economy of decolonisation.

Table 7.4   Share of the Portuguese colonies in Portugal's external trade (annual averages)

	Total imports (million escudos)	Total exports (million escudos)	Imports from the colonies (million escudos)	Exports to the colonies (million escudos)	% Share of total imports (%)	%Share of total exports (%)
1925–9	2539.2	884.4	366.8	104.0	14.4	11.8
1930–4	1939.2	852.0	192.8	103.8	9.9	12.2
1935–9	2207.4	1127.4	227.6	137.4	10.3	12.2
1940–4	2939.8	3146.8	902.6	512.6	30.7	16.3
1945–9	7976.4	4104.4	1252.6	1018.2	15.7	24.8
1950–4	9400.0	6660.0	1405.2	1643.6	14.9	24.7
1955–60	13220.0	8360.0	1746.6	2170.2	13.2	26.0

Source: Mitchell (1992).

As is evident from Table 7.4, the measures taken by the Salazar regime had little impact on the overall pattern of commodity trade between Portugal and her colonies during the 1930s: the colonial share of Portuguese imports actually fell and the share of metropolitan exports going to the empire rose only slightly. As intended, the proportion of the colonies' imports provided by Portugal rose over the decade: in Angola, it was 37 per cent in 1930–4, and 44 per cent in 1935–9. But this was substantially below the French share of imports into France's African colonies, and indicates the incapacity of the Portuguese economy to equip the colonies with many of their basic requirements. The overall figures conceal one important trend, because Portuguese imports for consumption from the colonies rose from 7 per cent in 1926 to a peak of 23 per cent in 1942. Nonetheless, it is clear that the colonies lacked the natural resources and ecological diversity to provide Portugal with more than a narrow range of products: cotton, sugar and vegetable oils accounted for three-quarters of their exports. Conversely, the home market was too small to absorb all Angola's coffee or the cocoa from São Tomé and tea from Mozambique. In the aggregate, the colonies were important as a source of supply only during the Second World War, and it was then that they became a major market for Portuguese exports. Even at the empire's peak economic utility to Portugal in the 1950s, however, the metropolis never did more than 22 per cent of its total trade with the colonies.

The aggregates conceal great variations in the trading pattern of different parts of the colonial empire and, more importantly, disguise the virtual imperial self-sufficiency achieved by the 1940s in the provision of sugar and cotton, a key raw material for the metropolitan economy. In the early 1930s, the colonial regime greatly extended a repressive system of forced cotton cultivation in Mozambique and, on a more limited scale, Angola. To encourage production, it offered concessionary companies in the colonies (but not African producers!) a price well above the depressed international level for raw cotton, and paid the differential as an export bonus so that the textile industry would not have to bear the cost. Simultaneously, the setting up of textile mills in the colonies was prohibited to protect metropolitan interests, and the regime moved to a policy of limiting colonial industrialisation to activities that either cut down on costly imports from abroad or increased the value of colonial exports sold to foreign markets. After a very difficult period during the Depression, the Portuguese cotton industry expanded rapidly on the basis of cheap colonial inputs and assured sales in colonial markets. Manufacturers entered a period of exceptional profitability in the late 1940s and early 1950s because colonial raw cotton was sold in Portugal at below world prices, while the price of piece goods in the colonies rose steeply. By the late 1950s, colonial cotton imports were nearly five hundred times greater by weight than they had been in the late 1920s, and the empire was meeting 80 per cent of Portugal's needs. Over the same period, the metropolitan textile industry acquired a dominant position in the African empire. In the 1920s only about a fifth of the colonies' cotton imports came from Portugal; by 1960 over nine-tenths of the cotton goods imported into Angola and Guiné were of Portuguese make, and in Mozambique the proportion was three-quarters. Unlike the situation in the French empire, this was not an instance of the colonial market sustaining an otherwise declining industry. Portugal in the 1950s was, in today's jargon, a 'newly industrialising' country where abundant cheap labour gave a comparative advantage in textiles manufacture. A small group of metropolitan firms invested the high profits of the 1940s and 1950s in technological modernisation that formed a springboard for launching a competitive industry onto international markets. Because of rising productivity, the real price of Portuguese cottons sold in the colonies fell substantially in the mid 1950s.

The other staple Portuguese industry which continued to look on the colonies as vital for its export was wine-making, but in this case one can detect an archaic branch of production 'sheltering' in a captive market. Portuguese wine-makers had customarily sold much of their ordinary wine to France for blending but, as imperial preference closed the

French market, they looked to their own government to make the colonies a 'reserved' outlet for their exports. The more extreme proposals of the wine lobby (such as the statutory payment of part of Africans' wages in wine) were rejected, but the government lowered the duties on Portuguese wine, kept the price of beer artificially high and tried to eradicate illegal production of alcoholic drinks. Partly as a result of these measures, but also because of the immigration of white settlers in Angola, colonial outlets became ever more important for producers of cheap wine. In the late 1950s, over 80 per cent of ordinary wine exports went to the colonies.

A tentative judgement on Salazar's version of the colonial pact would be that it complemented the regime's deflationary political economy fairly successfully and made a limited contribution to economic growth by raising demand for textile manufactures. It seems fair to say that the returns to the metropolis were more or less in proportion to the coercion of colonial labour: this was the most manifestly exploitative of colonial regimes, which refused to ratify the 1930 International Forced Labour Convention until 1956, and maintained compulsory cotton cropping until 1961. But it was a rather more dynamic and developmentalist colonialism than its many critics have allowed. By the later 1940s, the larger and better capitalised firms in Portugal, with profits boosted by neutrality during the Spanish Civil War and Second World War, were increasingly attracted by the idea of direct investment in the colonies. They could expect to cut transport and labour costs, and broaden the market for consumer goods. The regime relaxed its prohibition on colonial industrialisation, which was vociferously demanded by the white settlers. One set of light industries was established producing textiles, metal implements, foodstuffs, soap and other consumer items for rural Africans and poor townspeople (black and white). Another produced bulky intermediate goods such as sacking, cement and other building materials. The state supported this private industrial investment by providing energy and transport facilities, and launched ambitious development plans in the 1950s that entailed public investments broadly comparable to those made in the colonies of other European powers. In 1953–8 the state invested an annual average of approximately $20 million in the colonies, compared with five or six coming from the private sector. Even before the rapid and profound mutations in Portuguese imperialism that followed the 1961 Angolan uprisings, fundamental changes in colonial economic policy had been initiated.

Conclusions

This balance sheet of modern colonialism is more impressionistic than the language of accounting promises, and what should be major items are great gaps in the author's knowledge. However, enough has been said to revise the 'Cobdenite' view (well represented by Grover Clark's remarkable statistical compilation) that the colonies were sheer economic loss. They never fulfilled the exaggerated economic expectations of Leroy-Beaulieu or Ferry, but they were a major, integral part of the French economic ensemble by 1920, and allowed France to absorb the shock of the global economic crisis. Even a sceptical assessment of their economic worth should be qualified by a recognition of their value to the small colonial powers and to particular sectors of the large metropolitan economies. As an American analyst wrote in early 1940:

> It is the Indies which make Holland a world power. Supplying more than one third of the world's annual consumption of rubber, one fifth of the tin and one nineteenth of the oil, and possessing a practical monopoly of cinchona – to say nothing of its position in regard to sugar, tobacco, hard cordage, fibre, palm oil, bauxite, copra, spices, etc. – the Netherlands Indies have placed the mother country in the front rank of the 'have' powers (Keller, 1940).

I doubt whether Jacques Marseille's case for the colonial empire's contribution to French national economic growth before 1914 would withstand a counterfactual assault of the type so relished by Anglophone economic historians. He is right, though, to insist on the need for sectoral disaggregation of the national accounts, partly because it identifies the trades and industries with a stake in the political economy of colonialism and clarifies the relationship between colonialism and capitalist development in the first half of the twentieth century. It is striking how, among European capitalists, textile manufacturers – the quintessential representatives of capitalism in its competitive, individualist phase – had the most durable interest in colonial markets and raw materials, and punched the biggest political weight in making that interest felt. They clung to a resolutely Ricardian vision of an international division of labour between 'core' manufacturers and 'peripheral' primary producers, and correctly sensed that it could be sustained only by political subordination. The association between colonialism and what is misleadingly called 'monopoly capitalism' was weaker and, it would seem, differently phased, for the oligopolistic European firms tended to see overseas dependencies as sites for direct investment when they acquired tariff autonomy and their independence was in prospect.

8

THE POLITICAL ECONOMY OF DECOLONISATION

Introduction: The Complexities of Decolonisation

The use of a single word – decolonisation – to refer to the transfer of sovereignty from the imperial powers to their former colonies after 1945 may suggest a uniform process with a common set of causes. Were that true, it would make an account of the 'political economy' of decolonisation much easier to draw up. This suggestion is, unfortunately, largely erroneous: decolonisation in the Middle East, South and South-East Asia and Africa followed different chronologies, sprang from a variety of causes and took various forms. Japan's meteoric victories over the colonial powers directly and indirectly strengthened Asian nationalism and communism, which were about a political generation in advance of Africa. While the British empire in India, Ceylon and Burma was dissolving in the later 1940s, and the French and Dutch were fighting to restore their authority in Indo-China and the East Indies, European colonialism was having a new lease of life in Africa. Not that the imperial game was up in Asia: the British successfully reoccupied Singapore, Hong Kong and Malaya, and had short-lived illusions about the revival of the old 'concessionary' enclaves in China (Cain and Hopkins, 1993, pp. 275–81; Shai, 1980). The French and Dutch still attracted native allies, and the disparity between their forces and peasant insurrectionary movements (yet to be armed by the Soviet Union or communist China) remained considerable. Dutch 'police actions' against the Indonesian Republic were militarily successful and what persuaded the Netherlands to negotiate a transfer of sovereignty to Sukarno's republic was, primarily, American pressure backed up by the cessation of Marshall Aid (Ansprenger, 1989, pp. 254–57).

With serious qualifications, it is, nevertheless, broadly true that in Asia colonial economic and political structures were gravely weakened by the Second World War, while in Africa they were strengthened. The financial relationship between Britain and India had been reversed: India had accumulated considerable sterling balances in London, on account of unrequited exports of *matériel*, and was now Britain's largest single creditor. Any appearance of 'colonial' continuity with respect to the South Asian successor states after 1947 is superficial. Whitehall did not expect economic relations with post-imperial India and Pakistan either to aid domestic recovery or to greatly strengthen the Commonwealth as a hospitable external environment for British capitalism. Even the fact that India had become the largest overseas market for British capital goods was economically unwelcome. Engineering and other capital goods were, officials argued, needed to reconstruct the domestic economy, and if exported then they should go to hard currency areas (Tomlinson, 1985). Official pessimism as to the value of the post-imperial connection was born out by events: in 1946, the Indian market still accounted for 8.7 per cent of British exports but the proportion declined rapidly after Independence and in 1970 was less than 1 per cent. India attracted little of the exiguous funds available for foreign investment. The pattern of trade between the Indian subcontinent and the rest of the world had altered and it was no longer earning surpluses of hard currency that could be contributed to the common 'pool' of the sterling area. As the champion of 'neutralism', Nehru's India loosened the ideological bolts of the Commonwealth, and weakened its credibility as a British-led power bloc in international politics (Lipton, 1980).

Africa's strategic and economic value had waxed while South Asia's waned. World markets for African rubber, sisal and even coffee and cocoa recovered dramatically from their Depression lows when the Japanese cut off South-East Asian supply areas, and this favourable conjuncture continued after 1945 (Austen, 1987, pp. 205–6; Crowder, 1984, pp. 8–51). The British emerged from the war resolved to regroup their colonial empire around African territories where economic compensation could be found for the loss of India, Burma and Ceylon. Like the French and the Belgians, they regarded their African colonies as indispensable assets in the task of national economic reconstruction. Consequently, the 1940s witnessed 'the second colonial occupation' and a tightening of economic controls by the metropolitan powers which enabled them to squeeze and exploit their African colonies in ways never seen before (Fieldhouse, 1986, p. 6). Between 1945 and the late 1950s, Africa was more closely integrated into the economies of Europe than ever before. Yet, paradoxically, this period concluded with the European powers voluntarily abandoning the political instruments which reinforced such integration, though many of the economic and monetary ties (particularly those linking former French Africa to Europe) persisted until the early 1970s (Coquery-Vidrovitch, 1988b, pp. 105–33; Austen, 1987, pp. 204–9).

The Three Perspectives on Decolonisation

This chapter will try to combine three perspectives on African decolonisation. The first is that of the 'balance sheets' of the European colonial powers, and continues the analysis in Chapter 7. There is evidence – discussed below – that as the balances were scrutinised with greater care from this perspective, so the arguments for retaining colonies looked less compelling and decolonisation more attractive. Indeed, with respect to the French empire, the voluntary disengagement of private capital from colonial concerns appears to have preceded the lowering of the *tricolore* (Marseille, 1984a, pp. 128–33). The second perspective is afforded by the colonial economy itself, in which changes initiated by the colonialists unintentionally created the conditions for a transfer of power. In West Africa, accelerated development after 1945 typically precipitated a revolution of rising expectations, drew increasing numbers into urban wage labour, and broadened the popular basis of nationalism. Some of the most widely supported demonstrations of discontent in the whole colonial period occurred between 1945 and 1950, when protest movements assumed a more organised and more overt political form (Hopkins, 1973, pp. 268–9). Furthermore, with the retreat by expatriate concerns during the 1950s from certain activities they had previously monopolised, native entrepreneurs took over part of the colonial trading economy and so acquired a stake in it. A case in point is the relinquishing to local businessmen of bush trading stations by the giant commercial concerns in West Africa when their profitability no longer seemed sufficient. In the rather special circumstances of Kenya, rapid economic growth during the 1950s undermined the privileged position of the white settlers on mixed farms who had hitherto been allowed to represent all expatriate opinion. Newer European interests in commerce, industry and plantations were promoted, which were willing if necessary to abandon the settlers, and to ally with African leaders prepared to accept the private enterprise system and allow them to stay in business (Leys, 1975, p. 42). In brief, the striking changes in the political economy of late colonialism created the conditions for a conservative transition to post-colonial states in which many of the features and practices of the old regime survived. European governments appear to have assumed that by turning over political office to the most 'Westernised' Africans they would maintain the structures that had nurtured them (Austen, 1987, p. 226). These sentiments were echoed in at least some European business circles: during the late 1950s, Félix Houphouët-Boigny of the Ivory Coast (a wealthy planter who served in various French governments between 1956 and 1959) came to represent the kind of moderate African leader with whom the 'le parti colonial' was confident it could do business if and when independence came to French Black Africa (Pasquier, 1992, p. 310).

Our third perspective is afforded by the increasing interdependence and integration of the Western European economies since 1950, an economic and political transformation that has had no less an impact on Europe's relations with the 'Third World' than the decolonisation of the overseas empires. There were two strands to economic integration in Europe during the 1950s: one was the revival of multilateral trade among the liberal market economies that accepted Marshall Aid. The formation of the European Payments Union in 1950, of which Britain was a member, boosted multilateralism by allowing participating countries to offset trade deficits with one fellow member against surpluses with another. Intra-European trade expanded irrespective of the dollar shortage and Britain's participation meant that the sterling area (discussed below) was integrated into a wide zone of currency transferability. The second integrationist strand was the building of the common institutions now clustered in the European Union, and its most significant stages were the formation of the European Coal and Steel Community in 1951, of the Customs and Economic Union of the original Six in 1957, and its subsequent widening with the accession of new members in 1973 and 1986.

As far as the colonial and post-colonial world was concerned, European economic and institutional integration has had two contradictory consequences: 'associationism' and marginalisation. Under the Treaty of Rome, France secured the 'association' of her colonies (and Belgium's) with the EC to ensure free access to the Common Market for colonial exports, while in exchange the preferences enjoyed by French goods in the colonies were extended to the Six. The subsequent development of these accords into multilateral ties between former colonies in Africa, the Caribbean and Pacific with the European Community is discussed in the penultimate section of this chapter. The point to stress here is that it has done little to counter the marginalisation of the poorest, ex-colonial countries as far as the western European trading and investment bloc is concerned. From 1958 to 1973, the internal trade of the Common Market of the Six grew at 15 per cent per annum (while world trade increased by 9.5 per cent per annum) and as it did so the role of erstwhile colonies in Africa and Asia as markets and suppliers steadily diminished. Africa provided 11.5 per cent of EC imports in 1958, and only 4.9 per cent in 1971 (Grilli, 1993, Table 4.1, p. 141). The enlargement of the EC, and the accord of associate status to a large bloc of 'Third World' countries has not reversed this trend. For the former colonial powers, the complementary commerce with tropical dependencies which was a substantial proportion of their foreign trade in the early 1950s had become vestigial by 1980. For former colonies, the old metropolitan power became less important as a market and a source of imports. The investment ties between the metropoles and their former colonies have become equally tenuous because of a strong tendency to relocate overseas investment to industrialised countries.

  In delineating these three perspectives on the 'political economy' of decolonisation I am not arguing that the decisions to surrender European sovereignty were determined by economic factors and considerations. Scholars generally agree that there was little economic rationality or calculation behind decolonisation, and in negotiations with nationalist leaders, political and constitutional questions were certainly far more prominent than questions of commerce and investment (Fieldhouse, 1986, p. 231; Panter-Brick, 1988, pp. 73–104; Austen, 1987, p. 209). But decolonisation was not effected in an economic vacuum, and for both Britain and France the transformation in their external economic relationships between the later 1940s and the later 1950s profoundly altered the contexts and parameters in which imperial policies were formulated and decisions taken. In the years of post-war reconstruction and critical dollar and commodity shortages, metropolitan economic needs and colonial capacities were complementary: the colonial powers were willing to undertake the costs of accelerated development – in terms of investment in infrastructure and native welfare – because colonial primary producers promised a handsome return. By the later 1950s, the world of the late 1940s had been transformed. Britain's and France's industrial and dollar-earning capacities were greatly strengthened; the terms of world commodity trade had turned in favour of the advanced economies and the colonial hard currency earnings counted for less; 'imperial' economic blocs were being outmoded by the revival of multilateral trade. In these circumstances it had become much more difficult to define any positive role for the colonies in European economic advance (Porter and Stockwell, 1987, p. 27).

Colonialism in the Post-war World: France and Britain Compared

It is a paradox of France's post-war history that the nation was most committed to the empire when French capitalism and the state were least able to constitute an autonomous imperialist power. Gauged by the size of colonial trade and public investment in the colonies, colonialism was its zenith between 1945 and later 1950s. Yet liberated France was an impoverished economy in economic retreat from the wider world. In 1947, external investments were half of the value of foreign capital holdings in 1929 and less than a fifth in real value of those of 1914. Private foreign investments had to be requisitioned in 1946–7 to meet the balance of payments crisis caused by the outflow of dollars to pay for the capital goods imports of resurgent French industry. The traditional deficit in her foreign trade could no longer be filled by the income from capital invested abroad. Before the 1960s, there was little possibility for the export of private capital, and not till the beginning of the 1970s did capital exports reach levels comparable to those before 1914. The disparity between French strategic resources and political objectives became evident with the increasing reliance on US subventions for the Indo-Chinese war after 1949: at least two-thirds of the financial costs of the French war effort were being met by the United States by 1953 (Rioux, 1987, p. 214).

Despite her economic and military weakness, France was no more prepared than Britain to turn her back on the colonial past in 1945. In a remarkable disjunction between what a political community believes and the material resources at the disposal of the state, the idea of empire was seemingly more popular in France in 1944–5 than at any other point in French history (Ageron, 1991b, p. 103). It was as if the defeat of 1940, the end of French influence in central and south-eastern Europe, and the ignominious withdrawal from the former Syrian and Lebanese mandates under British and Arab pressure, all created a reflex determination to hold the colonial empire as a manifestation of French greatness. Every shade of the political spectrum except the communists believed that '*la France outre mer*' would provide a complement of force and energy to compensate France for her reduced role in Europe and the wider world. The premier Paul Ramadier spoke for a broad consensus when he declared in February 1947, 'France without colonies would be a servile France, condemned to being only a satellite' (quoted in Bouvier, Girault and Thobie, 1986, p. 262). At this time, few perceived any incompatibility between the planned modernisation of the French economy and retaining the colonial empire. Indeed, national economic planning and colonial development policy had evolved in tandem since 1940.

Even before the liberation of metropolitan France, the Free French movement had issued an unambiguous endorsement of the colonial 'mission' at the Brazzaville conference of the governors of French Black Africa, convened by de Gaulle in January 1944. The conference report flatly excluded any possibility of the political evolution of the colonies outside the French imperial bloc, at however remote a date. Admittedly, Brazzaville was not an entirely backward-looking occasion: it recommended the abolition of forced labour in the colonies (enacted in April–May 1946), and its commission reviewing the imperial economy warned against a return in the post-war world to the autarky that had prevailed before 1939. The integration of the colonies with the international division of labour was identified as a central objective of development. But the conference gave only cautious support to the idea of raising native living standards and purchasing power through the local industrialisation of primary product processing. Its proposal for a ten-year development plan to enable the colonies to compete better in world markets was less forward-looking than the development programmes prepared by Vichy officials (Marseille, 1984a, pp. 342–7; Coquery-Vidrovitch, 1988b, pp. 107–9). After the Brazzaville conference, the Provisional Government created the Central Fund for Overseas France (Caisse Central de la France d'Outre-Mer – CCFOM), in imitation of Britain's Colonial Development Fund, to provide credit for economic growth in the overseas territories where financial stringency had been the norm. The CCFOM promised a more liberal credit regime since it had the authority to issue colonial paper money and limit the autonomy of those colonial banks that had not yet been nationalised.

When the first national plan for modernisation appeared, its authors declared that the recovery of France was 'inconceivable' without a 'complementary' development of the overseas territories of the French Union, and they sought to integrate metropolitan and colonial economic objectives into a coherent whole. Though raising native living standards was given prominence, the core aims were those of the traditional 'colonial pact': the colonies were to furnish the metropole with cheap primary produce and their 'development' would consist mainly of an infrastructure facilitating the harvesting and export of agricultural and mineral products. Proposals for colonial industrialisation – which far-sighted officials had advocated in the 1930s as a solution to the structural crisis of overpopulation and underemployment in French Indo-China – were ignored (Marseille, 1984a, pp. 347–8). The real break with the past lay in the renunciation of loans as the basic means for financing colonial development, for it was acknowledged that debt payment had weighed too heavily on colonial budgets. The creation of the Investment Fund for the Economic and Social Development of Overseas France (FIDES) in 1946 simultaneously inaugurated colonial planning and a policy of financing capital equipment by outright grants and 'soft' loans. Individual colonial governments were required to submit plans indicating their investment requirements. In line with the predominant role of public power in the colonial economies since the 1930s, the planning law entitled the state to concert private economic activity, and eventually to supplement it by public companies or 'mixed' enterprises.

Under the two colonial development plans of 1947–52 and 1954–8, French public investment accounted for 83 per cent of the French capital placed in the empire and comfortably exceeded in real terms all the public investment of previous decades (see Table 8.1). In Black Africa, total expenditure was about three times greater than during the fifty years preceding 1939. Some authors have sought to debunk huge French investment as a 'myth', claiming that the largest amount of the funds invested emanated not from France but from taxation levied on Africans, and that a significant portion of the funds dispensed came from Marshall Aid (see, for example, Manning, 1988, p. 126). There is little substance to this charge. The planners had originally earmarked 2 per cent of the metropolitan budget for the development of overseas France but this proved inadequate to infrastructural needs, and actual spending accounted for 5.1 per cent of the budget in 1949. Metropolitan expenditure – mostly in the form of grants – totalled about 340 milliard francs under the first plan (not including grants to Indo–china) and more than the anticipated total of 348 milliards during the second plan. Additionally, subventions and 'soft' loans were made available to overseas territories so that they could balance their budgets. Spending appears to have peaked in 1955, when 9 per cent of the metropolitan budget was absorbed by colonial investment, debt charges and related items, and there were further expenses resulting from military operations. In that year, nearly a tenth of the taxes born by the French were in respect of expenditure in overseas France. Contrary to the claims of nationalist writers that most of the FIDES credits were recycled to France in the form of trading company profits and salaries, detailed calculation showed that 61 per cent were directly invested in the form of bridges, dams, hospitals and schools. It is true that investment on this scale led to a considerable additional burden on local budgets because of the rising costs of maintenance and administration; nevertheless, much of this burden was relieved through interest-free advances made by the CCFOM (Ageron, 1991b, pp. 117–20).

Spending on welfare also rose steeply, especially in Algeria where Muslim population growth was assuming Malthusian form and where the attempt to 'assimilate' Algerians to metropolitan citizenship led to huge increases in social security transfer payments. Payments of family allowances rose five-fold between 1946 and 1955. By the later 1950s, public spending in Algeria accounted for more than half of French public expenditure on the empire (Marseille, 1984a, p. 136). Under the predominantly left-wing governments of post-war France, protective legislation was extended to native workers, which indirectly increased the costs of development. The Moutet Code of 1947 introduced the principle of equal wages for equal work for European and native employees in the overseas territories. Moutet's successors suspended this entitlement under massive pressure from the Comité de l'Empire Français and employers of African labour, but it nevertheless contributed to raising labour costs on public works. The 1952 Code du Travail went further by proposing trade union rights for native workers, a forty-hour week, paid holidays and, again, 'equal wages for equal work' (Albertini, 1971, p. 428).

Table 8.1   French capital invested in overseas France (millions of 1914 francs)

| | Private funds | Public funds | | Total |
	colonial company issues	Loans	Credits for capital equipment	
Before 1914	1970.9	2098	2424.1	6493
1915–29	1623.9	676.2	231.5	2531.6
1930–9	799.8	3888.9	539.6	4728.3
1940–58	1989.8		10000.5	11990.3
Total	6384.4		19858.8	25743.2

Source: Marseille (1984a, p. 105).

Colonial development clearly imposed a far greater burden on the French taxpayer than on the British. R.A. Austen has calculated that, in 1960 US dollars, the total public development aid disbursed to the French colonies was $3448 million between 1946 and 1960. The comparable disbursement under the British Colonial Development and Welfare Acts and other legislation in this period was $1246 million (Austen, 1987, Table 8.1). Britain's economy was slightly bigger, so the relative burden on the British public purse that much smaller, while British colonies were more densely populated than the French, so the discrepancy in per capita expenditure was huge. Confirmation that France was committing a comparatively large proportion of her national product to overseas development can be found in OECD figures for net public aid as a percentage of GNP. In 1960, nearly all French aid was directed to territories in the French Union and accounted for 1.38 per cent of French GNP. For Britain, public development aid represented 0.56 per cent of GNP. Significantly, of the listed countries, only Portugal devoted a higher proportion than France of GNP to development aid (Chipman, 1989, p. 194).

France's theoretical gains from this expenditure was an exceptionally favourable position for her exporters in colonial markets, and access to colonial supplies that could be purchased in francs (thus enabling the French Treasury to conserve hard foreign currency). In the post-war decade, 37.6 per cent of total French exports were sold in the French Union, and it supplied on average 24.4 per cent of all French imports (Fitzgerald, 1988; see Table 8.2). For exporters, the empire was even more important than it had been in 1938 when it received 27 per cent of total French exports. The proportion of metropolitan French goods in the total imports of Overseas France had risen from 59 per cent in 1938 to 71 per cent in 1951, and the structure of trade remained typically 'colonial'. Agricultural products were on average 78 per cent of colonial exports to France in 1951–3 and manufactures were 84.1 per cent of metropolitan exports to the colonies in the same period. Two industries, textiles and metallurgy, provided about 36 per cent of metropolitan exports to the French Union in the early 1950s. The captive nature of colonial markets appears to have allowed French exporters much more scope to maintain profit levels. From 1949 to 1958 the volume and value indices of exports to the colonies advanced at just about the same rate (62 and 61 per cent) which contrasted sharply with the performance of exports to foreign markets where the volume index doubled while the value index rose by only 39 per cent. The principal colonial imports were wine, coffee, cocoa, tea, fruit and vegetables, and oilseeds and kernels: together, they accounted for about 55 per cent of all imports from the French Union (Bloch-Lainé, 1956, pp. 484–7, Tables III and IV).

Table 8.2   French colonial trade as a proportion of total French commerce 1946–56

	Exports to the French Union		Imports from the French Union	
	Worth (billions of current francs)	Share of total exports (%)	Worth (billions of current francs)	Share of total imports (%)
1946-8 (average)	106.4	42		
1949-51 (average)	420.5	38	335.8	21
1952-4 (average)	555	38	362.9	26
1955-6 (average)	540.2	32		

From the first of our perspectives, that of the French national economy, the commercial advantages of colonial trade were factitious. The reasons for this included the artificially high prices paid by French consumers for colonial produce and the fact that uncompetitive metropolitan industries were 'sheltering' in protected colonial markets. But the most serious drawback of colonial trade in national accounting terms was that it required the subsidisation of colonial budgets by the metropolitan treasury, as was clearly demonstrated when a team of economists under the former treasury official, François Bloch-Lainé, analysed the accounts of the franc zone in the 1950s. This defensive monetary union had been established in September 1939, and it ensured the interconvertibility of the colonial and metropolitan currencies within the franc zone but regulated exchange with currencies outside it. As in the sterling area and escudo zone, hard currency earnings were pooled. However, while Portugal gained because her colonies earned considerable amounts of foreign exchange, France lost because almost all the overseas countries in the franc zone had an unfavourable commercial balance in their foreign trade. They imported more from the dollar zone and from the countries belonging to the European Payments Union (except Britain) than they exported to them, and ran trading surpluses only with countries that had 'soft' currencies. Additionally, the overseas territories imported much more from metropolitan France than they exported, a commercial imbalance which could be sustained only by capital transfers. These were mostly public funds destined for infrastructural investment. There was little *net* private investment by French companies and individuals (since repatriated profits and disinvestment in the colonies largely cancelled out fresh capital inflows), and negligible foreign investment. The 'colonial pact' was now operating in reverse: the metropole furnished francs so that its dependencies could run large trade deficits and import the capital goods they need for economic development. Although North African nationalists denounced membership of the franc zone as the colonial monetary yoke, objectively it was a favour done to them and not a sacrifice imposed on them (Bloch-Lainé, 1956, p. 36, p. 44).

Trade in the franc zone was regulated by preferential tariffs on colonial goods entering France and quotas on imports into the colonies from outside the zone. Some goods (vegetable oil and cotton) were bulk-purchased by official agencies, though this had less significance than in the British colonies. Support funds, guaranteeing minimum prices for most exports from the Black African colonies, were instituted between 1946 and 1949. Since these operated by export levies, they proved unpopular with their supposed beneficiaries. In the mid-1950s, a new system of price stabilisation was introduced, the cost of which was borne largely by a central fund in Paris. As in the British colonies, native entrepreneurs engaged in the export economy became beneficiaries of the imperial marketing system, with a strong interest in maintaining the external orientation of the economy beyond formal decolonisation. But, underlying this similarity between French and British colonial development in post-war Africa, one broad difference is worth emphasising immediately. The French colonies were on the whole poorer, and more reliant on French public investment and officialdom, as well as French markets and French expatriate business. During the later 1950s, the proportion of the exports of French West Africa going to France rose from 61 to 69 per cent, and from Equatorial Africa from 62 to 66 per cent. (A further 10 per cent of French West African exports, and 7 per cent of Equatorial African, went to the rest of the franc zone.) In both territories, France provided over 60 per cent of the total imports in 1958 (Suret-Canale, 1972, p. 134). The British colonies, besides being wealthier, were becoming less dependent on the colonial power's markets in the run-up to independence. Ghana sent 30.7 per cent of its exports to Britain in 1955, and 21.5 per cent in 1960. Imports from Britain declined from 47 to 37 per cent of total imports during these years. Nigerian exports to Britain declined from 69 per cent of the total in 1955 to 47 per cent in 1960. Imports from Britain fell from 47 to 42 per cent (calculated from Mitchell, 1982). Even Tanganyika, one of the poorest colonies, was sending only about half its exports to Britain in the late 1940s, and by the eve of independence this had declined to just over a third. The modifications made to the French West and Equatorial African economies after 1945 had the effect of integrating the Federations more closely with the metropolis, whereas in British West Africa economic innovation sprang mainly from the expansion of the open economy itself, and so was self-financing to a much greater extent. This distinction had far-reaching political implications: it helps to explain why the Gold Coast and Nigeria took the lead in demanding and achieving independence, and why the French colonies, when offered independence in 1958, chose with the exception of Guinea, to remain temporarily within the French Community (as the federation of the metropolitan France and its overseas dependencies was styled in the Constitution of the Fifth Republic) (Hopkins, 1973, p. 289).

Britain's international economic position in 1945 was scarcely less transformed than France's: the country was reliant on American economic aid and, having liquidated most of its overseas assets, was now the world's greatest debtor, with liabilities to the rest of the sterling area totalling £3700 million. Net overseas investment income, which had long offset deficits in commodity trade, was less than a quarter of the pre-war level in terms of real purchasing power. Between 1946 and 1949, capital imports exceeded exports, and only the inflow of US loans and grants enabled Britain to send capital abroad (mostly to the sterling area). The price of economic dependence was made clear when, during negotiations for the fifty-year loan of $3750 million, the USA insisted on the convertibility of sterling and commercial non-discrimination in the sterling area from mid-1947. As Britain had done once, the US was now championing 'openness' and multilateralism in the international economy, and saw the non-convertibility of sterling and the imperial preference system as major impediments to the free movement of goods and capital.

In the event, implementing convertibility was a disaster: the rest of the world rushed to satisfy its insatiable demand for dollars on the London money market, forcing the British government to suspend convertibility in August 1947. The incident did as much as anything else to convince the political élite of the decline of British power. But it also reinforced a bipartisan conviction that the sterling area represented the only viable strategy for a trading economy with a high propensity to import that was pledged to full employment and to heavy domestic investment in housing and social welfare, and yet wished to insulate itself against the deflationary pressures of the dollar shortage. Recourse to the sterling area also promised to ensure the supply of materials whose shortage was a chronic anxiety for the Labour government. In this strategy, a rejuvenated colonialism, dedicated to rapid development, played a key role, not least because of the dollar-earning capacity of the colonies in the post-war world. As the new Chancellor of the Exchequer, Stafford Cripps, told the African Governors' Conference in November 1947: 'The whole future of the sterling group and its ability to survive depends . . . upon a quick and extensive development of our African resources' (quoted in Low, 1991, p. 170). Post-war economic vulnerability stimulated not a steady retreat from empire but a new spasm of 'constructive' colonialism.

The balance sheet of post-war colonialism was so closely connected with the fortunes of the sterling area that something must be said about its structure and function. Like the franc zone, it came into formal existence as a wartime measure to conserve hard currency earnings in Britain and the Empire–Commonwealth (except Canada, which formed part of the dollar zone), and was joined by some independent states after 1945. Member countries held their foreign exchange reserves in sterling and pegged their mutually convertible currencies to it. They were exempted from British exchange controls, so capital could move freely between them. Their governments had the right, denied to those outside the area, of borrowing on the London capital market. The area functioned as a multilateral trading system, except that dollar earnings were surrendered to a 'Dollar Pool' in exchange for sterling, and members could draw on the pool for their hard currency requirements when they made licensed imports from the United States. The USA put up with this 'dollar-discriminatory trading club', and financially supported Britain with Marshall Aid, because of an overriding political interest in strengthening the Western allies during the cold war (Strange, 1971, p. 62).

Whether a territory gained or lost from sterling area membership was generally determined by its political status. Dominions and independent states participated out of self-interest: most of their trade was conducted within the area and they gained from the exchange stability of the system, as well as access to steady supplies of hard currency. In the five years to 1950 they were net drawers on the Dollar Pool as well as substantial importers of capital from Britain. But the dependent colonies, which earned surpluses with the dollar area throughout the period 1945–56, were forced by virtue of their colonial position to surrender hard currency to the central pool. Given that the heaviest contributions were made by Malaya, the Gold Coast and Nigeria, it is hard to deny that Asian and African peasants laboured to support living standards throughout the 'white' Commonwealth (Newton, 1985, p. 178). Only a small proportion of the export surpluses earned by the colonies was reinvested locally. Most accumulated in Britain as sterling balances, together with the reserves of the Currency Boards and marketing agencies. Between 1945 and 1957, the colonies' sterling holdings rose from £411 million to £1281 million, the biggest increases coming during the Korean War stockpiling boom when exceptionally high prices were paid for primary commodities (Hazlewood, 1962, p. 187). Britain was in the anomalous position of continuously borrowing from its poorer dependencies funds that they could have used for their own development. By contrast, the holdings of the independent sterling countries were reduced in all but two of the years between 1946 and 1957. During the crisis of 1947, the British government had to restrict the right of its major creditor, India, to draw down its balance, but this was a negotiated and temporary arrangement. Subsequently, India, Pakistan and Egypt drew upon their balances at agreed rates to finance trade deficits and capital goods imports; in the 1950s, India financed half her deficit by running down her sterling balance.

Currency regulations and import-licensing had the intended effect of concentrating British trade within the sterling area. In 1936–8, the area had furnished 32 per cent of Britain's annual imports on average and received

41.4 per cent of British exports. The area provided 33.5 per cent of UK imports in 1946 and nearly 39 per cent in 1950. The proportion of British exports going to the sterling area rose from 45.6 per cent in 1946 to 50.8 per cent in 1949 (although it then fell back). Within the overall framework of sterling area trade, colonial commerce was proportionally greater than before the war. The colonies supplied 34.9 per cent of UK imports from the sterling area in 1946–50, as against 24.8 per cent in 1936–8; they received 26.2 per cent of British exports to the sterling area in 1936–8, and 31.1 per cent in 1946–50 (Sargent, 1952, pp. 536, 545).

Colonial supplies were particularly advantageous to Britain because they represented a saving of the dollars needed for capital goods imports and were acquired at less than world market values. By bulk-purchasing the major cash crops at administratively determined prices, and making their export a state monopoly, Britain manipulated the terms of trade with its colonies. Colonial producers were denied access to the international commodity markets that had reopened with the scrapping of US import-licensing and official price ceilings, and there was a growing disparity between the prices they received and those obtainable elsewhere. In early 1947, Britain was bulk-purchasing copra, palm oil and kernels for between two-fifths and two-thirds of their world market value, while the colonies were paying fully competitive prices for their manufactured imports. Development and welfare expenditure in no way compensated for their commercial losses: Nigeria, for example, was losing over £8 million a year, while its Colonial Development and Welfare allocation was £2.5 million. As the Colonial Secretary warned in March 1947, if this course were pursued then His Majesty's Government 'would be accused of imperialistic exploitation, the only difference between it and the economic exploitation of the 19th century being that the State was now the guilty party' (CO 852/989/3, 'Prices of colonial export products': draft Cabinet memorandum by Creech Jones, reproduced in Hyam, 1992). Resentment of this 'unequal trade' boiled over in the Accra riots and Nigerian strikes of 1948.

Ambitious proposals to exploit colonial resources (such as that for mechanised groundnut production in Tanganyika) dated from the end of hostilities, when the world appeared threatened by chronic food shortages, especially of oils and fats. Since expenditure under the CDW Act 1945 was mainly directed at basic social services and public utilities, the British government established the Overseas Food Corporation to promote colonial food exports to Britain and the Colonial Development Corporation to develop mineral resources and industrial crops where supply to Britain or other countries would assist the balance of payments. Until the convertibility crisis, the Treasury's attitude to their funding was typically parsimonious, but thereafter it acknowledged the national self-interest in sanctioning costly development to increase dollar-saving colonial supplies. Greater quantities of cocoa, cotton, coffee, tobacco, groundnuts and chromium would also promote reciprocal trade between the sterling area and western European countries with ready access to sterling. The disastrous Tanganyikan groundnut scheme absorbed £36 million in a futile attempt to provide the metropolitan housewife with edible fats (Low, 1991, p. 172).

The results of the 'new colonialism' on the ground were agricultural improvement schemes and the expansion of cash-crop production, educational advance and better sanitary measures, constitutional progress and local government reform. The market was extended by an increase in money earnings, physical improvements in communications, and greater government expenditure. As a consequence, entrepreneurs found it worth while to invest in local consumer goods industries (although import controls and shipping shortages in the immediate post-war years had given a prior incentive to manufacturing). Annual government expenditure in Tanganyika, for example, rose from £8.7 million in 1949 to £22.6 million in 1956, and effected 'a new level of governmental penetration of society' by what seemed to Africans a growing army of officials. Domestic exports doubled in real value between 1945 and 1955 and, with the cash crop boom, the money earnings of coffee and cotton cultivators brought 'new levels of rural prosperity'. The number of licensed motor vehicles rose about nine-fold between 1943 and 1957 (Iliffe, 1979, pp. 443, 453). Though not on the scale of the industrialisation undertaken by Kenyan Asians from the early 1950s, the beginnings of local consumer goods manufacturing were evident in late-colonial Tanganyika. In West Africa, the lead in establishing import substitution industries was taken by the giant trading firms (CFAO, SCOA, UAC), partly in response to the more competitive conditions of the expanded market. The value of Nigeria's manufacturing output, for example, grew nearly five times during the 1950s, as former importers competed to establish subsidiaries. Manufacturing was still a small sector of an overwhelmingly agricultural economy in the early 1960s – accounting for less than 5 per cent of GDP – but it was the fastest-growing, and attracting foreign investment away from trading and services. The expatriate firms moved into manufacturing in the hope that they could achieve sufficient savings in production and transport costs to undersell their new rivals. Though consumer goods for which there were mass markets were the main lines of production, other industries (such as cement) were started in response to transport costs and the local supply of raw materials (Kilby, 1969, pp. 11, 21; Hopkins, 1973, pp. 278–9).

The political economy of late colonialism included, as we have seen, a panoply of controls over export marketing that resulted in the punitive taxation of primary producers, and a crucial dimension of economic decolonisation was the bequeathing of these controls to the independent regimes, along with a policy of 'squeezing' primary producers in the name of development. Between the establishment of the produce marketing boards in 1947–9 and 1962, the state export monopolies withheld from Nigerian and the Gold Coast farmers between one-third and one-half of the commercial value of the yield of controlled crops (Bauer, 1973, pp. 643–650). The West African peasant agricultural sector accounted for about half the growth of real output, but received on average only about 12 per cent of total investment. Though the original beneficiaries of economic controls were the expatriate trading firms, as the system became more complex and 'politicised' it protected influential African traders. The emergent nationalist élites came to look upon the state-managed economy as a key part of their inheritance: they shared the European officials' impatience with 'peasant conservatism' and the only model of development with which they were familiar was an autocratically imposed one. In Tanganyika, for example, the African Association rarely met in the 1950s without demanding compulsion in some field (Iliffe, 1979, p. 443). Even before Nigerian independence, the corruption inherent in a high degree of administrative intervention in a developing market economy was evident in kickbacks by public works contractors to the leading political parties in the regions.

Economic Modernisation, European Integration and Decolonisation: The Basic Connections

If we concentrate for the moment on France, the coincidence between European integration and decolonisation is striking. The signing of the Treaty of Rome was closely preceded by the independence of Morocco and Tunisia and the voting of the *Loi-cadre* (outline law) devolving considerable political power to the dependent states of the French Union. The Treaty of Rome was fairly soon followed by the breakup of the French Community and the independence of the French colonies in sub-Saharan Africa. (Guinea, which rejected continued 'association' with France in the referendum of September 1958, became independent in October. The other Black African colonies became independent in 1960.) What, if any, were the common impulses behind integration with Europe and decolonisation? Integration was certainly not conceived as a diminution in the competence and authority of the French national state; on the contrary, it was a strategy for restoring French national power by tying the strongest industrial economy in western Europe, Federal Germany, in subordinate alliance. But though the traditional political objective of national security was the primary motive for integration, it also reflected the novel conception of national power as accountable in economic terms. As A.S. Milward has written, in the 1950s national income growth came 'to occupy in the national psyche of western Europe the place formerly occupied by the growth of national territory' (Milward, 1992, p. 41). Advocates of integration had done most to reshape the political agenda in terms of this new national self-consciousness: Jean Monnet, who proposed the 'High Authority' to run the ECSC in 1950, had drawn up the first plan for Modernisation and Equipment in 1946–7. Between these dates, he had come to see an integrated western Europe as offering the competitive market environment necessary for the modernisation of the French economy, especially its protectionist and 'Malthusian' manufacturing sector.

Trade liberalisation and economic modernisation in an integrated western Europe could not occupy a central place in national policy without the rationale and future of the colonial empire being called into question. In his important study, Marseille has traced how the empire came to be seen by officials within the French administration and certain capitalist groups as a drain on national resources and a restriction on the dynamic and competitive elements in French capitalism (Marseille, 1984a). The debate on the future of the colonial empire had its roots in opposing responses to the world depression of the 1930s: those representing an 'autarkic' tendency argued for preserving the colonies as sources of primary commodities and as a *chasse gardée* – or licensed game park – for French exporters and investors. Ranged against them were economic liberals whose primary objective was to strengthen the metropolitan economy by opening it up to international competition; in terms of the colonial political economy, this meant abandoning protection and lending support to local industrialisation. Furthermore, though France decolonised at a time when an unprecedentedly large proportion of her external trade was with the colonies, senior figures in the economic and financial administration and many business men had long been convinced that the colonial market was not only useless but an encumbrance to the modernisation of the French productive infrastructure. Decolonisation had none of the dire consequences for the national economy which 'le parti colonial' had predicted. (In fact, French external trade soared and the balance of payments went into surplus after decolonisation.)

Ostensibly, British decolonisation falls into a different pattern because the process was well under way when Britain first applied to join the Common Market in 1961 and was, with isolated exceptions, a receding memory by the time membership was secured in 1973. Until 1960, those willing to contemplate integration under a supra-national authority were isolated converts in the political class: the primacy of the Commonwealth – which supplied cheap food and reliable allies in national peril – was part of the 'Butskellite' consensus. But as early as mid 1956, the British government was planning to bring some coherence to economic policy by associating with France, Germany, Italy and other countries in an industrial free trade area which, it was hoped, would eventually embrace western Europe. The strategic objective – spelt out in Harold Macmillan's 'Plan G' – was to provide Britain with a unified market of the size required by the scale of modern technology, one in which her industries would be driven to raise their competitiveness (Morgan, 1980, vol. 3, pp. 9–10; Macmillan, 1971, ch. 3). No viable future could be seen for the sterling Commonwealth as an autonomous trading bloc. Although the wartime and post-war emergencies had temporarily bolstered imperial autarky, by the mid 1950s the British market was saturated with the primary products of the temperate dominions and tropical dependencies, and import-substituting manufacturing in Australia and elsewhere had reached an advanced state. There were no tariff advantages in the import of copper and rubber from the colonies because of Britain's adherence to the GATT agreements. (Their basic principle was the non-discriminatory regulation of trade: if one country reduced import tariffs on a particular item from a second, then all other countries adhering to the agreement could demand the same treatment.) For these reasons, the imperial preference system was crumbling away, with no hope of reinvigoration. The attraction of western Europe as a large, steadily more prosperous and integrating market in which British industry would be compelled to improve its efficiency was plain enough, and still more evident because the only alternative appeared to be closer attachment, as a minor partner, to the United States.

When the proposal for an industrial free trade area was discussed in Cabinet in September, the Colonial Secretary wondered whether the UK 'might not be pursuing irreconcilable objectives in attempting to assume leadership in Europe while remaining the centre of a powerful Commonwealth . . .' (CAB 128/30/2, CM 66(56)2). At the time, its proponents thought that Britain could have the best of both worlds: a large European market for its manufactures with continued access to cheap food imports from the Commonwealth and colonies. In the event, the Colonial

Secretary's apprehensions were well-founded. France blocked the proposal to associate the Messina powers with the industrial free trade area. The more limited European Free Trade Association that resulted from the reorientation of commercial policy could not fulfil the long-term objective of an extensive market in which to improve industrial competitiveness. From 1957, the growth of the Six not only stimulated trade among themselves, but even offered a market to British exporters that grew faster and became more important than any other, despite its increasingly discriminatory tariff. Trade with the EEC expanded at the expense of trade within the Commonwealth. Britain tried vainly to incorporate the Common Market Six in EFTA, and the failure of that initiative determined an application for membership (Pollard, 1983, p. 367; Miller, 1974, ch. 13).

I am not suggesting that decolonisation was caused by a reorientation of national economic policy towards Europe: British governments treated the colonies case by case, and resisted African calls for black majority rule wherever this threatened white settler interests (Darwin, 1988). But the 'turn' to Europe in 1956 represented a sea-change in perceptions of Britain's relations with the external world, and was bound to lead to a reassessment of the economic worth of the colonies. Harold Macmillan was the leading proponent of association with Europe, and one of his first acts as premier was to order an economic accounting for each colony to see what Britain would gain or lose by its independence (this is discussed below). There were two further reasons for calculating the costs and benefits of relinquishing formal control. First, British investors had since 1945 been unable or unwilling to furnish the underdeveloped colonies with funds on a scale commensurate with their development needs. Private investment in colonial loans floated on the London market was trifling, and to a remarkable extent the colonies were meeting their own capital loan requirements (Morgan, 1980, vol. 3, pp. 48–9). Since the state could not contemplate substituting public for private investment – or not in the amounts required – the implicit contract in the colonial relationship was breaking down. The metropolis was no longer a fit economic guardian of its colonial wards, and their insistent demands for funds created obligations it could do without.

Secondly, the colonies' role in Britain's external economic environment was being affected by the changing character of the sterling area and its impact on British policy. Until the Korean War stockpiling boom, the area functioned quite effectively in maintaining trade during the global dollar shortage, but the boom's sudden collapse proved a turning-point. Non-UK sterling countries used their accumulated dollar earnings to import considerable quantities of capital goods from the USA and, since their import prices were rising as their export prices fell, the area as a whole went into deficit with the rest of the world, confronting Britain with the sterling crisis of 1951–2. The independent sterling countries were set on industrialisation – often at the expense of imported British manufactures – and the British government was unable to reimpose collective fiscal discipline on them. There was an inherent tendency for the area to go into deficit with the rest of the world, and for its currency to be volatile. Partly as a consequence of the independent countries drawing down their reserves, a steadily greater proportion of total sterling reserves was constituted by the colonies' sterling balances. (They were about half the total sterling balances by 1958, compared with 27 per cent at the end of 1949.) In the late forties, these balances represented assets, but their worth was diminishing as international economic conditions changed substantially. The dollar shortage was much less acute, and the western European countries more than doubled their gold and dollar reserves between 1949 and 1956. A 'dollar-discriminating trading club' was losing much of its rationale, and the colonies' dollar-earning capabilities were becoming less valuable. The sterling area had always been considered an emergency measure to meet the war and post-war crises, and in 1952 Britain and its trading partners pronounced the return to full convertibility a primary policy objective. The new Conservative government and its allies in the City wanted to re-establish sterling as a general international currency and London as an open financial market-place (Strange, 1971, p. 64).

By this date, the Gold Coast was self-governed, its independence no longer a distant prospect, and its example was having a dynamic impact on the other African colonies. In these circumstances, the colonial sterling balances posed a dilemma for the policy of full convertibility: a precipitate running down of the reserves by successor regimes would render sterling more volatile and threaten the pound. India provided a warning of what might happen: like other sterling area countries, it expected the UK to supply the bulk of its foreign capital as a condition for participating in the British-led sterling area. When denied a development loan for its second five-year plan (1956–61), India simply ran down its sterling balances and unilaterally altered the law governing the size of its foreign currency reserves. India seemed to have set an example that other members of the area in Asia and Africa would be likely to follow as they accelerated the pace of economic development (Shonfield, 1958, p. 132). Faced with this dilemma, Britain might have repudiated its sterling obligations, but this would have sabotaged the strategy of incorporating former colonies into the Commonwealth. Britain preferred, instead, to accelerate a negotiated transfer of power to nationalist leaders prepared to follow the conservative monetary policies of colonial governments. Both the Malayan leaders with whom Britain was negotiating in the mid-fifties and Nkrumah agreed to remain within the sterling area and abide by the dollar pool. By moving with the nationalist tide in her dependencies, Britain hoped to benefit from the informal ties of the Commonwealth while simultaneously promoting sterling's wider, cosmopolitan role. The case for colonial or neo-colonial hegemony in Africa and Malaya had already collapsed when sterling was made fully convertible in December 1958 (Darwin, 1988, pp. 178, 204; Cain and Hopkins, 1993, p. 266).

Europe, and Belgian and Portuguese Decolonisation

The lesser colonial powers also decolonised while enjoying accelerated economic growth within an increasingly integrated western Europe, and it is worth asking what – if any – were the connections between the two. In the case of Belgium, there is no evidence that the problems of reconstructing the national economy and integrating it with the Six had any impact on policy towards the Congo. On the contrary, the political establishment saw no conflict between Belgium remaining a great African power and participating in European integration. On his 1955 royal tour, the king had spoken of Belgium and the Congo forming a 'single nation' (Stengers, 1989, p. 225). As in British and French tropical Africa, the colonialists decamped after a decade's intensive economic development (initiated in 1949 with the first ten-year plan) when the returns to metropolitan economic interests from the colony were as great as ever. The objective of making the colony more productive was certainly achieved, for the global tonnage of Congolese exports reached an all-time high in 1959. The colonial mining and plantation companies controlled by Belgium's giant financial institution, Société Générale, were more profitable on average than its metropolitan businesses, and their returns bolstered the financial bourgeoisie's position in the domestic power structure. The stock market value of the Union Minière peaked in 1955–6 (ibid., p. 233). The guiding philosophy of late colonialism was to move towards a less coercive form of rule and consolidate the stratum of native petty officials and clerical employees who identified with the colonial system. There is ample evidence the colonialists succeeded in this; for example, the young Patrice Lumumba eulogised Belgian rule in a circular addressed to évolué Congolese in early 1956 (ibid., p. 232). When the Treaty of Rome came into force, a Congolese national movement did not yet exist and few could have imagined that the Belgian parliament would unanimously approve Congolese independence in 1960. Though the metropolis had to subsidise the Congolese budget in the later fifties because of heavy public borrowing to finance economic and social development, and expected to do so for the foreseeable future, the legend that the Belgian élite calculated that the colony was becoming an economic burden best relinquished has no foundation in fact.

What could scarcely be anticipated was that European integration would enable Belgium to shrug off the economic losses entailed by the loss of the Congo. The adverse consequences were slight and short-lived for an increasingly European-centred economy. The financial institutions reoriented their operations towards investing in multi-national enterprises in western Europe and sponsoring mining companies in non-Third World countries (such as Canada and Australia). Zaïre remained very important in Belgium's network of international relations but, relative to the new dimensions of the Belgian economy, the economic weight of the old colonial connection diminished greatly. By the late 1970s, Algeria had surpassed Zaïre as Belgium's main trading partner in Africa (Peemans, 1980, pp. 257–86).

Portugal, the last and least developed of the colonial powers, experienced more sharply than any other the tensions between remaining in Africa and integrating with Europe. The Portuguese economy was more deeply enmeshed in colonial trade and investment than the Dutch had been and, unlike the Belgians, the Salazarist government chose to defend the colonial regime with force rather than negotiate with insurgent nationalism. But in doing so, it acted against metropolitan economic interests. Following the Angolan uprisings of 1961, the African territories became a drain on the public purse while in subsequent years the metropolitan economy turned away from the colonies and towards Europe (Clarence-Smith, 1985, ch. 7). Even the spectacular growth of the white population in the colonies and their rapid urbanisation failed to raise the stake of the Portuguese economy in colonial markets, since local food processing and import-substituting industrialisation restricted settler demand for metropolitan products. In late-colonial Mozambique, the secondary sector expanded dramatically: the single most important industry was oil-refining, but the colony also began manufacturing cement, bricks, tiles, asbestos sheeting, electric cables, steel castings, wire and consumer durables. The local chemicals industry produced insecticides, tanning materials, paint and pharmaceuticals. At Cabora Bassa, an international consortium undertook one of world's most ambitious hydroelectric power projects. The colonial economy became less reliant on metropolitan imports and markets, and more closely integrated with South

Africa, which was Mozambique's major trading partner and provided 89 per cent of all new inward investment by the early 1970s (Newitt, 1995, p. 533).

Meanwhile, the metropolitan economy had reoriented towards Europe. After joining EFTA in 1961, it became easier to expand traditional exports of textiles and wine to northern Europe, while the partial lifting of controls on foreign investment permitted major inflows of European and American capital. From the later sixties, France and Germany began to attract large numbers of Portuguese emigrants. This reorientation to Europe became especially marked in and around 1970 for two reasons: Portugal was granted associate EEC status in July, which required her to dismantle the structures that had reserved colonial markets exclusively for Portuguese exports, and lift restrictions on foreign investment in the colonies. At the same time, in an attempt to reform (and retain) the empire, Portugal granted more administrative autonomy to Angola and Mozambique, which began restricting metropolitan imports. The result was a sharp decline in trade with the colonies, notably Mozambique, while the major Portuguese corporations operating in the colony began to liquidate their investments and sell out. Portugal was one of Europe's fastest growing economies between 1960 and 1973 – gross domestic product grew about two and half times – but colonial markets were of marginal interest for the newer, dynamic industries at the heart of the industrial boom. The industrial oligopolies emerging during the 1960s did not invest in empire to any significant extent, which suggests that, as in France, a sector of the Portuguese bourgeoisie was losing faith in the imperial mission before formal decolonisation. On the eve of imperial collapse in 1973, pharmaceuticals, soap and railway materials were the only significant industries that relied on the colonies for a high proportion of exports, and even in these cases exports accounted for a small share of total output. When Britain, Portugal's most important market, reapplied to join the EEC it was inevitable that the Portuguese should do likewise, but they found the overseas territories were a major obstacle to concluding an agreement on full membership. The military coup of 1974 in Portugal unleashed forces that were to lead to a chaotic and often disastrous process of political decolonisation, but for some time it had already been clear that Africa was an obstacle on the road to Brussels (Clarence-Smith, 1985, p. 219).

The Economic Calculus in the Decolonisation Process

To what extent were the decisions to decolonise determined by a hard-headed calculation in Paris and Whitehall that the costs of formal rule outweighed any putative economic benefits? Was there any conscious anticipation that European economic interests would be better served in the long term by an accelerated transfer of power? These questions are, to be sure, simplistic: we have to assess different perceptions of costs and benefits held by discrete bodies of men. The costs of formal rule (if not borne by the natives themselves) fell on the public purse whose keepers conceived of a 'national' interest in the colonies that included economic elements but was not reducible to them. The economic benefits of formal rule accrued mainly to private interests whose business decisions were calculated in strictly cost–benefit terms. However plausible a coalition of public and private interests might seem, it has left no trace in the British official record or company archives. With respect to West Africa, it is evident that the 1948 Accra riots alerted the British government to the intense unpopularity of the expatriate firms, added to official unease about their stranglehold on foreign trade and prompted concern about the political liability they represented. As the Gold Coast's political development accelerated, the Colonial Office was little concerned with British business interests, and the firms were cold-shouldered by the colonial administration. The business community's declining political influence was signalled by its inability to secure continued representation in the Gold Coast Assembly after 1954. The Colonial Office's main objectives were to preserve the Gold Coast's participation in the sterling area and the Commonwealth once independent, and British business interests were not promoted in negotiations with African politicians. For its part, the expatriate business community accepted that there was no preventing constitutional change in the face of the rapid transformation of 'native' politics. Their influence over political decision-making in Britain's stable political system was limited compared with the Fourth Republic, where ministerial instability allowed greater scope for the intrusion of private interests (Fieldhouse, 1992, pp. 489–95). As the Gold Coast and Nigeria approached independence, the firms endeavoured to safeguard their local positions by propaganda, by patronising African education and by 'Africanising' their personnel. They were not passive in the face of political change, but they had to adapt from being an element of the colonial power structure to a pressure group competing for the goodwill of African politicians. The most powerful, the UAC, recognised that it would have to buy its way into good political relationships in the future, not by bribing individual politicians, but by cooperating with their determination to speed up economic, and particularly industrial, development (Stockwell, 1995, pp. 277–300; Fieldhouse, 1994, p. 346). There is no reason to believe that the clash of interests between a colonial administration determined to prioritise indigenous economic development and expatriate business was unique to West Africa: a similar conflict has been documented in pre-independence Malaya (White, 1997).

It was only during the months prior to Ghanaian and Malaya independence (and some years after the process had been recognised as irreversible) that the British government began to calculate the economic consequences of decolonisation. In early 1957, Macmillan asked the Cabinet Colonial Policy Committee for

> something like a profit and loss account for each of our Colonial possessions so that we may be better able to gauge whether, from the financial and economic point of view, we are likely to gain or lose by its departure. This would need . . . to be weighed against the political and strategic considerations involved in each case (CAB134/1555/CPC (57) 6, Macmillan to Lord President, 28 January 1957).

The four main items in the account were: the budgetary implications of decolonising a territory for the UK; the likely calls of any development plans on investment funds; the effect on the sterling area balance of payments; and the effect on British trade.

The budgetary implications were fairly straightforward: independence would relieve the UK of costs incurred through the Colonial Development and Welfare Vote, the Colonial Services Vote and the Colonial Development Corporation, then totalling £51 million per year. Since Ministers had decided against any regular pattern of government-to-government aid for independent Commonwealth countries, and against the CDC embarking on new schemes in them, the Exchequer burden would decrease with independence. But, the committee warned, the net saving would almost certainly be considerably less than generally assumed. The African territories nearest independence were least in need of Exchequer assistance, and in Malaya costly counter-insurgency operations would require British support for the foreseeable future.

The calls on investment funds anticipated as a result of independence were a more speculative matter whose consideration involved discussing ways of shifting the current as well as the future 'burden' of development. Only one-sixth of the Colonies' development expenditure was (in July 1957) being covered by CDW grants, the rest being met from local resources or external loans. The needs of colonial governments for London market loan finance were expected to run at £25 million to £30 million per year for the next few years, and the indications were that the market would be unable to meet all the calls made upon it. Total demands for investment from all colonial quarters were considered well beyond the UK's resources, public, and private, and to ease the 'cumulative strain' the committee contemplated surrendering some responsibility for colonial welfare, either by sharing this with other Commonwealth countries or by granting independence, which 'might place Britain in a stronger position to refuse requests for capital assistance'. Since the transfer of political responsibility for colonial territories to another Commonwealth power (such as Canada) was regretfully recognised as unacceptable to public opinion anywhere, independence was the only realistic way of easing the 'strain' (CAB/134/1551, Colonial Policy Committee Minutes, 5 June 1957).

Sterling matters clearly dominated the committee's deliberations, and it was in relation to them that decolonisation posed the biggest potential cost to Britain's national interest. In 1954–6, the colonies had a deficit with sterling area countries amounting to £28 million, but their surplus with the non-sterling area totalled £63 million, overall a satisfactory position as far as British trade and sterling were concerned. If they left the area after independence and began retaining dollar earnings and running down sterling holdings, then the consequences would be serious. But the Colonial Policy Committee saw no reason to believe that any of the candidates for independence would find it in their interest to do so. It saw a greater danger of a former colony departing from the area in a fit of pique were independence to be postponed. Britain had long encouraged its colonies to make maximum possible use of their sterling holdings for development and merely granting independence would not, it was thought, make any appreciable difference to this process 'except in so far as it must be expected that standards of prudence would probably fall . . . ' An ex-colony might pursue rash 'over-development' policies and run into public expenditure deficits, leading to a rapid fall in its sterling holdings and a considerable strain on the UK. The danger was considered serious only in relation to Ghana, Malaya and Nigeria, but the committee had no proposals to avert it: 'The running down of sterling balances represents a real but inescapable burden on the UK' (CAB/134/1551, CPC Minutes, 4 July 1957). The committee's cautious optimism was well founded: there was no precipitous run-down of sterling balances after Malaya and Ghana achieved independence, and both wanted to maintain the colonial currency system.

In any event, West Africa's trading position was deteriorating because of falling cocoa prices and its economic detachment from Britain was already in train by mid 1957. The region had received no direct lending from HMG over the past three years, nor had the area borrowed on the London market during the period. It had, in fact, repaid £10 million on earlier loans.

Considering the size of its population, private capital expenditure was low: it was estimated at £35 million in 1954–6 (£23 million from the UK and £12 million from non-sterling sources). The situation in East Africa, especially Kenya, was markedly different. With its white settlers and rapidly expanding Asian community heading a precocious commercial and industrial development, the territory was sucking in British goods, capital and official aid. East Africa had a deficit of £49 million on current account with the sterling area in 1954–6, and attracted a share of sterling capital disproportionate to its population.

As to the final item in the 'profit and loss' account, the implications of decolonisation for British trade, the Committee was reasonably sanguine. The trading balance was, of course, in Britain's favour, and, given the centrality of the balance of payments to economic policy, could not be lightly foregone. But as a proportion of total exports and imports, colonial commerce was diminishing with the upsurge in trade between the industrialised nations. Furthermore, over-dependence on sterling area markets that were growing less rapidly than world trade as a whole was officially recognised as contributing to the fall in Britain's share of world exports of manufactures since the early 1950s (*Board of Trade Journal*, March 1957, quoted in Shonfield, 1958, pp. 79–85). In 1956, UK exports to the colonies were £422 million, or 13 per cent of total exports (£343 million being manufactured goods), while the colonies furnished only 10 per cent of total British imports (though they did provide 17 per cent of imports of basic materials). Only a quarter of the colonies' total trade was with Britain. In Africa, the proportion was higher, but in the Far East lower: Britain provided only 18 per cent of Malaya's imports in 1955 and received 18 per cent of Malayan exports. The Committee saw no reason to anticipate that independence would adversely affect British commerce. British companies enjoyed few formal advantages over their competitors, and the intangible benefits of common trading standards were thought more important than the vestiges of imperial preference. The colonies were already liberalising their commercial policies and, even if granting independence did lead to the loss or weakening of established export markets, 'other and perhaps more valuable markets might be found if we made sufficient effort' (CPC, Minutes, 4 May 57).

Overall, the Committee concluded that

> economic considerations tend[ed] to be evenly matched and the economic interests of Great Britain were unlikely in themselves to be decisive in determining whether or not a territory should become

independent . . . [The] economic dangers to Great Britain in deferring the grant of independence after the country was 'ripe' for it would be far greater than any dangers resulting from an act of independence negotiated as an act of goodwill (CAB 135/1551, CP (O)(57)3, 4 July 1957).

Strategic considerations merely confirmed this equanimity, since colonial territories had fewer logistical functions in the modern world. Britain required air communications, bases, and, to a much lesser extent, manpower.

Ostensibly, the French had far more to lose from decolonisation than did the British because their overseas commercial and economic interests were highly concentrated in formal dependencies and 'protected' states constituting the franc zone. Trade with the zone had been much more stable than other French external commerce since the inter-war economic crisis. In 1959, exports to foreign countries had not yet reattained their 1927 real values, but those to the empire had grown three-fold in thirty years. In 1957, the Director of Economic Affairs at the Ministry of French Overseas Territories claimed that half a million people in metropolitan France depended directly for their livelihood on colonial commerce.

However, the commercial advantages of the colonies to particular industries and firms cannot be equated with advantages to the French economy as a whole. Broadly speaking, colonial markets had, since the inter-war economic crisis, 'propped up' technologically archaic industries in which global production was shifting to less developed, low-wage economies. The cotton textiles, paper, silk, soap, matches, mass-produced clothing and refined sugar industries all relied on colonial markets for overseas sales. The importance of these colonially oriented industries in terms of the total value added of French industry and total exports was falling overall, in line with their diminishing role in international trade. Preferential colonial outlets assured them a proportion of 'easy' sales and shielded them from competitive pressures to raise productivity and rationalise business organisation. Over 85 per cent of cotton exports went to the empire between 1949 and 1958. The medium-sized family firm was still the typical business organisation in the industry, and in 1952 a labour force of around 150 000 was dispersed among 1177 enterprises. Restructuring was impeded by colonial tariff protection, a fact clearly demonstrated when, following the loss of Indo-China, 176 cotton firms went into liquidation, and the productivity of the industry as a whole improved sharply (Marseille, 1984a, p. 356). The technologically progressive industries, such as motor vehicles, which sent a high proportion of their exports to the empire did so only because of commercial and monetary policies that had wrapped a protective cocoon around conservative industrial sectors. The most dynamic trend in world trade in the 1950s was the exchange of specialised, technologically advanced manufactures between industrialised countries, and French industry had to join this trend if it was to achieve export-led growth.

The overt and hidden subsidisation of colonial trade through supported prices and metropolitan subventions for colonial budgets magnified its disadvantages for the metropolitan economy. More than two-thirds of French agricultural imports were furnished by the colonies in the 1950s, but at supported prices around 50 to 100 per cent above those on world markets. As we have seen, when France's apparently favourable balance in colonial trade was scrutinised by economists and statisticians charged with the national accounting it proved spurious. The corollary of the French surplus was the growth of colonial trade imbalances which France financed by supporting local currencies tied to the franc. With rather less than a third of colonial exports leaving the franc zone in 1950, the 'gains' in hard currency from the monetary union did not compensate for its financial costs to France. Among the 'modernising' administrative élite, the colonial empire was increasingly seen as a legacy of the protectionist, 'Malthusian' past which encumbered the expansion of the more dynamic and competitive sectors of the national economy. A key technocrat recalled that no one on his team of statisticians was for the Indo-Chinese war, for the national accounting process had made clear to them that the colonial empire, far from being a source of wealth, was a very heavy charge (Claude Gruson, *Programmer l'espérance*, quoted in Marseille, 1984a, p. 351).

From the early 1950s, as the costs of divorce between France and her empire were first being seriously calculated, industrial and administrative circles were presented with a fairly clear-cut demonstration of how severing colonial links removed inhibitions on economic growth. After the Netherlands was forced to withdraw from Indonesia, the Dutch economy enjoyed a remarkable boom: it was, the business journal *L'Entreprise* declared in November 1955, 'an economy prospering without colonies'. Since the colonial débâcle, Dutch exports of high-value-added products (chemicals, machinery, optical instruments, electrical goods) had grown spectacularly. The retreating Dutch had discarded their sovereign obligations to repair war damage and ameliorate social conditions while maintaining certain genuinely beneficial economic links with the Republic of Indonesia. Their example appeared particularly instructive because the French state's obligations to its colonial citizens were proliferating from the later 1940s, especially in Algeria. Minimum-wage legislation and social security taxes on employers, which were entailed by the juridical union with France, discouraged private investment, while the formation of a local skilled labour force was handicapped by the freedom with which Algerian workers could move to metropolitan France with its higher wage levels.

A well-known journalist, Raymond Cartier, took up the high cost of sustaining French sovereignty in Africa in a series of essays in *Paris-Match* in 1956. Their gist was that France had squandered huge sums in unremunerative African projects, money that might have been far more productively employed developing the national economy. The political rewards for this munificence had been small, and since the left-wing nationalist challenge to French rule was strongest in the most developed territories, development aid seemed inherently in conflict with the promotion of France's national interest. Aid should only be granted, Cartier argued, after stern negotiations and never without securing certain political advantages (Albertini, 1971, p. 440). Cartier articulated a populist backlash against the obligations of sovereignty which alarmed moderate African leaders, such as Léopold Senghor. They feared that the African territories would be cut adrift from France without the economic and financial assistance necessary for viable state formation. Though Cartierism did not dissuade the Gaullist regime from wide-scale financial and developmental aid to Francophone Africa, it contributed to a different climate of opinion from that prevailing in Britain. As Lennox-Boyd informed his Cabinet Colleagues:

> [T]here exists in France a considerable body of opinion which holds that the country would be well advised to cut her losses by withdrawing her capital from those overseas territories which feel no more than a cupboard-love for the Metropolitan Government and to use it instead in Europe for projects which offer a better prospect of raising living standards in France itself. In the UK, there is no real equivalent to this current of feeling; indeed, with us the pressures, on both sides of the House, are rather in the opposite direction – to increase the flow of aid to the under-developed territories, for reasons of conscience, prestige, and international policy as much for purely commercial consideration (FO371/1331405, 'The Lessons of the Referendum in French Africa', 16 August 1958, quoted in Michel, 1992, p. 506).

Since the Algerian war, a tenacious political myth has made business circles, including those with direct investments in overseas territories, the appeasers of colonial nationalism, either as part of a strategy of accommodation with successor regimes or else as one of a calculated, 'Cartierist' programme of colonial disinvestment. The myth was common to the irreconcilable Right – for whom Indo-China and Algeria had been 'perdues par l'Argent' – and the Marxist Left – who credited 'Grand Capital' with having smartly anticipated the neo-colonialist order (Ageron, 1991b, pp. 122–4). The surest indication of expatriate capital's decommitment in advance of the transfer of power lies in the aggregate data on colonial assets assembled by Marseille, though it points to a restructuring and relocation of colonial business rather than a wholesale retreat. The trading accounts of 125 leading colonial firms between 1945 and 1954 showed that their profits were, in real terms, substantially below those enjoyed before the Second World War, while the value of their assets located in the colonies fell sharply after 1945–6. Taking the profit level of mining companies in 1938 as 100, in 1954 it was only 44; for commercial companies, the comparable index was 79.9 (Marseille, 1986, pp. 167–73). Expatriate *industrial* firms, however, followed a contrary trend: their profit level in 1954 was four times higher than in 1938 and the real value of their assets had almost tripled, which testifies to a partial reorientation of colonial capitalism away from the commercial and financial activities required for exporting primary products towards investment in manufacturing. Indo-China and Algeria, which had been the most profitable areas of the colonial empire up to the 1940s, witnessed sharp contractions in expatriate investment: the value of colonial assets in Indo-China, where business interests quickly recognised the long-term untenability of France's position, fell by two-thirds between 1946 and 1953. Such major corporations as the Banque d'Indochine relocated their liquid assets in France and French Africa (and in the bank's case the Middle East and South Africa). Though Algeria was politically quiescent before November 1954, the real value of expatriate business assets was significantly below their 1938 level for most of the post-war decade.

In Black Africa and Madagascar, on the other hand, the value of business assets grew considerably between 1945 and 1954, though we should note this was the main area of activity for only four of the 32 leading colonial firms both in 1929 and in 1958 (Marseille, 1984a, p. 132). The two trading giants, SCOA and CFAO, enjoyed a period of high and stable profitability between 1946 and 1950, but from that point the former's profit level fell steeply and the latter's more gently (Coquery-Vidrovitch, 1975, p. 599). Business *opinion* – as expressed in representative bodies and journals – reflected the 'Africanisation' of the empire, and regarded the prospect of independence, whether north or south of the Sahara, with alarm. The Central Committee for Overseas France, on which business interests were strongly represented, declared that 'Without Africa, the metropole will not prosper', and this prognosis was endorsed in April 1956 by the national employers' journal, *Patronat* (Pasquier, 1992, pp. 297–313). Massive unemployment was anticipated in France if colonial markets were surrendered and colons driven back to the mother country. Business circles were not unprogressive in terms of colonial politics, for they took the communist threat very seriously and hoped to cultivated moderate African leaders who proclaimed their 'dual attachment to France and to Black Africa'. By the mid 1950s, the most influential of their journals, *Marchés Coloniaux*, was advocating the reform of colonial political structures to make them more representative of native opinion and a federal association between France and its overseas territories. Initially, it welcomed the 1956 *Loi cadre*, establishing democratic rights and institutions in French Africa, as a step towards an association that would conjure away the spectre of independence whose 'illusions and dangers' *Marchés Coloniaux* constantly denounced.

What made business interests most apprehensive (apart from the communist threat) was the overseas territories exercising fiscal autonomy once independent. They insisted on the need to defend the imperial monetary union, the common hard currency fund, the preferential markets for French goods, and the investment facilities and guarantees. Businessmen generally accepted the necessity of protecting infant colonial industries and supported the continuation of France's public investment effort after the transfer of power. They also wanted to conserve the economic space of the French West African Federation (Equatorial Africa had always been a minor affair economically) and were alarmed by its 'Balkanisation' as power devolved to the assemblies and governments of the individual territories after 1956. There is no truth in the claim – advanced by theorists of neo-colonialism – that the West African Federation was broken up to ensure continued dependence on metropolitan capitalism. At a time when markets were enlarging and harmonising elsewhere, it seemed absurd to business interests that French West Africa was fragmenting into eight small markets. That each territory was likely to adopt its own regulatory code for foreign investments stiffened business suspicion of the 'centrifugal' form of French decolonisation. We should not attribute a unified colonial policy to business groups: some could not conceive of operating without some form of political 'cover' for their interests, but others were reconciled to independence by the late 1950s, prepared to forge links with the new African leaders, and no longer identified themselves with the old colonial power. Generally, though, business interests neither anticipated African decolonisation nor took any part in initiating, and like nearly everyone were disconcerted by, the rapid acceleration of history after the creation of the French Community in September 1958.

'Neo-colonialism' and Economic Decolonisation

Though most African states became independent between 1957 and 1964, their economies generally remained strongly marked by the colonial heritage, and their development heavily influenced by bilateral relations with the former colonial power until the early 1970s. The real break with the colonial economic past came with the call for a New International Economic Order enunciated at the Algiers non-aligned summit, the oil crisis precipitated by OPEC, and the emergence of a multilateral pattern of economic relations in which the European Economic Community was an increasingly important player. Until this 'second decolonisation', nearly all former colonies depended primarily on the old colonial power for capital imports and finance, and it was usually the most important supplier of manufactures. Except for Tanzania, British investment was more than half of all foreign investment in former British Africa in 1976. Among former French colonies only Guinea, with its US bauxite enclave, had another national investment source surpassing that of France. Similarly the dominant holders of foreign investment in Zaïre, Rwanda and Burundi were Belgian, and in Somalia Italian.

'Neo-colonialism' was most evident in former French Africa, where many states were scarcely viable as autonomous national economies and the new governing élites saw considerable economic and political advantage in continuing the financial ties with France and providing a hospitable environment for foreign, businesses predominantly French ones. With the exception of Guinea, they signed cooperation agreements that ensured a remarkable continuity of official institutions, administrative and advisory personnel, and channels of communication. Their essential economic features related to French investment in mineral exploitation, the maintenance of existing commercial relations affording reciprocal tariff preferences, and the continuation of the monetary links prescribed by membership of the franc zone. It was the last which tied the former colonies to France most closely. The value of the CFA (Franco-African Community) franc remained pegged to the metropolitan, and France guaranteed its unrestricted convertibility, circulation and transfer, while subsidising the state budgets of the poorest former colonies to ensure monetary stability. But in return France insisted on maintaining strict control over the new states' financial reserves which were deposited in French francs on account with the French treasury, and the practice of centralising foreign currency holdings in Paris was continued. The two issuing banks of the former French African Federations were, in fact, branches of the Bank of France, and French nationals were a third of directorates on one, and half on another. Virtually all their first national development plans, drawn up during 1961–2, were prepared by French experts, as were most of the second plans prepared during the latter part of the decade (Coquery-Vidrovitch, 1988b, pp. 118–24; Basso, 1992, pp. 255–79). Though certainly 'dependency', this was not one-sided exploitation, for a stable and convertible currency was a major advantage in attracting foreign investment. French personnel supplied the necessary expertise during the hiatus between formal independence and the 'Africanisation' of public and private administration. Conversely, the policy of 'co-development' pursued by De Gaulle for essentially political aims was financially costly: though the total of French overseas aid declined as a proportion of GNP from a high point in 1960, it remained about twice the average of Western donor countries.

In Senegal, the 'neo-colonial' country *par excellence*, the 'trade economy' based on cultivating groundnuts for the French market, which absorbed some four-fifths of all exports, persisted well into the 1970s. The French subsidised the groundnut price until 1968, and exports were diversified only through exploiting phosphate deposits. French capital continued to monopolise the industrial sector, which was already well established around Dakar by 1960. The CFAO and SCOA now participated in the industrial processing of raw materials and import substituting manufacturing. They were cosseted by a liberal and indiscriminate policy of tax exemptions, and granted the unlimited right to repatriate profits. African entrepreneurs began to compete with the Lebanese in wholesale trading, transport and building, but their only substantial industrial ventures before 1980 were in groundnut processing. The banking sector remained almost exclusively French and granted African entrepreneurs access to credit only on stringent terms. The privileged position of French interests was reinforced by the cultural hegemony of the French language and educational models. The French military discreetly protected the Senghor regime at critical moments. The state imitated the late colonial administration by investing heavily in large-scale infrastructural projects of doubtful economic value, and – with an adverse balance of payments – relied on foreign loans to finance them. A swollen and unproductive public sector imposed its own high cost on the economy. The state's indebtedness trebled in the fifteen years after independence, with a result that an increasing proportion of foreign exchange earnings was expended on unproductive debt servicing (Barry, 1988, pp. 271–94).

By contrast with France's economic tutelage of its African protégés, the former British colonies soon broke with the sterling area and the vestiges of colonial economic management. The East African territories fairly quickly dispensed with the Currency Board they had inherited from the colonial regime, and established their own central banks to oversee credit and monetary policy. To make access to savings easier for the purposes of investment, they adopted less stringent rules governing the central banks' foreign exchange reserves. Following the sterling devaluation in 1967, they diversified their foreign exchange holdings and in 1971 pegged their currencies to the dollar. Again in contrast to the Francophone states, the former British territories diversified their sources of foreign aid more rapidly, benefiting from a growing variety of development agencies. Tanzania led all Africa in its per capita receipt of foreign aid by the mid-1970s, and attracted assistance from new donors (such as Communist China and the Nordic countries) as well as the World Bank (Austen, 1987, p. 245). Unlike France, Britain studiously avoided interventions in its former colonies and the concept of 'neo-colonialism' is scarcely applicable to their state-to-state relations.

The 'real' transfer of economic power in Francophone Africa began around 1970 and was determined by pressures being exerted simultaneously in Africa and Europe. De Gaulle's departure was important, because he had closely supervised an emphatically étatiste policy of 'aid and cooperation' with the 'Third World', whose economic costs were justified in terms of the political advantages to France (Chipman, 1989). His successor, Georges Pompidou, brought to the direction of foreign policy the conceptions and priorities of a banker and businessman, and sought to scale down public development assistance to Francophone Africa while revitalising French private sector investment in the region. This chimed in with increasing scepticism – authoritatively voiced in the Gorse Report on aid and cooperation of June 1971 – as to whether official development assistance had much benefited either recipient or donor (Suret-Canale, 1987, pp. 74–6). Two-thirds of the credits granted by France to former colonies were absorbed by 'technical and cultural cooperation' from whose benefits most Africans were excluded. Considerable resources went into aiding Francophone education at secondary and university levels, though only an estimated 3 per cent of the population were competent French speakers. The economic record of the 17 states aided by France was unimpressive: in

11, per capita income growth had been less than 2 per cent a year between 1961 and 1968, a period when most less developed countries grew more rapidly. Some of the Sahel states were already experiencing 'negative' growth by the turn of the decade (Brett, 1985, pp. 185–86). Popular hostility to foreigners and neo-colonialism helped push political élites towards more radical economic nationalism and contributed to the fall of cooperative, pro-French regimes in Madagascar and Dahomey (Benin). Partly prompted by Algeria's decision to nationalise the oil industry in 1971, Togo took its phosphates sector into public ownership and Mauritania its iron ore mines. Several states became avowedly socialist, though political rhetoric was often merely smeared over post-colonial reality: even after a decade of official Marxism–Leninism in Congo, the primacy of the French business community was immediately apparent to the most casual visitor to Brazzaville (Young, 1983, p. 294). After the 1973 oil price shock, the Francophone African states were much more forthright in demanding revision of their cooperation agreements with France. On the French side, there was a franker public recognition (notably in the Abelin Report of 1975) that the political ambition to exert a dominant influence in Africa had to be adjusted to France's means and the policy of economic cooperation coordinated with other donor countries. The Africanisation of expatriate capital through the introduction of local public and private partners was recognised as inevitable and even desirable. A new – or at least revised – framework for multilateralism was being created in the Lomé agreements between the EEC and the Afro-Caribbean-Pacific states, and the development of the 'Eurafrican' market which counterbalanced the strongly bilateral character of French influence.

In the 1960s and '70s, the term 'neo-colonialism' was commonly used by African leaders to condemn the humiliating limits on their national autonomy, and by Marxists to analyse how hospitable regimes for external private capital in former colonies were leading to greater social polarisation and class conflict (Nkrumah, 1965; Leys, 1975). In retrospect, both discounted the capacity of even weak states in the 'Third World' to dictate the terms on which foreign entrepreneurs operated within their frontiers. Private economic power does not command political–military force on any significant scale in the modern world, and without it foreign corporate capital could not impose its own desired political forms and economic policies on post-colonial states, even when they were fissiparous and crisis-ridden. The failure of the Belgian finance companies to break the unitary structure of the independent Congolese state by fomenting the secession of mineral-rich Katanga is an illuminating example. This neo-colonialist strategy (which was supported by the Belgian Foreign Minister, Paul-Henri Spaak) foundered on an emerging African international order created by the acquisition of sovereignty by so many former colonies in 1960. The concert of African states, as well as both superpowers, recognised a paramount political interest in preserving a centralised, unitary Congolese state, and it was with this entity that the Belgian mining interests were forced to do business. In 1966, the Mobutu government extinguished the claims of the Belgian colonial corporations to mineral rights over nearly half the total land surface and took over the Union Minérale du Haut-Kantanga. This demonstrated to the Belgian financial groups that they could maintain a stake in the country only if they submitted to the objectives of the new regime. Henceforth, they cooperated closely with the Kinshasa government, and links were institutionalised through public development loans, credits and the financing of important technical assistance. These links could be disrupted by the Mobutu regime more or less as it wished. During 1973–5 – years of vigorous 'Third World' self-assertion – Mobutu proclaimed a 'Zaïrianisation' of the economy (which proved disastrous) and sought a more diversified set of foreign investors: American, Japanese, German, French, British, and Communist Chinese (Peemans, 1980; Young, 1983; idem 1988).

There were, of course, striking differences in the economic and financial relations that African states maintained with the former colonial powers, and in their public stance towards expatriate business within their borders. But it would be quite misleading to say of any of them (as theorists of 'neo-colonialism' were wont to do) that independence gave the new states juridical title but no real power over the economy. On the contrary, the new African countries inherited a state authoritarianism that offered wide scope for economic innovations – rather wider, in fact, than that available to their colonial predecessors who had inhibiting responsibilities to metropolitan constituencies and 'traditional' native interests (Austen, 1987, p. 224). In Africa, whatever the political complexion of the post-colonial state, the weakness of indigenous entrepreneurial groups inevitably enhanced the state's role in the economy, just as this weakness required heavy protective tariffs that effectively subsidised newly founded manufacturing industries. Professedly socialist regimes – such as Ghana under Nkrumah after 1960 – were overtly hostile to private enterprise whether foreign or Ghanaian, but even in free enterprise economies, such as the Ivory Coast and Kenya, the share of the public sector in entrepreneurial capital formation increased considerably after independence, reaching 50 per cent and 37 per cent respectively by the mid 1970s (ibid., p. 238). Between 1960 and 1974 there were 340 cases of nationalisations and take-overs (including many foreign-owned, resource-based industries) in sub-Saharan Africa – nearly two-fifths of the world total in that period, though the region has only about a tenth of world population. The only countries not to nationalise at least one substantial foreign enterprise were the Ivory Coast, Liberia and Gabon. The general trend was for the public sector in the new states to take over infrastructural enterprise and wholesale distribution, leaving private foreign capital to concentrate on mining, industrial agriculture and manufacturing for local markets. Certain states – Libya, Algeria and Tanzania – were determined to bring all foreign fixed assets into public ownership, but even where this political pressure was not exerted MNCs tended to move into joint ventures with the state or public sector companies, negotiating management and or technical contracts and selling arrangements. Foreign commitment to fixed assets physically located in Africa was thereby reduced, although control was maintained via the 'leasing' of knowledge and capital. The forms and instruments of African dependence on foreign capital changed, the substance persisted (Green, 1981, p. 333). The wide-scale controls over agricultural marketing which African states had inherited were extended into banking, insurance and petrol distribution, and more rarely into manufacturing (Adedeji and Ake, 1981, p. 30). Though the Ivory Coast was taken to be the model 'free market' African state in the 1960s and 70s, the government intervened in the economy in far-reaching ways: through its *caisse de stabilisation*, a substantial part of world price paid for Ivorian exports was siphoned off from peasant producers to the state. Thus, in 1977, a boom year, farmers received only about a quarter of the world price for their crops. The surplus was used to pay for as much as two-thirds of the current public sector investment whose main beneficiaries were public employees and the urban middle class. In Tanzania, socialist ideology, enunciated in the 1967 Arusha Declaration, determined nationalisation – with mutually agreed compensation – of the major means of production and distribution (including foreign-owned banks and industries) and state control of the economy through the central bank, the parastatal system and cooperative movement (Mushi, 1981, pp. 204–37). Even Kenya, whose new governing élite made the attraction of foreign investment a central feature of its development strategy, established exchange controls to limit the remittance of capital and earnings. Under what are admitted to have been 'quite effective' regulations, only capital that had been brought in from abroad, and earnings on it, could be remitted, while foreign companies were forbidden the use of local savings to 'gear up' their operations so as to enhance the profits attributable to foreign equity capital (Leys, 1975, p. 126). All in all, sovereignty palpably transformed the political context in which Western enterprises operated in the former colonies, enabling the new states to improve the division of rent (gross profits, interest charges, royalties, and licence fees) by taxation and other means, impose an indigenisation of local management, increase the local content of non-labour (as well as labour) inputs, and so reduce the 'enclave' features of foreign-owned enterprises. Where the state achieved a working accommodation with foreign enterprise, then the economic development of independent Africa was well served by any realistic criteria. Manufacturing output grew rapidly in the most favourably endowed states during the 1970s; in Nigeria, for example, the annual average growth was 12 to 13 per cent in real terms up to 1979 (Iliffe, 1983, p. 65).

The European Economic Community and the ACP

The connections between European integration and economic decolonisation, and the transition from bilateralism to multilateralism in the 'Third World's' relations with Europe, which have been recurrent themes of this chapter, are traceable to the institution of the Common Market. France insisted on 'associating' its overseas territories with the EEC (together with the Belgian Congo, Ruanda-Urundi and Italian-administered Somaliland) in the hope of shifting some of the financial burden of development onto the Community as a whole. After independence, eighteen African states (including Madagascar) chose to renew their association with the EEC through the Yaoundé accords of 1963 that aimed to promote the free movement of merchandise and capital. They were included in the free trade area inside the common external tariff and became, therefore, privileged suppliers of goods originating from outside the EEC. But in return for this preferential status, they agreed to open their markets to EEC exports without discrimination, though they were permitted to retain purely fiscal duties and certain protective industrial tariffs. The process of market liberalisation was eased by a transitional period, lasting up to 1968, when subventions and various special aids aimed at diversifying African export schedules were in force. The EEC committed itself to an economic and social investment programme in the overseas associated states, and set up the European Development Fund (FED) and European Investment Bank (BEI). It was some time before these multilateral agencies were effective, and their initial disbursements scarcely compensated associated countries for the loss of price support for primary exports in the French market. In time, they became conduits of development aid that duplicated the bilateral agencies of the European states (such as France's Fund for Aid and Cooperation – FAC). Between 1958 and 1971, France and Federal Germany both contributed a third to the FED (while the other third came from the remaining members of the EEC). French firms are reckoned, however, to have secured over 40 per cent of the markets and contracts created by FED expenditure in associated countries, so French economic interests gained on balance.

With Britain's accession to the EEC in 1973, 12 of her former African colonies, as well as 6 other African countries, became associated states, and were joined by 7 Caribbean and 3 Pacific countries. Accords of association now extended to the greater part of Africa. The signing of the Lomé agreement in February 1975 further enlarged the 'Afro-Caribbean-Pacific' (ACP) bloc, which numbered 60 states by 1980 (many of them 'micro-polities' with no realistic prospect of economic autonomy). Lomé also brought significant revisions in the mechanisms of EEC–ACP economic relations: it was now recognised, even in such fora as the Club of Rome, that participation in the international division of labour was not accelerating development in the poorest countries. Industrialisation, based on their comparative advantage in cheap labour, was identified as a key to economic survival, and Lomé quadrupled the sums available for financial and technical aid, while agreeing that these could now be used for effective industrial development. (Hitherto, economic aid had followed 'colonial' lines in being trade-related and heavily concentrated on infrastructure.) The principle of commercial reciprocity between the ACP bloc and industrialised Europe was abandoned: while the former's exports continued to enjoy preferential treatment, the reverse was no longer the case. A system of price stabilisation was introduced to compensate exporters when the price of certain agricultural products fell below the average for the preceding four years for price. Under the second Lomé agreement of 1979, the price support system was extended to a number of mineral products (copper, manganese, bauxite).

There can be no doubt that this European framework of multilateral development assistance has fulfilled the original intention of shifting much of France's financial burden onto broader shoulders, and has become an increasingly important source of aid for some of the world's poorest states. In 1960, French 'public' overseas aid amounted to 1.38 per cent of GNP (though included in this was aid to overseas Departments and Territories that are juridically backward regions of France). The average figure for donor members of the Development Assistance Committee at this time was reckoned to be 0.55 per cent of GNP. By 1969, total French 'public' aid had declined to 0.69 per cent of GNP, while the corresponding figure for DAC members was 0.39 per cent (Given in Basso, 1992, p. 274). The totals rather disguise France's decommitment from development assistance to its former colonies because the proportion going to overseas Departments and Territories - with only 1.2 million inhabitants in 1970 – rose from less than a quarter to a third of the total. From the recipient's perspective, the internationalisation of 'aid' is even more evident: in 1962, four-fifths of the total development assistance received by France's former African colonies was bilateral French aid, but in 1977 only two-fifths (Suret-Canale, 1987, p. 84).

Furthermore, the French political class could congratulate itself on having attracted non-French development capital to Francophone Africa while retaining the substance of French commercial paramountcy. Shortages of foreign currency among the associated states in the franc zone meant French imports tended to be favoured over those from other EEC countries, despite being generally more expensive. Though the proportion of imported French products did decline, France remained the most important supplier to her former colonies (as well as the most important source of foreign investment, except in Guinea).

Did the former African colonies benefit from the shift from bilateralism to multilateralism, from their subordination to a single European power to a more veiled dependence on a bloc of wealthy industrialised states? In the opinion of the respected Marxist historian, Jean Suret-Canale, the answer is an unequivocal 'no'. He describes the association of the former colonies with the European Community as 'nothing more than the instrument of a neo-colonial policy, more unrelenting in certain respects than the old colonial policy' (ibid., p. 68). This seems unnecessarily – even absurdly – dogmatic. We can agree that, for the erstwhile African colonies, their association with an integrating European involved losses as well as gains: they had to relinquish protected markets in the metropoles (with guaranteed prices for their export products) and align their prices with those on the world market, and it is doubtful whether the 'Europeanisation' of development assistance compensated, in real terms, for the relative fall in France's overseas aid programme after 1968. Yet why should sovereign states – under various political regimes – have sought association with the European Union if the consequences were as baneful as Suret-Canale maintains? Is it the case that all governing élites have acted solely in the class interest of the 'comprador' bourgeoisie from whom they are (supposedly) drawn? It would seem more plausible that the tangible benefits of association have persuaded post-independence rulers that participation in the 'Eurafrican' market is preferable to exclusion. The ACP countries' 'traditional' trade in tropical primary produce (such as cane sugar and bananas) has been protected from the competition of more efficient producers in Latin America and Asia by preferential tariffs and by guaranteed markets in France and Britain. At the same time, a number of the associated African states have been able to diversify their export schedules, their markets, and sources of supply: between independence and the first Lomé convention, exports of the former French colonies to EEC countries other than France rose from 14 to 27.6 per cent of the total, while imports from these sources rose from 8 to 16.6 per cent (ibid., p. 70). Since Lomé I, countries such as Mauritius, Kenya and Tanzania have expanded their 'non-traditional' exports of manufactures – chiefly clothing, cotton yarns and fabrics, and leather goods – under agreements which protected them from more competitive Asian producers. Though these 'non-traditional' goods tended to follow ex-colonial lines of trade – with France being the largest single market – Germany, Italy and the UK were also important destinations (Stephens, 1990, pp. 217–41).

Conclusions: Decolonisation and the Emergence of the 'Third World'

The decolonisation of the European empires and the emergence of the 'Third World' as a recognised grouping in international society were two phases on a single historical continuum. Politically, they marked an epochal change in world history by universalising the sovereign national state. With dwindling exceptions, all humankind was included within political entities accorded formal equality in the international states system, and with governments normatively empowered with secular authority over continuously-bounded territories. Of course, many peoples perfectly entitled to be considered 'nations' were denied or could not enforce claims to statehood. Two examples are the Baganda, who had a long tradition of statehood but were unable to extricate themselves from modern Uganda, and the Ibo of Biafra, whose attempted secession was defeated in the Nigerian civil war. Both were forcibly included within states where civil and human rights have, for long periods, been atrociously abused. But for all its lamentable failures to establish a legal order for civil society, the post-colonial state represented a caesura with both the era of empires and indigenous political traditions. It embodied – or was suppose to embody – the collective right to self-determination as a norm of political life. At the same time, all states were voicing the right to participate in the economic development that had brought mass prosperity to the former imperial powers. At independence, an explanation for the Afro-Asian countries' failure to develop hitherto lay readily to hand: their common historical situation, colonisation, had caused their common economic condition, under-development. 'Without exception', declared Kwame Nkrumah, '[the colonial powers] left us nothing but our resentment . . . When they had gone, the destitution of the land after long years of colonial rule was brought home to us' (quoted in Bauer, 1971, p. 632). It was a grotesque distortion of the historical record, but it articulated a community of sentiment among the disparate countries that were to form the Non-Aligned Movement.

When measured against its political import, the economic significance of decolonisation seems in no way comparable, whether our perspective is that of the ex-colony or former colonial power, or of the larger economic bloc forming in western Europe from the later 1950s. With the exception of Portuguese decolonisation, independence was granted when the metropolitan powers were undergoing their most sustained period of economic growth ever, and they effortlessly shrugged off any adverse commercial and financial consequences. (Portugal's withdrawal from her empire coincided with the world recession, and the country entered a severe economic crisis, though whether this was due primarily to decolonisation or to the leftward lurch of the Portuguese revolution is debatable.) With respect to France, the signs are that decolonisation removed impediments to economic growth: the fiscal burden of military and social expenditure was lifted; capital was repatriated and invested in the domestic economy; the archaic industrial sectors reliant on colonial markets declined more rapidly; industrial restructuring during the 1960s promoted heavily capitalised and internationally competitive enterprises engaged in high-value-added production. The number of French overseas subsidiaries rose from 83 during 1946–60 to 163 during 1961–77, but were heavily concentrated in Britain, the United States and Latin America, while only a handful remained in Africa. The commercial balance, which had been almost constantly in deficit before 1959, went into debit up to 1968 (when production and exports were lost through massive strikes) and was basically positive until 1973. France was able to absorb the largest repatriation in her history with the return of about 1.7 million French people from the empire, along with some 200 000 Vietnamese and Algerian refugees. There was no increase in unemployment; on the contrary, with gross domestic product growing by 5.5 per cent per year during the 1960s labour was in chronic demand, and this stimulated an influx of North African economic migrants to fill the demographic deficit in the French workforce. By 1985, immigrants from the Maghreb were as numerous in France as French repatriates. The French economy was transformed after 1963 by industrial concentration and the emergence of financial 'groups' who were actively remodelling the face of French capitalism. The giant corporation finally displaced the medium-sized family firm as the dominant form of business organisation. In terms of 'finance capital' theories of imperialism, the chronology of this transformation is indeed paradoxical: it seems almost as if finance capital had to wait for decolonisation before making its decisive thrust into the economy (Marseille, 1984a, p. 121).

As with all decolonisations, the severing of France's formal links with her empire rapidly affected her trade patterns. French exporters were much more successful than British in finding substitutes for the colonial markets (which absorbed more than a quarter of total French exports in 1960) *and* in maintaining their market share of the imports of their former colonies (Table 8.3). The uncompetitiveness of British exports meant that their market share would have declined irrespective of decolonisation, and the loss of exports attributable to the transfer of power in itself was equivalent to 5.2 per cent of total exports in the early 1970s. For France the proportion was 5.6 per cent. However, the volume of total French exports had grown 2.8 times, the volume of British exports only 1.8 times.

Table 8.3   French and British trade with colonies and ex-colonies 1960 and 1972

	1960 Exports to colonies or ex-colonies: Share of total exports (%)	1960 Market share of colonies imports (%)	1972 Exports to colonies or ex-colonies: Share of total exports (%)	1972 Market share of ex-colonies imports (%)
Britain	16.9	27	11.0	20
France	26.5	67	6.2	42

Source: Livingstone (1976).

Up to independence, Algeria was France's single most important trading partner, receiving 15.9 per cent of metropolitan exports in 1960 and providing 8.1 per cent of imports; by 1970 these figures had fallen to 3.1 and 3.3 respectively. French Black Africa provided 10 per cent of metropolitan imports in 1959 and received 8 per cent of French exports; by 1975 the corresponding figures were 3 per cent and 4 per cent respectively. Though there were specific factors affecting various 'colonial' trades, the general trend is quite clear: a stagnation or decline in the absolute values of trade between metropolitan countries and former colonies within a few years of the formal transfer of power and a very steep proportional fall within ten to fifteen years (Kleiman, 1976). Portugal experienced the same reorientation of its trade after 1970: during the later years of the Salazar–Caetano regime, the colonies furnished between 12 and 15 per cent of Portuguese imports and received between a fifth and a quarter of her exports. By 1985, imports from the former colonies were only about 1 per cent of total Portuguese imports and exports were about 4 per cent of the total.

The most recent statistics show a tendency for trade between integrated Europe and the ex-colonial 'Third World' to stabilise at a low level, despite the formal association of the ACP countries with the EEC and pledges on trade liberalisation. A telling measure of the commercial marginalisation of the world's poorest countries is that, in 1989, virtually the same proportion of EEC merchandise imports were from Switzerland (7.2 per cent) as from Africa (7.6 per cent). However, it must be emphasised that commercial relations between Europe and the less developed countries were and remain asymmetrical. The huge growth in the liberal market economies' reciprocal trade in manufactures has marginalised 'colonial' commerce as far as they are concerned, but for former colonies it remains a vital source of foreign exchange earnings. Africa's external economic relations remained set in a colonial mould in the sense that virtually all foreign trade continued to be with established markets outside the African continent long after independence. In 1970, only 5.3 per cent of the export and import trade in value terms was intra-African trade, and by 1977 this had declined to 4 per cent. Despite the self-professed 'socialism' of many regimes, the Communist bloc's share of African exports around 1970 was only 7 to 8 per cent. Independent Algeria still had a close trade dependence on France, which remained by far the most important supplier of imports in 1975, although by that date the premier market for Algerian products was the USA.

Since the 'second decolonisation' of the early 1970s, there has been little to differentiate the former colonies of Francophone and Anglophone Africa in terms of their external economic relations. Oil-rich Nigeria partly excepted, both sets of countries were equally dependent on the industrialised North for their foreign trade outlets and investment capital, and with export schedules dominated by a few primary products, equally vulnerable from the later 1970s to fluctuations in world economic activity (far more so, in fact, than during the world crisis of the 1930s, when colonial autarky helped shield African dependencies from the collapse of world trade). Throughout Africa, climatic and ecological deterioration, explosive demographic growth, and a reversal in the terms of trade for major exports contributed to the human disasters of the early 1980s, which television conveyed so vividly to Europe's living-rooms. That in 1984 practically every African nation could report substantially reduced mortality rates and rising life expectancy and literacy was less widely publicised (OECD, 1985).

With the calamities that befell sub-Saharan Africa during the 1980s, academic historians, economists and development agency officials began to probe more deeply into the long-term causes of the continent's backwardness. Even commentators with politically radical sympathies acknowledged that the indictment of colonialism and 'neo-colonialism' as the source of all woes was facile. Though profound differences remained between those prioritising the 'external' causes of Africa's economic crisis (the deteriorating terms of trade, protectionism in the industrialised North) and those for whom 'internal' causes were primarily determinant, there was considerable agreement that, all too often, the exercise of political power over the economy since independence had been disastrous. The catalogue of abuses included misguided fiscal and exchange rate policies, uncontrolled expenditure on projects with little economic rationale, the mushroom growth of state employment, endemic corruption and political clientelism, and the exploitation of primary producers by inefficient parastatal agencies. Not all post-independence states had experienced all these self-inflicted economic wounds in equal measure, but none had escaped them entirely. The agrarian policies pursued by African governments as part of the programme of import-substituting industrialisation were condemned on all sides: they resulted in very disadvantageous internal terms of trade for peasant producers, whose 'farm gate' prices were kept artificially low in relation to locally manufactured consumables. To raise food prices would have inflamed the underemployed working class on whose support most political leaders relied, and the monopoly state marketing boards 'squeezed' export-crop producers to finance industrial investment. Farmers were given no incentive to produce for off-farm sale nor to raise their productivity; agrarian stagnation or contraction occurred as population soared. Drought, the encroachment of deserts and the deterioration of fragile soils imposed severe environmental checks, but the causes of the food crisis which overtook Africa in the early 1980s were largely man-made, stemming from the failure of many countries to establish policies and institutions that would enable agriculture to flourish as a foundation for broad national development. Per capita food output declined at a rate variously estimated as 1.1 to 1.3 per cent a year *from* 1970. The increase in basic cereal productivity in Africa in the decade 1973–82 was less than one-third of that achieved in Asia. Before the drought of the early 1980s, grain production per capita in the 24 most seriously afflicted countries averaged about one-fifth less than in 1970 (OECD, 1985, pp. 5–8; Lofchie, 1987, pp. 85–109).

In the analysis of Africa's manifold crises a recurrent question – which can fittingly conclude this discussion – has been: how far were the policies of independent African states determined by political structures and practices inherited from colonial predecessors? Or, to phrase it differently, what real autonomy of economic decision-making did the independent African states enjoy? Catherine Coquery-Vidrovitch has argued that, given the authoritarian heritage of the colonial state, the transfer of power left no room for choice in independent Africa: to blame internal political decisions for economic mismanagement by one-party regimes would be a 'gross exaggeration of the data . . . ' In the absence of a constituted nation, she argues, 'the state could articulate its desiderata only by compulsive methods; the colonial economy had been a controlled, coercive economy. Quite naturally, the post-colonial economy, introduced into the same networks by the same agencies, acted in the same way.' In her analysis, the antithesis between the unitary model of the state imposed by colonialism and Africa's pre-existing pluralistic culture is at the root of the failure to constitute rationally directed polities as frameworks for economic development. The struggle to resolve the contradictions between state and culture, and bind together leaders and followers, bred the totalitarian cult of the charismatic leader and the mystique of tribalism. The state's mechanisms were constantly thrown out of gear by the use of political power to reward client groups, causing an escalation of corruption that resulted in situations of acute crisis (Coquery-Vidrovitch, 1988b, p. 133). There is much in her analysis with which we can agree, both in its general thrust and in its more detailed points. Yet it seems unwarrantably determinist, deeply pessimistic, and, on the relationship between the colonial and independent state, highly questionable. There were some continuities between the economic policies pursued by independent governments and their colonial predecessors (the use of marketing boards to extract much of the agricultural surplus is a signal instance) but, overall, independence brought a radical break with the past in economic management (Fieldhouse, 1986, pp. 240–5). For most of its short history, the colonial state had been the economic 'night-watchman' dear to liberal political economy, and its budgeting severely orthodox. Though the late colonial period was less financially restrictive and more interventionist, its innovations pale besides the expansionist economic and financial policies pursued after independence. State expenditure rose much faster than total product after independence, and by 1980 the public sector provided 50 to 55 per cent of non-agricultural jobs (compared with 36 per cent in Asia, 27 per cent in Latin America and 24 per cent in OECD countries). Despite increased taxation, governments resorted to foreign borrowing to finance investment on a scale quite disproportionate to their national resources. Debt service as a percentage of export earnings in sub-Saharan Africa increased from 6.8 per cent in 1975 to 19 per cent in 1983. Arms expenditure also rose quickly, and by the end of the decade accounted for about one-fifth of external debt (Young, 1994, ch. 1). There were, of course, many historical precedents for foreign borrowing to finance development, but state expenditure in Ghana, for example, was unregulated by the administrative apparatus, wasteful, and its public enterprises such a burden that it largely ruined the productive economy. Though this a somewhat special case of a relatively wealthy colony poised for capitalist development until turned in the opposite direction, almost entirely by the will of one man, massive misappropriation of economic resources by and through the public power has not been exceptional (Iliffe, 1983, p. 78).

It would be idle – as Coquery-Vidrovitch suggests – to envisage some 'genuine' process of decolonisation that would have involved a pure and simple rejection of the European type of state, but we must not conclude from this that independent African governments were constrained to followed an economic pathway laid out for them by the colonialists. They, together with many Western advisers, had exaggerated expectations of the pace of economic development, underestimated their material and human capital shortages, and made policy choices which in retrospect can be seen as economically counter-productive. They did not all depart from the models of political economy bequeathed by the colonialists in the same way, but the manifest ideological differences, say, between Ghana and the Ivory Coast in West Africa and Kenya and Tanzania in East Africa tend to disguise the extent to which all made radical departures from the past.

9

EUROPE AND THE 'THIRD WORLD' IN RETROSPECT

I

In the preface to this book, I noted when and how the terms 'Europe' and the 'Third World' became current, and we can fittingly close by observing their contrasting fortunes over the last generation. Fanon concluded his manifesto for the 'Third World' with a ringing invocation to 'Leave this Europe where they have never done talking of man, yet murder men everywhere they find them . . . ' The 'Third World's' destiny was to start 'a new history of Man, a history which will have regard to the sometimes prodigious theses which Europe has put forward, but which will also not forget Europe's crimes.' The wretched of the earth should cease paying ideological tribute to Europe by creating states, institutions and societies inspired by European models. Jean-Paul Sartre, who wrote the preface for Fanon's book, agreed that 'Europe is at death's door'. With the western European working classes now incorporated into capitalist society, the dialectic of historical transformation in Europe was exhausted (Fanon, 1967, pp. 251–5, 12).

In the late 1990s, this reads as a gross instance of philosophers misunderstanding the world they were seeking to change but, in its context, disillusionment with the idea of 'Europe' – even revulsion against it – was comprehensible. Given the brute facts of Europe's twentieth-century history, how could it signify moral progress? European humanism had been horrendously negated by the classification of millions of Europeans as 'sub-human' and their systematic murder; the conduct of a 'just war' debased by carpet bombing civilians. To many, and not simply those on the Marxist and Marxisant left, there were precedents for this inhumanity in the colonialist

306

segregation of 'natives' from Europeans and the ruthless slaughter of whole peoples when they opposed colonial rule. Liberals such as Hannah Arendt traced an ideological and political lineage from the racist imperialism of Europeans in Africa and Asia to racist totalitarianism within Europe. The genocidal violence of national socialism was anticipated by exemplary 'frightfulness' with which the Herero rebellion had been suppressed in German South-West Africa in 1904–5. It is true that some of those who resisted German and Italian fascism had looked to 'Europe' to supplant the discredited national state as a focus of political loyalty, but their hopes appeared naïvely misplaced in a divided post-war continent. The moral stock of 'Europe' was, if anything, further diminished by the relinquishing of responsibility for the continent's security to alliances dominated by extra-European superpowers and the failure of western European politicians to find a 'third way' through cold war rivalries.

For a fleeting period, the emergence of the 'Third World' as a recognised entity in international relations appeared to offer a dynamic alternative to Europe's frozen immobilism. The term was vested with overtones of revolutionary idealism (especially in France) but more directly associated with 'non-alignment', which became the common political denominator of 'Third World' states in the international system during the 1960s and 1970s. The neutralism they insisted on with respect to the antagonistic power blocs originated in the foreign stance adopted under Nehru by independent India. However, as more 'new nations' were represented at the non-aligned summits, so cold war issues were overlaid by hostility to persistent 'Western' imperialism (in Portuguese Africa, Rhodesia and South Africa) and by demands for a better return from the international economic system for poor countries. As early as the second Cairo Summit of October 1964, it was evident that with the loosening of the dominantly bipolar international system, the original, negatively conferred identity of non-alignment was losing its former sharpness, and anti-colonialism was now the core concern (Lyon, 1984, pp. 229–38). A pointer to the future at this conference was the raising of economic development as a common interest of the non-aligned and their pledge to strengthen the 'Group of 77', an association of less developed states formed at the first United Nations Conference on Trade and Development in March–June 1964 to challenge the industrial nations' dominance of world trade. There was growing evidence that the less developed countries were 'missing out' on the expansion of world trade and income, especially when their rapid population growth was considered. In almost half of them, per capita growth rates in the 1950s and 1960s were 1 per cent or less and, measured in constant dollars, the gap in average income between the OECD countries and LDCs roughly doubled (Brett, 1985, pp. 187–8). Raúl Prebisch wrote the keynote paper for UNCTAD (1) and his analysis provided intellectual grounding for the view that the international trading economy required restructuring if all were to share in development.

To adapt the terminology used in Marxist social class analysis, there was a brief moment in the early 1970s when the 'Third World' existed – or appeared to exist – 'in itself' and 'for itself'. A group of countries with a seemingly common, 'objective' position in the international economic system appeared united around a common programme of demands. These were watershed years for the global economy when the post-war boom, based on the hitherto unbroken expansion of world trade, gave way to much more difficult conditions. The Bretton Woods monetary system – in which the world's convertible currencies floated against a fixed dollar – broke down in August 1971 when the Nixon administration decided to leave the gold standard. Oil prices were expressed in dollars and the falling international value of the dollar meant a major loss in oil producers' incomes. This background is essential to understanding the great oil-hike of November 1973 when the producers' cartel, OPEC, experienced a sudden accession of international economic power in the aftermath of the Yom Kippur War. With the quadrupling of oil prices, and the temporary rise in other commodity prices, there now seemed a realistic possibility of the non-aligned using their control of strategic resources to bring about a restructuring of international economic arrangements on behalf of the developing countries. At their fourth summit in Algiers in August 1973 they had already opened the campaign for a more equitable pattern of world trade which culminated in United Nations General Assembly adopting (against stiff US opposition) the Declaration and Programme of Action on the Establishment of a New International Economic Order in May 1974. This represented a consensus of 'Third World' economic aspirations *vis-à-vis* the international order and a high-point of 'Third World' solidarity. The Declaration protested against global inequality – which left the developing countries, with 70 per cent of the world's population, receiving 30 per cent of the world's income – and called for a 'rational, just and equitable international division of labour'. The more specific demands were for a revision of the terms of trade between the developing and industrial states, improved access to the latter's markets through the progressive removal of tariff and non-tariff barriers, and preferential and non-reciprocal treatment for developing countries in all fields of international economic cooperation. The blunt criticism of the Western industrialised countries and their trading arrangements associated with the campaign for a NIEO was henceforth a central motif of the Non-aligned Movement whose spokesmen used the terms 'non-aligned', 'developing countries' and the 'Third World' without apparent distinction (Mortimer, 1980).

The 'objective' foundations of this coalition of poor states were transient and fragile, and whatever common interest they had in restructuring the world trading economy was outweighed by their conflicting economic interests in other areas. In poorer oil-importers, such as Tanzania, the steep rise in energy prices absorbed most export earnings by the end of the 1970s and imposed crippling costs on internal transport. Despite their rhetorical commitment to the NIEO, there was no real increase in economic co-operation between 'Third World' countries, and an estimated 70 per cent of their external economic transactions continued to be with 'First World' countries on an individual basis. Differentiation between developing economies was transforming the international division of labour, and obliterating the classical distinction between 'metropolitan' manufacturing economies and 'colonial' primary producers. The concentration of direct investment by multinational corporations in a relatively small number of 'Third World' countries accentuated their uneven development and widened the gap between 'middle-income' states and the poorest. Furthermore, the ideological solidarity of the Non-aligned Movement was being dissipated by wars within the 'Third World' – numbering over 140 between 1945 and 1989 and costing over 20 million lives – that were the counterpart of the long armed peace between the Western and Soviet blocs (Halliday, 1989, p. 11). Though some can be attributed to neo-colonialist interventions and others were exacerbated by the intrusion of the cold war confrontation into the 'Third World', many had communal, ethnic and nationalist causes and demonstrated the incapacity of the emergent nations to settle their disputes without the use of military force.

It would be grotesque narcissism to gauge the import of these tragedies by their cumulative effect on Western intellectuals, but they did have the consequence of disabusing many of the liberationist myths that had originally attached to the 'Third World'. France witnessed a particularly vociferous reaction against 'tiers-mondisme' from the late 1970s: Régis Debray, on the non-communist Left, damned it as the finest ideological 'swindle' of the epoch; on the Right, the 'Third World' was dismissed as an invention of the Parisian intelligentsia and an illusion that cloaked a Soviet quest for hegemony in Africa, the Middle East and Central America during the Brezhnev years. The concept of 'unequal exchange', which Marxist economists such Aghiri Emmanuel and Samir Amin had advanced to explain the exploitative character of international trade between the developed and underdeveloped economies, was scorned as an alibi for incompetent and often tyrannical political leadership. The view that the failure to establish and maintain viable polities was now a basic cause of 'underdevelopment' gained ground, greatly encouraged by the notoriety of the regimes of Idi Amin in Uganda, 'Emperor' Bokassa in the Central African Republic, Mobutu in Zaïre and, above all, the genocidal Pol Pot. It has been suggested that negligible support in France for the Live Aid concert of July 1985 was due to the discrediting of the notion of the 'Third World' (Lacoste, 1986, pp. 7–25). A noteworthy consequence of the reaction against 'tiers-mondisme' has been a revalorisation of European colonialism in Black Africa. What had once been condemned as a system of exploitation was now defended as a parenthesis of good government in the history of a continent where indigenous political organisations had failed to achieve the peaceful coexistence of myriad ethnicities. In a mordant polemic, Bernard Lugan, a leading Africanist, condemned the 'historical disinformation' which made the white man culpable for Africa's underdevelopment. 'Tiers-mondisme', by nourishing this sense of culpability, had – he argued – helped perpetuate a French cooperation policy in Francophone Africa that had the perverse effect of deepening African dependence on food aid and budgetary subventions. For fear of being dubbed 'colonialist', donor organisations had agreed to finance aid projects in whose viability they did not themselves believe. While 150 million Africans, or a quarter of the continent's population depended on international food aid in 1990, Black African states spent the equivalent to a third of their national product on arms (Lugan, 1991, pp. 57, 75–8).

There has not been a precise equivalent to 'tiers-mondisme' in English, and the 'Third World' has not been such a politically contested term. Nevertheless, the expression retains a considerable ideological charge and part of that charge comes from a historical mythology. I do not mean by this intentional falsehoods or distortions, but rather commonly accepted notions which orient us towards the human past and inform our understanding of its 'shape' and trajectory. In the sense I am using it, the idea of progress was a historical mythology in later-eighteenth- and nineteenth-century Europe. However vague the term 'Third World' has become in relation to present-day economic and political divisions in global society, it still invokes a past with a sharply defined narrative structure. In the mythology, the 'Third World' is a kind of residuum left over after the dialectic of European expansion and contraction had bound the continents into a single economic and political system, and divided human society into rich and poor, the powerful and powerless.

II

The strategy adopted in this book has been to formulate questions about the relationship between the development of Europe and the emergence of the 'Third World', and to attempt to answer them as far as the evidence permits. If the answers have been less clear cut than I or the reader might have desired this is principally because causal relationships are intrinsically difficult to specify for open-ended historical processes that rarely have clear beginnings and cannot be isolated for quasi-experimental investigation. This is especially true of two amorphous entities, which is why I have tried in a wide-ranging enquiry to home in on discrete issues.

To the great majority of economic historians, it will come as no surprise whatsoever to be told that European development was not organically and functionally related to 'Third World' underdevelopment (though this argument still goes marching on in Wallerstein's numerous publications). I agree that plantation slavery was a necessary (though not sufficient) condition for the commercial vibrancy of Atlantic Europe in the early modern era. Had it been sufficient, Portugal rather than the Netherlands would have been the world's greatest carrier before 1740. But it is difficult to see the mechanisms that 'underdeveloped' the lowland American tropics and African slave supply regions as necessarily related to the quantitative and qualitative shift in societal development that came with industrialisation. We lack the empirical data for definitive answers to key problems in European economic history before about 1820, but we cannot make it an article of faith that industrial development *required*, in the functionalist sense, slavery, colonial exploitation and economic retardation in other continents. This kind of counterfactual hypothesis is impossible to prove or disprove, but the evidence points, first, to an exceptional technological dynamism within western Europe that was quite independent of colonialism overseas. To illustrate how experimental techniques were being used to exploit Europe's abundant resources, we can cite the coke-fuelled blast furnace: it raised the annual production of iron to 15 kg per head in Britain by 1790 – a level of output that was probably fifteen times the global norm. It is merely one example of the exceptional dynamic within the western European economic space that stemmed from the high value placed on the rational manipulation of the human and material environment and the scope and effectiveness of private enterprise. Nowhere else in the world did technological creativity intermesh as tightly and effectively with economic production. (Landes, 1969, ch. 1, remains the best introduction to this topic.) Second, the evidence indicates that, within this economic space, population growth and rising incomes from agriculture were in themselves sufficient to form the extensive market needed to sustain industrialisation. To be sure, transatlantic demand did enlarge the market for British handicraft manufactures in the eighteenth century, and perhaps Britain would not have taken such an early industrial lead without that demand. But Britain was only the most advanced part of a single European economic community, and after 1815 its technological innovations diffused rapidly to the industrial regions of Belgium and northern France. The entrepreneurial and cultural preconditions for industrialisation were clearly present in Continental Europe, where development proceeded with negligible reliance on 'Third World' resources or markets. From the second quarter of the nineteenth century, the quantifiable data become more abundant, and they point consistently to Europe as an arena where industrialising economies traded with themselves, and drew upon each other's surplus capital. The division of labour was primarily between regional concentrations of high-technology manufacturing-and-mining, and areas of agricultural surplus. Trade in industrial goods from 'inner' north-west Europe to central Europe was a key mechanism in diffusing industrialisation because it typically took the form of the export of semi-manufactures (such as cotton yarn and pig iron) from regions of advanced technology to areas where there was an abundance of skilled but cheap labour. This proved a dynamic process, and by the 1890s technology transfers were creating industrial regions in 'outer Europe' (Pollard, 1981). Britain was semi-detached from Europe by reason of its far-flung export markets and the increasing flow of its investments to the Americas and colonies of settlement, but remained integrated within an economic community where *a* dynamic of growth remained cumulative, self-sustaining advances in technology and its diffusion across state borders.

European industrialisation was, very largely, an endogenous process which brought a fundamental discontinuity in the rate of economic change in human history. It raised the tempo of growth for a fringe of the world's population and introduced a profound caesura between states drawing on the material and symbolic resources of a new type of economy (embodied in the steamship and telegraph) and polities that could draw only on handicraft techniques and pre-scientific modes of communication. The sheer defencelessness of imperial China, the world's most populous state, in the face of minuscule Western forces in 1840–1 was a dramatic revelation of how great the gap had become. The continuation of European industrialisation did not 'require' – in a functionalist sense – the great irruption of European military–political power into Africa, Asia and the Pacific after 1875. It was not 'necessary' for capital accumulation; nor was it needed to secure markets and industrial raw materials. In fact, colonial imperialism was of small economic consequence one way or another for Europe, 'considered as one great country'.

For the 'peripheral' states and societies which have been exposed to European collective violence and to the peculiarly belligerent ways of Christian commerce for some centuries, inclusion as formal dependencies within the European states system had considerable economic consequences, not all of them detrimental. Internal order, the ending of slavery, famine relief, greater opportunities to use surplus land and labour in producing for export, internationally negotiable currencies and modern communications are not imperial fictions. We have discussed one case where European military–political power abruptly halted industrialisation 'from above' (Mohammed Ali's Egypt) but whether European rule generally 'retarded' modern development in the colonial world is impossible to prove. The contra-evidence from independent Latin America shows that sovereignty made a difference, but does it allow us to conclude that an independent Indian state (or states) would have developed much more rapidly than India actually did under the British Raj? Not if we are to credit the most all-encompassing explanation of why the Hindu social system locked India's agrarian civilisation into an equilibrium of cultural stability and economic stagnation – written, I hasten to add, by the Indian (and Hindu) development economist, Deepak Lal (Lal, 1988). According to Lal, the caste system persisted, in conjunction with the autarkic village community, because it fulfilled the economic function of maintaining adequate labour supplies in a decentralised system of control where the natural environment made agriculture chronically uncertain. Lal posits a fundamental changelessness in land–labour ratios, land use and living standards since the crystallisation of the caste system at the time of the Aryan invasions. The British, he insists, did little to disturb this ancient equilibrium, though without them the pace of change in the Indian economy would have been even slower than it actually was. Lal's central thesis is contentious, but its authorship should dispel the idea that exorcising the British ghost from the Indian past presupposes some personal identity with 'the West' or 'Europe'.

As European global dominance is brought into a longer-term historical perspective, its consequences for Asia and Africa can be more clearly seen as the imposition of 'cap-stone' military and bureaucratic institutions on indigenous polities and societies. Before the colonial empires were wound up, European capitalists had drawn the 'Third World' peasantries into labour and commodity markets to a rather limited degree. The corporations they headed had transformed specific regions (such as the Southern African mining zone) but touched others only superficially. They had sometimes been frustated by European colonial rulers, and perhaps more often their efforts to exploit local economies had been thwarted by indigenous or immigrant Asian entrepreneurs. When European political power was forced out by 'Third World' nationalists, the 'cap-stone' state institutions they had left behind were fairly soon used by political élites to assert national control over the local economy. The dominant classes in Africa's pre-colonial polities (which were lively memories in 1960) had enriched themselves and secured their political power by the control of external trade, and this deep-rooted historical tendency reasserted itself after independence. In this way and in so many others, the historicity of contemporary African and Asian states and societies is everywhere apparent. That they constitute a 'Third World' engendered and impoverished by European expansion is too crude and facile a thesis. We can no more ignore the well-documented material progress in the Belgian Congo than we can overlook the gross exploitation in Leopold II's private state. Real history is complex and more interesting than the simple terms in which it is often presented.

BIBLIOGRAPHY

Abbott, G.C. (1971) 'A Re-examination of the 1929 Colonial Development Act', *Economic History Review*, 24, 1, pp. 68–81.

Ade Ajayi, J.F. and M. Crowder (eds) (1976) *History of West Africa*, vol. 1, Longman.

Adedeji, A. (ed.) (1981) *Indigenization of African Economies*, Hutchinson.

Adedeji, A. (1986) 'The economic evolution of developing Africa', in A.D. Roberts (ed.), *The Cambridge History of Africa*, vol. 8, Cambridge University Press.

Adedeji, A. and C. Ake (1981) 'Historical and theoretical background', in A. Adedeji (ed.), *Indigenization of African Economies*, Hutchinson.

Adu Boahen, A. (1987) *African Perspectives on Colonialism*, Johns Hopkins University Press.

Ageron, C.-R. (ed.) (1986) *Les Chemins de la Décolonisation de l'Empire Français*, Editions du Centre National de la Recherche Scientifique.

Ageron, C.-R. (1991a) *Modern Algeria*, Hurst.

Ageron, C.-R. (1991b) *La Décolonisation Française*, Colin.

Ageron, C.-R. and M. Michel (eds) (1992) *L'Afrique Noire Française: L'Heure des Indépendances*, Editions du Centre National de la Recherche Scientifique.

Ajayi, J.F.A. (1968) 'The continuities of African institutions under colonialism', in T.O. Ranger (ed.), *Emerging Themes of African History*, Nairobi, 1968.

Alavi, H. (1975) 'India and the colonial mode of production', in R. Miliband and J. Saville (eds), *The Socialist Register 1975*, pp. 160–197, Merlin Press.

Alavi, H., P.L. Burns, G.R. Knight, P.B. Mayer and D. McEachern (1982) *Capitalism and Colonial Production*, Croom Helm.

Albertini, R. von (1971) *Decolonization: the Administration and Future of the Colonies, 1919-1960*, Holmes and Meier.

Albertini, R. von, (with A. Wirz) (1982) *European Colonial Rule, 1880–1940: The Impact of the West on India, Southeast Asia, and Africa*, Clio.

Aldcroft, D.H. (1968) 'Introduction: British industry and foreign competition, 1875–1914', in D.H. Aldcroft (ed.), *The Development of British Industry and Foreign Competition 1875–1914*, Allen & Unwin.

Alden, D. (1984) 'Late colonial Brazil, 1750–1808', in L. Bethell (ed.), *The Cambridge History of Latin America*, vol. 2, *Colonial Latin America*, Cambridge University Press.

Allen, G.C., and A.G. Donnithorne (1957) *Western Enterprise in Indonesia and Malaya*, Allen & Unwin.

Amin, S. (1974) *Accumulation on a World Scale*, 2 vols, Monthly Review Press.

Ansprenger, F. (1989) *The Dissolution of the Colonial Empires*, Routledge.

Anstey, R. (1975) *The Atlantic Slave Trade and British Abolition*, Macmillan.

Arasaratnam, S. (1991) 'Weavers, merchants and co: the handloom industry in South-eastern India 1750–1790', in S. Subramanyam (ed.), *Merchants, Markets and the State in Early Modern India*, Oxford University Press.

Arrighi, G. (1970) 'Labour Supplies in Historical Perspective: A Study of the Proletarianisation of the African Peasantry in Rhodesia,' *Journal of Development Studies*, 6, pp. 197–234.

Atkin, J.M. (1977) *British Overseas Investment, 1918–1931*, Arno.

Austen, R.A. (1979) 'The trans-saharan slave trade: a tentative census', in H.A. Gemery and J.S. Hogendorn (eds), *The Uncommon Market: Essays in the Economic History of the Atlantic Slave Trade*, Academic Press.

Austen, R.A. (1987) *African Economic History*, Heinemann.

Austen, R.A., and R. Headrick (1983) 'Equatorial Africa under colonial rule', in D.Birmingham and P.M. Martin, (eds), *History of Central Africa*, vol. 2, Longman.

Austen R.A. and W.D. Smith (1992) 'Private tooth decay as public economic virtue: the slave-sugar triangle, consumerism and European industrialization', in J.E. Inikori and S.L. Engerman (eds), *The Atlantic Slave Trade: Effects on Economies, Societies, and Peoples in Africa, the Americas, and Europe*,Duke University Press.

Baer, G. (1966) 'Land tenure in Egypt and the Fertile Crescent, 1800–1950', in C. Issawi (ed.), *The Economic History of the Middle East 1800–1914*, University of Chicago Press.

Bagchi, A.K. (1972) *Private Investment in India 1900–1939*, Cambridge University Press.

Bagchi, A.K. (1982) *The Political Economy of Underdevelopment*, Cambridge University Press.

Bairoch, P. (1973) 'European Foreign Trade in the XIX Century: the Development of the Value and Volume of Exports', *Journal of Economic History*, 2, pp. 5–36.

Bairoch, P. (1974) 'Geographical Structure and Trade Balance of European Foreign Trade from 1800 to 1970', *Journal of European Economic History*, 3, 3, pp. 557–608.

Bairoch, P. (1975) *The Economic Development of the Third World since 1900*, Methuen.

Bairoch, P. (1976) *Commerce Extérieur et Développement Économique de l'Europe au XIXe siècle*, Mouton.

Bairoch, P. (1980) 'Le Bilan Économique du Colonialisme: Mythes et Réalités', *Itinerario*, Pt 1, 1, pp. 29–41.

Bairoch, P. (1982) 'International Industrialization Levels from 1750 to 1980', *Journal of European Economic History*, 2, pp. 269–310.

Bairoch, P. (1986) 'Historical roots of economic underdevelopment: myths and realities', in W.J. Mommsen and J. Osterhammel (eds), *Imperialism and After*, Allen & Unwin.

Bairoch, P. (1991) 'Economic inequalities between 1800 and 1913', in J. Batou (ed.), *Between Development and Underdevelopment: The Precocious Attempts at Industrialization of the Periphery, 1800–1870*, Droz.

Bairoch, P. (1993) *Economics and World History: Myths and Paradoxes*, Harvester/Wheatsheaf.

Bakewell, P. (1984) 'Mining in colonial Spanish America', in L. Bethell (ed.), *The Cambridge History of Latin America*, vol. 2, *Colonial Latin America*, Cambridge University Press.

Barlow, C., and J. Drabble (1990) 'Government and the emerging rubber industries in Indonesia and Malaya, 1900–40', in A. Booth, W.J. O'Malley and A. Weidemann (eds), *Indonesian Economic History in the Dutch Colonial Era*, Yale University Press.

Barrett, W. (1990) 'World bullion flows, 1450–1800', in J. D.Tracy (ed.), *The Rise of Merchant Empires: Long-distance Trade in the Early Modern World, 1350–1750*, Cambridge University Press.

Barry, B. (1988) 'Neocolonialism and dependence in Senegal', in P. Gifford and W.R. Louis (eds), *Decolonization and African Independence: the Transfers of Power, 1960–1980*, Yale University Press.

Basso, J-A. (1992) 'Les accords de coopération entre la France et les États Africains: leurs relations et leurs conséquences au regard des indépendances Africaines (1960–1970)', in C-R Ageron and M.Michel (eds), *L'Afrique Noire Française:L'Heure des Indépendances*, Editions du Centre National de la Recherche Scientifique.

Batou, J. (1991) 'L'Égypte de Muhammad- Ali: Pouvoir Politique et Développement Économique', *Annales ESC*, 1991, 2, pp. 401–28.

Batou, J. (ed.) (1991) *Between Development and Underdevelopment: the Precocious Attempts at Industrialization of the Periphery 1800–1870*, Droz.

Bauer, P.T. (1973) 'British Colonial Africa: economic retrospect and aftermath', in P. Duignan and L.H. Gann (eds), *Colonialism in Africa, 1870–1960*, vol. 4, *The Economics of Colonialism*, Cambridge University Press.

Bayart, J-F. (1993) *The State in Africa: the Politics of the Belly*, Longman.

Bayly, C.A. (1983) *Rulers, Townsmen and Bazaars: North Indian Society in the Age of British Expansion, 1770–1870*, Cambridge University Press.

Bayly, C.A. (1985) 'State and Economy in India over Seven Hundred Years', *Economic History Review*, 38, 4, pp. 583–96.

Bayly, C.A. (1986) 'Two colonial revolts: the Java war, 1825–30, and the Indian "Mutiny" of 1857–59', in C.A. Bayly and D.H.A. Kolff (eds), *Two Colonial Empires*, Nijhoff.

Bayly, C.A. (1988) *Indian Society and the Making of the British Empire (The New Cambridge History of India, vol. II.1)*, Cambridge University Press.

Bayly, C.A. and D.H.A. Kolff (eds.) (1988) *Two Colonial Empires*, Nijhoff.

Beauchamp, J. (1935) *British Imperialism in India*, Martin Lawrence.

Bender, G. J. (1978) *Angola under the Portuguese: the Myth and the Reality*, Heinemann.

Bennett, G. (1971) 'British Settlers North of the Zambezi', in P. Duignan and L.H. Gann (eds), *Colonialism in Africa, 1870–1960*, vol. 2, Cambridge University Press.

Berg, E.J. (1964) 'Real income trends in West Africa 1939–1960', in M.J. Herskovits and M. Harwitz (eds), *Economic Transition in Africa*, Routledge & Kegan Paul.

Bernier, F. (1669) *Travels in the Mogul Empire, AD 1656–1668*, 1972 edn, Chand.

Berque, J. (1967) *French North Africa: the Maghrib between Two World Wars*, Faber.

Bethell, L. (ed.) (1984) *The Cambridge History of Latin America*, vols 1 and 2, *Colonial Latin America*, Cambridge University Press.

Birmingham, D. (1981) *Central Africa to 1870*, Cambridge University Press. (This is a reprint of Birmingham's chapters in *The Cambridge History of Africa*, vols 3, 4 and 5).

Birmingham, D., and P.M. Martin (eds) (1983) *History of Central Africa*, 2 vols, Longman.

Blackburn, R. (1988) *The Overthrow of Colonial Slavery*, Verso.

Blackburn, R. (1997) *The Making of New World Slavery*, Verso.

Blainey, G. (1965) 'Lost Causes of the Jameson Raid', *Economic History Review*, 18, pp. 350–66.

Bloch-Lainé, F. (1956) *La Zone Franc*, Presses Universitaires de France.

Blussé, L., and F. Gaastra (eds) (1981) *Companies and Trade*, Leiden University Press.

Bobrie, F. (1976) 'Finances Publiques et Conquête Colonial: le Coût Budgétaire de l'Expansion Française entre 1850 et 1913', *Annales ESC*, 31, 6, pp. 1225–45.

Booghaart, E. van den and P.C. Emmer (1986) 'Colonialism and Migration: an overview', in P.C. Emmer (ed.) *Colonialism and Migration*, Nijhoff.

Booth, A. (1990) 'Foreign trade and domestic development in the colonial economy', in A. Booth *et al.* (eds), *Indonesian Economic History in the Dutch Colonial Era*, Yale University Press.

Booth, A., W.J. O'Malley and Weidermann (eds) (1990) *Indonesian Economic History in the Dutch Colonial Era*, Yale University Press.

Botte, R. (1991) 'Les Rapports Nord–Sud, la Traite Négrière et le Fuuta Jaloo à la fin du xviii Siècle', *Annales ESC*, Novembre–Décembre, 6, pp. 1411–35.

Bouvier, J. (1976) 'Les traits majeurs de l'impérialisme français avant 1914', in Bouvier J. and R. Girault (eds), *L'Impérialisme Français d'avant 1914*, Mouton.

Bouvier, J. and R. Girault (eds) (1976) *L'Impérialisme Français d'avant 1914*, Mouton.

Bouvier, J., R. Girault and J. Thobie (1986) *L'Impérialisme à la Française*, Editions la découverte.

Bowser, F. P. (1984) 'Africans in Spanish American colonial society', in L. Bethell (ed.), *The Cambridge History of Latin America*, vol. 2, *Colonial Latin America*, Cambridge University Press.

Boxer, C.R. (1965) *The Dutch Seaborne Empire 1600–1800*, Hutchinson.

Boxer, C.R. (1969) *The Portuguese Seaborne Empire 1415–1825*, Hutchinson.

Boxer, C.R. (1980) *Portuguese India in the Mid-seventeenth Century*, Oxford University Press.

Brading, D. (1984) 'Bourbon Spain and its American Empire', in L.Bethell (ed.), *The Cambridge History of Latin America*, vol. 2, *Colonial Latin America*, Cambridge University Press.

Brading, D.A. (1991) *The First America*, Cambridge University Press.

Brandt (1980) Report of the Independent Commission on International Development Studies, *North–South: A Programme for Survival*, Pan.

Brandt (1983) Report of the Independent Commission on International Development Studies, *Common Crisis: North–South Cooperation for World Survival*, Pan.

Braudel, F. (1972) *The Mediterranean and the Mediterranean World in the Age of Philip II*, vol. 1, Collins.

Braudel, F. and F. Spooner, (1967) 'Prices in Europe from 1450 to 1750', in E.E. Rich and C.H. Wilson (eds), *The Cambridge Economic History of Europe*, vol. 4, *The Economy of Expanding Europe in the Sixteenth and Seventeenth Centuries*, Cambridge University Press.

Breman, J. (1992) 'The Hali system in South Gujarat', in G. Prakash (ed.) *The World of the Rural Labourer in Colonial India*, Oxford University Press.

Brenner, R. (1977) 'The Origins of Capitalist Development: a Critique of Neo-Smithian Marxism', *New Left Review*, 104, pp. 25–92.

Brett, E.A. (1973) *Colonialism and Underdevelopment in East Africa: the Politics of Economic Change, 1919–1939*, Heinemann.

Brett, E.A. (1985) *The World Economy since the War: the Politics of Uneven Development*, Macmillan.

Brown, J.M. (1985) *Modern India: the Origins of an Asian Democracy*, Oxford University Press.

Brunschwig, H. (1966) *French Colonialism 1871–1914: Myths and Realities*, Pall Mall Press.

Brunschwig, H. (1978) 'French expansion and local reactions in Black Africa in the time of imperialism (1880-1914)', in H.L. Wesseling (ed.), *Expansion and Reaction: Essays on European Expansion and Reaction in Asia and Africa*, Nijhoff.

Brunschwig, H. (1986) 'De l'assimilation à la décolonisation', in C-R. Ageron (ed.), *Les Chemins de la Décolonisation de l'Empire Colonial Français*, Editions du Centre National de la Recherche Scientifique.

Bull, H. (1984) 'European States and African Political Communities', in H. Bull and A. Watson (eds), *The Expansion of International Society*, Clarendon Press.

Bull, H., and A. Watson, (eds) (1984) *The Expansion of International Society*, Clarendon Press.

Burns, A. (1948) *History of Nigeria*, 4th revised edition, Allen & Unwin.

Butel, P. (1978) 'Les Amériques et l'Europe', in P. Léon (ed.), *Histoire Économique et Sociale du Monde*, vol. 3, Colin.

Butel, P. (1990) 'France, the Antilles, and Europe in the seventeenth and eighteenth centuries: renewals of foreign trade', in J.D. Tracy (ed.), *The Rise of Merchant Empires: Long-distance Trade in the Early Modern World, 1350–1750*, Cambridge University Press.

Cady, J.F. (1954) *The Roots of French Imperialism in Eastern Asia*, Cornell University Press.

Cain, P.J. and A.G. Hopkins (1993) *British Imperialism:* vol. 1: *Innovation and Expansion 1688-1914;* vol. 2: *Crisis and Deconstruction, 1914–1990*, Longman.

Cardoso, F.H., and E. Faletto (1979) *Dependency and Development in Latin America*, originally published in 1967, English translation, University of California Press.

Carey, P. (1976) 'The Origins of the Java War (1825-30)', *English Historical Review*, 91, pp. 52–78.

Cell, J. W. (1992) *Hailey: A Study in British Imperialism, 1872–1969*, Cambridge University Press.

Chandavarkar, R. (1985) 'Industrialization in India before 1947: Conventional Approaches and Alternative Perspectives', *Modern Asian Studies*, 19, 3, pp. 623–68.

Chandra, B. (1969) 'Reinterpretation of nineteenth-century Indian economic history', in M.D. Morris, T. Matsui, B. Chandra and T. Raychaudhuri, *Indian Economy in the Nineteenth Century: A Symposium*, Indian Economic and Social History Association.

Charlesworth, N. (1982) *British Rule and the Indian Economy, 1800–1914*, Macmillan.

Charlesworth, N. (1992) 'The origins of fragmentation of landholding in British India', in P. Robb (ed.), *Rural India: Land Power and Society under British Rule*, originally published by the Curzon Press, 2nd edn, Oxford India Paperbacks, 1992.

Chatterjee, P. (1986) 'The Colonial State and Peasant Resistance in Bengal, 1920–1947', *Past and Present*, 110, February, pp. 169–200.

Chaudhuri, K.N. (1968) 'India's International Economy in the Nineteenth Century: An Historical Survey', *Modern Asian Studies*, 2, 1, pp. 31–50.

Chauduri, K.N. (ed.) (1971) *The Economic Development of India under the East India Company 1814–58*, Cambridge University Press.

Chaudhuri, K.N. (1978) *The Trading World of Asia and the East India Company, 1660–1760*, Cambridge University Press.

Chaudhuri, K.N. (1983) 'Foreign trade and balance of payments (1757–1947)', in D. Kumar (with M. Desai) (ed.), *The Cambridge Economic History of India*, vol. 2 *c.1757–c.1970*, Cambridge University Press.

Chaudhuri, K.N. (1985) *Trade and Civilisation in the Indian Ocean: An Economic History from the Rise of Islam to 1750*, Cambridge University Press.

Chaudhuri, K.N. (1990) *Asia Before Europe: Economy and Civilisation of the Indian Ocean from the Rise of Islam to 1750*, Cambridge University Press.

Chaudhuri, K.N. and C. J. Dewey (eds) (1979) *Economy and Society: Essays in Indian Economic and Social History*, Oxford University Press.

Chipman, J. (1989) *French Power in Africa*, Blackwell.

Cipolla, C. M. (1970) *European Culture and Overseas Expansion*, Penguin.

Clarence-Smith, W.G. (1979) 'The Myth of Uneconomic Imperialism: The Portuguese in Angola, 1836–1926', *Journal of Southern African Studies*, 5, 2, pp. 165–80.

Clarence-Smith,W G. (1985) *The Third Portuguese Empire*, Manchester University Press.

Clark, G. (1936) *The Balance Sheets of Imperialism: Facts and Figures on Colonies*, Columbia University Press.

Coelho, P.R.P. (1973) 'The Profitability of Imperialism: The British Experience in the West Indies, 1768–1772', *Explorations in Economic History*, 1973, 10 pp. 253–80.

Cohn, B. S. (1969) 'Structural change in rural society', in R.E. Frykenberg (ed.), *Land Control and Social Structure in Indian History*, University of Wisconsin Press.

Cohen, R. (1971) 'From Empire to Colony: Bornu in the nineteenth and twentieth centuries', in V.Turner (ed.), *Colonialism in Africa, 1870–1960*, vol 3, *Profiles of Change: African Societies and Colonial Rule*, Cambridge University Press.

Cole, G.D.H. (1947) *An Intelligent Man's Guide to the Post-war World*, Gollancz.

Cole, J.I. (1993) *Colonialism and Revolution in the Middle East: Social and Cultural Origins of Egypt's Urabi Movement*, Princeton University Press.

Colson, E., (1971) 'The impact of the colonial period on the definition of land rights', in V. Turner (ed.), *Colonialism in Africa, 1870–1960*, vol. 3, *Profiles of Change:African Societies and Colonial Rule*, Cambridge University Press.

Cooper, F. (1981) 'Africa and the World Economy', *African Studies Review*, 24, 2/3, pp.1–87.

Coquery-Vidrovitch, C. (1975) 'L'impact des Intérêts Coloniaux: SCOA and CFAO dans l'Ouest Africain, 1910–1965', *Journal of African History*, 16, 4, pp. 595–621.

Coquery-Vidrovitch, C. (1977) 'L'Afrique Coloniale Française et la Crise de 1930: Crise Structurelle et Genèse du Sous-développement', *Revue Française d'Histoire d'Outre-mer*, 63, special number, pp. 386–423.

Coquery-Vidrovitch, C. (1979) 'Colonisation ou Impérialisme: la Politique Africaine de la France entre les Deux Guerres', *Le Mouvement Social*, 107, pp. 51–76.

Coquery-Vidrovitch, C. (1986) 'French Black Africa', in A.D. Roberts (ed.), *The Cambridge History of Africa*, vol. 7, *1905–1940*, Cambridge University Press.

Coquery-Vidrovitch, C. (1988a) *Africa: Endurance and Change South of the Sahara*, University of California Press.

Coquery-Vidrovitch, C. (1988b) 'The transfer of economic power in French-speaking West Africa', in P. Gifford and W.R. Louis (eds), *Decolonization and African Independence: the Transfers of Powers, 1960–1980*, Yale University Press.

Crafts, N.C.R. (1985) *British Economic Growth during the Industrial Revolution*, Oxford University Press.

Crowder, M. (1984) 'The Second World War; prelude to decolonisation in Africa', in M. Crowder (ed.), *The Cambridge History of Africa*, vol. 8, *c.1940 to c.1975*, Cambridge University Press.

Curtin, P. D. (1969) *The Atlantic Slave Trade: a Census*, University of Wisconsin Press.

Curtin, P.D. (1977) 'Slavery and Empire', *Annals of the New York Academy of Sciences*, 293, pp. 3–11.

Curtin, P.D. (1984) *Cross-cultural Trade in World History*, Cambridge University Press.

Curtin, P.D. (1990) *The Rise and Fall of the Plantation Complex: Essays in Atlantic History*, Cambridge University Press.

Darwin, J. (1988) *Britain and Decolonisation: the Retreat from Empire in the Post-war World*, Macmillan.

Dasgupta, P. (1993) *An Enquiry into Well-being and Destitution*, Oxford University Press.

Davenport-Hines, R.P.T. and G. Jones (eds.) (1989) *British Business in Asia since 1860*, Cambridge University Press.

Davies, N. (1996) *Europe: A History*, Oxford University Press.

Davis, L.E. and R. Huttenback (1988) *Mammon and the Pursuit of Empire: The Economics of British Imperialism*, Cambridge University Press.

Davis, R. (1962) 'English Foreign Trade, 1660–1700', in E.M. Carus-Wilson (ed.), *Essays in Economic History*, vol. 2, Arnold.

Davis, R. (1973) *The Rise of the Atlantic Economies*, Weidenfeld & Nicolson.

Deane, P. (1979) *The First Industrial Revolution*, 2nd edn, Cambridge University Press.

Dewey, C. (ed.) (1988) *Arrested Development in India*, Manohar.

Diaz-Alejandro, C.F. (1988) 'No less than one hundred years of argentine economic history plus some comparisons', in C.F. Diaz-Alejandro, *Trade, Development and the World Economy* (ed. A. Velaso) Blackwell.

Drake. P.J. (1979) 'The Economic Development of British Malaya to 1914', *Journal of Southeast Asian Studies*, 10, 2, pp. 262–90.

Drescher, S. (1977) *Econocide: British Slavery in the Era of Abolition*, University of Pittsburg Press.

Drescher, S. (1987a) *Capitalism and Anti Slavery: British Mobilization in Comparative Perspective*, Macmillan.

Drescher, S. (1987b) 'Paradigms tossed: capitalism and the political sources of abolition', in B.Solow and S.L. Engerman (eds), *British Capitalism and Caribbean Slavery*, Cambridge University Press.

Drescher, S. (1994) 'Whose Abolition? Popular Pressure and the Ending of the British Slave Trade', *Past and Present*, 143, May, pp. 136–66.

Drèze, J. and A. Sen (1989) *Hunger and Public Action*, Clarendon Press.

Drèze, J. and A. Sen (eds) (1990) *The Political Economy of Hunger*, 3 vols, Clarendon Press.

Duignan, P. and L.H. Gann (eds) (1973a) *Colonialism in Africa, 1870–1960*, vol. 4, *The Economics of Colonialism*, Cambridge University Press.

Duignan, P. and L.H. Gann (1973b) 'Economic achievements of the colonizers: An assessment', in P.Duignan and L.H. Gann (eds), *Colonialism in Africa, 1870–1960*, vol. 4, *The Economics of Colonialism*, Cambridge University Press.

Dumont, L. (1970) *Homo Hierarchicus: the Caste System and its Implications*, Weidenfeld & Nicolson.

Dunn, R. (1972) *Sugar and Slaves: the Rise of the Planter Class in the English West Indies, 1624–1713*, Cape.

Dutt, R.C. (1902) *The Economic History of India from the Rise of British Power to 1837*, Kegan Paul.

Dutt, R.C. (1906) *The Economic History of India in the Victorian Age*, Kegan Paul.

Edelstein, M. (1981) 'Foreign investment and empire 1860–1914', in R. Floud and D. McCloskey (eds), *The Economic History of Britain since 1700*, vol. 2, Cambridge University Press.

Edelstein, M. (1994) 'Imperialism: cost and benefit', in R. Floud and D. McCloskey (eds), *The Economic History of Britain since 1700*, 2nd ed, vol. 2, Cambridge University Press.

Ehrlich, C. (1973) 'Building and Caretaking: Economic Policy in British Tropical Africa, 1890–1960', *Economic History Review*, 26, pp. 649–67.

Elliott, J.H. (1963) *Imperial Spain 1469–1716*, Arnold.

Elliott, J.H. (1984a) 'The Spanish conquest and settlement of Latin America', in L.Bethell (ed.) *The Cambridge History of Latin America*, vol. 1, *Colonial Latin America*, Cambridge University Press.

Elliott, J.H. (1984b) 'Spain and America in the sixteenth and seventeenth centuries', in L.Bethell (ed.) *The Cambridge History of Latin America*, vol. 1, *Colonial Latin America*, Cambridge University Press.

Elliott, J.H. (1990) 'The seizure of overseas territories by the colonial powers', in H. Pohl (ed.), *The European Discovery of the World and its Economic Effects on Pre-industrial Society 1500–1800*, Franz Steiner.

Elson, R.E. (1990) 'Peasant poverty and prosperity under the cultivation system in Java', in A. Booth, W.J. O'Malley and A. Weidemann (eds) *Indonesian Economic History in the Dutch Colonial Era*, Yale University Press.

Eltis, D. (1983) 'Free and Coerced Transatlantic Migrations', *American Historical Review*, 88, 2, pp. 251–80.

Eltis, D. (1987) *Economic Growth and the Ending of the Transatlantic Slave Trade*, Oxford University Press.

Eltis, D. (1989) 'Trade between Western Africa and the Atlantic World before 1870: Estimates of Trends in Value, Composition and Direction', *Research in Economic History*, 12, pp. 197–239.

Eltis, D. (1993) 'Europeans and the Rise and Fall of African Slavery in the Americas: an Interpretation', *American Historical Review*, 98, 5, pp. 1399–1423.

Eltis, D. and L. C. Jennings (1988) 'Trade between Western Africa and the Atlantic World in the Pre-Colonial Era', *American Historical Review*, 93, 4, pp. 936–59.

Elvin, M.(1973) *The Pattern of the Chinese Past*, Stanford University Press.

Emmer, P.C. (ed) (1986) *Colonialism and Migration: Indentured Labour before and after Slavery*, Nijhof.

Engerman, S.L. (1984) 'Economic Change and Contract Labor in the British Caribbean: the End of Slavery and the Adjustment to Emancipation', *Explorations in Economic History*, 21, pp. 133–50.

Engerman, S. L. (1986a) 'Slavery and Emancipation in Comparative Perspective: A Look at Some Recent Debates', *Journal of Economic History*, 46, 2, pp. 317–39.

Engerman, S.L. (1986b) 'Servants to slaves to servants: contract labour and European expansion', in P.C. Emmer (ed.), *Colonialism and Migration: Indentured Labour before and after Slavery*, Nijhoff.

Engerman, S.L. (1994) 'Mercantilism and overseas trade, 1700–1800' in R.Floud and D. McCloskey (eds), *The Economic History of Britain since 1700*, 2nd edn, vol. 1, Cambridge Unversity Press.

Fage, J.D. (1969a) *A History of West Africa*, 4th edn, Cambridge University Press.

Fage, J.D. (1969b) 'Slavery and the Slave Trade in the Context of West African History', *Journal of African History*, 10, 3, pp. 393–404.

Fage, J.D. (1977) 'Upper and Lower Guinea', in R. Oliver (ed.),*The Cambridge History of Africa*, vol. 3, Cambridge University Press.

Fage, J.D. (1989) 'African Societies and the Atlantic Slave Trade', *Past and Present*, 125, pp. 97–115.

Fanon, F. (1967) *The Wretched of the Earth*, Penguin.

Farnie, D.A. (1979) *The English Cotton Industry and the World Market 1815–1896*, Oxford University Press.

Fasseur, C. (1986) 'The Cultivation System and its impact on the Dutch colonial economy and the indigenous society in ninteenth-century Java', in C.A. Bayly and D.H.A. Kolff (eds), *Two Colonial Empires*, Nijhoff.

Fasseur, C. (1991) 'Purse or Principle: Dutch Colonial Policy in the 1860s and the Decline of the Cultivation System', *Modern Asian Studies*, 25, 1, pp. 33–52.

Feis, H. (1930) *Europe:the World's Banker*, Yale University Press.

Fieldhouse, D. (1971) 'The economic exploitation of Africa: some British and French comparisons', in P. Gifford and W.R. Louis (eds), *France and Britain in Africa: Imperial Rivalry and Colonial Rule*, Yale University Press.

Fieldhouse, D. (1973) *Economics and Empire 1830-1914*, Weidenfeld & Nicolson.

Fieldhouse, D.K. (1978) *Unilever Overseas*, Croom Helm.

Fieldhouse, D.K. (1986) *Black Africa 1945–80: Economic Decolonization and Arrested Development*, Allen & Unwin.

Fieldhouse, D.K. (1992) 'British merchants and French decolonization: the UAC in Francophone Africa (1945-1960)', in C-R. Ageron and M. Michel (eds), *L'Afrique Noire Française: L'Heure des Indépendances*, Editions du Centre National de la Recherche Scientifique.

Fieldhouse, D.K. (1994) *Merchant Capital and Economic Decolonization*, Oxford University Press.

Fischer, W., R.M. McInnis and J. Schneider (eds) (1986) *The Emergence of a World Economy 1500–1914*, 2 vols, Franz Steiner.

Fitzgerald, E.P. (1988) 'Did France's Colonial Empire Make Economic Sense? A Perspective from the Postwar Decade, 1946–1956', *Journal of Economic History*, 48, 2, pp. 373–85.

Förster, S., W.J.Mommsen and R.Robinson (eds) (1988) *Bismarck, Europe and Africa: the Berlin Africa Conference 1884–1885 and the Onset of Partition*, Oxford University Press.

Frank, A.G. (1967) *Capitalism and Underdevelopment in Latin America*, Monthly Review Press.

Frank, A.G. (1973) 'The development of underdevelopment', in C.K. Wilber (ed.), *The Political Economy of Development and Underdevelopment*, Random House.

Frank, A.G. (1978) *World Accumulation 1492–1789*, Monthly Review Press.

Frankel, S.H. (1938) *Capital Investment in Africa: Its Course and Effects*, Oxford University Press.

Frykenberg, R.E. (ed.) (1969) *Land Control and Social Structure in Indian History*, University of Wisconsin Press.

Furber, H. (1976) *Rival Empires of Trade in the Orient, 1600–1800*, University of Minnesota Press.

Furnivall, J.S. (1944) *Netherlands India: A Study of Plural Economy*, Cambridge University Press, Amsterdam reprint, 1976.

Furnivall, J.S. (1948) *Colonial Theory and Practice: A Comparative Study of Burma and Netherlands India*, Cambridge University Press.

Furtado, C. (1976) *Economic Development of Latin America*, 2nd edn, Cambridge University Press.

Fynn, D.O. (1996) 'Early capitalism despite New World bullion: an anti-Wallerstein interpretation of imperial Spain', reproduced in D.O. Fynn, *World Silver and Monetary History in the 16th and 17th centuries*, Variorum.

Gadgil, D.R. (1971) *The Industrial Evolution of India in Recent Times, 1860–1930*, 5th edn, Oxford University Press.

Gallagher, J., and R. Robinson (1981) *Africa and the Victorians*, 2nd edn, Macmillan.

Ganiage, J. (1968) *L'Expansion Coloniale de la France sous la Troisième République*, Payot.

Gann, L.H., and P. Duignan (1971) 'Changing patterns of a white élite: Rhodesian and other settlers', in P. Duignan and L.H. Gann (eds), *Colonialism in Africa, 1870–1960*, vol. 2, Cambridge University Press.

Garner, R. L. (1988) 'Long-term Silver Mining Trends in Spanish America: A Comparative Analysis of Peru and Mexico', *American Historical Review*, 93, 4, pp. 898–935.

Geertz, C. (1963) *Agricultural Involution: the Process of Ecological Change in Indonesia*, University of California Press.

Gemery, H.A. and J.S. Hogendorn (eds) (1979) *The Uncommon Market: Essays in the Economic History of the Atlantic Slave Trade*, Academic Press.

Gibson, C. (1984) 'Indian societies under Spanish rule', in L. Bethell (ed.), *The Cambridge History of Latin America*, vol. 1, *Colonial Latin America*, Cambridge University Press.

Gifford P. and W.R. Louis (eds) (1971) *France and Britain in Africa: Imperial Rivalry and Colonial Rule*, Yale University Press.

Gifford P. and W.R. Louis (eds) (1988) *Decolonization and African Independence: the Transfers of Powers, 1960–1980*, Yale University Press.

Girault, R. (1979) 'Place et role des changes extérieurs', in F. Braudel and E. Labrousse (eds), *Histoire Économique et Sociale de la France*, vol. 4, pt. 1, Presses Universitaires de France.

Glantz, M.H. (ed.) (1987) *Drought and Hunger in Africa*, Cambridge University Press.

Goodman, J. (1993) *Tobacco in History: the Cultures of Dependence*, Routledge.

Goswami, O. (1986) 'The Depression, 1930–1935: Its Effects on India and Indonesia', *Itinerario*, 10, 1, pp. 163–76.

Green, R.H. (1981) 'Foreign direct investment and African political economy', in A. Adedeji, (ed.), *Indigenization of African Economies*, Hutchinson.

Greenberg, M. (1951) *British Trade and the Opening of China, 1800–1842*, Cambridge University Press.

Greenough, P.R. (1982) *Prosperity and Misery in Modern Bengal: The Famine of 1943–44*, Oxford University Press.

Grilli, E.R. (1993) *The European Community and the Developing Countries*, Cambridge University Press.

Gutkind, P.C.W. and I. Wallerstein (eds) (1976) *The Political Economy of Contemporary Africa*, Sage.

Habib, I. (1963) *The Agrarian System of Mughal India (1556–1707)*, Oxford University Press.

Habib, I. (1969) 'Potentialities of Capitalistic Development in the Economy of Mughal India', *Journal of Economic History*, 29, pp. 32–78.

Habib, I. (1978–9) 'Technology and Barriers to Social Change in Mughal India', *Indian Historical Review*, 5, 1–2, pp. 152–74.

Habib,I. (1982a) 'Agrarian relations and land revenue: North India', in T. Raychaudhuri and I. Habib, (eds), *The Cambridge Economic History of India, Vol.1, c.1200 – c.1750*, Cambridge University Press.

Habib, I. (1982b) 'The systems of agricultural production: Mughal India', in T. Raychaudhuri and I. Habib (eds), *The Cambridge Economic History of India*, vol.1, *c.1200-c.1750*, Cambridge University Press.

Habib, I. (1985) 'Studying a Colonial Economy – Without Perceiving Colonialism', *Modern Asian Studies*, 19, 3, pp. 355–81.

Hailey, M. (1957) *An African Survey: Revised 1956*, Oxford University Press.

Hall, A.R. (ed.) (1968) *The Export of Capital from Britain, 1870–1914*, Methuen.

Hall, D.G.E. (1955) *A History of South-East Asia*, revised edn, Macmillan.

Hall, J. A. (1985) *Powers and Liberties: the Causes and Consequences of the Rise of the West*, Blackwell.

Halliday, F. (1989) *Cold War, Third World*, Hutchinson Radius.

Halperín Donghi, T. (1982) ' "Dependency Theory" and Latin American Historiography', *Latin American Research Review*, 17, pp. 115–30.

Hamilton, E.J. (1929) 'American Treasure and the Rise of Capitalism', *Economica*, IX, 27, November pp. 338–357.

Hamilton, E.J. (1934) *American Treasure and the Price Revolution in Spain, 1501–1650*, Harvard University Press.

Hammond, R.J. (1966) *Portugal and Africa, 1815–1910: a Study of Uneconomic Imperialism*, Stanford.

Hammond, R.J. (1973) 'Some economic aspects of Portuguese Africa', in P. Duignan and L.H. Gann (eds), *Colonialism in Africa, 1870–1960*, vol. 4, *The Economics of Colonialism*, Cambridge University Press.

Hancock, W.K. (1942) *Survey of British Commonwealth Affairs: vol. II Problems of Economic Policy*, Oxford University Press.

Hanson, J.R. (1980) *Trade in Transition: Exports from the Third World, 1840–1900*, Academic Press.

Harms, R.W. (1981) *River of Wealth, River of Sorrow: the Central Zaïre Basin in the Era of the Slave and Ivory Trade, 1500–1891*, Yale University Press.

Harnetty, P. (1971) 'Cotton Exports and Indian Agriculture, 1861–1870', *Economic History Review*, 24, pp. 414–29.

Harnetty, P. (1972) *Imperialism and Free Trade: Lancashire and India in the mid Nineteenth Century*, University of British Columbia Press.

Harris, N. (1986) *The End of the Third World: Newly Industrializing Countries and the Decline of an Ideology*, IB Tauris.

Harwitz, M. (1964) 'Subsaharan Africa as a growing economic system', in M.J. Herskovits and M. Harwitz, (eds), *Economic Transition in Africa*, Routledge & Kegan Paul.

Havinden, M. and D. Meredith (1993) *Colonialism and Development: Britain and its Tropical Colonies, 1850–1960*, Routledge.

Hazlewood, A. (1962) 'The export and import of capital', in G.D.N. Worswick and P.H. Ady (eds), *The British Economy in the Nineteen Fifties*, Clarendon Press.

Headrick, D.R. (1981) *The Tools of Empire: Technology and European Imperialism in the Nineteenth Century*, Oxford University Press.

Headrick, D.R. (1988) *The Tentacles of Progress*, Oxford University Press.

Hennessy, A. (1992) 'The Nature of the Conquest and the Conquistadors', *Proceedings of the British Academy*, 81, pp. 1–36.

Herskovits, M.J. and M. Harwitz (eds) (1964) *Economic Transition in Africa*, Routledge & Kegan Paul.

Heston, A. (1983) 'National Income', in D.Kumar (with M. Desai) (ed.), *The Cambridge Economic History of India*, vol. 2, *c.1757–c.1970*, Cambridge University Press.

Hill, P. (1963) *The Migrant Cocoa-farmers of Southern Ghana: a Study in Rural Capitalism*, Cambridge University Press.

Hill, P. (1977) *Population, Prosperity and Poverty: Rural Kano, 1900 and 1970*, Cambridge University Press.

Hilton, A. (1985) *The Kingdom of Kongo*, Clarendon Press.

Hirst, P. and G. Thompson (1996) *Globalization in Question*, Polity.

Hjejle, B. (1967) 'Agricultural Bondage in South India', *Scandinavian Economic History Review*, 15, pp. 71–126.

Hobsbawm, E. (1969) *Industry and Empire*, Penguin.

Hogendorn, J.S. (1973) 'Economic initiative and African cash farming', in P.Duignan and L.H. Gann, (eds), *Colonialism in Africa, 1870–1960*, vol. 4, *The Economics of Colonialism*, Cambridge University Press.

Hopkins, A.G. (1968) 'Economic Imperialism in West Africa: Lagos, 1880–1892', *Economic History Review*, 21, pp. 580–606.

Hopkins, A.G. (1970) 'The Creation of a Colonial Monetary System', *African Historical Studies*, 3, 1, pp. 101–132.

Hopkins, A.G. (1973) *An Economic History of West Africa*, Longman.

Hopkins, A.G. (1980) 'Property Rights and Empire Building: Britain's Annexation of Lagos, 1861', *Journal of Economic History*, 40, 4, pp. 777–98.

Hopkins, T.K., and I. Wallerstein (1977) 'Patterns of Development of the Modern World-System', *Review*, 1, 2, pp. 111–45.

Hurd, J. (1983) 'Railways', in D.Kumar (with M. Desai) (ed.) *The Cambridge Economic History of India*, vol. 2, *c.1775–c.1970*, Cambridge University Press.

Hyam, R. (1988) 'Africa and the Labour Government, 1945–1951', *Journal of Imperial and Commonwealth History*, 3, pp. 148–72.

Hyam, R. (ed.) (1992) *The Labour Government and the End of Empire 1945–1951, Part II Economics and International Relations (British Documents on the End of Empire, Series A, vol. 2)*, HMSO.

Hynes, W.G. (1979) *The Economics of Imperialism: Britain, Africa and the New Imperialism, 1870–1895*, Longman.

Iliffe, J. (1979) *A Modern History of Tanganyika*, Cambridge University Press.

Iliffe, J. (1983) *The Emergence of African Capitalism*, Macmillan.

Iliffe, J. (1987) *The African Poor: A History*, Cambridge University Press.

Iliffe, J. (1995) *Africans: the History of a Continent*, Cambridge University Press.

Indian Industrial Commission (1919) *Report of the Indian Industrial Commission, 1916–18*, PP1919, vol. 17, Cmd 51.

Inikori, J.E. (ed.) (1982) *Forced Migration: the Impact of the Export Slave Trade on African Societies*, Hutchinson.

Inikori J.E (1987) 'Slavery and the Development of Industrial Capitalism in England', *Journal of Interdisciplinary History*, 17, 4, pp. 771–93.

Inikori J.E. (1992) 'Slavery and the revolution in cotton textile production in England', in Inikori and Engerman (eds) (1992).

Inikori J.E. and S.L. Engerman (eds) (1992) *The Atlantic Slave Trade; Effects on Economies, Societies, and Peoples in Africa, the Americas, and Europe*, Duke University Press.

Issawi, C. (1966a) 'The Economic Development of Egypt, 1800–1960', in C. Issawi (ed.), *The Economic History of the Middle East 1800–1914*, University of Chicago Press.

Issawi, C.(ed.) (1966b) *The Economic History of the Middle East 1800–1914*, University of Chicago Press.

Jewsiewicki, B. (1983) 'Rural society and the Belgian colonial economy', in D. Birmingham and P.M. Martin (eds), *History of Central Africa*, vol. 2, Longman.

Jha, S.C. (1963) *Studies in the Development of Capitalism in India*, Firma K.L. Mukhopadhyay.

Johnson, H.B. (1984) 'The Portuguese settlement of Brazil, 1500–80', in L. Bethell (ed.), *Cambridge History of Latin America*,vol.1, *Colonial Latin America*, Cambridge University Press.

Jones, E.L. (1987) *The European Miracle*, 2nd edn, Cambridge University Press.

Julien, C-A. (1978) *Le Maroc Face aux Impérialismes 1415–1965*, Editions J.A.

Katzenellenbogen, S.E. (1973) 'The Miners' Frontier, transport and general economic development', in P. Duignan and L.H. Gann (eds), *Colonialism in Africa, 1870–1960*, vol. 4, *The Economics of Colonialism*, Cambridge University Press.

Kawakatsu, H. (1986) 'International competition in cotton goods in the late nineteenth century: Britain versus India and East Asia', in W.Fischer, R.M. McInnis and J. Schneider (eds), *The Emergence of a World Economy, 1500–1914*, 2 vols, Franz Steiner.

Kay, G.B. (ed.) (1972) *The Political Economy of Colonialism in Ghana*, Cambridge University Press.

Kay, G. (1975) *Development and Underdevelopment: A Marxist Analysis*, Macmillan.

Keller, A. (1940) 'Netherlands India as a Paying Proposition', *Far Eastern Survey*, 9, 2, pp. 11–18.

Kennedy, P. (1993) *Preparing for the Twenty-first Century*, HarperCollins.

Kilby, P. (1969) *Industrialization in an Open Economy: Nigeria, 1945–1966*, Cambridge University Press.

Kitching, G. (1980) *Class and Economic Change in Kenya*, Yale University Press.

Kittrell, E. R. (1970) 'The Development of the Theory of Colonization in English Classical Political Economy', reprinted in A.G.L. Shaw (ed.), *Great Britain and the Colonies, 1815–1865*, Methuen.

Kiwanuka, M. S. (1970) 'Colonial Policies and Administrations in Africa: the Myth of Contrasts', *African Historical Studies*, 3, pp. 295–315.

Kleiman, E. (1976) 'Trade and the Decline of Colonialism', *Economic Journal*, 86, pp. 459–80.

Klein, M.A. (1971) `Chiefship in Sine-Saloum (Senegal), 1887–1914', in V.Turner (ed.), *Colonialism in Africa*, vol. 3, *Profiles of Change: African Society and Colonial Rule*, Cambridge University Press.

Klein, H. S. (1967) *Slavery in the Americas:A Comparative Study of Virginia and Cuba*, Elephant, 1989.

Klein, H.S. (1990) 'Economic aspects of the eighteenth-century Atlantic slave trade', in J.D.Tracy (ed.), *The Rise of Merchant Empires: Long-distance Trade in the Early Modern World 1350–1750*, Cambridge University Press.

Kling, B.B. and M.N. Pearson (eds) (1979) *The Age of Partnership: Europeans in Asia before Dominion*, University Press of Hawaii.

Krishnamurty, J. (1983) 'The Occupational Structure', in D.Kumar (with M. Desai) (ed.), *The Cambridge Economic History of India*, vol. 2, *c.1757–c.1970*, Cambridge University Press.

Kuitenbrouwer, M. (1991) *The Netherlands and the Rise of Modern Imperialism: Colonies and Foreign Policy, 1870–1902*, Berg.

Kumar, D. (1965) *Land and Caste in South India: Agricultural Labour in the Madras Presidency during the Nineteenth Century*, Cambridge University Press.

Kumar, D. (with M. Desai), (ed.) (1983) *The Cambridge Economic History of India*, vol. 2: *c.1757–c.1970*, Cambridge University Press.

Kumar, D. (1983a) 'Agrarian Relations: South India', in D.Kumar (with M. Desai) (ed.), *The Cambridge Economic History of India*.vol. 2, *c.1757–c.1970*, Cambridge University Press.

Kumar, D. (1983b) 'The Fiscal System', in D.Kumar (with M. Desai) (ed.), *The Cambridge Economic History of India*, vol. 2, *c.1757–c.1970*, Cambridge University Press.

Kumar, D. (1992) 'A note on the term 'Land Control'', in P.Robb (ed.), *Rural India: Land, Power and Society under British Rule*, originally Curzon Press, 1983 republished by Oxford University Press.

Laclau, E. (1971) 'Feudalism and Capitalism in Latin America', *New Left Review*, 67, May–June, pp. 19–38.

Lacoste, Y. (1980) *Unité et Diversité du Tiers Monde*, vol.1, Maspero.

Lacoste , Y. (1986) *Contre les anti-Tiers Mondistes et contre certains Tiers–Mondistes*, Editions de la Découverte.

Laffey, J. (1976) 'Les racines de l'impérialisme français en Extrême-Orient: à propos des thèses de J.F. Cady', in J. Bouvier and R. Girault (eds), *L'Impérialisme Français d'Avant 1914*, Mouton.

Lal, D. (1988) *Hindu Equilibrium*, 2 vols, Clarendon Press.

Landes, D.S. (1969) *The Unbound Prometheus: Technological Change and Economic Development in Western Europe since 1750*, Cambridge University Press.

Langer, W.L. (1950) *European Alliances and Alignments*, 2nd edn, Vintage.

Larkin, J.A. (1988) 'Philippine History Reconsidered: a Socioeconomic Perspective', *American Historical Review*, 87, 3, pp. 595–628.

Latham, A.J.H. (1978a) *The International Economy and the Underdeveloped World 1865–1914*, Croom Helm.

Latham, A.J.H. (1978b) 'Merchandise Trade Imbalances and Uneven Economic Development in India and China', *Journal of European Economic History*, 7, 1, pp. 33–60.

Lee, J.M. (1967) *Colonial Development and Good Government: a Study of the Ideas Expressed by the British Official Classes in Planning Decolonization*, Clarendon Press.

Léon, P.(ed.) (1977 owards) *Histoire Économique et Sociale du Monde*, 6 vols, Colin.

Leroy-Beaulieu, P. (1886) *De la Colonisation chez les Peuples Modernes*, 3rd edn.

Lewis, W.A. (1969) *Aspects of Tropical Trade, 1883–1963*, Almqvist & Wicksell.

Leys, C. (1975) *Underdevelopment in Kenya: The Political Economy of Neo-Colonialism*, Heinemann.

Lindblad, J. T. (1986) 'International trade and colonial economic growth: the case of Indonesia 1874–1914', in W. Fischer, R.M. McInnis and J. Schneider (eds), *The Emergence of a World Economy, 1500–1914*, vol. 2, Franz Steiner.

Lipton, M. (1980) 'Neither partnership nor dependence: Indo-British Relations since 1947', in W.H. Morris-Jones and D. Austin (eds), *Decolonisation and After: the British and French Experience*, Frank Cass.

Livingstone, I. (1976) 'The Impact of Colonialism and Independence on Export Growth in Britain and France', *Oxford Bulletin of Economics and Statistics*, 38, 3, pp. 211–18.

Lockhart, J. and S. B. Schwartz (1983) *Early Latin America*, Cambridge University Press.

Lofchie, M.F. (1987) 'The decline of African agriculture: an internalist pespective' in M.H. Glantz (ed.) *Drought and Hunger in Africa*, Cambridge University Press.

Lonsdale, J. (1981) 'States and Social Processes in Africa: a Historiographical Survey', *African Studies Review*, 24, 2/3, pp. 139–225.

Lonsdale, J. and B. Berman (1992) *Unhappy Valley: Conflict in Kenya and Africa*, 2 vols, Currey.

Louis, W.R. (1971) 'The Berlin Congo Conference', in P. Gifford and W.R. Louis (eds), *France and Britain in Africa: Imperial Rivalry and colonial Rule*, Yale University Press.

Louis, W.R. (ed.) (1976) *Imperialism: The Robinson and Gallagher Controversy*, Franklin Watts.

Love, J.L. (1980) 'Raúl Prebisch and the Origins of the Doctrine of Unequal Exchange', *Latin American Research Review*, 15, pp. 45–72.

Lovejoy, P. E. (1982) 'The Volume of the Atlantic Slave Trade: A Synthesis', *Journal of African History*, 23, pp. 473–501.

Lovejoy, P.E. (1983) *Transformations in Slavery: A History of Slavery in Africa*, Cambridge University Press.

Lovejoy, P.E. (1989) 'The Impact of the Atlantic Slave Trade on Africa: a Review of the Literature', *Journal of African History*, 30, pp. 365–394.

Lovejoy, P.E., and J.S. Hogendorn (1993) *Slow Death for Slavery: the Course of Abolition in Northern Nigeria, 1897–1936*, Cambridge University Press.

Low, D.A. (1991) *Eclipse of Empire*, Cambridge University Press.

Low, D.A., and A. Smith (eds) (1976) *History of East Africa*, vol. 3, Oxford University Press.

Lugan, B. (1991) *Bilan de la Décolonisation*, Perrin.

Lugard, J.F. (1922) *The Dual Mandate in British Tropical Africa*, Frank Cass reprint, 1965.

Lyon, P. (1984) 'The Emergence of the Third World', in H. Bull and A. Watson (eds), *The Expansion of International Society*, Clarendon Press.

Macleod, M. (1984a) 'Spain and America: the Atlantic Trade, 1492–1720', in L.Bethell (ed.), *Cambridge History of Latin America*, vol. 2, *Colonial Latin America*, Cambridge University Press.

Macleod, M. (1984b) 'Aspects of the internal economy', L.Bethell (ed.), *Cambridge History of Latin America*, vol. 2, *Colonial Latin America*, Cambridge University Press.

Macmillan, H. (1971) *Riding the Storm 1956–1959*, Macmillan.

Maddison, A. (1971) *Class Structure and Economic Growth: India and Pakistan since the Moghuls*, Allen & Unwin.

Maddison, A. (1990) 'Dutch Colonialism in Indonesia: a comparative perspective', in A. Booth, W.J. O'Malley and A. Weidemann (eds), *Indonesian Economic History in the Dutch Colonial Era*, Yale University Southeast Asia Studies.

Majumbar, R.C., H.C. Raychoudhuri, K.K. Datta (1960) *An Advanced History of India*, Macmillan.

Mamdani, M. (1996) *Citizen and Subject: Contemporary Africa and the Legacy of Late Colonialism*, Princeton University Press.

Mann, M. (1986) *The Sources of Social Power:* vol. 1 *A History of Power from the Beginning to A.D.1760*, Cambridge University Press.

Mann, M. (1993) *The Sources of Social Power*, vol. 2, *The Rise of Classes and Nation-states, 1760–1914*, Cambridge University Press.

Manning, P. (1982) *Slavery, Colonialism and Economic Growth in Dahomey, 1640–1960*, Cambridge University Press.

Manning, P. (1988) *Francophone Sub-Saharan Africa 1880–1985*, Cambridge University Press.

Manning, P. (1990) *Slavery and African Life: Occidental, Oriental and African Slave Trades*, Cambridge University Press.

Marks, S., and S.Trapido (1979) 'Lord Milner and the South African State', *History Workshop*, 8, pp. 50–81.

Marseille, J. (1974) 'L'Investissement Français dans l'Empire Colonial: l'enquête du Gouvernement de Vichy (1943)', *Revue Historique*, Oct.-Dec. 1974, pp. 409–32.

Marseille, J. (1975) 'L'Industrie Cotonnière Française et l'Impérialisme Colonial', *Revue d'Histoire Économique et Sociale*, 53, pp. 386–412.

Marseille, J. (1984a) *Empire Colonial et Capitalisme Français*, Albin Michel.

Marseille, J. (1984b) 'Les Relations Commerciales entre la France et son Empire Colonial de 1880 à 1913' *Revue d'Histoire Moderne et Contemporaine*, 31, April–June, pp. 286–307.

Marseille, J. (1986) 'Une approche économique et financière de la décolonisation: l'évolution des bilans des enterprises coloniales (1938–1954)', in C-R. Ageron, (ed.), *Les Chemins de la Décolonisation de l'Empire Colonial Français*, Editions du Centre National de la Recherche Scientifique.

Marseille, J. (1987) 'The Phases of French Colonial Imperialism: Towards a New Periodization', *Journal of Imperial and Commonwealth History*, 13, (Special issue on 'Money, Finance and Empire 1790–1960' edited by A.N. Porter and R.F. Holland), pp. 127–41.

Marshall, P.J. (1975) 'British Expansion in India in the Eighteenth Century: A Historical Revision', *History*, 60, pp. 28–43.

Marshall, P.J. (1987) *Bengal: the British Bridgehead*, *The New Cambridge History of India*, vol. II. 2, Cambridge University Press.

Martin, P. M. (1983) 'The Violence of Empire', in D.Birmingham and P.M. Martin (eds.), *History of Central Africa*, vol. 2, Longman.

Marx, K. (1853) 'The British Rule in India', June 25, 1853 and 'The Future Results of the British Rule in India', July 22, 1853, reproduced in *Marx-Engels: On Colonialism*, Moscow, 1959.

Marx, K. (1867) *Capital*, vol. 1, Penguin edn., 1976.

Mauro, F. (1967) *L'Expansion Européenne, 1600–1870*, Presses Universitaires de France.

McAlpin, M.B. (1974) 'Railroads, Prices and Peasant Rationality: India 1860–1900', *Journal of Economic History*, 34, 3, pp. 662–84.

McAlpin, M.B. (1975) 'The Effects of Expansion of Markets on Rural Income Distribution in Nineteenth-Century India', *Explorations in Economic History*, 12, pp. 289–302.

McAlpin, M.B. (1983a) *Subject to Famine: Food Crises and Economic Change in Western India, 1860–1920*, Princeton University Press.

McAlpin, M.B. (1983b) 'Price Movements and Fluctuations in Economic Activity (1860–1947)', in D.Kumar (with M. Dsesai) (ed.), *The Cambridge Economic History of India*, vol.2, *c. 1757–c.1970*, Cambridge University Press.

Meier, G.M. (1973) 'External trade and internal development', in P. Duignan and L.H. Gann (eds.), *Colonialism in Africa, 1870–1960*, vol. 4, *The Economics of Colonialism*, Cambridge University Press.

Mendelsohn, R. (1980) 'Blainey and the Jameson Raid: the Debate Renewed', *Journal of Southern African Studies*, 6, pp. 157–70.

Meredith, D. (1975) 'The British Government and Colonial Economic Policy, 1919–39', *Economic History Review*, 28, 3, pp. 484–99.

Metcalf, T. R. (1969) 'British land policy in Oudh', in R.E. Frykenberg (ed.), *Land Control and Social Structure in Indian History*, University of Wisconsin Press.

Meyer, F.V. (1948) *British Colonies in World Trade*, Oxford University Press.

Michel, M. (1992) 'L'Afrique noire, la France et la Grande-Bretagne en 1958: l'accélération des indépendances et la sauvegarde des "French and English Connections" ', in C-R. Ageron and M.Michel (eds), *L'Afrique Noire Française: L' Heure des Indépendances*, Editions du Centre National de la Recherche Scientifique.

Michel, M.(1993) *Décolonisations et Émergence du Tiers Monde*, Hachette.

Mill, J.S. (1848) *Principles of Political Economy*, 1892 edn.

Mill, J.S. (1859) *On Liberty*, Oxford University Press, 1975, edn.

Miller, J.B.D. (1974) *Survey of Commonwealth Affairs: Problems of Expansion and Attrition, 1953–1969*, Oxford University Press.

Miller, J.C. (1983) 'The paradoxes of impoverishment in the Atlantic zone', in D.Birmingham and P.M. Martin (eds), *History of Central Africa*, vol. 1, Longman.

Miller, J.C. (1991) 'A marginal institution on the margin of the Atlantic system: The Portuguese southern Atlantic slave trade in the eighteenth century', in B. L. Solow (ed.), *Slavery and the Rise of the Atlantic System*, Cambridge University Press.

Milner, A. (1892) *England in Egypt*, 7th edn, 1899, Arnold.

Milward, A.S. (1992) *The European Rescue of the Nation State*, Routledge.

Mintz, S. W. (1985) *Sweetness and Power: The Place of Sugar in Modern History*, Viking.

Mitchell, B.R. (1982) *International Historical Statistics: Africa and Asia*, Macmillan.

Mitchell, B.R. (1988) *British Historical Statistics*, Cambridge University Press.

Mitchell, B.R. (1992) *International Historical Statistics: Europe, 1750–1988*, 3rd edn, Macmillan.

Mommsen, W.J. and J. Osterhammel (eds) (1986) *Imperialism and After: Continuities and Discontinuities*, Allen & Unwin.

Money, J.B. (1861) *Java or How to Manage a Colony*, 2 vols, Hurst & Blackett.

Moon, P.T. (1926) *Imperialism and World Politics*, Macmillan.

Moore, B. (1966) *Social Origins of Dictatorship and Democracy*, Allen Lane.

Moreland, W.H. (1923) *From Akbar to Aurangzeb*, Macmillan, Oriental Books reprint, 1972.

Morgan, D.J. (1980) *The Official History of Colonial Development: vol. 2, Developing British Colonial Resources*; vol. 3, *A Reassessment of British Aid Policy, 1951–1965*, Macmillan.

Morineau, M. (1978) 'Le Siècle', in P. Léon (ed.), *Histoire Économique et Sociale du Monde*, vol. 2, *Les Hésitations de la Croissance, 1580–1740*, Colin.

Morley, J. (1879) *The Life of Richard Cobden*, 1906 edn, Fisher Unwin.

Morley, J. (1908) *The Life of W.E. Gladstone*, vol. 2, Lloyd.

Morris, M.D. (1963) 'Towards a Reinterpretation of Nineteenth-Century Indian Economic History', *Journal of Economic History*, 23, pp. 606–18.

Morris, M.D. (1967) 'Values as an Obstacle to Economic Growth in South Asia', *Journal of Economic History*, 27, pp. 588–607.

Morris, M.D. (1969) 'Trends and tendencies in Indian economic history', in M.D. Morris, T. Matsui, B. Chandra and T. Raychaudhuri, *Indian Economy in the Nineteenth Century: A Symposium*, Indian Economic and Social History Association.

Morris, M.D. (1979) 'South Asian Entrepreneurship and the Rashomon Effect, 1800–1947', *Explorations in Economic History*, 16, pp. 341–61.

Morris, M.D. (1983) 'The Growth of Large-scale Industry to 1947', in D.Kumar (with M. Desai) (ed.), *The Cambridge Economic History of India*, vol.2, *c.1757–c.1970*, Cambridge University Press.

Morris-Jones, W.H. and D. Austin (eds) (1980) *Decolonisation and After: the British and French Experience*, Frank Cass.

Mortimer, R.A. (1980) *The Third World Coalition in International Politics*, Praeger.

Munro, J.F. (1976) *Africa and the International Economy, 1800–1960*, Dent.

Munro, J.F. (1984) *Britain in Tropical Africa, 1880–1960: Economic Relationships and Impact*, Macmillan.

Mushi, S.S. (1981) 'Tanzania', in A. Adedeji (ed.) *Indigenization of African Economies*, Hutchinson.

Myint, H. (1973) *The Economics of the Developing Countries*, 4th edn, Hutchinson.

Myrdal, G (1956) *Economic Theory and Underdeveloped Regions*, Methuen.

Neal, L. (1990) 'The Dutch and English East India Companies compared: evidence from the stock and foreign exchange markets', in J.D. Tracy (ed.), *The Rise of Merchant Empires: Long-distance Trade in the Early Modern World, 1350–1750*, Cambridge University Press.

Neale, W.C. (1962) *Economic Change in Rural India*, Yale University Press.

Neale, W. C. (1969) 'Land is to rule', in R.E. Frykenberg, (ed.) *Land Control and Social Structure in Indian History*, University of Wisconsin Press.

Newitt, M. (1981) *Portugal in Africa*, Hurst.

Newitt, M. (1995) *A History of Mozambique*, Hurst.

Newton, S. (1985) 'Britain, the Sterling Area and European Integration, 1945–50', *Journal of Imperial and Commonwealth History*, 13, pp. 163–182.

Nkrumah, K. (1965) *Ne-colonialism: the Last Stage of Imperialism*, Nelson.

North, D. C. and R.P. Thomas (1973) *The Rise of the Western World: A New Economic History*, Cambridge University Press.

O'Brien, P.J. (1975) 'A critique of Latin American theories of dependency', in I. Oxaal, T. Barnett and D. Booth (eds), *Beyond the Sociology of Development: Economy and Society in Latin America and Africa*, Routledge.

O'Brien, P.K. (1982) 'European Economic Development: the Contribution of the Periphery', *Economic History Review*, 35, 1, pp. 1–18.

O'Brien, P.K. (1988) 'The Costs and Benefits of British Imperialism 1846–1914', *Past and Present*, 120, pp. 161–199.

O'Brien, P.K. (1990) 'European Industrialisation: From the Voyages of Discovery to the Industrial Revolution', in Hans Pohl (ed.), *The European Discovery of the World and its Economic Effects on Pre-industrial Society 1500–1800*, Franz Steiner.

O'Brien, P.K. and S.L.Engerman (1991) 'Exports and the growth of the British economy from the Glorious Revolution to the Peace of Amiens' in B.L. Solow (ed.), *Slavery and the Rise of the Atlantic System*, Cambridge University Press.

OECD (1985) 'Crisis and Response in Africa', in *Development Cooperation: 1984 Review.*

OECD (1991) Organisation for Co-operation and Development, *1991 Review.*

Owen, E.R.J. (1969) *Cotton and the Egyptian Economy. 1820–1914*, Clarendon Press.

Owen, E.R.J. (1981) *The Middle East in the World Economy*, Methuen.

Oxaal, I., T. Barnett and D. Booth (eds) (1975) *Beyond the Sociology of Development: Economy and Society in Latin America and Africa*, Routledge.

Palmer, R. (1977) 'The agricultural history of Rhodesia', in R. Palmer and N. Parsons (eds) *The Roots of Rural Poverty in Central and Southern Africa*, Heinemann.

Palmer, R. and N.Parsons (eds) (1977) *The Roots of Rural Poverty in Central and Southern Africa*, Heinemann.

Panter-Brick, K. (1988) 'Independence, French Style', in P. Gifford and W.R. Louis (eds), *Decolonization and African Independence: the Transfers of Powers, 1960–1980*, Yale University Press.

Park, M. (1799) *Travels in Africa*, Everyman edn, Dent, 1954.

Parry, J.H. (1967) 'Transport and trade routes', in E.E. Rich and C.H. Wilson (eds), *The Cambridge Economic History of Europe*, vol. 4, *The Economy of Expanding Europe in the Sixteenth and Seventeenth Centuries*, Cambridge University Press.

Pasquier, R. (1992) 'Les milieux d'affaires face à la décolonisation (1956–1960) d'après quelques publications', in C-R. Ageron and M.Michel (eds), *L'Afrique Noire Française: L' Heure des Indépendances*, Editions du Centre National de la Recherche Scientifique.

Pearson, M.N. (1979) 'Corruption and Corsairs in Western India', in B.B. Kling and M.N. Pearson (eds), *The Age of Partnership: Europeans in Asia before Dominion*, University Press of Hawaii.

Pearson, M.N. (1987) *The Portuguese in India The New Cambridge History of India*, I.1, Cambridge University Press.

Pearson, M.N. (1988) *Before Colonialism: Theories on Asian-European Relations 1500–1750*, Oxford University Press.

Pearson, M.N. (1991) 'Merchants and states', in J.D. Tracy (ed.), *The Political Economy of Merchant Empires*, Cambridge University Press.

Pedler, F. (1973) 'British planning and private enterprise in colonial Africa', in P. Duignan and L.H. Gann (eds), *Colonialism in Africa, 1870–1960*, vol. 4, *The Economics of Colonialism*, Cambridge University Press.

Peemans, J-P. (1973) 'Capital accumulation in the Congo under colonialism: the role of the state', in P. Duignan and L.H. Gann (eds), *Colonialism in Africa, 1870–1960*, vol. 4, *The Economics of Colonialism*, Cambridge University Press.

Peemans, J-P. (1980) 'Imperial Hangovers: Belgium – The Economics of Decolonization', *Journal of Contemporary History*, 15, pp. 257–86.

Perlin, F. (1983) 'Proto-Industrialization and Pre-colonial South Asia', *Past and Present*, 98, pp. 31–95.

Phillips, C. R. (1990) 'Trade in the Iberian empires, 1450–1750', in J. D. Tracy (ed.), *The Rise of Merchant Empires: Long-distance Trade in the Early Modern World, 1350–1750*, Cambridge University Press.

Phimister, I.R. (1974) 'Rhodes, Rhodesia and the Rand', *Journal of Southern African Studies*, 1, 1, pp. 74–90.

Pieper, R. (1990) 'The volume of African and American exports of precious metals and its effects in Europe, 1500–1800', in H. Pohl (ed.), *The European Discovery of the World and its Economic Effects on the Pre-industrial Society, 1500–1800*, Franz Steiner.

Pohl, H. (ed.) (1990) *The European Discovery of the World and its Economic Effects on the Pre-industrial Society 1500–1800*, Franz Steiner.

Pollard, S. (1981) *Peaceful Conquest: the Industrialization of Europe*, Oxford University Press.

Pollard, S. (1983) *The Development of the British Economy 1914–1980*, 3rd edn, Arnold.

Porter, A.N. and A.J. Stockwell (eds) (1987) *British Imperial Policy and Decolonization, 1938–64*, 2 vols, Macmillan.

Prakash, G. (ed.) (1992) *The World of the Rural Labourer in Colonial India*, Oxford University Press.

Prakash, O. (1976) 'Bullion for Goods: International Trade and the Economy of Early Eighteenth-century Bengal', *Indian Economic and Social History Review*, 13, pp. 159–87.

Prakash, O (1979) 'Asian trade and European impact: A study of the trade from Bengal, 1630–1720', in B.B Kling and M.N. Pearson (eds), *The Age of Partnership: Europeans in Asia before Dominion*, University Press of Hawaii.

Prebisch, R. (1950) *The Economic Development of Latin America and its Principal Problems*, United Nations.

Prebisch, R. (1967) 'The system and the social structure in Latin America', in I. Horovits, *et al*, (eds), *Latin American Radicalism*, Random House.

Rachid bencheneb (1986) 'L'Algérie à la veille du soulèvement de 1954', in C-R. Ageron (ed.), *Les Chemins de la Décolonisation de l'Empire Français*, Editions du Centre National du Recherche Scientifique.

Raychaudhuri, T. (1962) *Jan Company in Coromandel*, Nijhoff.

Raychaudhuri, T. (1982) 'The State and the Economy: the Mughal Empire', in T. Raychaudhuri and I. Habib (eds), *The Cambridge Economic History of India*, vol.1, *c.1200–c.1750*, Cambridge University Press.

Raychaudhuri, T. (1983) 'The eighteenth-century background', in D.Kumar (with M. Desai) (ed.), *The Cambridge Economic History of India, vol. 2, c.1757–c.1970*, Cambridge University Press.

Raychaudhuri, T. and I. Habib (eds) (1982) *The Cambridge Economic History of India*, Vol.1: *c.1200 – c.1750*, Cambridge University Press.

Raychaudhuri, T. (1985) 'Historical Roots of Mass Poverty in South Asia: A Hypothesis', *Economic and Political Weekly*, 20, 18, May 4, pp. 801–6.

Reid, A. (1990a) 'An 'Age of Commerce' in Southeast Asian History', *Modern Asian Studies*, 24, 1, pp. 1–30.

Reid, A. (1990b) 'The 17th Century Crisis in Southeast Asia', *Modern Asian Studies*, 24, 4, pp. 639–59.

Reid, A. (1993) *Southeast Asia in the Age of Commerce*, vol. 2, *Expansion and Crisis*, Yale University Press.

Reinhard, W. (1990) 'The West: economic change in the Atlantic Triangle', in H. Pohl (ed.), *The European Discovery of the World and its Economic Effects on Pre-industrial Society, 1500–1800*, Franz Steiner.

Remmelink, W. (1988) 'Expansion without Design: the Snare of Javanese Politics', *Intinerario*, 1, pp. 111–28.

Reynolds, L.G. (1985) *Economic Growth in the Third World, 1850–1980*, Yale University Press.

Rich, E.E. and C.H. Wilson (eds) (1967) *The Cambridge Economic History of Europe*, vol. 4, *The Economy of Expanding Europe in the Sixteenth and Seventeenth Centuries*, Cambridge University Press.

Richards, J.F. (1981) 'Mughal State Finance and the Premodern World Economy', *Comparative Studies of Society and History*, 30, pp. 285–308.

Richards, J.F. (1993) *The Mughal Empire, The New Cambridge History of India*, vol. I.5, Cambridge University Press.

Richardson, D. (1987) 'The Slave Trade, Sugar and British Economic Growth, 1748–1776', in B.L. Solow and S.L. Engerman (eds), *British Capitalism and Caribbean Slavery*, Cambridge University Press.

Richardson, P., and J-J van Helten (1984) 'The Development of the South African Gold-Mining Industry, 1895–1918', *Economic History Review*, 37, pp. 319–40.

Ricklefs, M.C. (1993) *A History of Modern Indonesia since 1300*, 2nd edn, Macmillan.

Rioux, J-P. (1987) *The Fourth Republic 1944–1958*, Cambridge University Press.

Robb, P. (ed.) (1983) *Rural India: Land Power and Society under British Rule*, originally published by the Curzon Press, 2nd edn, Oxford India Paperbacks, 1992.

Robinson, R. (1978) 'European Imperialism and indigenous reactions in West Africa, 1880–1914', in H.L. Wesseling (ed.), *Expansion and Reaction: Essays on European Expansion and Reaction in Asia and Africa*, Leiden University Press.

Robinson, R. (1988) 'The conference in Berlin and the future in Africa, 1884–1885', in S.Förster, W.J.Mommsen and R.Robinson (eds), *Bismarck, Europe and Africa: the Berlin Africa Conference 1884–1885 and the Onset of Partition*, Oxford University Press.

Robinson, R. (1986) 'The Excentric Idea of Imperialism, with or without Empire', in W.J. Mommsen and J. Osterhammel (eds), *Imperialism and After: Continuities and Discontinuities*, Allen & Unwin.

Robinson, R. and J. Gallagher (1976) 'The Partition of Africa', originally published in the *New Cambridge Modern History*, vol.11, reprinted in W.R. Louis (ed.), *Imperialism: The Robinson and Gallagher Controversy*, Franklin Watts.

Rodney, W. (1966) 'African Slavery and other Forms of Social Oppression on the Upper Coast in the Context of the Atlantic Slave-trade', *Journal of African History*, 7, 3, pp. 431–43.

Rodney, W. (1972) *How Europe Underdeveloped Africa*, Bogle-L'Ouverture Publications.

Rostow, W.W. (1960) *The Stages of Economic Growth: a Non-Communist Manifesto*, Cambridge University Press.

Rotberg, R.I. (1988) *The Founder: Cecil Rhodes and the Pursuit of Power*, Oxford University Press.

Rothermund, D. (1988) *An Economic History of India: from Pre-colonial Times to 1986*, Croom Helm.

Sachs, I. (1990) 'Growth and poverty: some lessons from Brazil', in Drèze and Sen (eds), *The Political Economy of Hunger*, vol. 3, Clarendon Press.

Said, E. (1978) *Orientalism*, Penguin.

Sanderson, G.N. (1975) 'The European Partititon of Africa: coincidence or conjuncture?', in G.N. Sanderson, *European Imperialism and the Partition of Africa*, Frank Cass.

Sargent, J.R. (1952) 'Britain and the Sterling Area', in G.D.N. Worswick and P.H. Ady (eds), *The British Economy 1945–1950*, Clarendon Press.

Saul, S.B. (1960) *Studies in British Overseas Trade, 1870–1914*, Liverpool University Press.

Sauvy, A. (1952) 'Trois Mondes, une planète', *L'Observateur*, 15 August 1952.

Schama, S. (1987) *The Embarassment of Riches*, Collins.

Schölch, A. (1976) 'The "Men on the Spot" and the English Occupation of Egypt in 1882', *Historical Journal*, 19, 3, pp. 773–85.

Schwartz, S.B. (1978) 'European Demands and Indian Responses in Northeastern Brazil', *American Historical Review*, 83, 1, pp. 43–79.

Schwartz, S.B. (1985) *Sugar Plantations in the Formation of Brazilian Society: Bahia, 1550–1835*, Cambridge University Press.

Scobie, J.R. (1971) *Argentina: A City and a Nation*, 2nd edn, Oxford University Press.

Seeley, J.R. (1883) *The Expansion of England*, 2nd edn, Macmillan, 1900.

Sen, S. (1992) *Colonies and Empire:India 1890–1914*, Sangam Books.

Shai, A. (1980) 'Britain, China and the End of Empire', *Journal of Contemporary History*, 15, pp. 287–95.

Shonfield, A. (1958) *British Economic Policy since the War*, Penguin.

Simmons, C. (1988) 'Arrested development in India – worthwhile epiphet, hostage to fortune or plain Utopianism?', in C.Dewey (ed.), *Arrested Development in India*, Manohar.

Simon, M. (1968) 'The pattern of new British Portfolio Foreign Investment, 1865–1914', in A.R. Hall (ed.), *The Export of Capital from Britain, 1870–1914*, Methuen.

Slicher van Bath, B.H. (1986) 'The absence of white contract labour in Spanish America during the colonial period', in P.C. Emmer (ed.), *Colonialism and Migration: Indentured Labour before and after Slavery*, Nijhoff.

Smith, A. (1776) *An Inquiry into the Nature and Causes of the Wealth of Nations*, Glasgow edn, Clarendon Press, 1976.

Solow, B. L. (1987) 'Capitalism and slavery in the exceedingly long run', in B. L. Solow and S. L. Engerman (eds), *British Capitalism and Caribbean Slavery*, Cambridge University Press.

Solow, B. L. (ed.) (1991) *Slavery and the Rise of the Atlantic System*, Cambridge University Press.

Solow, B. L. and S. L. Engerman (eds) (1987) *British Capitalism and Caribbean Slavery*, Cambridge University Press.

Specker, K. (1988) '"De-Industrialisation" in nineteenth-century India: the textile industry in the Madras Presidency, 1810–1870', in C. Dewey (ed.), *Arrested Development in India*, Manohar.

Steensgaard, N. (1974) *The Asian Trade Revolution of the Seventeenth Century: the East India Companies and the Decline of the Caravan Trade*, University of Chicago Press.

Steensgaard, N. (1981) 'The Companies as a specific institution in the history of European expansion', in L.Blussé and F.Gaastra (eds), *Companies and Trade*, Leiden University Press.

Steensgaard, N. (1990a) 'Commodities, bullion and services in intercontinental transactions before 1750', in H. Pohl (ed.), *The European Discovery of the World and its Economic Effects on the Pre-industrial Society, 1500–1800*, Franz Steiner.

Steensgaard, N. (1990b) 'The growth and composition of the long-distance trade of England and the Dutch Republic before 1750', in J.D. Tracy (ed.), *The Rise of Merchant Empires: Long-distance Trade in the Early Modern World, 1350–1750*, Cambridge University Press.

Stengers, J. (1989) *Congo Mythes et Réalités: 100 Ans d'Histoire*, Duculot.

Stern, S. J. (1988) 'Feudalism, Capitalism and the World-System in the Perspective of Latin America and the Caribbean', *American Historical Review*, 93, 4, pp. 829–72.

Stevens, C. (1990) 'The Impact of Europe 1992 on the Maghreb and Sub-Saharan Africa', *Journal of Common Market Studies*, 24, 2, pp. 217–41.

Stockwell, S.E. (1995) 'Political Strategies of British Business during Decolonization: The Case of the Gold Coast/Ghana, 1945–57', *Journal of Imperial and Commonwealth History*, 23, 2, pp. 277–300.

Stokes, E. (1959) *The English Utilitarians and India*, Clarendon Press.

Stokes, E. (1978) *The Peasant and the Raj: Studies in Agrarian Society and Peasant Rebellion in Colonial India*, Cambridge University Press.

Stokes, E. (1983) 'Agrarian Relations:Northern and Central India', in D.Kumar (with M. Desai) (ed.), *The Cambridge Economic History of India*, vol. 2: *c.1757–c.1970*, Cambridge University Press.

Strange, S. (1971) *Sterling and British Policy*, Oxford University Press.

Subramanyam, S. (ed.) (1991) *Merchants, Markets and the State in Early Modern India*, Oxford University Press.

Suret-Canale, J. (1971) *French Colonialism in Tropical Africa 1900–1945*, Hurst.

Suret-Canale, J. (1972) *Afrique Noire Occidentale et Centrale: III: De la Colonisation aux Indépendances (1945–1960)*, Editions sociales.

Suret-Canale, J. (1987) *Afrique et Capitaux*, 2 vols, L'arbre Verdoyant.

Tandeter, E. (1981) 'Forced and Free Labour in Late Colonial Potosí', *Past and Present*, 93, November, pp. 98–136.

Tarling, N. (1966) *A Concise History of Southeast Asia*, Praeger.

Third World Guide, 89/90 (1988) Third World Editors (General Editor: Roberto Remo Bissio) Montevideo.

Thobie, J. (1983) *La France Impériale*, Mégrelis.

Thobie, J. (1985) *Ali et les 40 Voleurs: Impérialismes et Moyen-orient de 1914 à nos Jours*, Editions Messidor.

Thomas, H. (1971) *Cuba: the Pursuit of Freedom*, Eyre & Spottiswoode.

Thompson, V. and R. Adloff (1973) 'French Economic Policy in Tropical Africa', in P. Duignan and L.H. Gann (eds), *Colonialism in Africa, 1870–1960*, vol. 4, *The Economics of Colonialism*, Cambridge University Press.

Thornton, J. (1992) *Africa and Africans in the Making of the Atlantic World*, Cambridge University Press.

Tinker, H. (1974) *A New System of Slavery*, Oxford University Press, Hansib Publishing reprint, 1993.

Tomlinson, B.R. (1978) 'Foreign Private Investment in India 1920–1950', *Modern Asian Studies*, 12, 4, pp. 655–77.

Tomlinson, B.R. (1979) *The Political Economy of the Raj 1919–1947: the Economics of Decolonization in India*, Macmillan.

Tomlinson, B.R. (1985) 'Indo-British Relations in the Post-Colonial Era: The Sterling Balances Negotiations, 1947–49', *Journal of Imperial and Commonwealth History*, 13, pp. 142–61.

Tomlinson, B.R. (1986) 'Foreign Investment in India and Indonesia, 1920–1960', *Itinerario*, 10, pp. 145–62.

Tomlinson, B.R. (1989) 'British business in India, 1860–1970', in R.P.T. Davenport-Hines and G. Jones (eds), *British Business in Asia since 1860*, Cambridge University Press.

Tomlinson, B.R. (1993) *The Economy of Modern India 1860–1970*, The New Cambridge History of India, vol. III.3, Cambridge University Press.

Tosh, J. (1980) 'The Cash-crop Revolution in Tropical Africa: An Agricultural Reappraisal', *African Affairs*, 79, 314, pp. 79–94.

Tracy, J. D. (ed.) (1990) *The Rise of Merchant Empires: Long-distance Trade in the Early Modern World, 1350–1750*, Cambridge University Press.

Tracy, J. D. (ed.) (1991) *The Political Economy of Merchant Empires*, Cambridge University Press.

Turner, V. (ed.) (1971) *Colonialism in Africa 1870–1960*, vol. 3, *Profiles of Change: African Society and Colonial Rule*, Cambridge University Press.

Twomey, M.J. (1983) 'Employment in Nineteenth-Century Indian Textiles', *Explorations in Economic History*, 20, pp. 37–57.

Vail, L. (1976) 'Mozambique's Chartered Companies: the Rule of the Feeble', *Journal of African History*, 17, 3, pp. 389–416.

Vail, L. (1983) 'The political economy of East-Central Africa', in D.Birmingham and P.M. Martin (eds), *History of Central Africa*, vol. 2, Longman.

Vail, L. and L. White (1980) *Capitalism and Colonialism in Mozambique: A Study of Quelimane District*, Heinemann.

Vellut, J-L. (1983) 'Mining in the Belgian Congo', in D.Birmingham and P.M. Martin (eds), *History of Central Africa*, vol. 2, Longman.

Verlinden, C. (1970) *The Beginnings of Modern Colonisation*, Cornell University Press.

Waites, B. (1993) 'Europe and the Third World', in B. Waites (ed.), *Europe and the Wider World*, Routledge.

Wakeman, F. (1978) 'The Canton trade and the Opium War', in J.K. Fairbank (ed.), *The Cambridge History of China*, vol. 10, Cambridge University Press.

Wallerstein, I. (1974) *The Modern World-System, I: Capitalist Agriculture and the Origins of the European World-Economy in the Sixteenth Century*, Academic Press.

Wallerstein, I. (1979) 'The rise and future demise of the World Capitalist System', in *The Capitalist World Economy*, Cambridge University Press.

Wallerstein, I. (1980) *The Modern World-System, II: Mercantilism and the Consolidation of the European World-Economy, 1600–1750*, Academic Press.

Wallerstein, I. (1983) *Historical Capitalism*, Verso.

Wallerstein, I. (1986) 'Incorporation of Indian Subcontinent into Capitalist World-economy', *Economic and Political Weekly*, 4 January, pp. 28–39.

Wallerstein, I. (1989) *The Modern World-System, III: The Second Era of Great Expansion of the Capitalist World-Economy, 1730–1840s*, Academic Press.

Ward, J.R. (1988) *British West Indian Slavery, 1750–1834: the Process of Amelioration*, Clarendon Press.

Warren, B. (1980) *Imperialism: Pioneer of Capitalism*, New Left Books.

Washbrook, D.A. (1981) 'Law, State and Agrarian Society in Colonial India', *Modern Asian Studies*, 15, 3, pp. 649–721.

Washbrook, D.A. (1988) 'Progress and Problems: South Asian Economic and Social History c.1720–1860', *Modern Asian Studies*, 22, 1, pp. 57–96.

Washbrook, D.A. (1990) 'South Asia, the World-System, and World Capitalism', *Journal of Asian Studies*, 49, 3, pp. 478–507.

Watson, I.B. (1981) 'Fortifications and the "Idea" of Force in Early English East India Company Relations with India', *Past and Present*, 88, pp. 70–87.

Watts, D. (1987) *The West Indies: Patterns of Development and Environmental Change since 1492*, Cambridge University Press.

Weber, M. (1948) 'India: The Brahman and the Castes', in H.H. Gerth and C.W. Mills (eds), *From Max Weber: Essays in Sociology*, Routledge & Kegan Paul.

Wehler, H-U. (1976) 'Bismarck's Imperialism, 1862–1890', originally published in *Past and Present*, reproduced in J.J. Sheehan (ed.), *Imperial Germany*, Franklin Watts.

Wehler, H-U. (1979) 'Introduction' to *Imperialismus*, 1970, English translation in C. Emsley (ed.), *Conflict and Stability in Europe*, Croom Helm.

Wesseling, H.L. (ed.) (1978) *Expansion and Reaction: Essays on European expansion and Reaction in Asia and Africa*, Leiden University Press.

Wesseling, H.L. (1988) 'The Giant that was a Dwarf, or the Strange History of Dutch Imperialism', *Journal of Imperial and Commonwealth History*, 16, 3, pp. 58–70.

Wesseling, H.L. (1996) *Divide and Rule: The Partition of Africa, 1880–1914*, Praeger.

White, N.J. (1997) 'The Frustrations of Development: British Business and the Late Colonial State in Malaya, 1945–57', *Journal of Southeast Asian Studies*, 28, 1, 103–19.

Wilber, C.K. (ed.) (1973) *The Political Economy of Development and Underdevelopment*, Random House.

Wilks, I. (1989) *Asante in the Nineteenth Century*, 2nd edn, Cambridge University Press.

Williams, E. (1944) *Capitalism and Slavery*, University of North Carolina Press, 1961 edn.

Williamson, E. (1992) *The Penguin History of Latin America*, Penguin.

Wills, J.E. (1993) 'Maritime Asia, 1500–1800: The Interactive Emergence of European Domination', *American Historical Review*, 98, 1, pp. 83–105.

Wilson, C. (1954) *The History of Unilever*, vol. 1, Cassell.

Winch, D. (1965) *Classical Political Economy and the Colonies*, Bell & Sons.

Worsley, P. (1964) *The Third World: a Vital New Force in International Affairs*, Weidenfeld and Nicolson.

Worsley, P. (1984) *The Three Worlds: Culture and World Development*, Weidenfeld and Nicolson.

Worswick, G.D.N. and P.H. Ady (eds) (1952) *The British Economy 1945–1950*, Clarendon Press.

Worswick, G.D.N. and P.H. Ady (eds) (1962) *The British Economy in the Nineteen Fifties*, Clarendon Press.

Wrigley, C.C (1976) 'Changes in East African Society' in D.A. Low and A. Smith (eds), *History of East Africa*, vol. 3, Oxford University Press.

Wrigley, C.C. (1986) 'Aspects of economic history', in A.D. Roberts (ed.), *The Cambridge History of Africa*, vol. 7, *1905–1940*, Cambridge University Press.

Young, C. (1983) 'The northern republics, 1960–1980', in D. Birmingham and P.M. Martin (eds), *History of Central Africa*, vol. 2, Longman.

Young, C. (1988) 'The Colonial State and Post-Colonial Crisis', in P. Gifford and W.R. Louis (eds), *Decolonization and African Independence: the Transfers of Powers, 1960–1980*, Yale University Press.

Young, C. (1994) *The African Colonial State in Comparative Perspective*, Yale University Press.

Zolberg, A. (1981) 'Origins of the Modern World System: A Missing Link', *World Politics*, 33, 2, pp. 253–81.

INDEX